C000126953

JUST ONE OF SEVEN

THE AUTOBIOGRAPHY OF

DENIS SMITH

JUST ONE OF SEVEN

THE AUTOBIOGRAPHY OF

DENIS SMITH

This book is copyright under the Berne convention.

No part of this book may be reproduced, sold or utilised in any form or transmitted in any form or by any means, electronic or mechanical, including photocopying, recording or by any information storage and retrieval system, without prior permission in writing from the Publisher.

© Denis Smith and Simon Lowe, 2008

The right of Smith and Lowe to be identified as the authors of this work has been asserted by them in accordance with sections 77 and 78 of the Copyright, Designs and Patents Act, 1988.

Know The Score Books Limited
118 Alcester Road
Studley
Warwickshire
B80 7NT
01527 454482
info@knowthescorebooks.com
www.knowthescorebooks.com

A CIP catalogue record is available for this book from the British Library
ISBN: 978-1-84818-504-3

Mixed Sources
Product group from well-managed
forests and other controlled sources
www.fsc.org Cert no. TT-COC-2082
FSC © 1996 Forest Stewardship Council

Printed and bound in Great Britain
By Cromwell Press, Trowbridge, Wiltshire

CONTENTS

ACKNOWLEDGEMENTS

Heartfelt thanks to:

My four assistant managers, Viv Busby, Malcolm Crosby, John Gorman and Kevin Russell. And not forgetting all the other staff who have supported me from office staff to scouts, players to physios, cleaners to press officers, programme sellers to Chief Executives. As a manager you really can only be as successful as your team and your staff allow you to be and I have been blessed with some wonderful and talented people both in my time as a manager and a player.

Also to everyone who helped me in putting together this project, especially Terry Conroy, Rob Mason, Simon & Glynis Wright, Gordon Banks, Lawrie Rampling, Nigel Johnson, Geraint Parry, Steve Buxton, Neil Reynolds, John Clegg, Norman Bartlam, Mick Brown, Steve Bould, Kevin Ball, Robin Herd, Keith Cox and Paul Collins.

A big thank you to all my former clubs, Stoke City FC, Sunderland AFC, Oxford United FC, Wrexham FC, Bristol City FC, West Bromwich Albion FC, and all the media outlets with whom I've worked over the years, especially The Sentinel, BBC Radio stations in all seven cities, Yorkshire Evening Post, Evening Chronicle and PA Photos.

All my family who helped me with my research, Simon Lowe, Graham Hales and everyone at *Know The Score Books* for putting together such a wonderful book and our two interview venues The Swan With Two Necks at Blackbrook, Staffs, and Warwick School.

There may well be other people I should thank and if I have not mentioned you in person it is only down to my awful memory for names. Thank you all the same.

Denis Smith
September 2008

DEDICATION

To Kate & our wonderful kids
and those special seven grandchildren

FOREWORD
BY GORDON BANKS OBE

What can I say about the lion-hearted Denis Smith that hasn't already been said a hundred times?

Playing with Denis was wonderful for a goalkeeper like me. I thought he was the strongest, bravest centre-half I ever played behind. He helped me keep clean sheets and build my reputation by risking life and limb to throw himself in front of a volley, at a cross or any shot that was coming my way. He would block the ball with any part of his body, which saved countless goals, as often it would be a shot I probably wouldn't have been able to save.

Denis was a tiger of a player and we relied on him to win tackles and headers. He did so ferociously and often put a centre-forward off by trying to reach a ball that really wasn't his, crashing into his opponent in the process. The striker would then think twice about challenging for the ball again. We had a very good understanding as Denis listened to my commands and would block any opponent who was trying to get to a ball I wanted to jump and claim, again putting his body on the line selflessly.

That bravery famously cost him all those injuries, the breaks, cuts, bruises, stresses and strains. I remember someone saying one year, when we came back for pre-season training and Denis was hobbling around the place getting over his latest injury, "ah, we can always tell when the football season is about to start because Denis Smith is walking about in plaster!"

There was one occasion when Denis arrived at the Victoria Ground with a bad back for a big cup replay against Manchester United. He was unfit to play and only popped into the dressing room to wish us luck, but instead of going up to the Players' Lounge he found himself being given a fitness test, somehow passing it even though he could barely walk, and ended up playing. That was typical of Denis's spirit. He wanted to be out there at all costs and never wanted to miss a game. That was often to his personal detriment.

He excelled the longer we went on during those runs to the latter stages of both the FA and League Cups in the early 1970s. His desire to win shone through and we looked up to him to help get us through the testing times which eventually lead to our victory at Wembley in 1972.

One of the things I liked about Denis the most was that, as well as being the toughest guy around, he was a great sportsman. When he flew into somebody in his usual fierce manner they knew they'd been tackled, and often would be found lying face down in the mud. But then he'd lift them up and ask if they were OK. The end of a brutal, physical ninety minutes would see him shake hands and put an arm round his direct opponent. He loved the cut and thrust of competition and the nature of his duels with strikers such as Derek Dougan, John Toshack, Francis Lee, Geoff Hurst, Denis Law, Martin Chivers and Kevin Keegan. In those days it was a lot more sporting than the modern game.

Football meant everything to Denis and I think that was why it was so special to him to help Stoke City win the first trophy in the club's history. It meant so much to us all, but I think it was all the more special to a local lad such as Denis.

Denis is also a great family man and loves his three kids and his grandchildren. We were neighbours for many years at Ashley, our children went to the same school and we enjoyed each other's company. He and Kate had a great dog called Bandit who would walk to school with the kids. At work Denis was one of the lads in our very strong group and enjoyed the jokes cracked around the dressing room. He also loved going on our regular Monday nights out on the town.

There was one thing which he didn't think was particular funny, but I did. Although we lived close together we tended to drive into the Victoria Ground separately as we often had to go off and do different things after training. I remember this particular very frosty, sunny day there was about an inch of ice on the road and with us being based out in country it was not gritted. I was taking my time as I could feel my car sliding around. But then in my mirror I could see Denis's car coming up at speed. He sat behind me for about a mile, but then got bored and so passed me, waving as he sped off. A couple of miles later I came round the corner to find he'd driven off the road and into the ditch. Naturally I waved back at him as he desperately tried to get me to stop as I sailed by! Of course I did pick him up and took him to a phone box to call for the RAC, but I didn't stop laughing about that for weeks.

Denis has obviously gone on to a long and successful career in management, though not always at the glamorous end of the game. He has made a difference at each and every club for whom he has worked, showing that same selfless dedication which I benefited from for so many years at Stoke City. Perhaps the greatest thing I can say about Denis is that in a sport in which transience is the norm, after all these years we are still good friends.

Gordon Banks
September 2008

INTRODUCTION

We were all together in the Restaurant Gilmore, near Uttoxeter, my brothers and sisters and I plus our partners. Unfortunately we were without one of my older brothers Graham and his wife Gladys who had passed away. We were out for something to eat just before my 60th birthday in November 2007. It was the usual chaos when we are together. Bedlam.

We were enjoying a lovely meal in a room on our own, but other diners kept coming in and asking if they could have an autograph from me or shake my hand. The meal kept getting interrupted, but I didn't mind. Eventually this lady came in asking if I would sign something for her and my brother Mick shouted across the room, "Hey love, he's just one of seven you know."

That remark resonated so strongly with me. I am one of seven wonderful siblings, I have been proud to play for and managed seven football clubs and as this book is about to be published I will become the very proud grandfather of a seventh fabulous grandchild. For some reason the symmetry and the symbolism seemed to click together and so I chose Mick's phrase 'Just One Of Seven' as my title, as I felt it summed me up so aptly.

For some reason the symmetry and the symbolism seemed to click together. As I was already underway with work on my autobiography and had yet to select a title, I chose Mick's phrase 'Just One Of Seven', as I felt it summed me up so aptly.

I've never really understood being famous and prompting reactions like the ones from the people in that restaurant.. To me that's left to stars like Elton John and Michael Jackson. I'm just good at what I do. I don't seek fame, I don't cultivate it cynically, I just deal with the consequences of having a high profile job in a community-based business. Sometimes, though, it brings lovely little surprises.

For example in 1997 Stoke City, my first club, were moving to a new ground and invited all their former players to a bash to celebrate the closure of the old Victoria Ground, where we had all made our names. I walked into the room along with my two sons Paul and Tom and spied Stoke's greatest ever servant and legendary England international winger Sir Stanley Matthews over near the bar holding one of his famed tomato juices, the drink which he claimed allowed him to keep playing until the age of 50 in the top flight of English football. I made a beeline for Stan, who was one of my boyhood heroes, and put my hand out to shake his. He turned towards me and with a twinkle in his eye shook my hand firmly saying, "It isn't, is it? It is! It's the great Denis Smith."

"Oooh, Dad!" came the inadvertent gasp from my sons.

That was one of the greatest moments of my life.

Almost the same thing happened to me soon afterwards when I was in London at a PFA bash. I met my protégé Steve Bould, who was celebrating Arsenal's double-winning achievement of 1998. I turned up at the swanky reception to find Steve and his defensive colleague and Gunners legend Tony Adams sharing a few laughs. Steve introduced me, "Tony meet Denis". Tony's eyes lit up. The great man offered me his hand. "Ah," he said, "So you're God are you?"

I'm always pleased when I've left a good impression, especially on people such as Steve Bould or Garth Crooks, Lee Chapman, Howard Kendall, Marco Gabbiadini, Kevin Ball, John Byrne, Andy (or should that be Andrew?) Cole, Matty Elliott, Lee Hughes, Darren Ferguson or Dennis Lawrence. I have had the pleasure of working with a lot of good young players, helping them to improve and go on to have great careers. It's been one of the great pleasures of the second half of my footballing career, in management.

There have been so many great moments along the way . . . promotions, fantastic Cup victories, winning at Wembley, the Millennium Stadium, the Nou Camp and Old Trafford, great comebacks and last minute dramas. But also so many more warm and funny stories involving personalities behind the scenes such as chairmen, coaches, assistants and other sporting greats like Ian Botham and Clive Lloyd.

I love football. It's in my bones and my blood. The game just seeps through me, and I've always loved my club, my local team: Stoke City. Ever since I was first taken to see them as a boy. I was hooked by the speed and sounds of the game, the intensity of the atmosphere, the ferocity of the tackling, the glory of the game. But of course it was all so very different then. The players were not millionaires living almost separate lives from their fans. They were paid well, sure, probably three or four times the average working man, but not enough to own a car. Players would catch the bus to the ground along with the fans, or even, god forbid, walk.

Wherever I have gone around the seven clubs I have served during my career I have found the same desire, the same joy and the same love for the job, the people and the area in which I have settled. I hope that supporters feel I gave them my all at each and every one of my teams – Stoke City, York City, Sunderland, Bristol City, Oxford United, West Bromwich Albion and Wrexham.

My career has unfolded because of this undying love affair with the game from winning national silverware as a teenager through lifting the League Cup at Wembley to the LDV Vans trophy at the Millennium Stadium. Each success was remarkable in its own way, each achieved against the odds with a team which many thought had no right to be there, each brought elation to so many people.

Celebrating my 60th birthday it all seemed to make sense to me. To produce a book which told the story of the ups and downs, the highs and lows, revisited the joys of victory and the pain of defeat, broken bones and the inevitable managerial sack.

I have endeavoured to be as open as possible in writing my life story. Despite my reputation, mostly on the field of play, as 'tough', or 'uncompromising', it has never been my style to be hostile or to backbite, I just say it as I see it. It might not be pretty, but it will always be honest. I am not motivated by seeking retribution for wrongs done to me decades ago. I merely want to give the reasons why events happened as they did and my opinion as to why they went either so well or so badly. The rest I leave to you.

I've had my fair share of controversies, success and failure. I've learnt from them all. I hope in sharing them with you I can enlighten and entertain as I tell the story of a life which began when Britain had rationing, national service, Clement Attlee as Prime Minister ... goal average, legal tackling from behind and two points for a win.

Chapter One

DIRTY DEN?

When Leeds tough guy Norman Hunter named me as the "hardest man in football" in the early 1970s I thought he'd got a screw loose. Don't get me wrong, in many ways I took it as a compliment. To be considered his team's most difficult opponent was quite an honour, but I never considered myself a hard man. I was never nasty or snide in the way I played football. I offered full on commitment.

Years later Steve Bould, himself quite a tough player in the famous Arsenal back four that clinched so much silverware under George Graham and Arsene Wenger and who as a young lad I had nurtured in my own image as he came through the youth ranks at Stoke, said that I was "the most fearless man in football."

I like to think that Steve was closer to the mark. I was brave. Some would say to the point of being stupid. I was fearless, throwing myself into challenges that many others thought better of and earning myself a catalogue of injuries in the process. I was someone who was prepared to do battle, who relished the contest and who wouldn't give an inch. And I was dedicated to winning – at all costs.

In my time, from the mid-sixties to the mi-eighties, that meant being physically tough. This was an era of full-on, bruising contact. There were plenty of self-styled hard men around. Chelsea's Ron 'Chopper' Harris, Manchester City's Mike Doyle, Liverpool's Tommy Smith and Norman himself. There were the tigerish little sods like Leeds pair Billy Bremner and Johnny Giles, and Manchester United's World Cup winner Nobby Stiles. And then there were the silent assassins, now they were the ones you really had to watch.

Me a hardman? That is other people's opinion.

I had, in fact, spent the first ten years of my life being something of a hard nut, but sport had allowed me to channel my aggression into my teenage years. I became Staffordshire County Boxing Champion at 15 and football in particular really gave me something positive to focus on. As a top flight defender I could look after myself and relished the physical side of the game. I wasn't scared of anybody but, as you'll see, there was far more to my game than kicking, whacking and elbowing. It's just that in the era during which I started playing professionally I had to learn to live in the dangerous world I was entering. Quite simply, you didn't survive if you were frightened. In fact I revelled in the challenge of competing with the very best. I loved it and I loved them. I had always relished anybody wanting to take me on, either on the pitch or in the street, because I didn't think anybody could. I would never look for trouble, but growing up where I did and being a budding professional footballer, it tended to find me and it was something I had to deal with by facing up to it.

I learned very early in my football career how experienced professionals would try to destroy you if you couldn't stand up for yourself. When I was 18 I played for Stoke reserves at Leeds and as soon as the game kicked off this little feller came up to me and, from the side, punched me extremely hard on my temple. As I reeled from this blow I managed to get my head up and, through my watery eyes, spied this figure, the number 4 on his shirt, sloping back into his position. For me it was a make or break moment. The gauntlet had been laid down and I had to decide whether to turn the other cheek – which would be interpreted as me bottling it – or meet fire with fire. It would be a decision that would shape the career that lay ahead of me.

So now I was gunning for this number 4. I walked up to him and grabbed him by the throat, telling him, "I am after you," then stalked back into my half. Throughout the rest of the first 45 minutes we kicked lumps out of each other.

In the dressing room during the break our coach took me to one side and said to me, "Do you know who you were kicking out there?"

I replied, "I ain't bothered who it is. He ain't gonna do that to me."

It turned out the man in question was a pitbull of a Scotsman called Bobby Collins, whose reputation in the 1950s through to the mid-sixties was as the hardest, meanest sod in the game. This man was the feller who taught Don Revie's infamous Leeds side every little trick in the book and he had obviously chosen me as his target for this particular match, in which he was recuperating from injury to get back into the first team. And so it went on. In the second half I cracked through Collins in a tackle, raising my foot into his groin. His foot was fairly high too. The referee didn't even give a free-kick. The question was now how he would react to this young pup taking him on at his own game. I'm sure those on the sidelines and my team-mates held their breath. What would Collins do now?

I already thought I knew the answer. And I was proved right. We both got up and got on with it. I had passed the test. And so we carried on. He kicked me, I whacked him. It was war for the entire second half.

Typically me, the well brought-up boy that I am, I went up to Collins at the final whistle, offered him my hand and said, "Thank you very much, Mr Collins."

"Nasty little bugger," I think his words were. "Piss off, or I'll break both yer legs next time."

Collins had obviously targeted me, even at that early age, because I had a reputation and I showed no fear, mainly because I hadn't got any. I was now a marked man, but that made me feel good. It meant I was a threat to opponents. That was confirmed shortly afterwards when, on my league debut for Stoke, which came at Arsenal in September 1968, I was detailed to mark the Gunners' striker Bobby Gould. Now Bobby was a fairly robust player, and not short of a word or two either then, or in his time as a manager. Here I was, a young whipper-snapper, giving him a few indiscriminate kicks during a very tight, tense game. It wasn't long before Bobby began some of his legendary moaning towards the referee about the treatment he was getting, which was hilarious considering how he gave it back to me, but I knew it meant that I had arrived and people at the top level of the game were taking notice of me.

That reputation was one which would develop over the next few years as I became one of, if not the most-feared hitman in football. It was a title I relished as it became my job to sort out opponents who, shall we say, fancied themselves.

Ron Yeats was captain of Liverpool. Their manager Bill Shankly loved him. He was always eulogising him to anyone who would listen as the perfect physical specimen and I believe Shankly even changed Liverpool's kit from red shirts with white shorts to the all-Red they wear today because it made Big Ron look even bigger. His thighs were made of solid teak, or so Shanks said. Yeats was a very big lad indeed, towering over me. But I relished taking him on the first time I played at Anfield. I was marking Ron and when the first corner came over I leaped and stretched every sinew to win it cleanly and head it away. Second corner comes in and I again got up higher than him and nodded it clear. By now I was thinking, "Who's this Big Ron Yeats?"

The next corner came over. Ron had given himself some room to take a run and let me get airborne before he came crashing into me from behind. Bang. He flattened me.

Fair play to him, he stuck around to lift me up, staring me as he did with a look that said, 'welcome to the real world, son'. I swear his massive hand enveloped mine and stretched up past my wrist as he pulled me off the deck. But that didn't put me off. I couldn't be out-psyched. I couldn't afford to be.

It became my job to mark, or sort out, the opposition's hard man, I suppose because I was good at it. Chelsea's Mickey Droy was a huge central defender. A man mountain, complete with a beard that only made him seem bigger. In fact my wife, Kate, tells me the only time she's ever screamed out loud to warn me from the stand that I was in trouble was the first time she saw me face up to Mickey, she was that worried about me. Because of his sheer size he was always going to present a challenge, but I developed a subtler way of dealing with him. Whenever I went near him at a free-kick or corner I'd put my hand on his shoulder, smile and then tell him how I was going to stand on his foot. It really disarmed him and you could see Mickey thinking "why is he telling me that?" But it was just a distraction to take his mind away from the set-piece. I never actually intended to do it: that really wouldn't be a sensible thing, to upset Mickey, but he would lose a bit of concentration and make mistakes. I found a way to handle him, and using that technique was a far better way of gaining an advantage.

Certain players I could intimidate with mind games to gain the upper hand. Recently I attended a game at Newcastle United and I saw one of their great heroes of my era, Malcolm Macdonald, having a drink with a few other former players including Peter Beardsley and their wives. As I joined them Malcolm said to his wife, "do you know this is the closest I've ever got to Denis without having a kick?"

His wife said, "he seems such a nice bloke."

Mac said, "he is off the field. He used to kick me from one end of the pitch to the other".

SuperMac, as he styled himself during his barnstorming and goal-packed career with the Magpies, Arsenal and England, was a very interesting case. You could have great banter with Malcolm as he is a very intelligent man, as he has proved with his subsequent media career. But my central defensive partner Alan 'Bluto' Bloor and I were always looking for a weakness in opponents and we used to talk to him all the time, wheedling away at his super confidence, which was the thing Malcolm really thrived on. For example if I won the ball in the air Bluto would loudly offer the opinion, "Denis, that silly sod can't jump." And then if the next ball was a through ball, Bluto would get there first and I'd say, "Bluto, he can't run either". We'd just keep at it all game. Incessant; never stopping. "Malcolm, if you can't jump and can't run, what can you do?"

There wasn't a lot of self-doubt in SuperMac's mind. But we'd chip away and one day his fellow Newcastle striker John Tudor turned round to us and said, "why don't you two leave him alone?" We knew we were onto a good thing then. It was a different kind of intimidation – mind games rather than brute force.

Manchester City's barrel-chested forward Franny Lee was renowned in the game for winning penalties he shouldn't have got. He would go over if a fly touched him and he was bloody good at making it look as if you'd brought him down. I really didn't like this reputation of his and took to telling him right to his face every time I played against him, "Look Franny. If you dive I am going to stamp on you." It did the trick. He never won a penalty against Stoke all the time I played against him. He knew that I would have carried out my threat if he'd cheated us.

I remember one game at Stoke in which Manchester City were leading 2-0 and our manager Tony Waddington told me to go up front for the last few minutes to see if we could pull anything out of the fire and as I trotted up Franny shouted, "Thank God for that. Now see how you like getting bloody kicked black and blue!"

Martin Chivers, was one player who found me quite intimidating. Martin was an integral part of the Spurs side which won the League Cup and the UEFA Cup in the early 1970s. He was a good goalscorer, regularly netting in the top flight. But, for a big lad, he was a bit of a wimp. Bearing in mind he was an England striker, he would mostly be found hiding just behind his centre-half Mike England for protection when

Tottenham visited the Victoria Ground. He rarely gave me any problems, and the interesting thing is that wasn't actually because of anything I ever did to him. I never needed to. My reputation was enough and his team-mates would often have a go at him for steering clear of me during games.

Mind you, Chivers did manage to get a small amount of his own back on one occasion. We were playing Spurs at White Hart Lane in October 1972 and I was expecting my usual easy afternoon against him. But Martin had obviously decided enough was enough. Perhaps he'd had his fill of the comments from his team-mates. He received the ball about 25 yards out and faced me up. I positioned myself to invite him to go down the touchline so I could deposit him in the paddock, but he saw me coming, leaned into me with his shoulder and dumped me on my backside. He then bent the ball superbly round our goalkeeper, who happened to be one Gordon Banks, which just shows the class that Chivers was capable of, while I watched, sprawling helpless on the ground.

The funny thing was, although I was gutted we'd conceded, I was actually pleased that he had finally faced up to me, that he was prepared to challenge me, to give me something to get stuck into. It showed he did have character and to me that was what the game was all about back then.

One of the biggest characters and toughest strikers I faced was Wolves and Northern Ireland's Derek Dougan. He was most certainly not someone who would ever let himself be intimidated or out-psyched by on-pitch chit-chat. The Doog was a legend in his own lunchtime. He could talk the talk, and to be fair he could walk the walk too. His partnership with John Richards was prolific. Dougan was quick, strong, good in the air and arrogant with it. Total self-belief, but you have to say he had good reason to be cocky. He was a talismanic, goalscoring hero at Wolves. He was always one to up the pre-match ante a little with some paper talk and some blabbing before the game. That wasn't my style. On this particular occasion we faced Wolves at Molineux and just before the kick-off we had a little chat. It went something like:

Me: "Afternoon Derek."

Doog: "Hello Smithy, my boy."

Me: "Going to be a difficult game today then."

Doog: "Yes, yes, but I'll sort you out early on, so I will."

Well, that was it. Red rag to a bull. Wolves kicked off, played it back and launched it forwards towards the pair of us. Derek leapt to head it on to Richards and as he did I came clean through the back of him in mid-air and connected with my forehead right on the back of his head. Bang. Dougan slumped to the floor in a heap. Out cold. He was carried off.

"That's that sorted, then," I thought. "Nice easy day." I was quite pleased with myself.

That story nearly had a very different ending though. Dougan left the field of play, as I thought, very dramatically on a stretcher. Next thing we knew a substitute was on.

Doog must have been more hurt than I thought, so at half-time I enquired as to how he was doing, only to learn from one of the Wolves back-room staff that Dougan had still not yet come round. Now I began to worry. Dougan was a tough character, although not beyond a bit of posturing to make me seem the villain of the piece. But on this occasion I had gone too far and I was worried. Thankfully by the time we came off at full-time Dougan was up and about, gingerly wandering around. It was a massive relief. I was a hard, hard player, but I didn't set out to maim, only to win.

Sometimes opponents proved less resolute. In the early 1980s Norwich City unearthed a gem of a striker called Justin Fashanu, who scored a welter of goals for the Canaries, including one belting left-footed volley on Match of the Day against Liverpool which won Goal of the Season, to earn himself a big money move to Brian Clough's European Champions, Nottingham Forest. But Justin was meat and drink to the likes of me. He just couldn't cope with my physicality, which I thought was ridiculous because he was a big lad himself, very chunky, highly skilled and a good goalscorer. He proved to be weak mentally, though.

I remember one particular occasion when we played Nottingham Forest, just after Brian Clough had paid over a million pounds to take him to the City Ground, which was big, big money in that era, Justin burst into tears on the pitch because of me. When you'd got that sort of price tag I was the kind of player who would test you out. So straight after kick-off I was all over him, both in terms of giving him a real buffeting in aerial challenges and in tackles on the deck – smack. I also got into him mentally, nicking the ball off him, not letting him settle, reducing his confidence, probing his weaknesses. Incredibly Justin snapped, went over to the touchline and asked Cloughie if he could come off. Clough would have none of it, as you can imagine, and barked at Fashanu to remain on the pitch. Justin took one look at Clough and then one look at me and burst into tears as he walked tentatively back towards me. I was in full-on game mode and I knew I had him in my pocket then. Clough was making a point, of course, both to Justin and the rest of his team, that he would not tolerate anyone who gave up the fight. He could be hard when he felt it necessary, which was a quality he always admired in me. It's harsh but it was Clough's job to win a football match, so he refused to substitute Fashanu, despite the fact he was in floods and, clearly, mentally he'd gone.

Justin's career stalled beyond repair under Clough, and that humiliating incident can't have helped.

Justin had a younger brother, Wimbledon striker John Fashanu, who became a star and one of the most physical players of the 1980s. He was mentally far stronger than Justin and loved the limelight, making a great deal out of his nickname being 'Fash The Bash'. He eventually went on to present Gladiators for ITV, of course. By this time I had become a manager and was in charge of resurgent Sunderland, although I'd only just passed 40. I'd got Sunderland up into the top flight from the old Division Three in just three seasons and had signed a young lad called Kevin Ball to play the anchor role. Now

Bally was a bit like me, physically strong, impossible to psyche out, and honest as the day is long. I loved him and so did the fans at Roker Park, but this particular day in 1990 he lunged at Fashanu with a tackle that, had it connected, would have been dangerous. It was overzealous, but not serious. Fashanu, however, did the dirty by diving over the challenge to make it look to the referee as if he'd been caught and then blatantly play acted that he had been severely injured. Kevin received a straight red card and we were suddenly down to ten men.

It was towards the end of the first half of the game and I was incensed. I was livid. He had cheated me, Kevin and our supporters. So when the players came off at half-time I followed Fashanu down the tunnel and grabbed him by the throat, throwing him up against the wall, hissing, "I've sorted your brother out, so help me, I'll sort you out if you ever do that to me or my players again."

I put Fashanu down – and he was 6 feet 1 inch of muscle – and turned my back on him and as I walked away I thought to myself, "Den, you've still got it, lad."

My players, many of whom were in the tunnel and witnessed the incident, were right impressed. I think they saw a side to me that they'd only previously heard about until then. With the advent of TV you can't get away with those sort of things in the tunnel nowadays, unless it involves pizza, of course.

There was a little follow up to that story which took the shine off it a bit, though. Before our next training session I went into the dressing room and someone pulled out a paper with headlines in the sports section saying 'Fashanu comes out – £1 million Justin, I am gay'. All the players have gone "blimey gaffer".

Of course now we know that Justin was a much more tortured soul than many of us had ever believed at the time. I personally hadn't given him the slightest thought, but when you realise now what he went through and how he eventually took his own life it brings home to you the knife edge on which some people live. It was not the last time I would be faced with human frailties turning seemingly rational, fit professional footballers into walking timebombs, but those have never been demons which have visited me. All I cared about was winning football matches.

******

Going onto the field of play means you are there to perform. It is a performance, a show. And by that I mean I used to take on a totally different persona once I crossed that white line to that which I had for the rest of the day. Just like an actor playing the part of a tough guy in a film, I would become your Rambo or you Terminator. That was my role. People who knew me couldn't understand how I was this nice, softly-spoken lad off the pitch, but this fiercely competitive man on it. But that was my work, my profession, my livelihood. And I was very, very good at it.

Obviously my targets would generally be the player on the opposing side who could do us most damage, either their major goalscoring threat, or their playmaker. But it didn't always work. There was one occasion when Everton's World Cup winner Alan

Ball was playing really well against us, running the game. There seemed to be nothing we could do about him, no matter what we tried, and that caused me to lose my rag. When the ball bounced between us, I launched myself with both studs showing at the little man's head. If I'd connected I probably would have removed his head from his shoulders, I certainly would have stopped him hurting us, and I would undoubtedly have been sent off. Fortunately for everyone, Alan ducked and I flew over him!

Liverpool were the pre-eminent team of the mid-seventies and, until his move to Hamburg in 1977, Kevin Keegan was their inspiration. He was a little wasp of a forward, buzzing around, making a nuisance of himself, but he was also very physical for one so small. He was 5 feet 7 inches of solid muscle who constantly gave us headaches, so it fell to me to sort him out. Early on in one game in 1974 I put Keegan and the ball totally fairly, but deliberately into the Boothen paddock, which ran along the side of the Victoria Ground pitch at the foot of the main stand, with the terracing starting well below the level of the pitch. But Keegan was made of stern stuff. He simply got up, dragged himself out of the hole he literally found himself in, came back on to the pitch, backed into me and called for the throw on to come into his feet. Now that's class.

In common with many visiting teams in the 1970s and 80s, Anfield was always a ground at which Stoke had problems producing our best form. In fact I never won there as a player, and I still haven't as a manager. It's the one ground that has haunted me throughout my career. I've won at Old Trafford, Wembley, St James' Park, Goodison Park, Highbury, White Hart Lane, the Millennium Stadium and even the Nou Camp, but I've never escaped from Anfield with a victory. Sometimes it was worse.

Despite my image, I was only ever straight red carded twice in my career, and dismissed for two yellows on two further occasions, and yes the first time was at Liverpool. We were under pressure from incessant Liverpool attacks and their winger Stevie Heighway went past our full-back Jackie Marsh yet again. Heighway was clean through, so I chopped him right in front of that mythical beast the Kop and it was so blatant the referee dismissed me, which in those days was a very severe sanction indeed. Just my luck, I was at the other end of the ground to the tunnel leading to the changing rooms and let me tell you that is one hell of a long walk! Especially with 40,000 scousers giving you stick.

In a strange kind of way I loved even that experience. I'm one of those weird people who loves the challenge. I relish it, so I loved going to Liverpool or Manchester United. I loved the big clubs and I loved the big crowds. I really thrived on it. Not every footballer is the same. I remember some years later sitting on the coach en route to Anfield with a young Garth Crooks, who was the only black player in Stoke's squad at that time, beside me and he had been worried sick in the build up to the game about the kind of racial abuse he might get from the terraces during the game because he stuck out amongst the team due to his colour. Garth said to me, "they are going to give me stick and have a real go at me".

I replied, "you're right. They will have a go at you, but I have to do something before they start having a go at me. You've got an advantage."

Garth hadn't thought of it like that and I always felt he was someone who stood up to the abuse better than others and I hope that little chat helped him get around the mental side of things and contribute to his career blossoming in the way it has.

The only other straight red I received was in the most cynical game of football I ever had the displeasure to be involved in. In 1971 Stoke took part in the Anglo-Italian Cup, a short-lived competition between the teams that didn't quite make Europe that season in both countries. It was set up after Swindon Town had won the 1969 English League Cup, but were not allowed to take part in the Inter-Cities Fairs Cup as they played in the then-Third Division.

In June that year we travelled to Rome to play AS Roma and it was quite an eye-opener. The Roma players kicked you on the sly, pulled your hair behind the referee's back, would punch and pinch your arms and legs while waiting for free-kicks and corners and, worst of all, spat at you. It was pathetic and hugely cynical on a level I had never seen before. It became obvious they'd identified Peter Dobing as a player who was vital to our attacking pretensions, but also one that could be intimidated. So they had a lad called Giacomo Losi who did nothing else but follow Peter all over the field, kicking lumps out of him. It was incredibly cynical, the first time we'd come across such deliberately negative tactics on that kind of level.

Of course it was my job to protect our creative talents, so I made sure I marked Losi at a corner. Sure enough straight away he was punching me, biting me and kicking me, you name it. So when the free-kick came in I jumped with him and timed my header to connect firmly with his temple, knocking him clean out, so they had to take him off. Job done.

We beat Roma 1-0 thanks to a John Ritchie goal and when the final whistle went suddenly seats rained down from the terracing around the pitch and the fans set fire to stuff up on the terraces. We walked off the pitch down a glass tunnel and I remember that there was this fan with a crutch and he stuck this crutch straight through a partition as we walked past, smashing glass all over us. The Polizia used tear gas to disperse the trouble makers, but that only meant that they were out of the ground and waiting for us when it was time for our coach to leave. There was a huge mob outside, with scarves wound round their faces, and all they wanted to do was gain some revenge for the game.

The authorities had called in army lorries and soldiers with rifles, which was not something we were used to, and we had to lie on the floor of the coach to get out safely. We went back to the hotel for a meal that night and got chatting with the waiters who told us that the disturbances were actually a political protest as rather than about football.

"I'd hate to see them really annoyed with us," I said.

But the competition was played on a home and away basis and so by the time Losi comes to our place he's ready to start again. Early on in the game he was kicking Peter behind the referee's back. Peter had had enough. He just turned round and punched the Roma player and was sent off!

The next corner this madman came over and had a go at me. But that was where he made his big mistake, because I had a quick look at the referee, made sure he wasn't looking, and chinned him. He went down in complete histrionics. I thought, "that's him sorted. No problem."

The referee incredibly hadn't seen either incident, but he couldn't miss what happened next. I was waiting on the near post for the corner when the next thing I know I get a thump in my back. So I just lashed out behind me, catching the miscreant – you can guess who it was – across his face, breaking his nose which began to bleed profusely. As he hit the deck screaming like a child once again, Losi still retained enough of his wits about him to kick me. The referee, having seen that, came over, took one look at Losi with his nose spread across his face and sent both of us off.

Needless to say my own supporters liked to use my reputation to wind up opposing teams. They'd sing:

"Six Foot Two, Eyes Of Blue. Denis Smith is after you!"

Often the Boothen End, the huge bank of terracing behind the 'home' goal at the Victoria Ground where I had stood as a lad to watch my heroes playing in the red and white stripes of Stoke, would warn opposing strikers:

"Denis is gonna get you. Denis is gonna get you."

It helped me in my psychological war against whoever I happened to be marking in that game. Often the centre-forward heard the chant and then the next time the ball came to them, normally with their back to goal and me breathing down their neck, they'd look for me coming, then take their eye off the ball for a spilt second, miscontrol it and I'd nip in to take it off them. Effectively that player would then be out of the game until they managed to put me and the chant out of their mind. That is an example of how a reputation can help make you a better player, not that I was a bad one.

I could pass a decent ball. In fact I thought in my heyday I was one of the best two centre-halves in the country, alongside Derby County's Roy McFarland, who if I'm honest, was always just that hair's breadth better than me. And yes that does put me above the likes of Smithy and Big Norm, not to mention Emlyn Hughes, Mike England, Jack Charlton, Dave Watson and Brian Labone. At Stoke we could play some great, flowing, passing football, with wide players who could beat men and create chances and central midfielders who could carve open opposing defences. Playing with the likes of Jimmy Greenhoff, Alan Hudson, Peter Dobing, George Eastham and Terry Conroy made me a better footballer simply because I was expected to attain the same standards of passing and ball retention as the rest of the team once I had done my bit and won the ball.

My first job, though, as a defender, was to stop the opposing team, which meant one thing was important above everything else – tackling. I could tackle. Not just in the brute force, physical fashion of Chopper or Tommy. When I did that it was out of choice and done to make a point to my opponent. But I could time my interceptions, slide in to win the ball on the run, harry players into blind alleys and then win the ball in the air and on the deck. Some players can tackle and some players, even though they call themselves defenders, can't. I could. Nowadays, with the added restrictions to how you can win the ball, there's plenty of players who can't tackle. Having been a manager since 1982, I've employed many of them! They will have other, positive attributes of course, but a defender's stock in trade is to win the ball and preferably retain possession.

Of course it's more difficult in this day and age when so many players go in with injury-causing challenges because they are themselves afraid of getting hurt, while cameras are everywhere, even at lower division games, replaying tackles which would have barely have brought free-kicks in my era.

This is only the end of a process which started when I was making my way in the game. Things changed massively for everyone in football before the start of the 1971/72 season when the FA outlawed the tackle from behind. People think that's a modern innovation, but there was actually a huge crackdown at that time. Not that the ultimate sanction of a red card was given to referees. At that stage it would be yellow for a really bad challenge, or for repeated offending. Before that it had been carte blanche. If you've ever seen a rerun of the 1970 FA Cup final between Chelsea and Leeds at Wembley you'll know what I'm talking about. Some time ago the football magazine FourFourTwo asked Premiership referee Dermot Gallagher to watch the game on DVD and write down what decisions he would have made. He ended up showing numerous red cards, and Chelsea's David Webb would have been sent off three times! Everyone knew that after the showpiece final of the season – the one game that was shown live in the season in those days – had proved such a bloodbath that things had to change. You had to adjust your game and some players couldn't. It finished them. I didn't find it a problem. For someone like me it meant I had to get cuter, to adapt to winning the ball as the forward controlled it, or turned, rather than diving in and whacking them. I loved that tactical challenge as much as the physical side of the game. I was pitting my wits as much as my brute strength and iron will against my opponents and, although I always played on the edge of the rules, I never actively went out to break them.

I remember one of our early games that season was West Ham away and there had been all this publicity about how tackles from behind had been outlawed and wouldn't be tolerated. I was marking Geoff Hurst, the hat-trick hero of England's World Cup victory in 1966 and the darling of Upton Park. I had already adjusted the way I tackled so that instead of coming through the back of players to make my point I would scythe through from the side. Not exactly subtle, but I had responded to the rule change and still maintained my advantage over Hursty. Geoff was normally fairly mild-mannered and was obviously a very good player, but that day he eventually lost it completely, partly I always thought, because he was expecting the kind of protection that referees give strikers today. So again he beat himself really, although my consistent tackling, winning the ball and taking the man from the side, played a big part in that. Because of that the referee couldn't book me and instead Geoff got so riled that, after yet another challenge when I won the ball, he turned around and kicked me. The referee blew the whistle, stopped the game, walked over to us and, without a word showed Geoff the yellow card. I'd won.

There are two other things that I remember about that game, two little stories that showed me that I'd done my job well. The next morning, one of the Sunday paper reporters wrote, 'Smith treated Hurst like an Upton Park crash barrier'. And I did. But it wasn't only Hursty who took a battering. I remember coming off at full-time. Upton Park was in uproar because of the way I'd treated their hero and the tunnel into the old main stand leading to the dressing rooms didn't have any cover on it, so people on either side of it could lean over and shout and scream and worse at you. I'll always remember as I was walking down the tunnel off the pitch there was this old lady, probably in her sixties, who bent over, screaming at me for hurting "Our Geoff" and whacked me on my head and shoulders with an umbrella. I got really battered. It was great! I killed myself laughing.

Hursty was quite a big lad, but he didn't have a mean streak like some centre-forwards. I started playing in the days of people like Aston Villa and Leicester striker Andy Lochhead. Now he was a hard, hard man. Tough as titanium. He'd make sure his elbows flew into your face as you rose with him to challenge for a header – the kind of thing that is banned now, but was commonplace in the mid-sixties. I remember playing at Filbert Street and going up for a ball, knowing that Andy, was coming in to challenge from an angle. As I hung in mid-air, a comfortable winner of this heading duel, I realised too late what was coming. Andy had timed his jump so that he was just a split-second late, meaning I could head the ball clear, but so that he would make contact with me close enough to that to make it look like a proper challenge. Except it wasn't. As I came back down to earth both his knees whacked me in the middle of my back knocking every breath out of me. It was an early lesson in improving my peripheral vision.

Joe Royle was another tough nut, who was very difficult to dominate physically. As a high ball came forward, the pair of us would jocky for position with him backing into me. I'd then try and get in front of him to intercept the ball and it would become a battle, sometimes with little regard to the arrival of the actual ball. It was all about supremacy and you could not afford to give ground in a pitch battle like that. Often coaches teach you in those situations to stay behind the centre-forward and try to win the header from there. "Goal side," is their mantra, but I think that can be wrong. If a centre-forward is backing into you then let him carry on going backwards and get round the front of him and get the rise on him to win the header. It worked well for me, although if you get run under the flight of the ball you are in serious trouble, risking letting you opponent have a free run on goal and a serious bollocking from your team-mates.

Later, in the mid-1970s, another centre-forward who challenged me physically was Joe Jordan, of Leeds and Manchester United. Big Joe could run all day and was bloody hard work. He was fearless and as he had no teeth, he hadn't really got anything to lose anyway! Joe relished the physical aspects of the game as much as I did. I remember him accidently catching me in the privates one game. It was a bad foul and it hurt, but I got up and started talking to Joe face-to-face and up in the press box they were thinking, 'here we go', licking their lips at the thought of a big scrap between the two of us. Nothing happened, though, and afterwards several journalists sought me out and asked me why. "What were you saying to Joe when he caught you?" they insisted on knowing.

"Nothing. It's alright, it wasn't a problem," I replied. But they wouldn't believe me. They thought I was going to give them some quote to start a war on their back pages.

"Come on, tell us," they insisted.

"Oh, well," I said. "If you must know I just said to him 'steady on Joe, mind me knackers, I'm on a promise tonight'".

John O'Hare, a Scottish international forward who won a League title with Derby in the 1970s was a very under-rated and extremely tough player. He was big and strong and backed into you, creating a physical barrier which you had to battle against. I relished the scrap with him. He was a very good target man, so good that Cloughie took him to Leeds and then Forest when he moved there.

Andy Gray, now known to millions as a Sky Sports commentator, was another tough Scot like John and Joe, who loved the physical duel, backing into you and feeling where you were in relation to him, then trying to control the duel from there. I always felt you had to be cuter than that and make players like Andy and Joe think more by occasionally dropping off to get a running jump, or sometimes coming round in front late to nick the ball away before it reaches them. If a centre-forward doesn't know what you're going to do he can't plan for it. If he is in control then his team-mates can play the same balls into him over and over again, running off him and gaining a huge advantage of starting playing halfway inside your half. If you win the majority of those balls they are living off scraps and you disrupt their best-laid plans.

There was always an element with players such as Andy, John and Joe that they would try to bully you, mentally as much as physically. But you couldn't let them. You had to be tougher than them. If you weren't, they would boss you and either score themselves or help their team win the game. I was utterly committed to not letting that happen, to winning my battles and contributing as much as I could to my team winning the football match. That was my job. If someone was to beat me, I was determined it would be through sheer skill alone.

One man who had my utmost respect on that score was George Best. He truly possessed genius on the ball. Realistically the only way to stop him was to aim your first tackle at his chest, but the chances were he'd feint one way with the ball glued to his feet and then wave you past as you dived into the space which he had just vacated.

To give you an idea what it was like playing against George Best, I remember on many occasions facing up to him as he got on the ball. And he had this thing where he would stop, just momentarily with his leg paused for a split second above the ball at the end of which dangled a foot which could do pretty much anything, and he'd look at you – right in the eye – and you'd think, "What is he going to do now?" You knew that even George didn't necessarily know what he was going to do next and you knew that he was capable of doing absolutely anything with a football. He proved that often enough in a wonderful career with Manchester United and Northern Ireland when he was, in my opinion, the most exciting player in this country.

Of course my first thought in that situation was, "I'm going to have you this time, Georgie." And there were many occasions when I did come out on top. But there were plenty when I didn't. Sometimes they hurt.

I remember he scored a goal against us at the Victoria Ground in an FA Cup 6th round replay in March 1972 when, with the score 0-0 in an otherwise very tight and hotly-contested match, he picked the ball up on the half-way line and accelerated inside our right-back Jackie Marsh – and that wasn't easy because Jackie was fast. Then he came inside and went round my centre-half partner, Alan 'Bluto' Bloor. Now that took some doing because generally if you pushed the ball past him Bluto would simply block you off and give away a free-kick rather than let you through. So now Best was bearing down on the edge of our area and I was the last man, covering behind Bluto. Before I knew it, George had left me on my backside as he wove his way into the box. Somehow left-back Mike Pejic had managed to do a fabulous job in coming across to cover behind me. Now Pej was called 'the claw.' He had more shirts off opposing players' backs without their permission than anyone I know. But in a flash Besty has done Pej like the proverbial kipper and then waltzed around Gordon Banks on the right side of our area.

Now, silly sod here has been daft enough to get up off the ground while this wizardry has been going on to hare back onto the line to try and stop George scoring. So I was now the only player between him and goal. It was one of those moments, when he stopped momentarily and looked me in the eye. I knew I was in trouble. And I was right. George advanced towards me and produced one of the most sublime pieces of foot-to-ball magic that I've ever witnessed. People thought that Best was very left-footed. Well I'm here to tell you that his right wasn't bad either. On this occasion he shimmied from left to right and back again, swivelling his hips like a Latin dancer. I was desperately trying to block his effort when it came, but he just toyed with me through sheer skill. As I dived to block what I thought was going to be his shot, he dummied one final time, with my momentum meaning I was now committed to going to ground. So I dived to the floor towards the left-hand post leaving the freedom of the penalty box for Besty to score. Except he didn't. Not straight away anyway. George, being George, didn't just tap the ball into the gaping net. No. He actually stopped it on the line, out of my reach, and with the rest of our defence and goalkeeper just dragging themselves off the ground where he had left them strewn in the Victoria Ground mud, swivelled to face them as if to say, 'watch this boys,' and back-heeled it in.

I mean, I thought I was a good defender and he had stitched me up like no-one else ever did in my career. Again, although I was very very annoyed we'd conceded a goal at the time, afterwards I didn't mind that much. George hadn't gone out to humiliate us, to take the Mickey professionally, he'd simply gone where his genius had taken him. You have to admire skill and brilliance that can create moments of magic like that. Anybody who can produce those sort of goals deserves to be hallowed, deified, exalted, call it what you want. We need players at the top of the game who can rise above the average to produce those kind of moments, much like a Rooney or a Gascoigne have in more recent times. It's part of what makes football a magnetic force in our world.

It was an absolutely brilliant goal, but I will say one thing. I scored a late equaliser in that cup tie and in extra-time we found the net again to win the game 2-1 and knock United out.

Chapter Two

TOMMY SMITH
WAS A PUSSYCAT

My era was crammed full of those players who have gone down in folklore as simple hatchet men. But I beg to differ. Yes we were hard as a breed, but we played within the existing rules of the time – mostly. I'm sure the likes of Chopper, Smithy and Norman get as frustrated as I do at times to think that because of our physicality we have gone down in history as one-dimensional players, although to be fair someone like Ron features high on the list of those who have perpetuated that myth. People think that's all you could do. It wasn't. We could play as well. The image of the violence is perpetuated by some high profile occurrences that happened to be shown on TV while the regular, untelevised fare in the top flight would see some wonderful football played within the rules as they stood at the time – it just so happens that they, when compared to today, were very lax when it came to punishing physical, and what is now called dangerous or excessive, play.

Having said that there were occasions when I saw some very cynical men at 'work'. Stoke's Welsh international midfielder Roy Vernon 'did' Arsenal's double-winning captain Frank McLintock in a match at the Victoria Ground with a studs up flying challenge. Now Frank could look after himself, but he was carried off that day thanks to this naughty challenge Roy put in. These days you think of Frank as the avuncular guy who features on Sky Sports' Soccer Saturday, but that day he was kicking up a stink about how Roy had whacked him and so Frank came into the players' lounge brandishing a bottle, looking for Roy and we had to calm him down and send him out.

Those occurrences, however, were actually very rare indeed and some of the men who have become renowned for dishing out stick were not quite what their modern day reputations would have you believe.

Everyone knows Ron 'Chopper' Harris was Chelsea's hardman. Sure, he could dish out some stick with the best of them – he was a hard man and took no prisoners – but his reputation is bigger now than it ever was then, boosted by a fair amount of publicity on his own behalf! Ron loves to bang on about how hard he was, but in fact the real hard men in that Chelsea team were David Webb and Ian Hutchinson. Webb was one of the hardest lads I ever played against. He was unbelievable. Built like the proverbial outhouse and with a 'take no prisoners' attitude. And you didn't mess with Hutch. Fellow striker Peter Osgood could be naughty, he would stamp on you, but if you started messing Ozzie about Hutch would be in to sort you out. If you had a battle with Hutch you knew you would come out with a hell of a lot of bruises.

Tommy Smith was a pussycat. He loved having a fearsome reputation as much as Chopper loved his, feeding off the hype created by being an integral part of Bill Shankly's successful Liverpool side which created a legendary club that has gone on to be the multi-million pound business we know today. But Tommy was far more than a just a beast of a tackler. He could play. He was good enough to play for England and should have played more. Again, like Ron Harris, he could put in some horrendous challenges when riled, but that was seldom in my experience. He ruled on reputation as much as anything.

I got on really well with Tommy. In fact the respect between us was mutual and over the course of our careers we developed something of an affinity. He actually used to love me whacking Emlyn Hughes, his own team-mate! I don't think there was any love lost between them and Emlyn was a very different personality to Tommy. He was extrovert and wore his heart on his sleeve. It was between the two of them for the captaincy and I don't think Tommy was overly chuffed that he lost out. So I'd stick a couple of challenges in on Emlyn early in the game and more often than not Tommy would shout from 40 or 50 yards away, "do it again, Den!"

I remember one particular game when Emlyn, who was pretty vocal at the best of times, finally cracked after I'd put an early thundering challenge in on him and he leapt up, literally foaming at the mouth like a rabid dog, and screamed at the referee: "Ref, this man is mad. He's a blinking lunatic!"

I calmly turned to the referee and said: "Look at me, ref. Now look at him." He did and saw what looked like a deranged inmate from the film One Flew Over The Cuckoo's Nest. "Now tell me who is mad?"

Now Emlyn's nickname was 'Crazy Horse' and he really loved it, lapping up the adulation that the Kop and the papers would give him, but as he and I stood looking daggers at each other that day, Tommy piped up in the background: "who's the animal?" Everyone in hearing distance fell about!

Of course Emlyn's very early death, having become one of the nation's favourites sports personalities by captaining a team on Question Of Sport for so long, was a real tragedy. But he was a real pain in the arse on the field, always moaning and cajoling referees.

Later Bob Paisley put together a midfield packed with real tough nuts like Jimmy Case and Graeme Souness. They were always far more prone to be naughty and go over the top than Tommy Smith ever was. You never messed with the midfield at Liverpool. They could all play but they could all look after themselves, so you had to be sensible as there was no point in trying to intimidate them, but they needed to understand that was a mutual thing, and believe me they didn't take kindly to people standing up to them. Generally speaking I came to an understanding with them and we just got on with the game, which was probably a good thing.

To me Tommy Smith was always the top man at Liverpool, with that great sense of humour he has. How could you not love the man who used to give Jimmy Greaves, the mercurial Tottenham goalscorer, a copy of the menu at the Liverpool Infirmary whenever he arrived at Anfield for a match?

Norman Hunter was just like Tommy. He was the one with the big reputation in that Leeds side managed by Don Revie that everyone loved to hate at that time. But that isn't strictly true. Sure, Norman would go through you and knock you about, but he was never looking to seriously damage you. Norman's role in that Leeds side was to step in when someone retaliated against one of the smaller, but nastier Leeds players such as Giles or Reaney who would go around dishing out dreadful stick left, right and centre and then find themselves on the receiving end of some like-minded retribution. But Norman was by no means the animal that football myth has painted him. He was hard but fair, but if you earned his respect then you both knew where you stood and everything was OK.

You might think it strange but I didn't hate Leeds at all, even though they were one of our direct opponents for silverware and bragging rights. In fact I loved them. If anything they were my second team. I thought their footballing ability was second to none. Yes they could intimidate you, but only if you allowed yourself to be intimidated. That Leeds side have become legendary – Bremner, Giles, Charlton, Collins, Hunter, Reaney. They knew every trick in the book, and invented some new ones too like World Cup winner Big Jack Charlton, who famously kept a 'little black book' in which he noted names of opponents on whom he needed to put one over to gain 'revenge'. But the main difficulty to combat was that as a team they organised their violent tendencies systematically, something which hadn't been done so well before, and made sure they got, as the old phrase goes, their retaliation in first. They were cute about it too. Basically early on in the game someone like Johnny Giles or my introducer to the harsh reality of professional football Bobby Collins would go over the top of the opponent's best player in an attempt to put him out of the game. Meanwhile all the other members of the team would gang up and take it in turns to have a go at one opposing player after another. Sometimes it would be in a tackle, other times off the ball. With many players and many teams it got into their psyche and they were beaten before they went onto the pitch because they didn't fancy matching Leeds' intimidation tactics. We struggled at Elland Road, but at home, at our wonderful Victoria Ground, packed with partisan supporters, we often stuck it right to them, although it was always a battle.

In fact the last players you might expect to have caused me problems in that Leeds side would probably be the goalscorers Allan Clarke and Mick Jones. But Clarke managed to put one over on me simply because I wasn't expecting it from him. We were playing at Elland Road this particular day and just before half-time Clarke and I went for a bouncing ball. I swung a foot to clear it and comfortably beat him to the ball, but Clarke hung his boot out high and tensed his leg so that when I followed through with my kick I whacked into his rigid, studs-up foot with my shin. He knew exactly what he was doing, but it was clever because nobody saw it as the ball was flying through the air towards the other end of the pitch. It hurt I can tell you. But, being the self-styled hardman, I could hardly let it show. So I got through to the break without further mishap, but when I got into the dressing room I pulled down my sock and my shinpad fell out in two pieces. It had shattered right down the middle where Clarke's studs had made contact. Thank God I was wearing them or that would have been my leg.

Full-back Terry Cooper was equally adept at going over the top in the tackle. I remember in one game he did it twice to our right-back Jackie Marsh, hurting him badly. After the second time, which left Marshy limping, I said to the ref, "if he comes near me there is no way I'm going for the ball." Shortly afterwards Terry made one of his rangy runs into our half, but overran the ball just enough for it to be equi-distant between us, so I thought, 'Right. I'm going to get you back for hurting my mate, Jackie.' So I went flying over the top of the ball into Terry, but, instead of giving him a fearsome whack, we actually clashed the soles of our boots because both of us had been going in so high. That probably saved both of us a red card, serious injury, or both.

Johnny Giles, as has been well-documented by other players who have written about that era and in particular that Leeds team, was the real nasty one. He was the one who kept his nose clean in front of the referee, but would then give you a sly one off the ball. He would also happily go over the top when you went into a challenge with him. In fact he was brilliant at it. He could do it extremely well and everyone knew it, so you were always careful how you tackled him, because if you weren't he'd stamp on you to lay down his marker. He did it to protect himself as he was relatively small and being a talented player attracted a fair amount of stick. Giles was a superb footballer, he could pass accurately and run all day in midfield. In fact all those Leeds players were top, top footballers. You didn't get much better on the left-hand side of midfield than Eddie Gray for example. They had a hell of a side. Often they were a joy to watch, but they'd also got that physical side to them if it proved necessary, and to them that was if their opponents didn't roll over and die.

I had a similar role to Norman and it was my job to look after the players in my Stoke team that would win us the game by scoring goals. Players like John Ritchie, Stoke's all-time leading goalscorer and his partner in goals Jimmy Greenhoff, a sublime footballer whose skills complemented Ritchie perfectly, Alan Hudson, a midfield maestro who developed into the best player I have ever seen, Terry Conroy, an Irish winger with the vim and vigour of Norman Wisdom – and the sense of humour to go with it – Peter Dobing, a cultured inside-forward and captain of our League Cup-winning side and 'Gentleman' George Eastham, an old-fashioned playmaker who could slice open defences with one visionary pass.

I may have put in more than my fair share of shuddering tackles on opponents and I may have used my physicality to intimidate those who were mentally weaker than me, but I never once did it nastily, never once on the sly to really hurt someone by taking them unawares. That wasn't my style. In fact I wasn't a bad player. Good enough to be called up for several England squads at my peak and in fact I firmly believe I was one of the two best centre-halves in England at that time, although the whims of England managers of the era and my continuing injury problems meant I would never be given the chance to show what I could do on the highest stage. But to reach that level in my era required a certain amount of brute force and physical prowess. It was the kind of behaviour that has rightly been stamped out of the game for good now. In my day, the kind of tackle which Birmingham City's Martin Taylor carried out on Arsenal's Eduardo in February 2008, which resulted in a triple break in the poor Croatian international's ankle and lower leg would probably not have seen its perpetrator receive anything more than a stern ticking off from a referee, even a stickler such as Clive 'The Book' Thomas. It would have been seen as just an unfortunate mis-timed tackle – just like the challenges which sadly ended the careers of both Ritchie and Dobing in their early 30s. That's how I have lived my life on the pitch as a player and throughout my subsequent 25-year career in management. Football is a bear pit in which the survival of the fittest is the prevailing law. The rules may have changed in my 50 or so years in the game, curtailing some of the rough stuff that went on in my early years, but in every way those men who could cope with the rigours of the game were, and still are, the ones who succeeded and win things.

But this assumption that there was all-out war breaking out on pitches up and down the country between the hard men in teams back in the 1970s simply isn't the case. In fact I very rarely got involved with what pundits and fans would call the other 'hard men'. Partly because I was rarely on the same part of the pitch as them, as we would almost always be defenders who patrolled their own halves and wouldn't come into direct contact with each other too much, but also for the simple reason that there'd be no use kicking Tommy Smith because all you would do is rile him and believe me you don't want to wound that particular animal.

In fact the ones you really had to watch – and this holds true for management as much as for my playing days – are the people in the game who you don't expect to put the boot in, literally and figuratively, but will when you least expect it. Some of the names who were more than happy to do this would surprise you. I'll give you an example. Denis Law. For all his wonderful artistry with a ball, Denis could look after himself. I know this from painful personal experience. He was a blinking hard lad, Denis, a hard lad. He could look after himself. But he was also brilliant to play against.

The first time I played against United was at Old Trafford in March 1969 and Waddo detailed me to mark Denis. This team were reigning European champions, so it was a stiff test for a young lad just making his way in the game. Right from the kick-off we came together, centre-half marking centre-forward. Stoke were attacking and so we were left in the centre circle in our half pretty much on our own and like a fatherly old pro Denis asked me, "you enjoying it, son?"

And I, well brought up and used to calling senior pros such as Gordon Banks and George Eastham "Sir", replied: "Yes thank you, Mr Law".

I was thinking to myself: 'This is what it's all about. What a nice fellow. It's a joy to be on the same field as him,' when out of the blue Denis, having made sure no-one was looking, smashed his elbow into my face. Another lesson learnt!

That was all about Denis wanting to find out what I was made of, trying to give himself an easy day. If I wouldn't fight and come back at him he knew he would have an easy life both during that match and in all subsequent meetings. He was testing me as he thought a youngster like me might crumble. He was wrong. I gave as good as I got that day and after that first meeting Denis was brilliant with me every time we met. I would batter him a few times, but he used to simply get up and smile and then give it me back and get on with the game. He was a brilliant footballer, a great player on the ball all right, but a damned hard one too. In those days all the real top players could all look after themselves. Bobby Charlton, for example, could look after himself as well. You didn't upset Bobby. Bobby would top you by showing his studs in a lunging challenge on you if he thought you were getting naughty with him. He wouldn't do that unless you were getting naughty, mind. He didn't go looking for it, but he could look after himself.

I loved the likes of Denis and Bobby because people like them didn't carry any animosity off the field and let it become personal. They knew it was a battle on the pitch as much mentally as physically. As soon as the game kicked off you would set your stall out against your immediate opponent, whoever that might be – Law, Best, Hurst, Peters, Keegan, Toshack, Radford, Worthington, Bowles or Currie. They would be saying: "I am going to take you on and beat you today." I would be saying: "You think you can batter me, that you can beat me for pace, or for skill, that you can out-tackle me, but you can sod right off. Let battle commence." That was my attitude.

Chapter Three

JUST ONE OF SEVEN

I began my apprenticeship to become one of football's tough guys fairly early in life.

I formed my first gang at the age of three. You might think that's a tad early to start the life of a criminal mastermind, but it wasn't about that. It was about being a group of kids who came together and took on all-comers. I had this gang – and it was my gang – and I ruled the roost. When someone came along to challenge us, we sorted them out. We beat up Tubby Hawkins and his mob. They were our main rivals and we did them. Even then I was ultra-competitive. It may only have been at nursery school, but where I came from you got your retaliation in early and made sure you were top dog. If we wanted to play in the sandpit we played in the sandpit. Simple.

I was always the leader. It wasn't a conscious thing, other kids just wanted to be associated with me because we had fun and we won things, like football matches and fights. I had this fierce determination not to be beaten at anything. We continued this through juniors and seniors at Sandon Road Junior School, now called the Grange, up to the age of 11.

There was a reason why I needed a gang. I came from a council estate at the south of the city of Stoke-on-Trent. Stoke's an unusual place. It is constituted of six towns, Hanley, Burslem, Longton, Tunstall, Fenton and Stoke itself. It only became a city in the mid-1920s when the mayors of each town came together and managed to get a royal charter. It was then that the football club which I would later play for became known as Stoke City, rather than plain Stoke. Of course the area is world-renowned as The Potteries, the birthplace of the famous brands of Wedgwood, Spode and Minton, but for us, in the immediate post-war years, the legacy of that heyday of pottery and china production was a city covered with a permanent smog from the antiquated potbanks that littered the landscape.

One of my earliest memories is going out into the thick, black smog which occasionally took a solid grip of Stoke with an old pram and collect the coal off the tip and bring it back to the house to burn to keep warm. I also recall that at times when I was very young dad worked in the pits, so we used to get some coal, which helped. I remember getting 10 bob each for picking potatoes all day on a farm. We would all do that as a family to earn a little and then be allowed to take some potatoes to take home as well.

In Stoke you were either a potter or a miner, went into the forces or to prison. You don't get much more working class than that. The pay was average to say the least and the work bloody hard. But, for all that, I always felt that people I knew were relatively happy with their lot. There wasn't a lot of unemployment and not much disparity between what people earned. We were a community, all in the melting pot of life together.

I came from the south end of Longton, the most southerly of the six towns. The area was called Meir and the Meir estate was a large council estate packed with working-class families. The houses on Ryder Road had been new when Mum and Dad first moved in soon after marrying in the 1930s, but by the time I was growing up, just after the end of the War, ours at no. 1 was 20 years-old.

In that kind of environment it was only natural that, as kids, we used to hang out in gangs all the time. There were no distractions such as Nintendo, X-box, or even television (we were too poor). It was a different age, in which we made our own group entertainment, normally with boxes and some string, invented games, played tag or, more often than not, football.

Even at home I had plenty of competition, although in a nice way. I was one of seven kids, three brothers and three sisters. I was next to the youngest and so was looked after by my eldest sister Joyce. She was 16 years older than me and so effectively brought me up. That was how it was then, the oldest sister would bring up the younger kids while the parents worked to bring in a living wage for such a large family.

After Joyce came Ron and Graham, 18 months apart. Then, a five-year gap to Beryl, another two years to Mick, then me four years later, when Mum was 35 and Dad in his 40s, and finally Susan another three years after that.

Incredibly we lived in a three-bedroomed house – actually, saying that, it was two proper bedrooms and a box room. From the earliest time I can remember we were packed in like sardines. It would probably be called poverty now, but we had a ball as kids. There wasn't a happier household than ours. No matter that she had seven hungry mouths to feed, Mum never complained about her lot, and we certainly didn't. To us our living conditions were normal.

Sleeping was a squeeze. In our room there was Graham in the corner in his own single bed, while Ron, Mick and I slept in a double. They called me 'the hot water bottle' because I was the youngest and so would be sent to bed first to warm the sheets up before they came in later on.

Susan was always in with Mum and Dad because she was the youngest, and later, Beryl, as the other young daughter, had to share with them too, sleeping in a bed with

Susan. This was because she had been evicted from her place in the double bed in the box room with Joyce, because our eldest sister had gone and got married, so she now had her husband Ralph and, fairly quickly, their baby daughter Marilyn in that room. At that point there were eleven of us under that one roof. We were a fairly big family, but it wasn't uncommon on that estate to have that many folk squashed into one house. It was just how it was.

Joyce got married young, just as our parents had. That was the way in those days. The only option was for them to move into our already busy house, but no-one minded. In fact we enjoyed having a baby around, especially us younger ones. I was only four years older than Marilyn and it gave me someone else to play with. I didn't feel in any way deprived. Living like this felt carefree and fun. It was great.

Our house was run like a military camp. It had to be. It was always spotless and our things were always ready for us when we got up or before we went to school. There was no room for mess, which meant Mum was always occupied with cleaning or washing. That may be why Joyce had to look after us young 'uns, as well as Marilyn; Mum spent so much time cleaning. I think it was probably force of habit with her.

She had been brought up extremely strictly in a convent in the 1920s from the age of 4 and had gone into service aged about 14 and married my Dad at 18. She stopped having to work in service then and began a family, but even then she just worked. She was unbelievable. Non stop. Cooking, cleaning, washing. As a kid I just accepted it, but now I know how tough it can be looking after a family, I truly appreciate how much she did for us, and how proud she was of her home and family. She was determined that we would have a good life and that nobody could talk about those Smiths being dirty. We were scrubbed, in particular our fingernails were scrubbed. We were also brought up to be polite and mind our Ps and Qs. She was quite single-minded in that sense and it rubbed off on us. I prized politeness above most other qualities from an early age.

When she was ill just before she died at the age of 62 in 1975, she used to come round our house and we'd find her making the beds. And I'd say: "Mum, what are you doing? Stop working. You're ill." And she'd reply: "I'm not working. I'm just making the beds."

She didn't talk much about the experiences in the big house near Longton where she was a servant throughout her teens. It's one of my regrets in life that I never got into enough discussions with her about her youth and how she grew up. She never raised the subject and unfortunately she died just when I was getting to an age when you would perhaps start getting interested in your family history. What I do know has been gleaned from my older siblings.

Having grown up in the convent, Mum was a Catholic, although she didn't bring us up in the faith. I suppose she was what I would call a 'poor catholic'. She didn't have any money and so wasn't that cared for by the catholic community. They didn't ignore her exactly, but they didn't come running with too much help either. She'd had a bad time in the convent as a young girl, although she once told Kate, my wife, that she wouldn't talk about it. I think that experience was what drove her to be the way she was and why she wanted us to have freedom as kids.

But she worked so hard. When I close my eyes and think about her, I always picture my mother on her knees every Sunday morning scrubbing the front step. I suppose it is a classically stereotypical northern town picture to paint, but she did. If you go back into the fifties, those were the kinds of things you saw in places across the north of England like Stoke.

Not only was our front step scrubbed on a regular basis, so were we. When we came back from a day's playing in the streets, fields, puddles or sandpits, we would have the tin bath in front of the fire which would be filled, probably more regularly than you would think, and we would take turns to scrub ourselves in it. Being the sixth meant it could be pretty dirty by the time it came to my turn! We did eventually have a bathroom put in downstairs, replacing the coalhouse just off the kitchen, but not until the early 1950s. The only toilet we ever had was right by the back door.

I'll always remember when we had the bath fitted. It was quite a big thing for us and when it came to my turn to have my first bath in it, I got my clothes off and was just about to step in when I peered over the rim and saw a fin swimming around in the bath. Now I was only about six and it was well before the Jaws books and films came out, so I wasn't that scared at the prospect of what might be lurking beneath the surface, but I wasn't exactly happy and shouted for Mum to come quick. Anyway, before she could reach me my elder brother Ron rushed in to fish his prize capture from his day on the riverbank out of the tub, where he'd put it for safekeeping. I can still see it; an eighteen inch-long pike.

Ron was different like that. As well as fishing, he was into his motorbikes. He would often take his bike to pieces in the kitchen, cleaning it bit by bit and then reassemble it. It could take him all day, with Mum fussing around him, making sure he didn't make a mess. Imagine trying to live round that.

I'll give you another example. The other day I got home and there was a message on the answerphone so I switched it to play to listen. It clicked in and this voice said, "Oi, Den," and put the phone down! Nothing else. Thankfully I could hear his dog barking in the background so I knew it was Ron!

Being such a tight squeeze meant that we weren't allowed to spend any time inside the house during the day. If the weather was even remotely hospitable, we were sent outside, partly because Mum wanted us out of the house so she could clean it and also so we wouldn't mess it up again when she'd made the floors sparkle and tidied our rooms. But I was young and carefree and loved spending my life outdoors. It was perfect. I used to cycle wherever I wanted, going out at 9 o'clock in the morning and coming back in when it was dark. I'd got total freedom to come and go in daylight as long as I was in on time for tea.

Us younger ones were positively discouraged from coming inside. I remember once trying to get in for a drink of water and Joyce, my eldest sister, had just finished mopping the kitchen floor and she said: "if you're coming in, you're staying in" and I said: "right, I'm not coming in then" and scooted back off outside to play some more.

There was, perhaps not surprisingly, no central heating in the house. We used to have the old fire with an old-style range and often in the hearth we'd keep little chicks we'd got off the rag and bone man. We'd rear them for eggs and then, eventually, as something to eat. I remember they would run around the back garden in the summer. But having chicks in various stages of development meant the house would be even more cramped than it already was! Put it this way, there wasn't really any room to go anywhere or sit anywhere. We only had two rooms downstairs – the kitchen and the living room. Unless you were quick you literally could not sit down. We didn't have enough chairs – just four round the dining table – so we couldn't all eat together. We used to eat in shifts.

Again Mum was unbelievable. There was a butchers down in Leacroft Road, close to where we used to play football, and the elder siblings would come in from work and Mum would ask them what they want and then walk down to the butchers and get it, come back and cook it. Thinking about it now, really she was basically a slave, but that was her life and she was happy doing it. Her family was her world.

We were also tight for space in the lounge. There was a two-seater settee and then a chair where my dad sat. There wasn't an inch of room in the house, so there really wasn't much point being inside unless you absolutely had to. Every Sunday morning, when Mum had put clean covers on the settee, she'd put the dining chairs on top so none of us could sit on it and get it dirty.

That suited me because there wasn't really anything to stay in for anyway. Not for a kid like me. I can remember Scalextric coming out and thinking "wow", but other than that there was nothing. We weren't able to have a television until very late in the fifties when they came down in price. We did eventually get one, but there wasn't a lot on anyway to interest us kids. It was the era of Andy Pandy and Watch With Mother, rather than Transformers, Tracy Beaker and Grand Theft Auto. I can't remember watching television in the house because I was never in that often. I was out.

They were very different times. There was no fear of strangers or anything like that. Without any worries, we could play all day in the street, which had only just been metallised with tarmac, and had previously just been dirt and earth because no-one owned a car in the neighbourhood.

Cars were rich man's things even in the 1950s. In fact, the only vehicles we would see would be the coal wagon, the rag and bone cart and the milk float – and the chances were that they were still horsedrawn. Certainly the rag and bone man had a horsedrawn cart. You wouldn't see any private cars. My brother got one of the first ones on the estate – a green Morris – and that wasn't until the very late fifties. So that meant we could play all day long in the middle of the street. It was great. We built trolleys out of old prams because everyone used to have those big Victorian-style prams, the kind you'd pay an arm and a leg for now. We would take the wheels off them and get pieces of wood and make trolleys. We loved flying down the hill of Ryder Road on them. Then, when the snow came – and it did come regularly – we would turn them into sledges and spend all day sledging. The thing I remember about that was that the snow stayed there for days because there was nothing to melt it or turn it into sludge. No cars, no global warming, just endless, frozen days. I believe all that give me fantastic energies so I could run for fun. I was forever out and I was never still.

As a childhood it was brilliant, fabulous. We spent all our lives playing games. Everything from football to cricket to marbles. It could get quite competitive; in fact marbles could get very competitive. As one of the younger ones, I wasn't that great at marbles, so I used to lose all mine in the games. But fortunately for me Beryl was a brilliant marbles player and she used to win them all back for me. Beryl was one of the lads in many ways, so much so that she taught me how to whistle. You know, the full-blooded wolf whistle kind of whistle with two fingers in the mouth. It's turned into something I've used all my life, especially as a manager on the touchline. I can make a hell of a noise! You need to in order to get things across to players either in training or during a game. It's been an invaluable skill, one of the best things I've ever learned and that is all down to my sister.

Actually my siblings were very important to helping me turn out OK. As you may have gathered, I was always a tearaway. But with so many older brothers and sisters I really didn't want to do anything that overstepped the mark so much that it upset Mum or Dad because it would mean Joyce or Ron or Graham getting on my case. They'd soon let me know if they weren't happy.

What wasn't stereotypical about us was that we had a very loving family. I never got beat, there was none of that, as is often painted about the working class at that time. My parents loved us all unequivocally and devoted their lives to helping us better ourselves, right from the very start. My Dad went out to work in warehouses as a labourer at Wardle's and then 16MU Stafford, an ammunition works, and at Seddons. He ended up organising the logistics for them as a sort of foreman.

They were a very hard working couple dedicated to giving their kids the best they could, meaning they had to give up so much. For entertainment he and Mum would go out together one night a week, Saturday night, and have two halves each. They never kept any alcohol in the house aside from a bottle of sherry at Christmas. Just occasionally dad would ask me to go to the bookies for him on a Saturday. This was at a time before bookies were strictly legal and the place I had to go was just down the back street. He'd give me a little slip and some money, send me down this back alley between terraced houses and get me to put on a couple of bets on the horses for him but that was about the limit of his flamboyancy. The rest of their very hard-earned money was spent on us.

By the time it came to me wanting football boots because I was getting serious about playing and was showing a good deal of aptitude and skill, Joyce and Graham were working on the pots. Graham was a foreman at Crown Staff and Royal Worcester. He could be a tough customer. They used to send people to Graham if they wanted to get rid of them, not only because he was tough, but also because he was extremely polite. But apparently he was a nightmare to work with. If you did everything right you were fine by him, and in fact most people loved him. But if you didn't, you were moved on. Simple as that. Both Joyce and Graham were bringing money into the house, so I got spoilt really and was able to have things that they hadn't because there were several wages coming in.

We didn't exactly have much money, but we did OK. I don't think any of us felt any amount of hardship. We always had plenty of food. It might just have been a plate of potatoes, but there was plenty of it. I never went hungry, so I never felt deprived. I knew I was well looked after and well fed because, when I was approaching my teens and became more conscious of such things, I saw some signs of the deprivation elsewhere on the estate. My clothes might have got dirty and torn quick as you like, but that was because I was always throwing myself headlong into all sorts of mad games with the odd scrap here and there for good measure.

As we got a bit older and were allowed to roam a bit more, our gang used to go up to a big flat expanse of land round the back of Sandon Road Junior School which had been Meir aerodrome, but fell into disuse after the war. Near there were Cromwell's Caves, which were really just holes hollowed out of a hill. We used to go up there, tie ropes to trees, and swing like Tarzan for hours on end.

But perhaps there was something more of the Huckleberry Finn childhood about the way we grew up. Things were so simple. I mean I learned to swim in the river Leigh. It wasn't the Trent, thank god, which has always been a polluted body of water that snakes through the city and was used to drive the industry which kept Stoke going through the years. I learned in a small river called the Blithe out in the countryside. We used to get on the train at the Meir, and take it out south-east towards Uttoxeter and then get off just south of Blythe Bridge. Then we'd run to the place where we'd blocked up the river to form a pool. I had often been there with the boys. But when it came to learning to swim I didn't have anything as fancy as lessons. In fact no-one really showed me what to do. My brother Mick just simply threw me in … sink or swim. I soon learned.

Now it might sound like an idyllic childhood – and in many ways it was – but there was another way in which it prepared me fantastically well for life in football. It was hard. Very hard.

I decided from a very young age that I wanted more than what the majority of my peers accepted as their lot in life. I knew that the estate would constrict me and I had ambitions, and I already knew in which direction those ambitions lay – football.

Chapter Four

FOOTBALL FIRST

As a kid, like millions of others through time immemorial, I became obsessed by playing football in the street and would spend endless hours kicking a ball around, either with my mates or on my own. I was football daft. The house in which I was brought up had a big side wall to it, so I could stand on the lawn just whacking the ball or heading the ball against that wall all day long. Doing that day in day out meant my skills came on and when I played for my first school team, Sandon Road Juniors, I was good enough to play anywhere. I was, for quite a time, the best player, but then as others improve you then find your natural place and discover what you're really good at. I was a natural defender, aggressive, a tough, clean tackler, a good reader of the game and I could pass the ball too.

Standing out so much meant the school made me team captain and then put me forward for trials for the Longton representative team. I injured myself during the trial so they didn't take me on, but they did pick another couple of lads from my school team, so, never one to take no for an answer, I went back with them, with my boots and shorts, to their first training session. This was where being utterly single-minded helped me. When people tell me I'm not good enough that's their problem. Instead of believing them, I was totally convinced they had got it wrong and so when the training session came along I just turned up with my boots, ready to play. They let me join in and I soon became part of the team.

For me football was already more than having a kickabout. Not only was it the channel for my natural aggression, from the age of 11 I decided I was going to be a professional footballer. Not only that, I'd fallen in love with my club – Stoke City. My dad took me down to watch the side in red and white stripes that had fallen on hard times in the 1950s, following an era in which they had been contenders for the League title and boasted the most famous footballer in the world among their ranks – Stanley Matthews.

I first watched Stoke around the age of seven from the boys' enclosure in one of the paddocks on the side of the ground. My early heroes were the likes of Frank Bowyer, an inside-forward who was one of the best volleyers of the ball I have ever seen, and a gritty centre-half called Ken Thomson, who was an iron-man centre-half and captain of the 1950s side that I loved to watch buffeting opposing forwards.

Then there was Don 'Ratter' Ratcliffe, who was a young winger in the late 50s. He was bloody mad, much like me, famous for being a bundle of energy. In April 1963 Stoke played Real Madrid in a friendly at the Victoria Ground to celebrate the club's centenary and Don absolutely ripped apart Madrid's left-back Vicente Meira. The fans loved Don and when he set off on one of his runs, legs going in a blur, head down, they used to shout "Open the gates, he's coming. Keep running, Ratter"!

When I got into my teens, having graduated to stand in the Boothen End, the vast kop behind the goal which rivalled Liverpool's home banking for fervent support, I was able to cheer on my heroes with my mates from very close proximity. Everything about a matchday captivated me, from the camaraderie amongst the fans and players, who mingled freely in those days, to the passionate support of my team. For every home game we'd get on the bus and then go down and put in 1s 6d entrance money. It became a wonderful habit. I had fallen totally in love with football. In fact I thought about pretty much nothing else. I became obsessed with players, history, the folklore of football, as well as playing the game as often as I possibly could.

If I think back to a player I modelled myself on – a question I am often asked – it wouldn't be any professionals. Not Billy Wright, then England captain, nor even Neil Franklin, who I was too young to see play in his pomp for Stoke and England in the immediate post-war years when he won a record 25 consecutive caps, something no England player had previously come close to. No, in fact the player I modelled myself on had much humbler origins. Around the age of 10, just when I was seriously considering football as a career, I used to go and watch my brother-in-law, Beryl's husband Joe Lynch, play for Stone Lotus works team. I'd go on the bus and spend the afternoon with him. Joe had been brought up in Ireland and played right-back. But alongside him in the Stone Lotus defence was this dominating presence. His name was Atholl Still and he was quick and strong and he used to win everything. He was a proper centre half, the first I'd been able to watch close up. I think he played sort of semi-pro. I used to think be like that, when I was older, I wanted to be like that. He had a shock of black hair and he controlled his back line and his opponents with an iron will. I liked that and, perhaps without realising it, took it on board.

I knew that my ambition would lead me to spread my wings, and to that end I began to make connections from off the estate in my early teens. I knew I couldn't stay involved in the gangs that ruled the turf in my immediate area, so I got to know people from other parts of the city, lads that I shared interests with and shared the same kinds of ambitions as me in terms of making something of themselves. By the time I was 14 or 15 my friends all came from other areas of Stoke. And I was right. Of the people who I teamed up with then, one of them, Dr Chris Boumford, is a professor in Canada, another, Alan Merry became a top businessman in Stoke and then emigrated to Australia, while a third, Graham Rushton, became a very good schoolteacher and he ended up going Down Under too. Much as I love Stoke, and it was a great place to grow up in, it is not somewhere that you can truly spread your wings and gain recognition. Gone are the days when the eyes of the world would focus on what Stan Matthews or Gordon Banks would do in a red and white shirt, or what Josiah Wedgwood or Thomas Minton were producing in their Potteries. The heydays of industry and sport seem a long way off from twenty-first century Stoke, but more of that later.

It's interesting. I developed from the tearaway who'd organised those gangs as a real young kid, to just about the most sensible, driven youth on the estate. By then the others called me 'Grandma' because if anyone suggested doing something a bit on the naughty side, like taking someone's back gate off its hinges just for a laugh, I'd now be the one saying: "Think about it. That could be your Grandma's." Those of us that became friends in our early teens shared that sense of responsibility. I'd got that in me by the age of ten.

In fact my new group of friends' interests moved on quite quickly from territorial gangs to having dreams of how our talents could take us out of Stoke-on-Trent. Like any teenagers in the late fifties those dreams centred on sport and rock 'n' roll. Early on we wanted to form a musical group because our friend Chris Boumford was very talented on the piano and another mate Alan Merry could play the guitar. The only problem was that left the jobs of singing and playing the drums and I couldn't do either. In the end we had a few practices, but nothing came of it. But I think it was an early example of how we saw our horizons widening.

I do remember that this particular escapade did have one happy side effect. Chris ended up playing piano in a few local pubs, particularly The Ring Of Bells, The Bluebells Of Scotland and The Vine, at the age of 16 or 17 and it meant that, thanks to him, we could all get pints. So we'd be in these pubs as young teenagers with all these burly miners, colliers and potters, getting sozzled and having sing-songs around the piano.

Now one of our lads, Reg, whose parents owned the Waterhead pub on the estate, had a party piece in which he would be able to drink a pint of beer straight down by opening up his gullet. It was pretty amazing. He would have beer races with these grown men and win more pints for us that way. The only problem was that he could only take a couple before he was hammered. I stopped drinking by the time I was eighteen, which ironically was the age at which you were allowed to buy alcohol. By then my football had started to get a lot more serious and I was being selected for the city representative teams, so my social life began to revolve around my sport rather than the pub.

Football had become my life, so much so that I knew it was where my future lay. If I'd known then what I knew now, about the wastage of teenagers whose dreams are shattered by poor coaching, injury or straightforward competition, I may have had second thoughts, but I was so driven, so focussed that I had convinced myself that nothing was going to get in my way. And I'd already made my mind up that I was going to be good enough to emulate my heroes. I was going to wear the red and white of Stoke City.

Two of my friends from off the estate had ended up going to the Grammar school, but I caused something of a controversy both at school and in my house when I refused to take the 11 plus entrance exam. It wasn't that I didn't think I could do it – I was considered reasonably bright at Sandon Road Junior School – but Longton High School, where I would have gone had I passed the exam, were a rugby-playing school. They didn't play football. I couldn't countenance that. I couldn't waver from my chosen path and going to the Grammar school, while good for my education, would have meant not playing football, so it wasn't an option for me.

Mum and Dad weren't happy. Despite the fact that going to Longton High would have meant them affording the uniform and all that went with going to a school like that, they wanted me to go. They had never had that kind of opportunity and were desperate for me to give it a go and improve my lot in life by becoming a Grammar School pupil. But it didn't matter to me one iota. So I went to Queensbury School and played football.

By the time I was 14 and playing in the City Boys team for the 1961/62 season I had an ally in my quest to make football my life – my Dad. He'd been a decent and fanatical player as a youth, but hadn't reached a higher standard than local football, although he had represented his unit while on National Service in the Army. I understand that his father had come down to England from southern Scotland around the turn of the century and had played at a decent amateur level himself, possibly for Queen of the South. But in fact my ability may have come more down my mother's line. She was one of 13 kids and one of her brothers was apparently a very good footballer. I think he played at a good level that's definitely where my athletic side comes from. And a cousin of mine on that side of the family, Dave Bullock, was also a good amateur player. Having said that, Dad was apparently aggressive as a player, but because none of my other brothers were any good, now I was his last chance to fulfil a dream which I suppose most fathers must hold for their sons. He'd watched as my three elder brothers showed little interest in sport. Mick was, according the sports teacher, a hell of a good cross country runner, but I think Mick was more interested in pub games like darts, dominoes and cribbage. He later gave up darts because it was too energetic!

I, however, was into every kind of sport imaginable. I ran for the school, district, city and county, enjoyed most athletic disciplines including cross country, 800 yards, long jump and high jump and was a very good boxer, representing Staffordshire up to Under 15 level. I was a frenzied fighter, a terrier in the ring, more of a street brawler than a boxer and I learned a very important lesson around this age when I sparred with a guy named Glyn Blundred, from Meir, who became all England Champion. Glyn made me appreciate the art of Boxing. I could fight and if I'd taken him outside he wouldn't have lasted five minutes, but he had real talent as a boxer, and had learned ringrcaft. After a few rounds inside the ropes with him I knew that if I came up against someone with my attitude and his talent I'd have get severely beaten, so when the inevitable clash between the two sports happened I chose to concentrate football.

Dad watched near enough every game in which I played from schoolboy up. He never interfered, never got in the way, was never the kind of 'pushy parent' you see on so many touchlines these days. In fact he was pretty much the opposite. All I would get from him was for him to say: "seen you do better" on regular occasions. If I got a "not bad" I knew I'd done well. He wasn't exactly over-effusive, but the school of hard knocks would serve me well.

I still had plenty to overcome. To start with I was small, only about 5ft 2 ins at the age of 14. In fact, when I met Kate, my wife, I was almost 15 and she was 14 and she was the same height as me! I then grew about eight inches in the next two years. It was quite a late growth spurt, but not unheard of in our family. When Ron, my eldest brother, first went to work he had to stand on a box to reach the production line and he then grew to 5 ft 9 ins. The same happened in the next generation. My eldest son Paul was small up to the age of 15, but now he is 5ft 10 ins. Being that small at 14 for me was a problem at times because I was told I was a centre-half, but you know you can't play centre-half at that size, so I played right-back or left-back. I didn't care particularly where I played at that time, I just wanted to be involved and have people watching me as I worked my way through the various representative teams. And in a funny kind of way, looking back on it now, being small helped because I had to leap higher if I wanted to win balls in the air and it also meant I had to be quicker, and, importantly, it sharpened my desire to compete.

By 16 I had a good pedigree to base my determination on. In 1961/62, the Stoke-on-Trent City boys team won the English Schools Shield, which was a massive competition in those days. It pitted the best youth players from all over the country head to head, much like the FA Youth Cup, then in its infancy, does on a club by club basis. The Schools Shield though was for all the schools in a particular area, so we represented the Potteries. We were a good side. In fact the following season we became the first team ever to defend that trophy. But at that standard I wasn't head and shoulders the best player. That honour fell to a guy called Bill Bentley. Bill was huge for his age. He's the same size as he is now as when he was about 11 when we first played together for Longton schools. He could play too. He was the main man, who would also play for and captain England schools as he trod a path seemingly towards football stardom. He was even being touted as the next Duncan Edwards.

There were quite a few good players amongst a very talented squad, including my mate Alan Merry. In fact I was one of the few in the team that didn't get picked for the

Staffordshire County side, which peeved me a bit. It could have been because I was actually playing a year above my age group, which was why I was able to play in two Schools Shield winning sides at Under 15 level. About seven of the others did win selection for the County, which at that time included the areas of Wolverhampton and Walsall, and that was understandable, they were good.

For example, among that group was a kid from the rough end of town like me called Jackie Marsh. Jackie and I would grow up in football together winning trophies as we did so. He would become my room-mate for years at Stoke City, and although we were very different personalities and had totally different outlooks on life and being a professional footballer, the camaraderie we developed from the age of 11 kept us closely together and became a very important factor in the success of Stoke City's homegrown defence which won the League Cup in 1972.

That Stoke-on-Trent Boys team were very fortunate in that we had former England international striker Dennis Wilshaw in charge. Dennis had been a star in Wolves' great post-war and 1950s side which had dominated domestic football and made the first forays into international club competition with a series of high profile floodlit friendlies against foreign opposition. Of course the most famous of those was the 3-2 victory over Honved on a foggy night in December 1954 at Molineux when the entire nation crammed round their TV set to see if the Wanderers could take revenge for the Hungarian national team's 6-3 thrashing of England at Wembley just over 12 months previously. Dennis played his part in their incredible comeback from two goals down to become 'Champions of the World' – or at least so Wolves claimed. He was a great forward, who scored 10 goals in just 12 games for his country – and yet with a strike rate like that he wasn't considered an automatic choice! I remember one particular game he played for England at Wembley. It was against Scotland in 1955 and Dennis raced through the Scots' defence to score four goals in a 7-2 thrashing.

Dennis was a remarkable man in many ways. Despite being an international striker with England's top club of the era, he wasn't a full-time player. He was one of the last semi-professionals. Like his Wolves team-mate Bill Slater, Dennis worked in education as a senior school teacher during the week, training at every opportunity, and then turning in performance after dazzling performance as Wolves became one of the best sides in the country.

Unfortunately for Dennis, Wolves manager Stan Cullis believed that players became spent forces after the age of 28, so in 1957 he was told he could move on. That was good news for Stoke City, though. Dennis had grown up in the city as a lad and the club's scouting network had missed out on him just before the war, Wolves stealing him from under their nose. But now Stoke manager Frank Taylor persuaded Dennis to return to his roots, take a job in a local school and coach the city boys team in his spare time. City were struggling in the Second Division at the time and needed more goals in the team and Dennis provided them, scoring 108 goals in 49 games. But he could create too and he was one of the most popular players of that era. I can remember him taking corners down at the Boothen End of the Victoria Ground with me and other members of the City Boys' team shouting at him, "Hello, sir!" He would just give us the eye as if to say, "Shut up."

Dennis scored a total of 167 goals in 340 games before his career was ended in January 1961 by Newcastle centre-half Bill Thompson, who broke his leg in a tackle so badly that, after countless surgical procedures it ended up an inch shorter than the other one.

Because of this experience and his natural ability as a schoolteacher he was a fantastic coach for our city team. He made us play like a professional team, even though we were all under 16 years of age. Under him we won the national trophy in two successive seasons, sweeping all before us and to celebrate we threw this gent of a man, a recent England international, in the baths!

I think Dennis appreciated the fact that I simply loved playing football and that I was left-sided, which has always been a plus. I could tackle and I could head, I could run and I wanted to play. I also always turned up no matter what. I mean the journey from Meir to where we trained the other side of Hanley was about three or four bus rides, but I would get there come rain or shine on time and always first with my boots on. I think he saw an hunger in me that he understood. He put me in the team a school year ahead which was fantastic. He was a great bloke for Stoke football and lads like me and John Marsh from the council estates.

No team had ever defended the trophy successfully before and we managed to do it. Dennis was undoubtedly the guiding force behind our success. And then, of all the stupid things, along came some idiot do-gooders who said it was too elitist, and Dennis was told to stop picking the best kids because others were getting passed over and people were complaining that he wasn't taking any notice of anyone else. Why should he? He was a winner. He was picking the best kids and having this fantastic success and then it was taken away from him by ridiculous people who didn't know the first thing about serious competitive sport.

I think sport is good for your development as a person. You learn how to lose as well as win. You learn that you're not always going to be the best at everything, but you find out what you're best at. Everybody's got strengths. It doesn't have to be sport, it could be writing, but if you want to write the greatest novel you're going to be competing against somebody because somebody else is also trying to achieve that. So there's always a competitive edge no matter where you are with these things. It has become absolutely farcical.

All that ill-conceived non-competitive nonsense was the start of a huge downhill turn in school sport in this country which has had a long term impact on sport at all levels, both amateur and professional, which I believe we have not recovered from and my not even be able to do so before the 2012 Olympics. Nearly half a century of standards dropping and regular failure because of these idiots who were worried about some kids being excluded. Well, I've got news for anyone who thinks that sport isn't competitive. You're wrong. And it's not just sport. To be good, to be the best at anything, you have to be better than other people. That's not a negative thing. It's just a fact of life. Now I take the point that those who aren't necessarily inclined to take part in a particular sport will be marginalised by being picked last and not feeling that they can compete, but there are many ways to make sport fun, and what should have been done is that those kids should have been included so that they could get something out of it, keep fit and develop some of that competitive spirit which would help them in every walk of later life.

It certainly helped me become a top level footballer and a manager who has been in charge of over 1,000 games.

If I hadn't had that drive I think I could have been one of those cast onto the scrapheap of professional football. Things went well to start with. As one of the stars of the team, I had done really well in those trophy-winning teams to establish the fact that we were the best in England – bar none – and impressed a few of the scouts who watched the two-legged final against in at the end of the 1962/63 season in which we hammered Bristol. Both Tottenham and Portsmouth wanted to take me on. They had scouts like all football clubs who'd come and knock on your door and sit with your mum and dad trying to persuade them to sign for their team. It was a huge compliment. Spurs were one of the biggest and best clubs in the country then. Bill Nicholson's men had won the first double of the twenty-first century in 1960/61 and had retained the FA Cup, something which only one other side, Newcastle United, had done since the war.

We had beaten Tottenham in the semi-finals of the Schools Shield, so they'd obviously seen me there. Portsmouth, on the other hand, although not a top flight team, having been relegated at the end of the fifties, a decade after winning their back-to-back League titles just after the war, were renowned as having the best youth set up in the country at the time. Had I signed, I would have been there alongside people like Ipswich and England captain Mick Mills and Roger Jones, the goalkeeper who later signed for Stoke and played with me in the team which won promotion back into the First Division in 1978/79. So it was great to have this interest from top clubs taking me on as an apprentice. I was flattered, but even this wasn't going to divert me from my chosen course. That, as far as I was concerned, was set. The issue was that Stoke City – my club – didn't seem that sold on me. They only took on so many full-time apprentices each season – about seven I think from that team group –and I wasn't one of them. They only offered me amateur terms.

Now I had a problem, not least because I was so loyal to my club, and so single-minded, that I was determined to become a Stoke player. I didn't want to go to London, or the south coast. I only wanted to play for Stoke. There is a kind of passion in all of us that are fans that drives us to play for our boyhood teams. Maybe these days kids don't necessarily support their local sides, so David Beckham, for example, can fulfil his boyhood dream by playing for Manchester United alongside his hero Bryan Robson, but in my day, it was all about playing for your local club. Just as with my determination not to go to a rugby-playing school, I wouldn't dream of joining any other club. It was Stoke or nothing.

But all the club would offer me was the chance to have a job as a plumber's apprentice with one of the Directors' Companies, so I could earn some money during the day and then train two nights a week and vie for a place in the A team.

So I started as a plumber's mate at a company owned by Percy Axon, who would later become Chairman of the club, hoping to impress with my football quickly enough to be taken on more permanently. That didn't exactly go to plan. The plumber I was assigned to was a big, rough lad, who obviously had to ask me to do things for him, mostly very menial tasks like finding a screwdriver or carrying something, or we'd be up on roofs fixing the flashing around chimneys with no safety net, no harnesses or anything. But the problem was that he treated me like dirt. He wouldn't say please or thank you – things which I prized highly thanks to my upbringing as I said before. He would gruffly say: "Fetch that." Now I'd dealt with bullies and the like all my life, standing up to them and for myself, so I'd got the confidence to reply: "Say 'please'". This plumber would retort: "I don't say 'please'" and I'd say: "Yeah, you do".

Remember at this stage I was this skinny 16 year-old, so it was quite a spectacle for me to be so bolshie and in is face, demanding an apology, and everybody on the site used to come and watch us have these barneys and laugh because this plumber was a monster of a bloke and there was me demanding: "say 'please'. My mum and dad say 'please', why can't you say 'please'?" On top of that I was fairly useless at plumbing anyway, and I didn't enjoy it at all. I used to have to be up at 6 o'clock in the morning to catch the bus to get to wherever in the Potteries we were working and then on Tuesdays and Thursdays I would get down to the Victoria Ground after a full day's work for 7 o'clock at night to train. That wasn't ideal from my point of view. In fact I only lasted about 12 months and then I went.

I had to be careful, though, because blowing my apprenticeship with the director's company could have affected my status as an amateur at Stoke, so I had to find work – and quickly. Fortunately for me, my brother Ron worked at the Lotus shoe company in Stone, between Stoke and Stafford, as a swing man. Now a swing man, rather like the job of the same name in musical theatre, means you can do all the jobs on the line, so if someone wanted to go to the loo, or was sick for the day, he filled in, allowing the production line to keep running smoothly.

My sister Beryl, her husband Joe, and brother Mick worked at Stone Lotus too, as I said before. The shoes would start to be made in the clicking room, where Mick worked. Here the material was cut according to the pattern for the particular design of shoe. They then moved through to the finishing room where Beryl worked stitching the shoes together. Finally the shoes moved on to the making room which housed what was called 'the track'. This was where the soles and heels were added and the final product was put together in a box and checked.

Eventually Ron went on to be the foreman because he knew all the jobs inside out and it was he who got me a job.

I started as a Clicker. It might not sound like much of a job now, but it was a five year apprenticeship and I did well, working my way up until soon I was getting £20 a week, while the other lads who'd stuck at the plumbing or at entry level at Lotus were only getting £6. That was partly because I always had the attitude that if I am doing something, coming into the factory from 8am till 5pm, I might as well work instead of sitting down in the loo and reading the paper like others did. So I progressed because the management saw I was committed and I could have had a solid career there. At one point they started to bring these machines in for cutting and consequently laying off workers, so all the young lads were worried about their futures and I got myself elected as spokesperson to lead a delegation in to have a word with the manager. But when we got in there, I turned round and there was only me. The others had bottled it. So in the end I was left arguing my own case. I told the boss I wasn't happy with the new arrangements and he appreciated my honesty and gave me the best jobs going, while the others remained stuck on machine jobs.

In the end, though, I only did twelve months at Stone Lotus, although they wanted me to stay because of my positive attitude, but I didn't even consider it. That was because things were happening for me at Stoke City.

Chapter Five

THE MOST INJURED MAN IN FOOTBALL

Throwing yourself bodily into every single challenge in your career has one serious drawback. Somewhere along the line, either through stupid belief in your own infallibility, a misjudgement, revenge or retaliation from a victim, you are going to get hurt. It might not be too serious, but you have to be prepared for pain.

As a kid I was fairly oblivious to it. If you see my legs, I am covered in scars from where I used to slide tackle on concrete, crash one of those makeshift carts we made or fall off a rope, but fortunately just across the road right opposite our house was the Doctor's and they would patch me up and I'd rush back out again to play and get myself into yet more scrapes. I used to drive my mother daft with all the cuts and bruises, I couldn't help myself and I was always itching to get out there and get involved in whatever was going on. When I first broke my leg at the age of 14 I 'recuperated' by playing football in the street on crutches with my leg in plaster.

I never lost that spirit of total and utter commitment and it would earn me the official tag of 'The Most Injured Man In Football' in the Guinness Book of Records. When I was a lad, holding a world record that was featured in that esteemed publication was an ambition which many youngsters across the country, and indeed the planet, held. Normally you'd want to be in there for being fastest, biggest, strongest, or for something like having toppled the most dominos, laid most sixpences in a line or sung Kum-Ba-Ya simultaneously in the biggest choir. But funnily enough when I heard I'd got in it I wasn't that chuffed.

I didn't buy a copy of the 1976 edition which listed me as 'The Most Injured Man In Football'. In it they listed 17 different injuries I'd picked up to that point. There would be plenty more.

It sounds pretty gruesome now, but I really didn't think too much of it then. Injuries had to be extremely serious to stop me playing, partly because of determination, partly pride and partly because I couldn't afford to lose my place in the team.

I'd never tried to count all my injuries up until I came to write this book, as if you do that kind of thing while you are still playing then mentally it could begin to get on top of you. Football is all about your last performance and then working towards your next game. The past is the past. If you want to win you have to deal with it, put it behind you and get on with preparing properly for the next game. And yes, that is 'taking each game as it comes'. Having said that, now I look back I think the Guinness Book of Records undersold me a bit. I have had at least 28 breaks or major operations – and those are the ones I can remember – not to mention having over 200 stitches in my face over my career. I have broken almost any bone you could mention, including both legs, ankles, knees, toes and fingers, during the remainder of my career. I smashed my nose, cut my face to ribbons on numerous occasions, had my lips and ears slashed by flying boots, suffered debilitating back injuries, plus damaged ligaments and tendons and had a plate inserted into my neck, and one into my arm.

As my career progressed I undertook countless injections, treatments, minor and major surgical procedures and each time I fought back. That's the way to deal with any kind of injury, have the belief that you are going to be OK, that you will be as good as new.

Have you ever had to fill out one of those forms at the doctors where they ask if you have ever been in hospital for treatment before? I had to do that recently and Kate was sitting with me saying, "you've forgotten this," or "you haven't put that down." I said "Oh God I'd forgotten about that." For example I often forget that I have a plate in my neck. You might think that would be something that would be at the forefront of your mind, but I do tend to forget these things. I've had that many scars that people look at me now and think they are wrinkles. I was constantly cutting myself, particularly my face. I'd just pop off for stitches, and Stoke's physician Doc Crowe would stitch me up in the tunnel and I'd go straight back on again.

As any pro footballer from that era will tell you the physical toll cumulatively on knees and ankles means by the time you get to 50 they are pretty much shot. For example, I had my first cartilage out when I was 16 and my last after a young Marco Gabbiadini did me one day in training when I had taken over as manager at York in 1984. "Take that, boss!" So I've had no cartilages for 20-odd years and obviously that's going to have an effect. Surgical techniques were not what they are now when sportsmen can rehabilitate in half the time and come back almost as good as new. But even so it's the cumulative effect that eventually gets you. Take Alan Shearer and Michael Owen. Neither ended up with that first burst of pace that had made them into top players. Both had to adapt and become more rounded forwards, but they also used their experience to get into regular goalscoring positions. Good players can do that, but it is easier in the modern era when the surgeons can get you back onto the pitch in better nick than ever before.

Mind you, I've seen progress get hijacked along the way. I remember the first time I had an injection. They were all the rage to stem the pain and allow you to get though a game in the mid-70s. We were playing Newcastle away and I split my eye just above the socket, so blood was gushing out. Because we were away from home, in those days we didn't take our own medical team, so we relied on the home side's and I remember standing in their dressing room, while this guy faffed around preparing a pain-killing injection. I said, "What are you're doing, just stitch it up."

"We've got to put this in," he said.

I knew his game, though.

"Sod off. You're just pissing about so I don't get back out there." And I leapt off the table as soon as I was stitched and hared back onto the pitch.

You could say that I didn't really help myself too much, being far more concerned about the game than my own personal condition, but that was me. In the mid-70s there was a real hardman called Bobby Murdoch at Middlesbrough. He was one of Celtic's Lisbon Lions European Cup-winning team in 1967 and moved to Ayresome Park late in his career and became mentor to a certain Graeme Souness, one of the hardest men of his generation, broke my shin pad and cut my left shin to ribbons with a studs up challenge. It hurt like hell, but I couldn't show it. I carried on playing until half time and when I came into the dressing room Micky Bernard was sick because he could see my shin bone. It was all hanging out. I told Doc Crowe, "Just strap it, cause I'm gonna do the bastard." Murdoch may have done me a treat but I wasn't going to come off. There was revenge to be had.

At one stage as a teenager it was suggested to me that I might have to give up playing because I might have brittle bones. Fortunately I didn't listen, and I certainly didn't have brittle bones, or any other disorder that might preclude me from playing football – I was just a blinking nutter. That wasn't only on the football field either. My headlong leap into life took in all spheres of being a teenager which meant regularly getting into fights. In fact one teacher at my Secondary School told me that if I went on the way I was going I wouldn't live much longer. I remember him telling me: "You're crackers. There is no way you'll live until you're 30." He was serious. Stoke was a dangerous place. There were knives and the beginnings of drugs on the streets and some lads around who fancied themselves. I suppose the problem was that one of them was me. I was never into going out there to make trouble. In fact if you met me you'd think I was quite a quiet bloke – softly spoken, quite happy with life – but if you rile me, if you threaten me, if you get in my face, if you make it you versus me, then there is only going to be one winner.

Stoke might not have been Chicago's gangland, but growing up there through my teens did give me a lot of street-nous. I remember once walking up a dark alley on the way home one night. I must have been about 16, and cocky enough to be outside my own estate on my own despite it being late at night. I came up against four lads, one of whom brandished a knife. It wasn't too overt, but he made sure I knew he was holding it. Now there is one rule of thumb you should always follow when faced with a situation like that – always hit the one with the knife. I did. He went down. The other lad left me alone and I got home safe and sound. You don't stop to ask questions if a knife comes out.

Being a minor local celebrity as my football career took shape marked me out sometimes, making me a beacon for trouble-makers. Coupled with that, as with pretty much any urban area, there are clear demarcations in Stoke-on-Trent as to where you should and shouldn't really go unless you 'belong'. I came from one side of the A50. If I ventured over the other side of the road, to what was called Meir Square, around the big cinema called the Broadway, I would have been taking my life into my own hands.

Then there was Blurton, a nearby council estate, where my girlfriend at the time Pam Clarke lived. I think I was about 15 or 16 when I walked her home one night. On my way back home this gang of about eight lads saw me walking along on my own. As I approached them they lined themselves across the road, blocking my passage. I don't think they knew who I was, but they knew that I didn't belong here and I would pay for my insolence in venturing onto their turf. Again, as with that youth with the knife and Bobby Collins a few years later, I had a decision to make. I could run, I could supplicate to whatever punishment they tried to dish out, or I could take them on. Now, as I said, I don't believe I was ever deliberately violent. I was cute enough to know not to make the first move, but I knew that if I kow-towed to this mob they would pounce on me. I sized them up and walked directly at the two tallest ones in the middle as if I hadn't got a care in the world, looking directly at them. Bold as brass, exuding confidence. They were so surprised they stepped aside and let me past. I think they thought I was going to turn and run. Far from it, although I hate to think what they could have done to me if I'd got that particular tactic wrong. I'd have taken any of them one-on-one and won hands down, but one-on-five would even out the odds somewhat.

When I was older and in the Stoke City first team, people I played against would meet me off the field in the players' lounge and couldn't believe I was the same person. You know, they thought I'd be walking around with an axe in my pocket. But I am actually a fairly quietly spoke, quiet and reasonably shy person. I just know how to stand up for myself. In fact when I was about 11 I had to stop actively fighting because I used to beat everybody and no-one would go up against me. I knew I could do it, so I just moved on to something else. I've been in that fortunate thing all my life I've not been frightened of anybody. I learnt how to walk away early on. If they thought I was a coward that was their problem. I knew I wasn't.

I think if I'd realised how dangerous the things I was doing were I would probably have stopped myself, but it was just the way I was. I just react in a particular way, and that is to stand up for myself. I still do and it can be a problem when you get to my age because I will walk in areas that people tell me not to walk or down dark alleys. Nothing bothers me. That kind of bravado was what prompted that teacher to comment that I wouldn't make it past 21, later some of my Stoke colleagues insisted I wouldn't make it past 30, but as I write this I've just celebrated my 60th birthday, so at least I proved them wrong.

It's a tough upbringing, but so many footballers have come out of one of those estates around North Staffordshire and been successful. Aside from the likes of Stan Matthews, there's Garth Crooks, Adrian Heath and Lee Chapman, who all started off at Stoke and went on to huge things – sadly at bigger clubs while the Potters spiralled into debt and almost oblivion through the 1980s and 1990s. Then from Port Vale there has been Robbie Earle, who made his name with Wimbledon and now works for ITV and Mark Bright. The key thing is that all of these men have all been motivated to make the most of their talents, to fight tooth and nail to be successful, by the desire to better themselves. That stems, I fully believe, from where they grew up. It did for me anyway.

Arsenal's Steve Bould, centre-back partner of Tony Adams in that all-conquering Gunners team of the early 1990s, came from Blurton, where I'd met that mob on my way back home. When I was manager of Sunderland I received a phone call from Arsenal manager George Graham who was interested in my opinion of the young Stoke centre-back. I knew him very well as he'd come through the youth ranks at the club during my final years there and was happy to recommend him as a two-footed, footballing centre-half, comfortable on the ball, while simultaneously wishing I could have afforded him to come to Roker Park.

"But has he got a nasty streak?" George wanted to know.

"Oh, yes," I replied. "He's from Blurton."

George knew what I was saying. It sealed the deal. Bould signed for £390,000 and went on to repay that fee in spades, winning three league titles and the FA Cup and the Cup Winners' Cup as part of the famous Arsenal back four, coincidentally or not alongside another player George signed from Stoke, although not a local, Lee Dixon, now a regular pundit on the BBC's Match of the Day.

Leaving aside the numerous scrapes from messing about as a kid, my serious injury problems started during my two years playing for the City of Stoke-on-Trent boys team which won the National Schools competition. In my first season playing in the Under 15 age group I broke my leg halfway through the first game in a typical, full-blooded tackle. It wasn't a nasty foul or anything, just a tackle that ended with me with a busted tibia. I just took it as something I had to overcome, so rehabilitated quickly – young bones always heal quicker – and got myself back fit and in contention to play again by the end of the season. I hadn't learned though. Halfway through my return game, I threw myself into a tackle and – snap – the same leg went again. So I'd played just two half games and broken my leg each time, which effectively meant I missed the whole season as I was out for six months on each occasion. That was a major blow for someone with my kind of self-absorbed ambition.

Thankfully I made a pretty full recovery both times, but it didn't stop me from accumulating a list of ailments you might expect to find associated with a combat battalion in Afghanistan during my career.

All these football-related injuries were minor fare compared to the thankfully few major problems I have faced in my life, although one of those would lead to the happiest and most constant relationship in my life – falling in love with the woman who would become my wife, Kate. Queensbury School was co-educational, but in my school year the sexes were kept separate in the classroom. Kate was a school year younger and by then the Headmaster had decided to have boys and girls in the same classes. Anyway we lived reasonably close to each other and would often be in the same group of kids walking home at the end of the day and I think she took a shine to me because I was the captain of the football team, something of an athlete and Head Boy. At the time she was more interested in me than I was in her because she was that bit younger and at one point, when she was 14 – and a much sought after girl herself, may I add – and I was 15, she asked me out and I said "no". Needless to say I have never lived that down!

But even though I did date a couple of other girls on an occasional basis – and she other boys – because of my total dedication to football, nothing remotely serious ever developed. It was the same with Kate for a while. Even after I finally gave in to her and we started seeing each other for about 12 months we were on and off, but I actually knew deep down that I was going to marry her even though I was still so young and we would have periods when we didn't see each other, usually due to my training schedule.

In fact it would be football in a roundabout kind of way that would bring Kate and I together. At this stage I had just turned 17 and was still working as a plumber's mate and playing for Stoke's youth team. Another of the lads picked me up to go to the Victoria Ground for a game in his Hillman Minx, one of those little runarounds with an engine in the back. I sat in the passenger seat and neither of us wore seatbelts as it just wasn't a thing you did back in 1965. As we drove along chatting about the game suddenly this ambulance, which I understand was racing along the other carriageway to a call out, overtook a car and crashed head on into us. The impact catapulted me straight through the windscreen. In those days windscreens were made from real glass and it shattered, leaving shards embedded into my throat, which was slashed to pieces, along with my face. I was knocked out for a while and was pretty beaten up when I came to.

In so many ways we were lucky, especially given the lack of seatbelts. The crash itself could have killed us, let alone the flying glass doing serious damage, but of all things we had hit an ambulance and the medics were unhurt, although shaken. But they were incredibly professional and simply got on with the job of patching us up so they could take us into hospital and get full attention.

Typical of me, when we got to hospital my first thought was not to get myself fixed up properly but to phone Stoke's chief scout Cliff Birks to let him know I was going to be late. Not unable to make it, you notice, but late. I could barely talk because of my throat and yet I was determined I wasn't going to miss the game. Cliff actually thought I was pulling his leg!

After I'd been fully put back together an ambulance took me home. Now my Mum had become used to ambulances dropping me off for different reasons and the first thing she said to me when I went through the door with bandages all round my throat and all over my face from the glass cuts was, "That's it I hope you're going to pack it in then".

She thought I'd done it playing football. Of course it could never have put me off my sole, burning ambition, but I was confined to the house for a while to recuperate properly and the fact that some of Stoke's youth team players had been injured in a car crash had made the Evening Sentinel's headlines. Kate read the story and came to visit me at home, bringing me a Mars bar because she knew I loved them and we got back together from then and that was it. It took at least 12 months for the compensation t come through but I got £250 and that proved to be the major catalyst as £250 then was a deposit for the house. So it enabled us to get married and we bought our first home for £2,365, with Kate's dad giving us some money to pay for furniture and various bits and pieces. Times were different in that we couldn't have lived together without being married but the money allowed us not to have to live with one set of parents as my older sister had been forced to do. By that stage too, I had just been taken on as a full-time professional by Stoke, and the club were able to help with the mortgage on the house, giving me a loan to help finance the mortgage which I paid back bit by bit from my monthly pay packet, so everything was rosy.

We got married on the morning of Saturday 7 October 1967 at 10.30 at Normacot C of E Church and I played in the afternoon because I didn't want to lose my place in the reserves. After changing out of her wedding dress Kate came down to the game to watch me play against an Everton side featuring Joe Royle and Jimmy Husband up front. The game didn't go too well as Jimmy got hat-trick, but we then had our reception in the evening. It was a great day, bar the result, but we weren't able to go away on honeymoon because we'd just sunk all our money into the house. I had literally only got a quid left in the bank at that point. I suppose that's another example of how times have changed. Not worse, not better, just different.

Throughout my career things just seemed to happen to me. I couldn't keep out of trouble. I broke my leg again before I got into Stoke's first team. I was by now a regular in the reserves and our goalkeeper, a lad called Paul Shardlow, dived across it during a game as I stretched to block a goalbound shot. His full weight landed on my outstretched shin, which was planted in the mud, and it snapped. By now I had become used to recuperating from such setbacks. It was, after all, the third time I had broken a leg, and it wouldn't be the last, but it was the only occasion on which one of my own team busted me up. I mean, my own goalkeeper!

Mind you, I was my own worst enemy in many ways because I was so determined to play despite any injury I might be carrying, sometimes having one injury would lead directly to me getting another. I broke my right ankle in early 1971, but because we were in the middle of an FA Cup run I kept it in plaster during the week, took it out each Saturday, injected it with cortisone, played the game, and put it back in plaster before leaving the ground.

At the start of all this we were embroiled in a mammoth tie with Huddersfield Town and it affected my mobility, so my body couldn't necessarily do what my brain was telling it. I can remember I was struggling to reach a ball crossed into our box, so I just dived full length to block it. Town's Frank Worthington was just getting set for a volley. Frank was such a skilful player. He brought so much joy to the game. He had the skill to produce pieces of brilliance and the temperament of a true goalscorer. He was also a complete maverick on and off the pitch, but that's another story. He had one of the best scoring records against Stoke during my time at the club. That, I am sure, was down to his inner belief.

Now Frank was a wonderful volleyer of a ball and he was winding up to hit this cross as it dropped about 12 yards out. I knew it was going to be a goal, so I just threw myself bodily at the point he would connect with the cross to just get something in the way. I wasn't quite quick enough as my legs wouldn't move because of the injury and Frank's follow through smashed into the side of my face, splitting my right ear so that the lobe was hanging off and had to be stitched back on. That didn't hurt so much because it's not that sensitive an area, but there was a lot of blood.

By the way, I blocked Frank's shot and we finally got past Huddersfield in that game, a fourth round second replay on our way to Stoke's first FA Cup semi-final appearance for over 70 years, winning 1-0. But more of that later.

Some Stoke fans thought I had some sort of prodigious powers of recovery because I always seemed to come back so much more quickly than other players. I don't think that was necessarily the case physically, although it may be true mentally. I think the case which often gets cited to me when fans talk to me about this is a tie later in that FA Cup run in 1970/71 when we faced a sixth round replay at the Victoria Ground against Manchester United. This was the game I referred to earlier when George Best scored a wonderful individual goal and I took revenge by heading an equalizer and we won in extra-time.

But it so nearly didn't happen that way. We had a very heavy schedule at that time because we had so many games to cram in and I had damaged the muscles in my back slightly in training on the morning of this particular game. It was nothing too serious at first, but, after going home for a lie down, when I tried to get up my back was completely rigid. Nothing I could do could free my muscles and I was pottering about the house with a stoop, unable to stand upright. I rang up the club and ruled myself out of the game, but said I would get down to the ground to give the lads moral support. I couldn't drive, though, so Kate helped me into the passenger seat and drove.

There was a massive crowd rushing to the Victoria Ground that night. It would actually prove to be the third largest gate the famous old ground ever had of over 49,000, and we couldn't get close to the Vic, so she let me out of the car a quarter of a mile away. As I got out something strange happened. My back clicked and I could at least stand up again. So I told Kate I'd go into the dressing room to wish everyone good luck and would see her in the players' lounge for a drink before kick-off.

When I got into the dressing room Waddo asked me how I felt and I explained how I had felt the tweak as I got out of the car and immediately Waddo pounced saying, "step up on there", pointing to the bench. I stepped up and Waddo and his coaching staff looked at my back intently. This went on for a few minutes and they poked and prodded me and asked me how it felt before Waddo declared, "You look alright". That was my fitness test – and before I knew it I was having another inection, pulling on a shirt, hearing my name being announced to the crowd over the tannoy and walking down the tunnel with the rest of the players.

This was all much to the surprise of Kate who when last she saw me had bade farewell to a cripple. And then to go and score the winner in a pulsating cup tie in extra time made it an incredible night. It was another example of how times have changed. Imagine if Manchester United risked Cristiano Ronaldo or Wayne Rooney in similar fashion. The club would get sued!

I think that my strength, fitness and athleticism, coupled with my inner fighting spirit got me through those all those crises. I trained every day until I was 50 and the last injury I got was when I was manager of Oxford. Even then I liked to put it about a bit and I clattered into a few of the opposing team in a practice match we were playing. So one of them, centre-half Phil Gilchrist, decided to take a bit of revenge on me and clattered me back, right over the top. That made me finally decide it was probably the end of the line for me to be competing in training regularly with players 25 or 30 years my junior.

Perhaps strangely, the worst injury in my career came not from a break, or because of a rash challenge. Far from it. It happened when I contracted septicaemia through a graze on my leg. Septicaemia is a bacterial infection of the blood which if not treated sees the bacteria multiply to damage blood vessels and induce the kind of drop in blood pressure, faintness and potential damage to major organs which affected me. It's potentially fatal if not dealt with.

It all started because Waddo had asked the Fire Brigade to pump water onto the training pitch at the back of the Victoria Ground. It was a favourite trick of his to water the pitch so that visiting teams would get bogged down at the Vic, while we trained all week in those conditions and were ready for them. But this water was pumped from the nearby murky, sewage-strewn River Trent onto the training pitch and it infected a minor gash I had picked up in my shin. When I got home that night I didn't feel or look well at all. Kate was worried and rang the doctor, who happened to be one of our neighbours. This girl was about the same age as me and she gave me a quick examination and pronounced that I'd got flu. I was certainly delirious as later that night I apparently came down the stairs from my sickbed and proposed to Kate, which seeing as we'd been married for several years by then was a bit unnecessary. That worried Kate enough to ask this doctor to come back and she gave me a full body examination then and found the tell-tale red line of a vein going up into my groin. That showed where the bacteria had infected my blood and she realised that if the infection reached my heart I would be toast. I was shipped off to North Staffs Royal Infirmary sharpish.

When I got there they did a load of tests on me and discovered that the infection had reached my heart. By this time I was no longer really conscious of what was going on, but they thought I was a goner, that I wouldn't survive and told Kate she shouldn't go home. Se actually thought this was it. Meanwhile they pumped drugs into me to fight the infection, trying to get it under control. Goodness only knows what Kate was going through while all this was happening. My wife has been through so much in her life, most of it because of my love and desire to play football and manage clubs. But I think she will always think back to that night and thank her lucky stars that the doctors were wrong. My body fought the intruding bacteria and gradually won the battle. I eventually regained consciousness and learned about what had been going on around me while I had been completely out of it. Thankfully I don't remember anything, I was in such a state. I shudder to think of what Kate must have gone through while I remained oblivious to the severity of the situation.

That wasn't my only near-death experience. The second one arrived while I was manager at York. My ankle was giving me gip. It actually felt as bad as if I'd broken it, but I knew I hadn't as I had all but finished playing now. It was actually right at the end of the season in which we'd won the Fourth Division with a record 101 Points and so we went on a club trip to Magaluf to celebrate. While we were abroad my ankle swelled up really badly so one of the directors took me to the hospital, where they took an X-ray of my leg. When the doctor came back with it he was laughing! I couldn't understand what was so funny as my ankle was getting worse by the minute. Anyway the doctor asked how I was still alive with all the breaks I had in my leg, ankle and foot! I told him I'd been a professional footballer, but that my ankle really hurt now. He told me that all the breaks he could see were old ones and that there was nothing wrong.

It was some sort of infection, though they never, ever found out exactly what it was. By the time we got back to England I was so bad that I was rushed into York General Hospital where I remained for weeks. The surgeons operated several times on my ankle trying to cleanse it of whatever had got into it. They cut it open, cleaned it out, stitched it up, but nothing seemed to have any effect. In fact my ankle is still discoloured black now. They even took a bit out of my spine to see if they could establish what was wrong with me. I lost over two stone in weight and was obviously very ill. Half the time I hadn't got a clue what was going on. I was out of it either with fever or on drugs. It was bad, whatever it was. In fact there was one point when the doctor told some club officials that I would not be coming back to work. I don't know whether he meant that I was on the point of dying or simply being crippled, but it wasn't good. I was only 37 and I'd been written off twice!

Having said that, I survived both times. The doctors told me they didn't quite understand how, but I believe it was a combination of my boisterous childhood and my will to get better. Conscious or not, my desire to get well again, to get back to normal, to provide for Kate and my family, and to get back to what I love doing held sway.

Chapter Six

A MATTER OF

LIFE AND DEATH

The great Bill Shankly is oft-quoted as having said that 'football isn't a matter of life and death – it's more important than that'. But for some people it is precisely that. Life and death.

I know that I was a lucky one – despite all the trauma, the injuries, the near-death experiences, and the upsets in my career I would never let myself wallow in anything like self pity. I couldn't. I had experienced what giving up the fight would mean as I had seen the devastating effects of what a death does to a family, friends and a community as, at a relatively young age, I saw one of my playing colleagues die in front of me.

In 1968 Stoke had a young goalkeeper called Paul Shardlow. He was the understudy to England World Cup winner Gordon Banks and was a very promising talent. He was also the keeper who had broken my leg in that reserve team game, but that was all forgotten as we were good mates.

In the summer of 1967 Stoke City had taken part in an attempt to promote football, or soccer, in the USA by taking part in a tournament with the likes of Aberdeen and Wolves, with each club representing a city. Stoke were based in Cleveland, Ohio, thanks to a feller called Norman Low who had been a scout for the club, but had since emigrated to America, and were called the Cleveland Stokers. I hadn't been part of the squad because I was five years younger than Paul and had yet to make my first team debut, but Paul had been over in the States and on the strength of that had been invited back the following summer to gain great experience by playing for the club who were then taking part in the first season of the NASL. During his summer in the USA he had played with good players such as Argentinian international defender Ruben 'The Hatchet' Navarro, who had played in the 1962 World Cup, and veteran Spanish goalscorer Enrique Mateos, part of the great Real Madrid side of the late 1950s. He'd even made history as part of the Stokers team which defeated a Santos side featuring

Pele and even saved a penalty to preserve a 2-1 victory. His stay ended prematurely, though, when he dislocated his shoulder in training. They had done various checks on him as part of his recuperation and in retrospect we were all surprised that no-one had picked up the problem that would take his life.

Paul had returned from the States with all this flash gear he'd bought out there as the dislocated shoulder had meant he'd had plenty of time to spend shopping, and he'd come in to training wearing trainers and tracksuits and baseball hats. Every morning before training I changed next to Paul and so I would give him plenty of verbals about the gear he was wearing as it was relatively rare back then.

Training always started with jogging in pairs around the training pitch out the back of the Victoria Ground and this particular day, 14 October, Paul and I were paired up as the squad jogged around. Goalkeepers are always big fellers and so aren't particularly good at running as it's not really what they train to do, but they joined in warm up before splitting off to do their own specialised training. We were chatting away as we jogged when Paul just keeled over and collapsed. My first reaction was to say, "get up you silly bugger," but there was no response. He was out cold and his eyes had this strange look to them. I shouted for help and Fred Street, the club physio who would go on to work with Arsenal and England and was highly qualified, raced across to give assistance. Fred gave Paul mouth-to-mouth to try to resuscitate him. An ambulance was called, but before the paramedics could get to him he'd gone. His heart had given out and it turned out he had a defect which had never been picked up before. There wasn't any routine scanning of professional footballers back then, but he had been through all that treatment in the USA without anything being spotted.

Paul was just 25 years old and was a promising keeper with hands like shovels, and a fantastic cricketer, who was good enough with bat and as a spin bowler to play for Staffordshire. I just couldn't understand how a young, fit professional athlete like him could die so young. His death affected me very badly. I was devastated and it was a massive influence on me. You know when you say your hair falls out with shock? Well big lumps of mine came out as I struggled to come to terms with it. It made me think a lot more about the future and also the present and I realised that I was in a privileged position and that I had to make the most of what was to come my way while I could because you never know what's round the corner. I also realised that you get so dramatically engrossed in football – and if you want to work in the game in any capacity and have a career it has to be your life, no question – that sometimes you lose sight of many of the things that really matter in life. There is a big world out there and football is very narrow and I determined that I would keep my eyes and mind open.

At the time Kate was pregnant with our first child, who would be born in April 1969. We named in him Paul in honour of my friend who lost his life that day.

Despite all the progress in medicine and monitoring of players, people are still dropping down dead even now. Just after Christmas 2007 Motherwell captain Phil

O'Donnell died on the Fir Park pitch. It is incredible to think this can still happen, but it can because the demands of the modern game puts a lot of pressure on organs, especially on the heart and if there is any defect of any sort the relentless pounding that delicate organ takes may eventually tell. Obviously it's well known that players have regular medicals, particularly when transferring between new clubs, and I believe these should be taken further and developed into a bespoke monitoring programme. I think the problem with footballers is that everyone thinks they are so fit that there can't be anything wrong. That's true to a level, but it's only when you are under intense pressure that these things show up and they don't monitor you at those times. When you have your medical at a new football club you are fairly relaxed and feeling positive, you are not under pressure. It's the same when players are training. Even a strenuous workout doesn't drive you to the limits.

Nowadays managers have a much more focussed programme than the players. It's run by the League Managers Association (LMA) and I, while manager at Wrexham, have been subject to it since its inception. Crudely it involved running on a treadmill and working on a gym bike to push yourself to the limits to see how the heart reacts. It's been interesting because when the managers started doing it they discovered that 40% or so had got some sort of defect. Some not a bad one, but some a significant issue. There have been plenty of high profile cases of heart conditions amongst managers – think of Scotland boss Jock Stein, who died on the bench during an international in September 1985 and Graeme Souness and Gerard Houllier, who both had heart problems while in charge of Liverpool, so it's important that the monitoring is developed even more to catch problems early in their development.

It's beginning to come in to other areas of the game too. For example Everton have recently started implementing the same monitoring system with all their coaching staff. They are the first club to do so, but as yet there is still not a comprehensive monitoring programme for players. It is all done very much on an ad hoc basis, club by club. Obviously players are generally fit lads and they have ECGs during medicals when they change clubs, and maybe once a year at those clubs that can afford it, and they wear heart monitors whilst training, but they do nothing under stress which would help identify players with problems. Motherwell, for example, would have trained wearing heart monitors, but no-one spotted that Phil O'Donnell had a problem because they are looking for different things and it is not whilst under the kind of extreme pressure that match conditions can produce.

At least if there is a regular programme instituted anomalies such as Paul Shardlow's inability to run long distances without struggling would be questioned and further investigation could take place. That kind of programme could save lives. I wonder whether it could have saved Paul.

Very very sadly Paul's death would not be the only one I would experience at first hand amongst my close colleagues and have to deal with during my football career. They would prove to be testing times which make a man of you as much as anything which might go on out on the pitch, be played out in the newspapers or earn any individual or club glory during their career.

When I took my first managerial post at York City in 1982, I inherited a half-decent squad, although one that was completely demotivated. A classic example of this was a big, black striker called Keith Walwyn. Keith was the loveliest man; kind, polite, honest. None of which are qualities you want in your typical barn-storming centre-forward during the 90 minutes of a game. He was an old-fashioned centre-forward - big, bustling, brave. He always gave you 90 minutes and he was feared by the opposition not because he was dirty in any way but because he was such a handful. I believe he could have easily played at a higher level.

He'd begun his career at Chesterfield a couple of years earlier after arriving from his home Caribbean island of St Kitts & Nevis and was so big, strong and powerful, yet he would not harm a fly deliberately. It was also strange because he was such a nice, gentle lad and spoke with a bit of a squeaky voice, when you'd expect this huge mountain of a man to have a deep, booming voice. Everybody who knew Keith had a tremendous liking for him and a tremendous respect. He didn't have a vicious bone in his body.

By the time I came across him in 1982 he was 26 years-old and I realised pretty quickly that if I could get him to play he'd cause defences huge problems in Division Four. I had to get into him mentally, building him up, turning him into the beast I wanted him to be once he crossed the white line. It didn't take much work because he would often go up for a cross with the centre-half and goalkeeper and flatten both of them. He would land and look round and think 'what happened to them?' People would just bounce off him and would be lying there, strewn on the turf – he simply didn't realise the power he had. It was just a question of getting him to realise what huge natural advantages he possessed. Keith had bundles of talent and tremendous physical prowess, power and pace, but he didn't understand how good he was.

Our success at York was in no small way down to Keith coming to the party, putting himself about and reaping the rewards. He scored 25 goals in 1983/84, the season in which we became the first team ever to break the 100 points barrier. In all he netted 140 goals in 291 games for the Minstermen, and also starred for Carlisle and Blackpool, but he was forced to quit full-time football in March 1991 after developing heart problems just after joining Kettering Town, which came to light when he collapsed while playing against Altrincham, and he ended up having a pacemaker fitted. Despite being such a mammoth man in outward appearance, internally there was obviously something wrong. It's interesting that he too – just like Paul Shardlow – had a heart problem but didn't realise.

There was possibly a clue in his eldest son, James, being born with a heart defect. As a baby he had to survive an operation to move the organ from the right side of his chest to the left in which his survival chances were only given as 50-50. Typically Keith and his wife raised more than £10,000 for the Killingbeck Hospital in Leeds where the successful treatment was carried out. In April 2003, after a dozen years of living in the Preston area and running a small shop, Keith himself went into hospital for a procedure which had been deemed necessary but he didn't pull through the operation. It seems astonishing to think that this lion of a man could succumb at just 47 years-old.

Liz, his wife, phoned me to ask if I would give a eulogy at Keith's funeral – well, what do you say? I was honoured to be considered worthy of talking about such a fabulous man. Someone who was an example to everyone he ever met, and all his fans at Chester-field, York, Carlisle, Blackpool and Kettering. The funeral, near Blackpool, was naturally an extremely emotional day. All the ex-players were there from York – John Byrne, John MacPhail and many others. Keith was so well liked, so I wasn't at all surprised. When it came to my turn to speak, as I stood up I spotted the fact that Keith's youngest son had come with a number nine shirt on. That was one of the most difficult moments of my life, trying to hold it together. I talked about Keith and what a good man he was. He was a gentle giant, so talented and as a person such a nice bloke. I was so pleased to be asked to do that because I hadn't actually spoken to Keith in years, that being the nature of football. I always think when someone dies young people are prone to say all sorts of nice things and some of them are tongue-in-cheek, but as far as Keith is concerned he was a bloody good bloke and one of the best centre-forwards York City ever had.

Keith's memory lives on at Bootham Crescent, where one of the hospitality suites bears his name, while York City fans have inaugurated their own personal tribute to the great man as inter-supporters group trophy they play-off for; the Keith Walwyn trophy.

There is a nice footnote to Keith's death. His younger son, Matthew, is making his way in the game and in May 2008 he was on the bench for Lancashire side Kirkham & Wesham for the FA Vase final against Lowestoft Town at the new Wembley Stadium. Matthew came on as a 79th minute substitute with his team 1-0 behind. He struck an 84th minute equaliser, and then an injury-time second, to win the game and the trophy for the first time in his side's history. He's obviously a chip off the old block.

Early death is a devastating event. There is often a feeling of desolation and waste. None more so than the loss of one of my former players in the prime of his football career. Martin Aldridge was only 25 when he died at the wheel of his car whilst returning home from a fixture at Rushden & Diamonds, where he was at that time on loan from Blackpool.

I had signed Martin on a free transfer from Northampton Town in December 1995 when I was in charge of Oxford. Many people questioned what I was doing as the Cobblers were below Oxford in the league at the time, but I'd seen his goalscoring record and I believed he could do the hardest job in a football team, putting that ball into the back of the net. It's what everyone is seeking and I thought this 21 year-old could produce the goods. We were vying for promotion to Division One at the time, while Martin had scored 17 goals in 70 games for the Cobblers in Division Three, so he was faced with a definite step up in class. Martin hit double figures in the higher divison after we went up, with his crowning glory being a hat-trick against Sheffield United in December 1996.

His all round game wasn't that great, I'd be the first to admit. He was the kind of striker that didn't work hard, didn't add extra strings to his bow, he just sniffed out chances in the box. Sometimes I thought he had that sixth sense that all good strikers have – the one that's like that comic strip Billy's Boots. But often supporters and other players couldn't see that gift. All they could see was what they thought was a lack of effort. But irrespective of that, his goals brought him a certain level of hero worship at Oxford.

When I moved to manage West Brom in December 1997 Martin fell out of favour under my replacement Malcolm Shotton. Within a month he'd been farmed out on loan to Southend, and then he was released from his contract in the summer of 1998. He signed for Blackpool and finished as their top scorer in 1998/99 under Nigel Worthington, but fell out of favour again and joined Rushden on loan in January 2000 when new manager Steve McMahon arrived at Bloomfield Road.

On 30 January 2000, Aldridge left Nene Park following Rushden's 6-0 Conference win against Northwich Victoria for which he had been an unused substitute. He was driving home towards Northampton on the A45 when his Peugeot was involved in a collision with a BMW travelling in the opposite direction. After being cut free from his car, Martin was taken to Northampton General Hospital with serious injuries. He died early the following morning aged just 25.

It was a very poignant time for me because I was in the process of rejoining Oxford United, the club I'd signed Martin for in my first stint and my first game, on 3 February 2000, saw us face Martin's parent club Blackpool in an emotionally draining fixture at which both sets of fans mourned a young hero. Martin's uncle and other family members were also present as club guests and there was considerable emotion in the dressing rooms amongst players who had almost all known Martin. Everyone remembered the slight young striker in their own personal way that day. On both benches players and staff who had counted him as a friend fought back tears. The Oxford chaplain gave a poignant eulogy before the game and I remember visiting Blackpool supporters draping a 'No. 9 Aldridge' tangerine shirt behind the Cuckoo Lane goal at the Manor Ground. It was a significant moment as Oxford fans had also come out in force to remember their former hero. It was as emotional a day as I can remember. Seldom has a minute's silence been more deafening. Or more moving.

Afterwards, having watched as my first game of my return – on any other day a vital relegation battle – had ended in a 1-0 victory to the visitors, I gave an interview in which I tried to sum things up in proportion. "We're upset about the result. but in the wider context of things, does it really matter? We lost a football match. But a young man has lost his life."

I was honoured to be a pall-bearer at Martin's funeral in Daventry the following week. It was such an incredibly sad day.

I was on holiday in Thailand in June 2008 when I heard the news that Sunderland's Academy goalkeeping coach Tim Carter had died. Kevin Ball, a man whom I had signed for Sunderland many years earlier and who had since become a legendary player and now coach for the club, rang me to give me the shocking news.

But it was only when I returned to attend Tim's funeral that I learned more about the apparent suicide of this 40 year-old who had the rest of his life ahead of him.

Being found in the bushes in a secluded part of Stretford, Manchester by a dog walker was a far cry from the career as a young goalkeeper I had helped Tim build when I signed him from Bristol Rovers in 1987 after he'd been something of a young prodigy, winning three England youth caps and making his league debut by 18. He played his part in Sunderland's resurgence which I was busy masterminding at the time, making over 50 appearances for the club, mostly as understudy to Iain Hesford and Tony Norman. He went on to play for a further seven clubs including Hartlepool, Millwall and Birmingham.

Tim was only a young lad when I signed him, but he made a good career for himself. He was such a pleasant lad, with a lovely nature and was very popular with the other players. After playing he had gone on to make his mark in coaching. He'd worked as first team goalkeeping coach at Sunderland with Mart Poom and from that he'd been invited to coach the Estonian international goalkeepers. In the summer of 2007 he'd been moved across to the Sunderland Academy to work with the kids there to make room for Roy Keane's former team-mate from Manchester United Raimond van der Gouw as first team goalkeeping coach.

I don't know if this has anything to do with how Tim was feeling about his life, but his four year-old son has cerebral palsy. Apparently when he was born there was a delay getting oxygen to the baby. It was only about 20 seconds or something, but it affected him permanently. It is a terribly sad condition and not something you'd wish on your worst enemy, let alone a lad with such a nice family. They were learning to live with the condition, though, and had placed him in special schools and had just moved house to a specially built a bungalow in Durham which had been converted to suit the young lad.

I attended the funeral along with all of Tim's ex-colleagues from my time at Sunderland, but nobody seemed to know what he was doing in Manchester. At the time of writing it seems strange and there has been no resolution to it. Kevin Ball told me that Tim had said to him that he was OK with moving across to work at the Academy, but Kevin has been knocking himself about over it as he feels as if he should have seen something if Tim was unhappy. Kevin was distraught. He said, "I was with him every day, I should have seen something. Suicide just seems totally out of character."

At the funeral it seemed as if everybody was saying the same. Who knows whether Tim chose to take his life because of anything to do with football, or personal issues in his life, which we may not even know about. Whatever the truth, it is a tragedy which I cannot help think joins those others which could have been averted.

Chapter Seven

LAND OF
SMOKE AND GLORY

One thing injuries never did was temper my full-blooded commitment to playing football, particularly in the tackle. My style was always all-action, totally committed, much the same as John Terry plays today. I had that kind of steel in me, but, admirable though it may be, it did pose a problem for me in my drive to become a professional footballer. I kept breaking bones, gashing myself or smashing my nose, which prevented me from playing for long periods. None of this impressed my manager at Stoke City, Tony Waddington, a man who loved the beautiful version of Pelé's game.

Having signed for the club as an amateur and emerged through the rite of passage that was my plumber's apprenticeship and my time on the production line at Stone Lotus shoes, I now wanted to fulfil my burning desire to sign professionally for First Division Stoke. The problem was, Waddo didn't rate me. Try as I might he just didn't seem to want to take the risk with me, even though I was now playing regularly in the reserves.

Naturally I thought I was good enough to earn a contract. I thought I was the best young player at the club, but this was now the start of the 1966/67 season, I was already 18 and I hadn't been signed. Being an amateur, though, gave me more rights back then because I had freedom to move and I decided to take the bull by the horns one day and present Waddo with an ultimatum. So, I knocked on his door.

"Come in," he said.

I did.

"Yes?" said the Stoke City manager.

"I'm leaving," said this 18-year-old know-it-all.

"What do you mean you're leaving?" came the response.

"I'm going somewhere else," playing the only card available to me. I was always fairly to the point in conversations such as this.

"You're not paying me and you know I'm good enough. I'm going to sign somewhere else."

This was a high stakes strategy. If Waddo dismissed me out of hand, sending me off to sign for my mythical other club, I'd have no choice but to clear my locker and attempt to do just that. But he looked me up and down for a moment and eventually said: "There might be a place in a game for a player like you."

Relief.

He continued: "What are you on?"

"Twenty quid a week," I replied. It wasn't bad money at Stone Lotus.

"Well, I can't pay you anywhere near that," he said flatly.

"What can you pay?"

"Twelve quid," said Waddo.

"Done."

So I signed professional terms, leaving my job and taking a 40% pay cut. The maximum wage for footballers may have been lifted thanks to the efforts of the PFA and my new team-mate George Eastham, who Waddo had signed from Arsenal for £35,000 straight after the World Cup finals, but my first basic wage at Stoke was a mere £12 per week.

Waddo was being quite cute. He knew I was committed and that I was a good athlete. Perhaps his concern was that I wouldn't develop to play at First Division standard, but I thought I could play. It was interesting that as I got older, people in the game, including many journalists, thought I could only do certain things because they saw merely my tackling and competitive streak. Then they started really looking at me and saw I could actually play. In training I used to do skills as well as anybody else. I could pass as good with both feet over 20/25 yards. With my left foot I could drop them in there all day 10 out of 10. With my right it might have been 9 out of 10. It was just that my job was as a defender, so I learned to be as effective as I could be.

Mainly I think Waddo took the punt on me because he had been convinced by my catalogue of injuries that I was a bit mad, so I didn't mind getting taking stick and giving it out. He also knew I had the drive to make a success of myself, and so he might as well give me the opportunity. Plus if he rejected me, I'd more than likely come back to haunt him. Once I put pen to paper on that contract he controlled me. I was a Stoke player and did not have a say over my own future. That's how it was for footballers then. The Bosman ruling which allowed us to have control over our careers only came into effect in the mid-1990s. Back in 1967 we were little more than tethered serfs. I was deliriously happy with that, though!

Tony Waddington was Mr Stoke City. After his playing career with Manchester United had been brought to a premature end by injury and a short spell coaching at nearby Crewe, he had joined the club as coach in the late 1950s and taken over from manager Frank Taylor in the summer of 1960. He was very shrewd in the transfer market and turned the fortunes of the ailing Second Division club around by bringing in a bevy of older, experienced, quality players, unwanted by the top clubs who deemed them to be over the hill, and created a team known as the 'Old Crocks'. It featured players such as Dennis Viollet, rejected by Manchester United at the age of 28, and 31 year-old Jackie Mudie, an FA Cup-winning centre-forward with Blackpool, Burnley's 31 year-old Irish midfield maestro Jimmy McIlroy, Everton inside-forward Roy Vernon and goalkeeper Jimmy O'Neill, both 28 when purchased, and, of course, in his greatest coup, that galvanised the club into winning promotion in 1962/63, the incomparable Stanley Matthews, who played in the top flight of English football up to his 50th birthday.

By the time I came onto the scene in the mid-sixties Stoke were an established First Division side and had just persuaded England's World Cup-winning goalkeeper Gordon Banks to sign as he had been ousted from the Leicester City team by the prodigious young talent of Peter Shilton. Banks was one of a number of star players including former England forwards George Eastham and Peter Dobing, striker John Ritchie and homegrown England starlet Tony Allen in defence. The team that Waddington was putting together was full of talent and on its day could take on all-comers. It lacked a bit of consistency and belief to challenge for the top honours and had a perennial problem because of his transfer policy of needing to be renewed every two to three years as players reached the end of their careers, but Stoke City were a force to be reckoned with. The arrival of the world's best goalkeeper proved that the club was beginning a new era and one in which Waddington aimed to produce a team good enough to challenge for silverware.

Now the problem for me was that, amidst all these internationals and flair players, Waddo thought I was a hooligan, a thug. He'd heard the stories about me fighting on the streets and seen me hurling myself into challenges that had proved dangerous to myself, let alone others on a football pitch. Perhaps he had a point, although Waddo did have a record of liking a tough tackler in his team as he had proved with both Eddie Clamp and Eddie Stuart in the 1962/63 promotion side. Having been a manager myself all these years I can understand his reticence to throw me in with the sharks in top flight football, but I had to find a way to convince him to promote me into the first team.

Flushed with the success of bartering my way into a professional contract, I had become a firm fixture in the Potters' reserve side. I was now 19, almost 20, not exactly young for a footballer – especially when you consider that Stoke's youngest ever player, Peter Bullock, had made his first team debut aged 16 years 163 days just nine years earlier in 1958. But a more salient fact about Bullock, interesting though his early stardom may be, is that he never made it in professional football. As with so many fabulous young talents he made an initial impact, but could not sustain his levels of performance. When I became a manager I appreciated what it takes to keep young players going through a long, hard English season. Talent alone is never enough to make a career. Any successful footballer in Britain needs so much more; desire, commitment, physical conditioning, a competitive nature, single-minded focus and the mental strength to regularly bounce back from disappointment. And that's just to keep your first team place, let alone progress and allow your natural talent to blossom. I was lucky in that I had those qualities in abundance.

Being in the reserves meant that in training down at Newcastle Town's ground I would be up against the first team attackers, players like Peter Dobing, George Eastham, Roy Vernon and Harry Burrows. These were all established players, many of whom were internationals to boot, but it didn't bother me. Even in training I just got stuck in. I could tell they didn't like it. Neither did Waddo. He was worried I would injure one of them seriously and cause him selection headaches.

It all came to a head one particular day. I remember there was a cinder cycling track around the training pitch we used at Newcastle-under-Lyme and Roy Vernon got on the ball, turned to face me and tried taking me on with some fancy stepover or trick that just acted as a red rag to a bull. I took him out with a full-blooded tackle, depositing him onto the track as he tried to go outside me. Frank Mountford, our coach, raced over, shouting, "Calm down, calm down," as Roy writhed in agony on the track with cinder burns all the way up the back of his thighs and onto his buttocks where his shorts had ridden up. I replied, "Look, if he wants to play tell him to get his arse back on the pitch. If he doesn't then tell him to sod off and get changed. But whatever happens he ain't gonna take the mickey out of me."

Waddo wasn't too happy with me for that. In fact for a time he actually banned me from playing against the first team in case I carried on crocking them, but the one side effect it had was that the first teamers began to tell the manager that I was so difficult to cope with and that they hated facing me so much I might be worth giving a go in the first team.

They simply didn't want to play against me, they'd rather have me on their side. Eventually it hit home with Waddo. At the time Stoke were struggling down near the bottom of the league after making a bad start to the 1968/69 season and people like Peter Dobing and George Eastham would go knocking on Waddo's door saying, "Play that idiot".

I was trying to displace either Tony Allen, a former England international full-back, who had now converted to play at centre-half, or Willie Stevenson, a former Liverpool centre-half who Waddo had picked up in December 1967 for £50,000. I was also competing to get into the team with a local lad a couple of years older than me called Alan Bloor, who had already been given a run of games to stake his claim, and a feller called John Moore, who played a couple of games but ultimately never made the grade.

Eventually, in early September 1968, Waddo was convinced enough to give me a go, and what a match he picked for me to make my debut in – at Highbury to face unbeaten league leaders Arsenal. I remember the game very well. The crowd at Highbury always seemed very close and they were quite vocal. Arsenal had gone through something of a lean spell in the Sixties, but new manager Bertie Mee was building a team that would become one of our major rivals over the next few seasons, and that would go on to win the double in 1971. As I've already said I gave Bobby Gould, their centre-forward, a tough time and he gave me back plenty of stick, which showed me that I was doing my job as I was getting to him. I remember gritty central defender Peter Simpson also complaining to the referee about me and if Peter thought you were tough then you were. He'd had plenty of practice himself.

But the game held a twist for me that was to prove a lesson in the harsh reality of life in the top flight. Just before half-time Arsenal's Jon Samells burst into our penalty area with the ball and I, slightly unused to the furious pace of the game, mis-timed my challenge on him and brought him down. Penalty. I'd given a spot-kick away in the first half of my first game.

To make things worse Terry Neill scored the penalty and Arsenal won the game 1-0.

Aside from that blemish I was happy with how I'd played, and even happier when I saw the following day's press in which I was given a lot of 9 out of 10 marks.

That rosy glow didn't last long. Just two weeks later we played away at Ipswich. We lost 3-1 and I give a couple more penalties away. I was in bits. I can remember crying practically all the way home on the train. I thought I'd blown it. I'd done so well in all other aspects of the game, but I was utterly frustrated with myself because I'd been handed this opportunity and messed it up. To give one penalty away at Arsenal, yeah okay I could live with that because I'd played so well. But to then give two more away in the very next game looked a lot like carelessness even to the most myopic of Denis Smith fans.

My final lesson in my harsh introduction to top flight football was that I was dropped by Tony Waddington. I can still remember him telling me, "You're not in, son." That hurt. I would not be given another chance for a full five months, during which I was expected to prove my worth in the reserves. At that stage Tony thought he'd got better players to battle relegation. In such situations you need experience and he persevered with Tony Allen, who he had converted from left-back, where he had won three England caps in his teens, to centre-half. Tony was hell of a good player, who was blessed with an innate ability to read the game. Tadge, as he was known, was a very different type of player to me. He wasn't a big tackler. His skill was to intercept and nick the ball off opposing strikers. Alongside him Alan Bloor cemented his place as the other centre-half and took on the mantle of being the more dominant partner.

I wasn't surprised to be left out and I had to live with it. I know now that Waddo was looking for a response. Fortunately I had it in me to put the disappointment behind me. I was helped in that by 'Bluto' Bloor, who was brilliant, encouraging me to keep my head up and keep at it. I knew he was right. This was the opportunity I'd dreamed of and I could have thrown it all away by getting too down on myself. Possibly under the scrutiny young footballers receive today I may not have got another chance. Equally not having blanket TV coverage meant we didn't have as much knowledge about our opponents and so we had to learn and think on our feet during games as we discovered what tricks the likes of Best, Law, Radford, Bell, Summerbee, Worthington or Osgood had up their sleeves. Once you'd played against them a first time you had some data in the bank for the next occasion, but the process was more gradual than in the modern era. We were given small dossiers on opponents on occasions, but they didn't contain too much information and my education generally took place on the pitch.

I also had a steep learning curve in my new environment of the first team dressing room where I was getting used to being on first name terms with men who I had previously only known as Mr Banks, Mr Eastham and Mr Ritchie. The atmosphere in our dressing room was great the vast majority of the time, but any professional football club is a place of work and, although we mixed and had great social lives together, it was a professional relationship. I always equate the dressing room to having brothers and sisters. Of course you mix with them, of course you love them, of course you rely on them, but whether you like them all the time is another matter. What was important was that a bond that developed over the next few seasons that allowed us to drag ourselves away from the foot of the table in that 1968/69 season to challenge for honours.

Five long months went by until I was eventually brought back into the side in March 1969 after impressing in the reserves. But the team's form was still very up and down, they had just lost back-to-back games against Sunderland (1-4) and Chelsea (0-1) and I found myself back in the team in place of Bluto, who was carrying a knock, for a home game against Leeds United, who were flying near the top of the table at the time and would eventually win the first Championship in the club's history that season. That match which is etched into my memory. I marked striker Mick Jones and he gave me a torrid time as he bagged a hat-trick and we slumped to a 1-5 humiliation. That was another salutary lesson. I felt unwell before the game with some stomach bug and I shouldn't have played really, but having got back into the first team picture I wasn't about to give up my chance easily, so the Doctor gave me some drugs and said, "you'll be fine". I believed him and went out to play and got torn to pieces by Mick, who was a fabulous talent and never really given the recognition I felt he deserved in that great Leeds side under Don Revie. But my illness is no excuse for the performance. If you are out there on the pitch then there are no excuses and there is nowhere to hide. Needless to say I ended up back on the bench, although Bluto's continuing injury did give me more opportunities to stake my claim before the end of the season.

Through togetherness and sheer bloody-mindedness Stoke survived that 1968/69 season and I played 10 out of the last 15 games, mostly alongside Willie Stevenson. I was delighted to get into the first team, but my place was still by no means secure at this stage and I was even occasionally used in emergencies as a striker. This wasn't as crazy as it sounds as whilst in the youth and A teams I had been played up front now and then and once scored in seven consecutive games. Waddo, I think in desperation as much as anything, tried me there when he had run out of other options and I remember I played up front at Leicester with David Herd, a Scottish international striker who had been brought in from Manchester United. David had scored two goals in the 1963 FA Cup final, as it happens against a Leicester side including one Gordon Banks. The Leicester we were facing now in 1969 were one of our relegation rivals, perhaps distracted by reaching the Cup final again that season, although they would suffer the double trauma of losing that final to Manchester City and demotion to the Second Division. We faced each other in March 1969, with points at a premium and the pressure on. Being typically me, I was chasing all over the place, challenging defenders, putting myself about, and after about half an hour I was beginning to get fed up with what I felt was Herd's lack of effort. I was working my socks off for him and the team, but as far as I could see he wasn't really bothering. So I shouted to him, "You gonna shift your arse, or what?"

David, now a wily old campaigner of 35, looked me up and down and replied in that terse Scots way of his, "Son, it's no use running if you don't know where you're going."

I tell you what, that was brilliant. That stuck with me. It made me think about my game and what I was actually trying to achieve, when I conserved energy and when I burst into life. It's such a simple concept and a simple thing to say, but it had a big effect on me as a young player. You've got to take things like that on board and not just shrug it off because someone like David, while he may have been a tad on the sarcastic side, had plenty of experience to pass on to the likes of me.

Needless to say I didn't cut it as a striker, as that goalless game – albeit a vital point to edge us closer to survival – proved, although I would score plenty of goals in my career. But it did add a couple of weapons to my armoury in terms of understanding what attackers hate when I finally did cement my place in the team in a defence which would become synonymous with the success that Stoke City would enjoy over the next seven years. As I've intimated the late-Sixties was a very much a transitional period for the club, especially in terms of the defence. Several different players got the opportunity to show what they could do, but eventually a first choice back four emerged – one that would stake its claim as the best defence in the club's history and remain together throughout those halcyon seasons.

We were all home grown youngsters and playing for our club, so bringing it success was a deeply-ingrained desire. At its heart were myself and Alan Bloor, while at right-back was Jackie Marsh, my pal who'd come up through the ranks of the City Boys team with me, and at left-back was another local lad Mike Pejic, a tough-tackling, athletic player with a mean streak to rival Stuart Pearce's.

'Bluto' Bloor was a great lad, who was born just 200 yards from my house, so we were both Meir lads from the estate. I'd known him for a long time because he was the same age as my elder brother, Mick. Bluto was class, but he never sought the limelight and so was one of those players people often forget about that are actually vital to the make up of a successful team. To be fair to him I took a lot of the credit for the success of our partnership and he did a hell a lot of the work. He was a far, far better player than people remember, but that's him. Alan was always quite happy to just do his job and go for a quiet pint. He didn't want to be a star. He's a very unassuming type of fellow and he was quite happy for that to be the way it was.

He was a joy to play with. He made my job easy. It seemed to me that he was always there, he read the game so well. When I made mistakes, he cleaned up, especially when I was settling in early on. He'd got good pace for such a big man and, as I was the one who man-marked and attacked the ball, his role was to clean up the bits and pieces. Often he'd tell me, "Den, go in and get your face smashed and I'll pick up the bits!" He didn't go in for the tough guy thing, although he wasn't to be messed with and he could look after himself quite happily, but he didn't get involved as much as I did. He was quite a bright lad, Bluto!

I always wanted to be attacking the ball. In either penalty area I would throw my head at anything and then dive in after the follow up, it was suicidal really. I've always wanted to be the extrovert as such. That was my nature. I wanted to be seen, to be noticed. Alan just wanted to do his job. The fact Alan and I were so different meant we complemented each other perfectly and worked brilliantly together as a partnership.

Alan and I were very close on the field, but off the field I generally knocked around with Jackie Marsh, my long-term room-mate on away trips, because we'd grown up together and played as schoolboys since the age of 13. Jackie got into the side a year or so before me and played 30 games in that 1968/69 season. He was a great attacking full-back, whose crossing was up there with the best of them. I'd compare him today with Manchester United and England star Gary Neville – he was that good. He wasn't the best defender in the world. His tackling left a bit to be desired in that he'd generally aim for the knees and occasionally would make contact at waist height or higher!

Jackie was great fun socially, always cracking jokes at 100 miles an hour. I'll always remember he was famous amongst the squad for not being able to make a decision. I'd ask him, "what are we going to do tonight, Jack?" and he'd reply, "what do you want to do?" It would go on like that for perhaps half an hour with me ending up giggling at his lack of decisiveness before I'd eventually cave in and reveal where we'd already decided to go anyway! It was great because it meant I got to decide where we'd go out every time.

At left-back was a totally different character, although an equally adventurous player, Mike Pejic. Where Jackie was a laugh a minute, Pej never spoke to anybody. Before he came into training each morning we would lay bets on whether he would say anything. There weren't many takers when it became apparent he was so withdrawn. In would come Pej and all he would say would be, "Morning" and then when he was leaving he'd just say, "See ya" – and that was it. That's all you got out of him. It's amazing he's gone into management and coaching. He managed Chester City and then was assistant coach at Stoke in the 1990s, whilst also working as an FA youth coach in the North East. There he helped the likes of Jermaine Defoe, Aaron Lennon and Stewart Downing come through. He now runs Plymouth Argyle's Academy, after having done the same for Stoke for a long period. I would never have believed he had it in him back then. He lived in the hills up on the moors near Leek, miles away from everybody. He would come into training dressed like a gentleman farmer and he sometimes used to turn up to matches in his Land Rover with his two sheep dogs sat in the front.

But for all that I would trust him Pej my life – as long as I was on the same side. No-one was going to go past him. We used to call him 'The Claw' because he would grab hold of players when they did manage to beat him and he'd rather give away a free-kick than let someone get clear down the wing to do us damage.

He'd been a hard nut from day one when we'd begun playing together in the Stoke youth sides aged 17. Like me, though, it did cost him a few flesh wounds here and there. I remember we were playing in the youth team at Notts County and Pej went to head a ball clear and collided with his own goalkeeper, who punched him for good measure. The ball fell in the mud right next to Pej's head and unfortunately as an opposing player tried to smash the ball into the net he whacked his foot right into Mike's face. The boot cracked into his nose full on. Blood splattered everywhere. When I went across to have a look, all I could see were mangled bones and claret oozing out onto the pitch. He got it put into plaster afterwards, but it was a right mess, and remained so for quite a long time.

Where many would have held back after that, it didn't ever stop Pej from full commitment to every challenge though. I remember a first team game in the mid-70s when Pej and Dennis Tueart had a running battle which ended up with both of them ignoring the ball and kicking each other on the Victoria Ground pitch. Pej got his marching orders after really overstepping the mark by head-butting Dennis.

But Mike was not just tough guy. He had been a left winger who had played for England Schools and then been converted to a flying, all-action left-back. He was quick and his crossing was equally as good as Jackie's and his left foot hit a mean dead ball too. After winning eight England Under-23 caps, he was good enough to be selected for the full England side at the end of the 1973/74 season, under the caretaker-stewardship of Joe Mercer, after Alf Ramsey had been sacked. Allegedly Mercer got fed up with what he saw as Pej's surly nature and dropped him, but he also had a bad game against Scotland at Wembley which would turn out to be his last. Then, as I will reveal later happened with myself, any thoughts Pej may have had of rejuvenating his international career under the new England manager were kyboshed by the appointment of Leeds manager Don Revie to the job.

I've always wanted to be number one. That's always been my attitude. As a kid at school I had to be the best fighter because that was what life was all about then and then, from age 10, I wanted to be the best at football. I always wanted to be the leader. I never wanted to take orders off anybody. I've always wanted to give them, so I controlled that back four. That was my job. I was a pain in the backside to the others, to be honest, always talking and shouting. I realise now, having been a manager, how important that is. I would always be looking for someone like me because many don't want to do it. They don't want the responsibility. I love the likes of Spencer Prior, John MacPhail, Phil Gilchrist and Matty Elliott. But when I was playing I just thought it was natural. I didn't realise it was a special skill. I just thought it was my job to talk to people and organise people.

The Stoke back four of Marsh, Pejic, Bloor and Smith first played together on 13 September 1969 in a 4-2 home win over Sunderland and we would remain together until Pej was sold to Everton in February 1977. Opposing forwards hated playing against us because we were all physical players and could look after ourselves. We were a tough proposition.

While that defensive unit was key to the longevity of Stoke's success over the next few years, Tony Waddington also employed what in the modern game would be called a defensive midfielder 'sitting' in front of us to offer extra protection. Two players were called upon to fulfil that role. The first was a lad called Mike Bernard. He was a fantastic character – a scouser with all the usual wit and banter that heritage entails. Bernie was not lacking in confidence. He was a funny lad. Great to have around the dressing room. If I tell you that since finishing playing he's been a publican a couple of times you'll know what I mean. He was a good player too, tigerish in the tackle and a decent passer of the ball. But he was a tough, tough guy. I genuinely believe if the situation had called for it he would kick his own grandmother. He certainly took no prisoners. Fans at the time didn't realise how important he was because Mick used to break up opposition attacks and upset their pattern of play.

How he came to be picked up is an interesting tale. When I was in the youth team we played Shrewsbury up at Northwood School and absolutely slaughtered them 10-1. The club's Chief Scout Cliff Birks, who was responsible for spotting and bringing into the club countless players over the years, attended the game and the next thing we knew he'd persuaded one of the opposing players – a certain Mike Bernard – to sign. It proved to be a fantastic spot as he became one of the most influential players in Stoke's rise and rise over the next three or four seasons. But those of us who played that day and graduated along with Micky into the Stoke first team never let him forget that day!

The other defensive midfielder was Eric 'Alfie' Skeels, a man who eventually made 606 appearances for the club, setting a record which I believe will never be broken. The strange thing was that for long periods Alfie never seemed to be the first choice and yet he holds the record for playing more games for Stoke than anybody else. But that sums 'Alfie' up. He could play anywhere across the backline or midfield and go do a decent job on the wing. You need someone to fill in any position and Alfie could do the job. He was probably helped by the fact that teams were only allowed one substitute in those days and so the manager was delighted to have someone in the squad who could fill in anywhere in times of need. He was possibly the ultimate utility player and certainly a manager's dream. He trained well and was a strong character in his own quiet way, never wanting to be beaten. Much like Bluto Bloor, Alfie was a very unassuming chap. He was just 5 feet 9 inches tall, but could compete with forwards five or six inches tall. On the ball, he was two-footed and played neat, simple passes. He so rarely ever made mistakes and became known as 'Mr Dependable'. Incidentally he was nicknamed Alfie because he used to bring his little dog down to training with him, and the dog's name was Alfie, so it stuck.

I find it incredible that he's the club's record appearance holder and yet he's not a player that lives long in the memory of the fans. Of course it was a different era when players would remain with a club for their entire career, as the majority of that Stoke squad did, but even so Alfie gave outstanding service to the club and should be lauded much more for his contribution.

As a defensive unit we were relatively young back in 1969, and with youngsters you tend to get a fair bit of arrogance. Yes, we thought we were good, but we did make mistakes too and thankfully we had the good fortune to have the world's greatest goalkeeper behind us to dig us out of any holes we might get ourselves into.

No defender could feel more comfortable than playing in front of Gordon Banks. Not only was he capable of pulling off brilliant saves, one of his most important attributes was his positioning. He always seemed to be able to read what the opposition were doing and be in the right place at the right time. It was wonderful for us defenders. If the ball was played over the top, you knew exactly where he would be. He would come out and collect on the edge of his area or clear from outside the box. People don't realise how important the understanding is between a goalkeeper and his defenders.

Another of Gordon's great strengths was communicating with his defenders. You always knew exactly where he was because he would constantly tell you and he would tell you where opposing forwards were if you were under pressure. He was a massive part of our success and a massive influence in the dressing room with his positive winning attitude. He was great for young professionals to be involved with and every time I stepped out onto the pitch with him between the sticks I felt that the pressure was immediately on the opposition who must have been thinking, 'oh no, we've got to beat this defence AND Gordon bloody Banks today.' It was a massive thing psychologically.

He's the greatest goalkeeper I've ever seen. His anticipation, his athleticism – everything he did was top class. And he read things as if his mind was like a computer. I remember playing at Tottenham when Ralph Coates sped down the wing and crossed the ball in for Martin Peters. It went over my head and I slipped as it did so, leaving me lying helpless face down in the dirt. As Banksy was pretty much standing next to me when Coates hit the cross I knew he couldn't have reached the ball so I just assumed that a goal would be scored, but the next thing I know Gordon's got the ball in his hands and Martin is looking puzzled. I said to him, "Mart, what happened?"

Peters said, somewhat bemusedly, "he saved it."

I couldn't believe it. One minute he'd been standing next to me at the near post, the next he had anticipate the cross and got across to deal with the shot. I'd fallen over.

Banksy was simply absolutely amazing. Time and time again people would hit shots and he'd just catch them, often being so well positioned he didn't have to dive. It must be so deflating for a striker when you've hit the ball as sweet as anything and see somebody just go "thanks very much" and catch it. It didn't surprise the people who played with him because we saw it every day in training, but it surprised everybody else.

Gordon had won the World Cup with England in 1966, and joined Stoke just a year later when Leicester manager Matt Gillies decided that the youthful talent of one Peter Shilton deserved a permanent place in the first team, so made Banksy available for transfer. Tony Waddington pounced to seal a deal to bring him to the Victoria Ground and it brought one of the world's most high profile players to the club. Along with George Eastham, Peter Dobing and John Ritchie we were a good side with big heroes. Everybody wanted to see Gordon Banks and later, in 1972, we signed Geoff Hurst, giving us probably the highest profile squad on the planet, including two of England's three biggest heroes of 1966. On a global scale we were certainly up there with the likes of Liverpool and Manchester United and were invited to travel the planet playing exhibition matches. Tours were also one of the few ways for clubs to generate income during the close season when there are no regular home games to generate money to pay wages. We went on some fabulous tours, travelling all over the world. The places we visited were often unusual. Even somewhere like Kinshasa, capital of the Democratic Republic of Congo and the second largest French-speaking city in the world.

At the end of the 1968/69 season I didn't even have a passport and, with me still not really considered a regular first teamer, it came as a shock that the club wanted to take me on tour. This was my first trip abroad of any kind and the first time I'd been on a plane, so to visit a place like the Congo was an incredible eye-opener.

It was made all the more difficult for me because Kate and I had just had a baby. Paul was a mere 10 days old and here I was being whisked away to play football in some place I genuinely had not heard of until then. I was away for three weeks in total and that is a long time when you've got a 10 day old baby. It was tough on both Kate and me, but that's the job.

It seemed as if I was fated not to be around Paul much, because I'd even managed to miss his birth. Kate had been in the hospital for a while with the baby due and late one night they told me that nothing was going to happen in the immediate future, so I might as well go home. The buses had long since finished running and I hadn't got a car, so I walked across the city and up to the Meir, which must be nearly five miles. By the time I got home it was gone three o'clock in the morning.

Despite this being at the tail end of my first season in Stoke's First Division side, we didn't have a phone in our new house either, so when I got up the next morning the first thing I did was to walk down to the local phone box to make a call to see how Kate was. I couldn't believe it when I heard that she'd had Paul. I was a dad and I hadn't known it for six hours!

It didn't stop there either. Our second child was born while I was on tour with the club in Italy. Because I'd missed Paul's I was desperate to be there and had secured permission to fly back at the drop of a hat should Kate show any signs of going into labour. We'd decided that Kate would have a home birth for this labour so that I would definitely be there, and here I was, on the end of a phone in a hotel in Italy, hearing that her waters had broken with no warning and could I get back sharpish! I think I was in the airport waiting to board my plane when Becky was born.

But that was the job. There were no ifs or buts about it. You got paid to play football and I prided myself on playing every game on tour. I didn't ever want a game off. Sometimes we could have 10 games or more and I'd play every game.

Naturally football tours in that day and age threw up some fantastic tales. Wherever we went we always got invited to both the British and American Embassies, and they would throw fantastic parties. In Kinshasa we had a reception at the British Embassy before the game and then played in stifling heat. It was at least 90 degrees in the shade, and we were out there in the sun. We came up with a simple plan. George Eastham was the best player in the side, able to keep hold of the ball under pressure from defenders, so let's give it to him. He was also the oldest player in the side, but that didn't really come into our thinking! "Give it to George" became the mantra for the day. And lo and behold he had a storming game and we won 2-0.

Refereeing was always interesting in these games and on that afternoon we saw a classic example. At 1-0 up we were awarded a penalty. Harry Burrows was our penalty taker then. His technique was simply to blast it as hard as his fantastic left foot could propel the ball towards goal. It worked the vast majority of the time. On this occasion he was facing a goalkeeper who obviously hadn't heard of the Law of the game which forbids goalkeepers to move off their line until the ball is struck at a penalty kick. As Harry ran up to let loose his thunderbolt the keeper ran out just as fast and when Harry made contact with the ball the goalie was about two foot away and smothered the shot. Amazingly the referee allowed it, but the keeper did pay for his endeavours by taking the full force of the shot in his stomach! Another thing I remember from that game is that we were protected by a phalanx of troops holding rifles ringed around the pitch to keep the packed and excitable crowd under control. Because of the heat we'd had bottles of water placed all around the touchline so we could keep hydrated. The crowd were getting thirsty and demanding the water which was meant for us, and so to avoid a riot the soldiers took to selling our water to the crowd.

I was always very curious about the places we visited, and unlike many footballers, I wanted to find out more and see as many of the sights as I could. I remember in Kinshasa we were invited to the American Embassy for a party and by that stage I'd had enough drinking so I just wondered off through the backstreets, crossing the river over into Brazzaville, the capital of the Republic of Congo on the facing bank of the River Congo. As I walked around what was effectively a shantytown, I could see people looking at me thinking, "who's this white fella?" That was perhaps not the brightest thing to do, to wander off alone, but I always figure that if I can walk around the Meir at night I can walk around anywhere. The thing that struck me as I explored the area around the riverfront was that I barely saw anyone aged over 40. It really stood out to me and I began to understand how life expectancy and living standards might not be the same the world over as they were back home.

After Congo we moved on to the Ivory Coast, played a game there and then went to the Canary Islands for a week's holiday. Fully rested, we flew to Spain and played all round the country, the pinnacle being a specially arranged friendly against Barcelona. I think it was a Spanish holiday that day so there were about 90,000 fans inside the Nou Camp. For a 20 year-old like me it was fantastic, absolutely amazing. Just to be in the stadium was incredible, but to play so well and take a three goal lead at half-time was beyond anyone's wildest dreams. David Herd, with two, and Harry Burrows scored the goals as we completely outplayed Barcelona in their own backyard. It was ridiculously easy, in fact. At half-time George Eastham, who was then Waddo's assistant, decided to bring himself on as he wanted to be a part of this fabulous performance we were putting on. I was at the back telling our midfielders to hold back, cover and keep things tight so we could hold our lead, while all they cared about was bombing forward and getting their names on the scoresheet. Barca, chivvied along by a stadium full of very irate supporters who hadn't given up their holiday to watch these upstarts from England beat their favourites, played far better in the second half and got back to 3-2, but a rearguard action kept them out and we held on for a famous victory.

You won't be surprised to hear that we had a fantastic night out after that great win. Myself, Jackie Marsh and John Farmer painted the town red and white and flopped into bed as dawn broke. The next day we were due for an early start to travel to Pontevedra over on the Atlantic coast on the other side of the country. Not that I'd been a goody-goody because I'd had a drink or two to celebrate, but I was the only one who woke up. The other two simply wouldn't stir. So I had a shower, packed my stuff and tried to rouse them again. I still couldn't get them to wake. So I grabbed them one by one and stuck them in a cold shower, leaving them in there as I packed their cases. That did the trick for Jackie, but John was utterly incapacitated. So about half past eight in the morning Jackie and I carried John down the stairs, tiptoed with him past the breakfast room's open door in case one of the management saw the state of our right back and out to the waiting coach. We put John down right at the steps and told him "right, we are going to let you go now. You've got get up these steps and sit down". Up the steps he tottered with John following him with his arm steadying John as if he was a ventriloquist's dummy. We sat him down on the back seat to keep him out of the way for the daunting 13 hour coach journey along the north coast of Spain.

We stopped in the hills for lunch at a tiny restaurant and we manage to get John off the coach and sat down at the table, but then the waiter put a big bowl of fish soup in front of him, with big lumps of fish sticking out of it. That was it for John. He disappeared back to the coach!

Having great players meant that the club's name also attracted great opposition to the Victoria Ground to play friendlies. In 1963 the great Real Madrid side, which had dominated the first decade of the European Cup, played a match to celebrate the centenary of Stoke City. Then in 1965 a special match to bid farewell to Stanley Matthews on his retirement was beamed all around the world. The game featured two scratch teams which included a host of world stars including Ferenc Puskas, Alfredo di Stefano, Lev Yashin etc

My first taste of such glitz and glamour came in September 1969 with the visit of Santos, and probably the greatest player of all Pelé. At that time the great man was at the height of his powers having won two World Cups and taken the world by storm with his goalscoring prowess and ability on the ball. He was also only nine months away from playing in probably the greatest team of all – the 1970 Brazil side that swept all before them to lift the trophy a third time. Several of that team played for Santos in this friendly before a packed Victoria Ground.

It soon became apparent to me that one of the reasons for Pelé's ability to have more time on the ball than any other player was because Santos would get the ball to him in advanced positions and then his nearest team-mates would block our players from getting near the great man. You went to challenge him and somebody would block you off to give him room to play. It was like American football. I'd never come across this kind of tactic before. They blocked us off and he played. And boy was he brilliant! He scored two goals with rasping drives from the edge of the box and produced some wonderful touch football with his fellow attackers. It was a scintillating display, and an education for me.

Santos won the game 3-2, although I actually got the ball into their net right on half-time with a header from a corner, but the goal was disallowed. I still haven't got a clue why, although I already had the feeling that whatever happened Santos would win this friendly!

In 2006 Kate and I were on holiday with my two grandsons, and I asked them, "who was Brazil's most famous player?"

"Pelé," they correctly replied.

"I've played against Pelé," I ventured.

"Yeah, alright Grandad," they laughed.

"I have," I insisted.

"Yeah, right." They wouldn't believe me no matter what I said.

Anyway when we went back off the holiday, my son Paul googled the game and in the match report it said there I had scored a goal right on half time and no-one had any idea why it was disallowed. Fortunately I've also got two photos of me playing against Pelé, so my grandkids do believe me now. The unfortunate thing about those photos is that both show me not getting in my tackle in time to stop the great man scoring.

In the summer of 1969 Tony Waddington made two inspirational signings. Firstly, in June, he re-signed a player that many of us had been surprised he'd let go in the first place. John Ritchie had been signed from Kettering as a teenager and scored 64 goals in 110 games as Stoke established themselves in the First Division in the mid-Sixties. He was a tall, rangy striker, who had a good turn of pace for a big man, and unerring will to win, but for some reason Waddo thought he'd be better off looking elsewhere for goals and sold Big John to Sheffield Wednesday for £70,000 in November 1966. I was a youth team player at the time and remember the consternation it caused amongst supporters. But now Ritchie, who had never settled at Wednesday and significantly had never moved out of the Potteries, was returning to Stoke for a knockdown £25,000. Waddo had pulled yet another transfer coup out of the hat. He'd resigned Big John and made a £45,000 profit into the bargain.

Then in August he spent £100,000 to prise a 23 year-old striker called Jimmy Greenhoff away from Birmingham City. Waddo was looking for the ideal foil for Ritchie and had heard that Greenhoff had become disillusioned after just a year at St Andrew's under Stan Cullis. The pair's arrival galvanised the side and John and Jimmy netted 23 goals between them over the season, with Harry Burrows finishing as equal top scorer with Big John with 14 goals.

The 1969/70 season generally went very well for me as well as the club. On 17 September I scored my first goal for the club to set the seal on a 3-1 win at West Brom and two weeks later I bagged two at West Ham in a 3-3 draw. I remember the first of those two goals really well because it nearly didn't get awarded to me. A corner came across and I leapt and headed it down back across the goal the way it had come so it bounced right on the line and into the net. But chasing it in was David Herd and when it crossed the line he wheeled away with his arm upraised claiming the goal. Typical bloody striker, someone else does all the hard work and he claims the goal! I wasn't having that, though, so I claimed it too and after the game, in the dressing room, David came across and admitted defeat. "You can have it. I've got enough goals son!" he said.

At the end of September, following a 2-0 victory over Manchester City, we sat fifth in the league table. We were sixth after a 1-0 win over Derby on Boxing Day, but a ten game streak without a win in the New Year saw us drop down into mid-table to finish ninth. One of those matches was our visit to Chelsea, a game which was to provide me with a less enjoyable dispute with Peter Dobing.

We had played really well to earn a goalless draw and were holding on to the point comfortably going into injury time when Peter picked up a loose ball in midfield, just inside our half. He was facing our own goal, looking directly at me. I fully expected him to turn and whack the ball long into the corners to keep it away from our goal and kill time. But he didn't. As I lost concentration he feinted to do what I, and everyone else, expected him to do, but then clipped the ball back towards me. Except I'd begun to squeeze out and the pass Peter played instead found Ian Hutchinson from Stamford Bridge, who raced through unhindered to accept the present and score past Banksy to win the game.

An argument ensued in the dressing room with Waddo wading into Peter for playing what on the face of it seemed to be a poor backpass.

"Why didn't you play it forward?" Waddo demanded.

Peter retorted, pointing at me, "Is he playing or not? If he's playing he should be expecting a pass. "

I wasn't. I'd switched off. I thought he was going to turn and play the ball forward to kill time. But I knew that Peter was right. He was keeping possession of the ball by playing it back to me, from where it could have gone back to Gordon, who at that time was allowed to pick it up and that probably would have seen out the few remaining seconds. Instead we lost. And it was my fault. I learnt. And quickly. I didn't want to be sitting in our dressing room getting slaughtered like that.

By this stage Tony Waddington had appointed George Eastham as his assistant to replace our former midfielder Jimmy McIlroy, who had decided to move back home to Burnley to become a journalist on the local paper. Waddo used George as a sounding board, although he always had one simple mantra when it came to management – pick good players. I can remember Frank Lord, the former Crewe, Rochdale and Plymouth centre-forward coming in at the end of his playing career to get some coaching experience and Waddo would watch his sessions, which always involved him trying to 'improve' players and say, "what's he doing?" He'd pull Frank aside and say, "Leave them alone. Look Denis Smith can defend and George Eastham can pass. Just get them fit and let them go out and play."

The game was very simple to Waddo. What he did was pick good players and play them in their correct positions, building enough rapport and cohesion to make a team. It sounds simple to say it, but he was of course absolutely right. When I got my first managerial job at York City I spoke to Tony and asked him what I should do to be a good manager. He replied by saying, "you want to be a good manager?"

"Yes."

"Then sign good players. But if you want to be a great manager, sign great players". And he's right. It's that simple.

******

Our trainer at Stoke was a real character by the name of Frank Mountford. Frank had been about forever. He'd joined the club during the Second World War as a 17 year-old star centre-forward and scored an incredible number of goals in the war leagues. When the war ended he reverted to centre-half, as he used to tell me, because he had got fed up being kicked and wanted to do the kicking himself. He played in the Stoke team that came within one victory of winning the title in 1946/47 and was a firm fans' favourite during the next 15 years as a wholehearted player. He became one of the old-school style trainers, always there with bucket and sponge in hand and a motivating word to get you up and going again. By motivating I mean he'd tell you what a wimp you were and there was nothing bloody wrong with you!

Frank was a different class. He loved a drink, especially the odd tot of rum, but if you needed something then Frank would sort it for you. He doubled up by doing the fitness coaching, so he'd have us running and take us for five-a-sides. I remember one session when Adrian Heath whacked a long ball up front and it went over his target Lee Chapman's head and Frank barks, "get it into his feet". Next time Inchey again whacks it far too long.

"Into his feet," shouts Frank. But it happened again.

"Right," said Frank, frustrated. "You come and stand here and see what you think about it." So now Frank was whacking balls over Inchey's head shouting, "what do you think about that?"

Inchey moaned, "well, I'm only small. I can't get them".

Frank made his point. "It's no good up whacking the ball up there. Keep it down".

Waddo had by now introduced another young talent into the team, Irish firebrand winger Terry Conroy, a player with a mercurial change of pace and the whitest, palest legs you've ever seen. With TC, as he became universally known, alongside the experience of George Eastham, Peter Dobing and John Ritchie, we had blended into a formidable side, with a strong will that was very difficult to beat.

We began the 1970/71 season well and were almost unbeatable at home, not conceding a goal until mid-October and not losing at the Vic until late February in a season which developed into our first serious tilt at major silverware. We signalled our intent with a 5-0 thrashing of Arsenal, which was made all the better by being televised that night on Match of the Day. TC scored the goal of the month in that game – it was an absolute belter from 25 yards, as he's forever telling me! John Ritchie was inspired that day, too, scoring twice, the second seeing him dribble into the box and around four players before planting a left foot shot past Bob Wilson into the far corner.

Even Alan Bloor netted a rare goal as the side which would eventually go on to win the double was put to the sword. We were irresistible that day and Arsenal had the proverbial nightmare as Terry ran riot down the wing and Greenhoff and Ritchie, now forming a truly formidable partnership, ripped the heart of their defence to shreds.

As good as we were that day in attack, we were equally strong handling Arsenal's strikeforce. Bluto and I had one of our best games together that afternoon keeping John Radford and George Graham quieter than church mice. Strong at both ends of the pitch, we were now a formidable side and the Boothen End, the huge Kop behind the goal which had become the spiritual home of Stoke supporters, rewrote Land Of Hope And Glory in our honour:

Land Of Smoke And Glory
Home Of Stoke City
High higher and higher
On to victory

We were still drawing too many games to become serious challengers in the league, but in cup competitions we never gave up. In those days penalty competitions had not been invented, so Cup ties went on and on, through replay after replay, until someone emerged victorious. I've already mentioned the battles we had with Huddersfield and Manchester United that season as we progressed through the rounds of the FA Cup. They were tough, intense ties that attracted huge crowds. The 49,000 we had at the Vic for the replay with United created an electric atmosphere that still sends a shiver down my spine even now. Those games really gave us the taste for glory. I loved big crowds, and the bigger the game, the bigger the opportunity as far as I was concerned. Sometimes that can get to players, but I lapped it all up and wanted more.

We didn't make life easy for ourselves. We'd lost to Millwall in a second round replay in the League Cup earlier in the season and when we drew them again in the FA Cup third round we thought, 'here we go again.' But we just squeezed past the Lions 2-1. The draw for round four paired us with fellow First Division club Huddersfield Town and their flamboyant striker Frank Worthington. The first game at the Vic was a belter, which finished 3-3, while the replay at Leeds Road ended goalless after extra time. So we had to meet again at the neutral venue of Old Trafford on a Monday night in February to fit the game in. Incredibly there were over 39,000 there to see us nick it 1-0 thanks to a Greenhoff goal.

It was during this marathon tie that I fractured my ankle, as I previously mentioned, but I was desperate to play. Waddo was keen for me to play too and he was a past master at getting performances out of players that should have been lying on the treatment couch rather than taking the field. If you were carrying an injury he would take you off for a chat and tell you "you're alright". He was quite incredible like that. Even if you were limping and couldn't put any weight on your ankle or carrying your arm limply by your side you would be fired up and ready to go. I had some fitness tests where I could hardly walk, but I had an injection so I couldn't feel the pain and played anyway. You want to go out and perform, even though it was all based on adrenalin most of the time.

The following Saturday was the fifth round and we were now up against another First Division club, and a very good one at that, Bobby Robson's Ipswich, featuring players like Mick Mills and Colin Viljoen. We were by now suffering from fatigue having played so often and the first game was fairly tight and uneventful, finishing 0-0 at the Vic. Three days later we met again at Portman Road in a fierce encounter. It was an extremely tense game once again, which was decided late on when I was left unmarked to bullet a far post header into the far top corner. I've got a great photo of this goal in my archives at home and it's one of my favourites. I'm bent almost double at the waist, having put so much of my upper body strength into the header. I was delighted to have scored and it proved to be a vital goal.

So now we were in the last eight and the draw proved kind to us – or so we thought – when we came out of the hat with Second Division Hull City. We were delighted and fancied our chances all the more. I have to admit I hadn't heard of their strikers Ken Wagstaff and Chris Chilton. Perhaps that was a little bit of the kind of arrogance that creeps into top flight clubs, not keeping abreast of what's going on further down the ladder. As far as we were concerned avoiding Liverpool and Spurs, who had been paired together, Arsenal and Everton meant we were in with a fantastic chance.

We arrived on Humberside to face Terry Neill's Tigers on a snowy day made for a cup upset. Thinking about it now it was the kind of day that dawned when my York side dumped Arsenal out of the Cup in 1985. The pitch was white all over and Hull tore into us. We were thrown by the entire situation and the intensity of their onslaught. Never mind the fact that they were a division lower than us, they gave us a right going over and the two strikers, Wagstaff and Chilton, gave myself and Bluto as hard a time as any top flight pairing ever did. Wagstaff was a chunky bloke, but had a fair turn of speed, while Chilton was a classic centre-forward who was a fantastic header of the ball. They combined brilliantly and Wagstaff helped himself to two goals to put them in a 2-0 lead. They gave us a torrid 90 minutes in front of a seething crowd of 41,500 crammed into Boothferry Park. I recall that the following day a Sunday newspaper published a fantastic photograph of me and Chilton diving to head a ball. We were both completely horizontal to the ground, stretching for the ball, both with our arms around one another's necks. It was voted as the Sports Photograph of the Year in 1971.

Despite Terry Conroy rounding Hull keeper McKechnie right on the whistle to make it 1-2, half-time that chilly March day was not a time to be in the visitors' dressing room at Boothferry Park. It was make or break time to say the least. We could feel the Cup slipping from our grasp and we had come through far too much to let it go without a fight. Heated words were exchanged, "what the hell are we doing coming here and losing to these?" being among the more printable sentiments. We knew that we had to get a grip on the two strikers, but Waddo also made a few organisational changes and asked us to get the ball to TC so he could take on their full-backs on either wing. Terry was approaching his best form of his career and we knew he could murder opponents given enough of the ball.

It worked. As snow fell we played one of the best halves of football that we ever put together. We drew level on 70 minutes when John Ritchie scored and we finally ended Hull's feisty resistance when Ritchie netted again. This time he headed home at the far post from a cross from a quickly taken throw in that was incorrectly awarded to us which the Hull lads contested and lost their concentration just a bit. It was a hell of a comeback, and one that gave us added belief in ourselves. That was an example where the arrogant belief in our own abilities pulled us through. It was what had got us into trouble too, mind you, as we hadn't done any research into who we were playing against. Because we were essentially a young side our arrogance was vital to us. We kept going and we didn't think we could lose.

On Monday morning we were pulled out of the semi-final draw hat with Arsenal. Now we really believed we could win the FA Cup. The last time we had faced them we'd won 5-0. We were superconfident.

Cup fever had been brewing in the Potteries throughout our run. Stoke City had seen relatively little success in its history for a club which had been founder members of the Football League. The club had only once previously reached the FA Cup semi-final, in 1899. Over 70 years later the anticipation of our big day, which was scheduled to be at Sheffield Wednesday's Hillsborough, brought huge queues for tickets outside the main Boothen Stand. Success-starved supporters were gorging themselves on these good times and no-one wanted to miss out.

The morning of Saturday 27 March 1971 dawned bright as thousands of Stokies, clad in red and white, streamed over the Pennines and into Sheffield. The place was packed. Our fans had been given the home end, which at that time had no roof and so it was a glorious sight as we walked out onto the pitch to play Arsenal. Because both of us played in red and white it had been decided that we would both play in our change strips, so we were clad in white from head to foot.

Our build up had been perfect. Nice and relaxed and full of fun and frolics to relieve any tension. On the pitch we'd lost at home to Manchester United the previous Saturday, but frankly the league had gone for a burton by this stage. We couldn't get into Europe and we'd got enough points in the bag not to be dragged into the relegation fight and while we would never play any game without 100% focus, we knew that our season all came down to this day in South Yorkshire.

We started well. Arsenal's dangerman was a big centre-forward called John Radford, who top scored for them that season with 21 goals, but Bluto and I really had his number that day. The Gunners were ineffectual going forward and we were controlling the game. Sometimes in football you get the feeling that everything is moving inexorably your way and the first half of that game saw a succession of events which left me thinking we were nailed on for a first ever Wembley appearance. On 22 minutes we won a corner. Harry

Burrows swung it in to the near post and I ran in to try to get a flick on. The ball deflected off me and into the six yard box, but Arsenal got it half clear back out towards me. I launched myself into a tackle with Arsenal midfielder Peter Storey and as I slung out my left foot to block the ball I though he pulled out of the challenge. 'Interesting,' I thought. 'A fifty fifty with Peter Storey and he's just disappeared.'

Storey did make a late poke at the ball as he realised he should actually get to it first, but all he succeeded in doing was hitting it against my ankle. The ball ballooned up and crazily right into the very top corner of Bob Wilson's goal. It flew in, causing the Stokies in the 55,000 crowd to go absolutely bonkers. Brian Moore called it "an absolutely freak goal" in the commentary. He was dead right, but I didn't care. I'd touched the ball last. It was my goal and we were 1-0 ahead.

Then it got better. Bluto easily dispossessed Graham on the half-way line and laid the ball out to Mike Pejic on the left. Pej chipped the ball forward for Harry Burrows to flick on for the charging Ritchie to race onto. John was beaten to it by Peter Simpson, however, who nodded it down to what he must have thought was the safe feet of Charlie George. But Charlie dinked a backpass in the direction of Bob Wilson only to find that John had continued his run on and was now behind Simpson, but hidden from George's view. As the ball trickled back towards Wilson, Ritchie pounced, waltzed round Wilson and netted before launching into one of the most memorable celebrations in Stoke's history. Both arms held aloft, with fists clenched, waving them around frantically, he ran at full pelt along the goal line then down the touchline back into our half. It's a moment that those there will never forget and I am delighted that it has been captured in the statue which commemorates John's achievements as the club's record goalscorer which was unveiled on the first anniversary of his death in February 2008.

How football fortunes sometimes change so radically. At that moment Charlie George was the villain of Arsenal's season. Surely that backpass had cost them a place in the Cup final? As fate had it, further twists would conspire to give Charlie the opportunity to win the double for the Gunners with a spectacular Wembley strike for which he is now world famous. For me, as we went into half-time totally in command, I could just not see how Arsenal could possibly get back into the match. We had played as well as we'd ever played as a team in that 45 minutes.

It was one of those games when you just don't want half-time to come. Our fans were buzzing and we felt we were going to steamroller the Gunners again. I remember thinking after the second goal, 'hang on, we could do another five nil here.'

But that Arsenal side were a tough bunch. Their fighting qualities, which had obviously improved since our September stuffing, were as strong as ours. Very early in the second half Arsenal presented us with a chance to absolutely nail their coffin shut when another poor backpass left Jimmy Greenhoff one on one with Wilson. Jimmy however did not retain his cool quite as well as Big John had. Instead of using his neat footwork to go round the keeper, he opted to shoot early from the edge of the box. The ball went straight at Wilson, who had spread himself, and it hit him, but seemed to have gone past him. The impact knocked Bob off balance and he fell backwards and sat on the ball, stopping it from entering the net. It was a moment which would eventually cost us dearly.

The tide began to turn when on 49 minutes we failed to properly clear a left wing cross. A defensive header fell short to the edge of the area and Peter Storey, whose weak challenge had lead to my goal, cracked it with his right foot. The ball rocketed towards me and I felt it flick off my leg as I tried to stop it. It took the smallest of deflections on its way past me, but it was enough to take the ball beyond the diving Gordon Banks and into the far corner of the net. Arsenal were back in it.

I suppose looking back that was the moment when the whole balance of the tie shifted. Until then Arsenal had been out of it, but now our mentality had completely changed. We had everything to lose and we dropped back to protect our single goal lead. Arsenal on the other hand were buoyed by that goal and took advantage of our gingerness, grabbing the game by the scruff of the neck. We still had 40 minutes to hold out and inevitably the Gunners gained a huge amount of heart from that goal and began to crank up the pressure. We clung on doggedly and actually restricted them to very few chances. The minutes clicked by and Wembley edged closer as the pressure grew and grew. The tension was unbearable, especially for our supporters. We knew that the ninety minutes was up because there was a big clock at Hillsborough attached to one of the floodlight pylons and it was showing ten to five. We were deep into injury time and both sets of fans were in enhanced states of excitement and agitation. It was all hands to the pump time as far as we were concerned.

But then came a chain of events which I still shake my head at disbelief at today. As the frantic play continue, with Arsenal not really looking like creating a clear cut chance, the referee gave a dubious free-kick for a foul by Pej on Storey. We really didn't like the decision as it was a 50/50 challenge and the ball was now on the edge of the box, giving them the option of shooting or crossing into a packed penalty area. We protested long and hard about the decision, partly to waste time and partly to put the Gunners off. It didn't really achieve either as they organised quickly and slung the ball into the box. Gordon Banks shouted "Mine" and I relaxed because I knew he would claim the ball, which he did with a big leap to catch it above his head. I thought our goalkeeper had possession and would take his time to clear. George Graham had other ideas. The Scottish forward, who'd done nothing all game, ran in and threw himself into the back of Banksy as our keeper was still in mid-air. It was a blatant foul for everyone to see. But incredibly referee Pat Partridge waved play on. That should never ever have been allowed. As plain as the nose on your face it should have been a free-kick.

As I'd felt Banksy would hold the ball I had stepped off my man, John Radford, by about a yard and so wasn't as tight to him as I wanted to be. The ball slipped out of Banksy's grasp as he collapsed under the weight of Graham's barge, and bounced towards us. I did the only thing I could do and reached out with my hand to flick the ball away from the foot of Radford as he wound up to lash it into the goal. Fortunately for me Partridge was behind me so my body concealed my misdemeanour and stopped me giving away a spot-kick. But I felt that was justice for what had gone on before.

The Arsenal players didn't. Now it was they hounding Partridge, who had only awarded them a corner after a subsequent shot had been battered away to safety. There was no respite for the referee because in one ear he had Radford and the Gunners mob screaming about my handball and in the other Pej leading the protests from our side about Graham's foul on Banksy. It only all calmed down when we all realised that there was a corner still to face up to. It had to be the last action of the game. How there was enough time to take it I will never know.

The ball came across into the packed penalty area. Three Arsenal players rose with me and another Stoke defender and Frank McLintock's head climbed highest to arrow the ball towards the bottom corner of the net. It beat Banksy, but not Josh Mahoney, who flung himself to his right to punch the ball off the line and just wide of the post. This time, however, Mr Partridge did not miss the infringement and awarded Arsenal a spot-kick.

It was another of those 'what if' moments that football throws up. Josh, for whatever reason, had moved a coupled of feet along the line and so had had to dive to punch it away. If he'd stayed on his post he'd have kicked it clear, but he'd moved. It was a good save, to be fair. One which Banksy would have been proud of, but there is no logical reason why Josh should have left his post. It was one of the most crucial and costly moments in Stoke City's history.

There is no word or phrase to describe how you feel at a moment like that, and heaven only knows how Josh felt. It's one of the incredible things about football that it can eat you up and spit you out as the tale of such a tumultuous game unfolds. I remember looking forlornly around as Arsenal players celebrated the award of the penalty as if they'd won the Cup! A couple of them were dancing around, and the ball still wasn't in the back of the net yet.

Incredibly it was Peter Storey once again who stepped up to take the penalty. He had been at fault for our first goal, had netted the Gunners' first and now had the chance to take the semi-final to the most unlikely of replays. I was able to look – just. But I felt so helpless. His penalty wasn't the best as he didn't hit it well and it passed about four feet to Banksy's right, but Gordon had shifted his weight to his right hand side and rendered himself unable to react. I don't think I've ever seen a footballer look so crestfallen as he did at that moment.

Somehow Arsenal had levelled at 2-2 and, while they celebrated like schoolchildren, the referee blew the whistle to end the game. Our Wembley dream had been snatched from us in the cruellest of fashions. My gut reaction was that we'd been robbed. To start with the game should have been over, then there was the non-free-kick and then the foul on Gordon. We had been 2-1 up in the 95th minute of an FA Cup semi-final. Every boy's dream was gone.

I think it's nigh on impossible to cope with that kind of turnaround mentally, especially when it's the first time you've been in that position. We thought we'd won that game. We thought we were in the final at Wembley. Somehow we weren't.

But we hadn't actually lost. We still had a replay at Goodison Park the following Wednesday night to get ourselves up for. It was an almost impossible task. Quite frankly we weren't in the game. George Graham scored with a flying header, which found the top corner in the 13th minute, and Ray Kennedy's tap in early in the second half sealed our fate. The 2-0 defeat didn't hurt as deeply as the fury which still raged within us about the first game, but in moments like that it crosses your mind as to whether you will ever get a chance like that again. Nearly forty years later I ask myself how history could have been different if we'd gone on to that Cup final and beaten Liverpool, earning further global exposure and lifting the small club complex which has always plagued Stoke City supporters? But we'll never know.

Somehow we had to find a way to recover from this crushing blow. Gordon Banks was one of the most professional players that ever lived and even he found it very difficult to cope with what had happened. We won only two of our last 11 league games that season. To be honest our hearts and minds couldn't adjust to what had gone on.

Strangely the day of the semi-finals was the same day we were supposed to play Arsenal in the league. That fixture was put back to the penultimate match of the league season, which by then the Gunners needed to win in order to stay in with a chance of lifting the title. We were determined to put an end to their double aspirations, but they nicked a 1-0 result and then won their last game, away at Spurs, to win the league and travel to Wembley still in with a chance of becoming only the second club this century to achieve the double of League and FA Cup. A 2-1 victory in extra time over Liverpool wrote them into folklore, while I could only watch and think of what might have been.

Little did I know that yet more heartache at the hands of the Gunners lurked around the corner – but at least there would be some glory to savour first.

Chapter Eight

WEMBLEY GLORY

Nobody fancied coming to play at the Victoria Ground, with the Boothen End in full cry, the pitch a bog and a hostile atmosphere. The Vic epitomised what the seventies were all about in British football. Virile hostility on and off the pitch, combined with enough maverick skill to whet the appetite of a generation of football fans. Every club had a bank of terracing upon which congregated the hardcore, vociferous support. Liverpool's Kop, Manchester United's Stretford End, Highbury's North Bank and Chelsea's Shed, they were all fervent, noisy throngs. But our Boothen End gave as good as it got.

That bank, packed full of supporters, provided us with true inspiration as we established Stoke City as a top five team in the First Division in the mid-1970s, a period in which the likes of Manchester United and Tottenham Hotspur languished in the Second Division. We were a very good side. We regularly finished in the top five of the First Division, reached the FA Cup semi-finals in consecutive seasons and won the first trophy in Stoke's long and distinguished history, the League Cup in 1972. It was arguably the most glorious era of this great club and I consider it an honour to have been able to be a part of making it happen.

We went into the 1971/72 season with a renewed sense of determination borne of the heartache of that last-ditch failure to reach the FA Cup final. We had been so close to glory and success that we knew how badly we wanted to touch it. We knew we were a very hard side to beat and now felt that we were good enough to repeat what we'd achieved the previous season in one or other of the cup competitions. As it happens we'd manage it in both.

The Football League Cup was only eleven years old and until 1967 had not even been given the honour of a Wembley final, so it was still a competition very much in its infancy, and was very much inferior to the FA Cup, something which hasn't really changed.

Our journey to Wembley and an appointment with destiny began at the unlikely venue of Southport. The Lancashire coastal resort was hardly a hotbed of football, but the Division Four team, managed by Jimmy Meadows, proved a surprisingly tricky nut to crack. Southport had a big, strong side featuring a centre-forward called Eric Redrobe – I remember he was like a wardrobe coming at you, physically strong and built like a castle buttress. It was a hard game, which we only just managed to squeak through 2-1 thanks to a late goal by Jimmy Greenhoff. That may have been in part because Tony Waddington, in the time-honoured manner of early League Cup rounds, rested certain players and allowed their deputies a rare first team run out. Gordon Banks, for example, was replaced by England Under 23 international John Farmer, while Sean Haslegrave was given a game in midfield in place of George Eastham and Josh Mahoney featured instead of Terry Conroy.

In the third round we were drawn away at Oxford's Manor Ground and survived another tricky tie thanks to another Greenhoff goal, which salvaged a 1-1 draw. Oxford were 14th in Division Two at the time, and we were surprised by the quality of their play. Gerry Summers was the manager and a certain Ron Atkinson captained the side. They had a decent team and obviously fancied their chances at their tight, unwelcoming ground. The 15,024 crowd created a huge din when John Evanson scored their late equaliser, and we had to do it all again a couple of weeks later. This time we had enough to get past them as Ritchie and then a superb Sean Haslegrave volley scored the goals in a 2-0 win.

One of the key factors in our growing success was the strike partnership of Ritchie and Greenhoff. Both were among the goals, and often they were providing them for each other, and with the pace of Terry Conroy and the guile of Dobing and Eastham, we had a very potent attack. For about three season, until John's career was ended by injury, they were a devastating pair. It was interesting because they were very different characters. John was a determined, single-minded kind of guy, who was never happy unless he'd scored.

We could win 5-0 and if he hadn't hit the net he could be a moody bugger! But that was his strength too. Big John just loved scoring goals and for such a big man he could finish in all sorts of ways – pass them in, volley them in, head them in. Jimmy, however, was completely different. Blessed with sublime skills, and a wonderful ability to hit volleys cleanly, Greenhoff was less of an out and out striker, and more of a link man in the way Wayne Rooney is today. I would say Greenhoff was that good too. Like Rooney when Jim scored goals they were usually worth seeing because he struck the ball so sweetly. I would say he is the best volleyer I've ever seen. He struck them so sweetly – but, like Rooney, that was also a problem. Jimmy scored great goals, but he didn't really score enough. He averaged about 12 to 14 in a season, which is not enough for a striker of his quality.

The problem with Jimmy was that as a person he was an extremely shy, nervous type of lad. He needed confidence to play, and when fans shouted his name you could see his chest puff out and he would lift his game. At those times he could be unplayable. Equally, sometimes when all wasn't going well, Jimmy would deflate. He was quite a complex character and a completely different animal to Ritchie. John had the inner belief to think he was the top striker around. Jimmy wasn't sure.

He would be a nervous wreck before each game and it could get to him during a match too. I remember him missing a penalty in the mid-1970s, and it affected Jimmy. Peter Shilton was our goalkeeper at this point, and wasn't happy with the way Jimmy had taken the penalty. So in the first training session afterwards I had a little bet with Peter that Jimmy wouldn't beat him with each of ten spot-kicks. Peter liked a gamble and was obsessive about not conceding, even in training. He really put every effort into trying to save each penalty, but Jimmy smacked all ten into the four corners of the goal giving Shilton no chance. There was no pressure, of course, but it was an unbelievable performance and just reiterated to me Jimmy's ability to do almost anything with a football. Come match days it became more difficult because of the pressure. That was Jimmy's nature again. His talent was awesome, but talent isn't everything, a truly great player needs temperament and fitness to go hand in hand. Jimmy would be thinking fans had come to watch the game and to criticise him. I would think people had come to praise me. It's just a different nature.

Goals are the lifeblood of any successful team. You need a minimum of 40 goals in a season from your front pair to give you any sort of chance of a trophy. Then you need others to weigh in. During our glory years you knew that TC would get 7 or 8, Peter Dobing could hit double figures, I would get four or five and the likes of Mahoney and Hudson would find the net too. But without your main strikers contributing the bulk you are going to struggle. Luckily for us John and Jimmy were in their pomp.

Our strikeforce came up trumps again when John Ritchie scored in a much more routine 2-0 home win in the replay to get us past Oxford. In the fourth round we came out of the hat with Manchester United. This would prove to be the first meeting of seven that season, including two in the league, three in the League Cup and two in the FA Cup, all of which were titanic battles and only one of which, the inconsequential league match at the end of the season, we lost. At the time we were showing how difficult we were to beat, but struggling to put sides away, and a surfeit of draws dogged our league form which saw us marooned in mid-table without a say in the title race, or the danger of relegation.

Despite the forward line being Best, Law and Charlton, this was not the halcyon United team which had won the European Cup so splendidly at Wembley against Benfica in 1968. Those that remained had aged and were drawing to the close of their careers, George Best excepted. George, though, was beginning to suffer from his demons, and was not at the peak of his powers. When I look at their line up and see the names of Francis Burns, Steve James and Alan Gowling, I know that for a great club like that they'd got a poor side, but I'm not giving them that as the reason why we knocked them out of both cups!

The first meeting in the League Cup was at Old Trafford. It was a tight game and we thought that John Ritchie's goal with 15 minutes to go might nick us a win. John had a header ruled out for some trivial offence that we didn't understand, so it was frustrating when, with five minutes left, Gowling netted a header to earn United a draw we thought they didn't deserve.

We really fancied ourselves at home against anyone, but I got injured in a hard-fought match against West Brom before that return and missed the goalless replay. I was back for the second replay, which we'd won the toss to host. Over 42,000 packed into the Vic on a passionate night. Best put United 1-0 ahead at half-time, but we fought like devils to get a foothold back in the game and Peter Dobing levelled things up with 20 minutes to go. The game really began to change in our favour when Waddo pulled off one of his masterstrokes by bringing on 35 year-old George Eastham for Josh Mahoney at half-time. Waddo rarely made substitutions as early as that, but he recognised on this occasion that we needed a bit more guile in midfield. George had been a wonderful player, but was now reaching the twilight of his career. He had taken to spending the summer breaks in South Africa, where his father, George Eastham snr, also an England international, now lived. George jnr would eventually set up his own team and sports business over there. In 1971, he didn't return to Stoke until towards the end of October and his return lifted the squad because we knew he was a quality passer of the ball who could be used sparingly to maximum effect.

Against United George galvanised our attacks and took some of the whirlwind pace out of the game, concentrating on retaining possession. It was a tough, bruising match, but George created Dobing's equaliser and then laid a cross on a plate for John Ritchie to head home the winner in the 88th minute. The Vic exploded with passion at the final whistle. We'd disposed of one of the biggest names in football, and finally gained a scalp we'd been seeking for years. It was a major moment for us as it showed we did have what it takes to win, and not be permanent nearly men.

Our captain that season was experienced forward Peter Dobing. Peter was one of those sublime players who could see openings and then exploit them. On his day he could tear a defence to shreds with his incisive, accurate passes. He was a tremendous talent, quick, strong, with a beautiful left foot. He loved to play balls inside the full-back for our wingers Terry Conroy and Harry Burrows to run onto. Sometimes they wouldn't anticipate the pass and the full-back would get back to cover and often the crowd would blame Peter for that, but it could also be the wingers not anticipating perfectly-weighted throughballs.

He was a very strong man and we used to call him Powerful Pierre. I think he'd been in the PTI in the army during his National Service. He also had something of a temper too. He didn't like being kicked and if someone targeted him he could either disappear or he could retaliate. But Peter did have a streak of inconsistency in him. If he didn't want to play then he'd get his metaphoric cigar out and coast through a game. You were never sure what you were going to get from him. Sometimes he would decide he was going to run things from just inside the opposition's half – and he was good enough to be able to do that, especially if that gave him the space to play in. I remember him scoring a hat-trick against Leeds in 1967. He ripped England's World Cup-winning centre-half Jackie Charlton to shreds as he single-handedly won this game 3-2. I think Waddo gave him the captaincy because he felt the responsibility which went with it would galvanise Peter to play to his full capacity more often than not. I do believe he sometimes had the attitude in league matches that because we were in mid-table and we were doing well in the cups it didn't really matter how he played, but he did have a real competitive edge when it came to the cup competitions.

Peter was another complex character. He was a very quiet, unassuming captain. He was never someone who motivated by giving long speeches or even personal chats really. Since finishing playing he has become something of a recluse as he now suffers from agoraphobia. He hasn't attended any of our recent get togethers because of that illness, which is a real shame.

Having finally disposed of United to reach the quarter-finals we were ecstatic when the draw paired us with Third Division Bristol Rovers. Our confidence was sky high by now and we were seriously thinking that Wembley was an attainable objective. Beat the Pirates and we would be just a two-legged semi-final away from the Twin Towers. After our endeavours to reach this stage – we had already played six matches, which would be enough to reach Wembley in the normal run of affairs – we were not going to let Rovers' victories in earlier rounds over Sunderland, Charlton and QPR worry us.

We played some sublime football at Eastville in a first half display that simply swatted Rovers aside. At least I think that's what happened. Strangely I don't actually remember. What I do know is that I scored the second goal that night with a header, but in the act of scoring I knocked myself out by clashing heads against a defender and after that I can't remember anything. I played the remainder of the game but can't remember a single second of it, or being on the bus home afterwards. But I know I scored and that we were 4-0 up and cruising before Rovers scored twice late on when we'd taken our foot off the pedal, but I don't remember a single second after that incident.

I couldn't play for a bit after that as the after effects of being concussed left me without any real balance and I felt uneasy on my feet. The feeling lasted for nearly three weeks and I played just one out of the next five games. It was very unsettling. I just couldn't stand up. Every time I did stand up I fell over. My balance had gone totally. It gradually eased, and I remember thinking, 'I feel a bit better this morning I'll take Becky – who had just arrived as our second child – round to the local shops.'

I gingerly walked the few hundred yards to the shops, hanging on to her pram, probably steering slightly erratically. I arrived, and as I bent down to put the brake on and pick Becky up, two old ladies came out of the shop. They took one look at me, swaying as I gingerly bent over to pluck my sleeping second born out of her blankets and said, rather too loudly, "look at that drunk. It's disgraceful!" I hadn't shaved because I couldn't shave, and I had put on the easiest, baggiest clothes imaginable, so to all intents and purposes I looked like a whino. They thought I was drunk in charge of a child!

I hoped to be back for the first leg of the League Cup semi-final against West Ham in early December as by then I was not feeling bad. But on the afternoon of the day before the game I went to Stone as Kate suggested I get out of the house and go shopping for a few bits and pieces. I thought I got on fine, but just after I arrived back home, the phone went. It was Waddo, who said, "are you alright?"

"Yes, I feel a lot better," I replied.

"The thing is," he continued. "I know you've been in Stone because I've had several fans phone up telling me that you were swaying around as you walked down the street and that I shouldn't pick you yet because you're not right."

I hadn't noticed a thing!

I obviously wasn't yet capable of playing a full ninety minutes, so did not play as Stoke met West Ham for the right to play the winners of Chelsea versus Tottenham at Wembley. We took an early lead at a foggy Victoria Ground when Jimmy Greenhoff latched on to a loose ball in the box and cracked a shot against the post which Peter Dobing followed in to slot home. But we reckoned without West Ham forward Clyde Best. Clyde was a big, physical lad. He kicked me in the face once as I was heading a ball clear and I really felt the full force of his boot. I still have the scar on my right cheek. He was one of the first high profile black players to make an impact in the top level of our game and was awarded the MBE for services to Bermudian football in 2006, rightly so in my opinion as he was one of the vanguard of Caribbean players to come over here and make an impact. He also coached their national side and proved an inspiration to many thousands of youngsters on the island. On this occasion he caused a right nuisance of himself. Waddo had chosen young defender Stewart Jump to replace me alongside Alan Bloor and I think Best got the better of him as the game wore on. Jump fouled Best to hand West Ham a penalty, which Geoff Hurst lashed home to equalise. In the second half Best scored the winning goal to give the Hammers a 2-1 League to take back to London. The turning of the tables by such a strong team left us utterly deflated. Were we going to miss out again? It was worse in some ways for me because I was unable to play and have any influence on what was going on. At least this time the tie was two-legged so we had our chance to redress the balance, but we felt that we'd have to play extremely well to claw back the goal deficit at Upton Park. As it happened the away goals rule had not come into operation at that time, and neither had automatic penalty shoot-outs in cup ties, so we travelled to West Ham knowing that any kind of single goal win would mean a replay.

I was still not yet fit enough to take my place in the team so little Alfie Skeels stood in for me and had a wonderful game as we snuffed out the Hammers threat. As the game wore on they tightened up a bit as Wembley approached. We knew what they were going through, having suffered at the hands of Arsenal just a few months before, and ramped up the pressure until, in the 77th minute, the breakthrough came. The ball was played to the far post where Big John Ritchie lurked to chest it down and ram home a great right-footed volley low into the net. We were back on level terms and the game remained tight right up until the end of 90 minutes and all the way through extra-time.

With just three minutes to go in that extra period, and a replay looming, a long hopeful ball was punted down West Ham's right flank and into the penalty area. Mike Pejic appeared to have beaten the Hammers' flying winger Harry Redknapp to it, but at the last minute he allowed it to roll through to Gordon Banks, who was expecting Pej to clear it. An almighty kerfuffle ensued and Redknapp seized on the confusion to nick the ball away. Banks, worried that he'd concede the decisive goal, felled Redknapp from behind. It was a ridiculous mix up really and I've never been privy to what went on between Banksy and Pej, but they had a massive fall out on the pitch about it. I do wonder whether that was a little bit of gamesmanship on their part too. You always want to delay the taking of a penalty as much as you possibly can and that argument certainly achieved that. It took forever for Geoff Hurst, Banksy's World Cup-winning team-mate, to get the ball onto the spot and for everyone to be out of the area ready for the kick which would decide our fate. Up in the stand I could see several of the West Ham team turned away from the action, not daring to look. It was a horrifically familiar scenario. Not seven months earlier we'd faced a similarly late spot-kick to dash our Wembley dreams in the FA Cup against Arsenal, now here we were again.

The crucial duel was between Gordon and Geoff. Clearly they knew each other extremely well, and heaven knows how many penalties Geoff may or may not have taken against Gordon during England training camps, but just perhaps the one he'd scored in the first leg of the semi-final at the Victoris Ground played a part in what happened next. That first kick he'd simply lashed down the middle, rendering Gordon's dive useless. On this occasion Geoff took his barnstorming long run up and whacked the ball once again almost straight down the middle of the goal. Banksy dived to his right once again, but this time he was ready for what Hurst might do and he somehow managed to fling up his arms, keeping them rigid and strong, and fisted the exocet which Hursty had unleashed up and over the bar.

Fantastic. Absolutely unbelievable. Gordon had no right to save that shot. It was simply incredible that the net had not ballooned and West Ham weren't at Wembley. We'd gone from thinking we were out to still being in with a shout, which gave everyone in the squad a huge lift. It was an incredible save as it looked as if he'd changed direction in midair. Hurst's kick was sweetly struck and fair flew towards the net, so must have carried a hell of a force behind it, and yet Banks still found the strength, after all the tribulations we'd been through in semi-finals, to parry it over the bar. For me it is up there with that save that everyone talks about against Pele in 1970 in Mexico and convinces me that Gordon was a genius, whose like we have not seen since.

Mind you every time I see Banksy I tell him he should have held onto it!

******

The contrast between that penalty at Upton Park and the one the previous year at Hillsborough could not have been more marked. We'd suffered so cruelly just nine months earlier at the hands of Arsenal in the FA Cup semi-final and now here we were on the other end of things. We felt the tie had swung back in our favour in that moment. It was a huge confidence boost and, although we really fancied our chances now, we weren't taking anything for granted.

Eventually I recovered my equilibrium and was back in the team on 27 December against Manchester City, finding the back of the net with a last minute tap in a 1-3 home defeat by title-chasing Manchester City.

The West Ham saga continued with a stale replay at Hillsborough which finished goalless and went to extra time, but nothing could have prepared anyone for the drama that was to unfurl at Old Trafford in the second replay. The game was scheduled for Old Trafford, which was a little harsh for the Hammers, but the major problem was that all the rain which had fallen had turned the pitch into a total quagmire. It made for an exciting match though. It was a thrill a minute for the 49,247 crowd – and against a London club at that! That was an incredible attendance and a great atmosphere.

On the half hour Hammers goalkeeper Bobby Ferguson came out to collect a through ball at the feet of the onrushing Terry Conroy, who inadvertently caught him on the side of the head. Ferguson went down badly injured and had to be carried off. With Peter Eustace, a midfielder, their substitute, West Ham had to reorganise until their keeper could re-emerge and surprisingly chose to put captain Bobby Moore in goal. I was very surprised at this decision because to me Bobby Moore was the best defender in the world.

His performance in the 1970 World Cup is the best defensive display you'll ever see. I drooled over it. He read the game with sublime ease. He wasn't a tackler like me, he would glide in and steal the ball away from attackers, and stride out of defence to set his forwards on the attack. He was also West Ham's captain and I thought they missed him for those vital, mad minutes while he was between the sticks for them.

A couple of minutes later we won a penalty after a wayward backpass left John Ritchie through on goal. He was felled by full-back John McDowell and Mike Bernard stepped up to take the penalty. 'Surely this is 1-0,' we thought. After all Bernie had only got to beat a stand-in keeper. But Moore somehow managed to outsmart Bernard and dived to his right to parry the ball. But this was where the craft of being a goalkeeper comes in. When Banks saved a penalty he parried the ball up and over the bar. Bobby pushed it out and right to the feet of Mike Bernard who had run on in after hitting the spot-kick. Mike smashed the ball into the net, and we finally did have 1-0 lead.

It didn't last long, though. Some bloke called Smith scored an own goal a few minutes later to put West Ham right back in it. Now I have to hold my hands up here. I really can't remember this incident. I do tend to block out goals we conceded and I just can't recall what led to me putting through my own net, but it was the first of a couple of goals we conceded as Trevor Brooking lashed in a shot to put West ham 2-1 ahead right on half-time. In injury time before the break, Peter Dobing made is 2-2 to end a dramatic half.

We started the second half on the offensive and early on Terry Conroy lashed home a drive to make it 3-2. TC was flying that season. He was absolutely unplayable, as he was in several spells in his career when he was fully fit and in form. He was so quick he used to go past people. They knew what he was going to do, but they couldn't stop him. He would drop his shoulder, knock it past the player and then was gone in a flash of ginger sideboard and with his skinny white legs pumping. He crossed great balls in too. I must have scored quite a few goals off his crosses and corners, so have a lot to thank him for. He was fantastic in the dressing room too. A real laugh a minute, and he would act as our social secretary, bringing the disparate members of the squad together.

There had been five goals in 17 minutes and at that stage we felt there would probably be more. The conditions were atrocious, we were covered in mud from head to foot, and as the game wore on it became difficult to tell the two teams apart. The tension grew just as it had against Arsenal as we clung on to our lead. This time, though, we remained mentally strong and kept West Ham at bay in the deepening quagmire. As the match moved into extra-time our supporters were celebrating riotously and I just remember thinking, 'blow the whistle. Blow the whistle!' We were keeping the ball safely at the back, but in that last minute if it had come anywhere near me it was going as far away from home as possible. I was determined we were going to stay in the lead.

Then, when the whistle went, we joined in the celebrations, caked in mud. I remember coming off the Old Trafford pitch that night. I realised I was frozen. You don't normally come off a football pitch cold because of all the effort you expend, but that night my feet, hands, everything was ice cold because it was had been so wet.

I remember there was that brilliant picture of Banksy on the front of the next home game programme, turning round to the fans behind his goal at the final whistle, with his fists clenched – yes!

Stoke City were at Wembley in a major cup final for the first time in the club's history. It was an incredible feeling.

It was obviously one shared by the vast majority of the 350,000 residents of the Potteries because when I got home the place was going bananas.

It was a waste of time trying to get into my drive at Meir Heath because of the number of people parked there who were after tickets – family, mum and dad, friends, relatives, neighbours, former neighbours, school friends, you name it. We'd finally made it through to the final on the 26 January so six weeks of mayhem ensued. We were only allowed so many tickets and I had to find a way to satisfy everyone.

We'd actually not long moved house and one of the first things we'd done was to have new windows put in, but they hadn't yet finished and so some were still covered with plastic sheeting. Becky wasn't very old and not sleeping so Kate was over-tired all the time. I was dealing with a new house, new baby and tired wife, and the hundreds of people who wanted tickets. It was a nightmare! Some people understood. Our old next door neighbour, Alan, who has now become a good friend, didn't pester us at all. He actually queued all night at the Vic to get tickets instead of joining the queue for the revolving door to ask me for tickets for the game. I couldn't believe it when I found out. I said to him, "what're you doing?"

He said, "I wasn't going to ask you, Denis. I understand everything that's going on for you." So instead he'd spent all night queuing for a ticket amidst the frenzy of supporters desperate to see Stoke's big day.

Reaching finals in that day and age meant several things – new suits, sponsorship deals, a ton of extra press work to do and, of course, recording a Cup final song. I'm not sure how it came about, but before we knew it we were making a record with Jackie Trent and Tony Hatch. They were a husband and wife song-writing team, and Jackie hailed from Stoke-in-Trent. Tony had made a major impact throughout the 1960s writting Petula Clark's smash hit song 'Downtown' and The Searchers' 'Sugar and Spice' amongst many others, and would go on to pen both the Crossroads, Emmerdale and Neighbours theme tunes. He was known as 'The British Burt Bacharach'. They wrote this fantastically catchy song for us called 'We'll Be With You' and we recorded it as best we could, with a large group of backing singers, and without any of us doing any cringeworthy solo lines. The song sold like hotcakes in Stoke and we got it up to no. 35 in the charts. It's still sung today at the Britannia Stadium, along with other Stoke-specific favourites such as the fans' own adopted theme tune Tom Jones's 'Delilah'.

The first sponsorship deal we ever had at Stoke was for the final. Adidas offered us plenty of money to wear their boots. Now I loved my Puma boots and didn't want to wear Adidas ones. Sometimes people don't understand how important boots are to a footballer. Your boots are your work tools. They're very personal. It's like a carpenter and his chisel. I think having worked at the shoe factory helped me appreciate that. I understood the difference in quality, and I was also very particular about how my boots were cleaned. It got so I wouldn't let any apprentice clean them. I used to do them myself, and change my studs. I felt that preparing my boots helped me prepare to play. I was pretty unique in that. We didn't earn the many thousands of pounds that players do today for our boot deal for the Cup final, but it brought in a bit extra.

Boot technology has obviously progressed massively in the years since then. As a manager I've become more and more concerned about the lack of protection they offer and it's been no surprise to me to see the spate of injuries such as the Rooney and Beckham metatarsal problems. Most players wear Nike now, and their entire rationale over the last decade or so has been to make the boots lighter, more comfortable and to increase the ability to produce shots which bend. It's become an obsession to produce new innovation, so we've had blades and the such like. A lot of that has merely increased the propensity for players to pick up injuries that were just non-existent in my day. For example the modern trend is to have soles that bend, but I prefer solid soles so the boots don't crumple in a challenge and crush your foot. They are meant to protect you and I feel they don't offer as much as they used to, particularly when the front of the boot curls up and creates pressure on the toes, the most vulnerable part of the foot. The 'innovation' of blades replacing studs has led to more players turning their ankles for example. It's become a manager's nightmare because the money the manufacturers and sponsors offer is so persuasive.

In the midst of all the final fervour, we were still progressing nicely in the FA Cup, after a third round victory over Chesterfield. Between qualifying for the final and playing it we played three more cup ties, defeating Tranmere 2-0 in a fourth round replay, after a 2-2 draw at Prenton Park, then facing up to the previous season's quarter-final opponents Hull, this time in the fifth round. This time our passage was much more comfortable as we raced to a 4-1 home victory thanks to goals by Greenhoff (2), Conroy and Ritchie. But it wasn't just the cup ties. We also played another three league games, one of which was a belting 3-3 draw against Ipswich. I scored the late equaliser in that game with a flying header in amongst the boots. It was one of my favourite goals, and another one against Bobby Robson's side. It was a hectic period to say the least and all those cup replays were catching up on us, affecting our league form, which now saw us in 12th position.

We had never experienced anything like this pile up of fixtures, aside maybe from the old heads of Banksy, Peter Dobing and George Eastham, so adrenalin got us through. Everybody was on a Wembley high.

Our opponents were to be FA Cup holders Chelsea, who would win the Cup Winners' Cup that season, defeating Real Madrid after a replay in Athens. The Blues were a fabulous, stylish team with the likes of Peter Osgood, Alan Hudson and Charlie Cooke posing a serious threat to our first piece of silverware. At the back they had a steely defence of David Webb, Paddy Mulligan and Ron 'Chopper' Harris protecting England's number two keeper Peter Bonetti, although in my opinion what had happened in Mexico in 1970 when Gordon was taken ill and Peter had something of a nightmare in the quarter-final of the World Cup when England lost a two-goal lead to lose to West Germany, showed the difference between the two. Still, the final promised to be one hell of an encounter. Could we upset the bookies' favourites, the self-styled Kings of the Kings Road?

To prepare us for the final Waddo took us down to stay at the Selsdon Park Hotel in Surrey for the week. On the Wednesday night, after a good training session, we were invited to a party at the house of Tony and Jackie Trent. It was full of glitterati and that was our last piece of relaxation before focussing on the task I hand. We had a few beers and chatted to some celebrities, mostly in the music business, but the next day we were up and ready for training.

In those days away from it all everybody talked. My conversations generally would be with people like Jackie Marsh and Pej, Bernie, TC and Josh Mahoney, the younger members of the squad. Basically we were all thinking it was a great adventure.

Taking us away from it all was a good move. As new boys in the world of playing one off finals to actually win a major prize I know understand that it gets you away from everything. As I've already described my own house was so chaotic I felt I couldn't go home. Every Tom, Dick and Harry was in the house. So it was difficult to deal with. Once we were away everybody was fairly relaxed and those of us who'd had all the insanity of the scramble for tickets because we were local boys felt as if we could begin to focus on the task in hand.

I remember Jackie, who I roomed with, saying, "Den, I'm so glad I'm away from it all because I now feel I've got not decisions to make," In fact all Jackie had to concentrate on was the card school. That kind of entertainment was never really for me. I'd always read a lot so I would rather be reading books, anything to try to take my mind off what was looming ahead, namely the biggest single game in Stoke City's history.

I've never ever had any trouble sleeping. Waking up, yes. Sleeping no. I would never sleep during the day, but I always sleep well overnight and when I go to bed I go bang out and wake up the next day fully refreshed. That's been one of the great things I've always been able to do. Sure, as a manager, there's been the odd night when I've lain there thinking, 'I should have done this or I could have changed that,' but for the most part I'm a good sleeper.

The other aspect to my relaxed approach to Wembley was more based on my youthful arrogance because I had now firmly convinced myself that I'd be going back every year. I really thought we were on the cusp of something magnificent at Stoke. I truly believed it, and still do believe that with more luck, a few breaks of the ball, and a couple of extra players to strengthen the squad in the right areas at the right time, Stoke would have been a top force to be reckoned with. As it was we did as well as any team the club has had, but in the lead up to that first final I genuinely thought that we would be competing for silverware for most of the rest of my career. I was still only 23. I could have almost another decade of trophies to lift, again and again.

It helped having the likes of Banksy around because obviously Gordon had played there regularly for England, as had George Eastham, while Peter Dobing had played in the 1960 FA Cup final for Blackburn. I remember George dispelling the myth about the pitch sapping your legs to me one evening. At the time the press would always go o about how it would drain the strength out of you, but George told me, "no. That's rubbish. It's to do with you mentally. Don't believe that stuff because then you might allow yourself to let it happen, to use it as a subconscious excuse." George was full of experience and when he spoke, which was relatively rarely about that side of things, you tended to listen.

Banksy was also very relaxed about Wembley, although he was desperate to win for the simple reason that he had never won a domestic trophy. He had lost the 1963 FA Cup final with Leicester to Manchester United and even though he'd won the World Cup with England at the stadium in 1966, he did not have a domestic honour to his name. This was a massive thing for him. I'd got to know him much more when we moved to Ashley later on as he had lived in the village for some time and we became next-door neighbours. He and his wife Ursula were very good to Kate and the family and so Gordon and I associated more and I understood what this piece of silverware, the League Cup, derided at its inception, and by many in the years since, meant to the greatest goalkeeper the world has ever seen. Never let anyone tell you that it's a worthless trophy. It meant everything to Gordon Banks and he was excited and motivated in equal measure.

On Cup final morning I woke up and realised that finally today was the day. We all had our routines and we stuck to them as much as we could. I had breakfast and read the papers to absorb something other than the reality of what I was about to do. I remember Pej being much more restless and constantly saying how he wanted time to go quicker as he wanted to get on that coach and get to the stadium. Perhaps the pressure was beginning to build.

Before I knew it Waddo had called the team meeting in which he laid out our plans for the game and confirmed the team, which held no surprises as we had no injuries. Tony was not a great tactician. His genius lay in his ability to put a good jigsaw puzzle together. He'd be able to slot the pieces in the right place by selecting the right players in the squad and the right starting eleven to go out there on the pitch. He was no rousing speechmaker. He would simply say, "go out and be solid. Don't allow them too much room, and keep the ball by giving it to the likes of George and Peter early on. You know your jobs, enjoy it."

That was it in terms of a team talk. I'm pretty sure he pulled Jackie and Pej aside and told them not to venture forward too early in the game, but aside from that there was little other tactical instruction. He was more interested in relaxing us to play our own game.

Everybody had to attend the pre-match meal around noon. I was always a poached eggs and toast man, but a lot of the lads would have steak. That's obviously changed massively in the modern era as diet has assumed more importance in the maintenance of performance in athletes such as footballers.

Then it was onto the coach and across London to Wembley. Arriving at the stadium was moving and exciting. There would be a crowd of 97,000 in the ground that day, the biggest attendance ever to watch a Stoke team play a competitive fixture, and it felt like they outnumbered Chelsea's fans two to one. As we drove up Wembley Way in the coach a lump came to my throat as I saw all those Stokies, draped in red and white, who were already there well ahead of kick-off to roar us on. There was a mass of people, but before we knew it we were through them and into the bowels of the stadium, disembarked and into the dressing rooms. I think it was vital we had the older heads amongst us at that time as George, Peter and Gordon just moved among us younger ones chatting about this and that. We walked out to inspect the pitch and realised how good the turf would feel underfoot. It had rained, and it was a grey March day, but the pitch was perfect.

I found the whole experience quite magical, and my mind did allow itself to hark back to some of the Cup finals I'd watched as a kid on our battered old black and white TV. Of course I didn't know then that it would be the only time I'd play at Wembley, although as a manager I would return. For now I was desperate to perform in front of this special crowd and told myself that this was my time, my day.

I was marking Peter Osgood, who was one of the hottest strikers around at that time. In my opinion he should have won far more than the five England caps he earned and should never have been bombed out of Chelsea so early either. Peter was a talented forward and was one of those players who would always find a way to get something on a ball in the box, so if you failed to clear you would be in trouble. He also had a swagger to him, as had Alan Hudson. They were such a talented pair and I knew we would be in for a tough afternoon.

The old Wembley had a kink in the tunnel so you walked up and over a brow and into the stadium. The first thing to hit us as we started up the slope was the sound of the fans, buzzing like bees with anticipation. Although I was second in line behind captain Peter Dobing, we could not yet see them, but the noise built as we emerged into the light and voluminous sound of the colourful stadium. For me that was the best sight I'd ever seen. The far end from the tunnel was crammed full of red and white. Scarves, shirts, faces Fantastic. It all added to the noise. I'm sure having your fans at the far end to the tunnel gave teams an advantage in that stadium because it just took over your senses, and it was a while before you thought to look around because it was so captivating, so Chelsea's players, whose fans were at the tunnel end and so were behind them as we walked out side by side, can only have felt intimidated. It certainly gave me and the rest of the Stoke team an incredible lift and I momentarily thought of the city itself sitting desolately empty as this part of north west London burned with anticipation of some silverware to return with.

When you are preparing for a match as big as the first final in your career you naturally run through different scenarios, ideal and otherwise, that may occur during the game to prepare yourself for how you will react. In our wildest dreams we couldn't have expected the start we made. Right from kick-off we controlled the game and pressed Chelsea back, retaining possession exactly as we'd planned. And then, suddenly, a chance. From a throw on the left hand side, level with the edge of the Chelsea penalty area, Dobing looped the ball in. I had gone forward to try to get a flick on at the near post, but Peter Bonetti leapt above me and batted the ball out to the edge of the area. It fell straight to the feet of George Eastham. George flicked it straight back in to the centre of the goal towards Jimmy Greenhoff, leaving Bonetti totally stranded as he was still picking himself up off the floor. Jimmy couldn't quite beat John Dempsey to the ball six yards out, but the Chelsea defender's clearance only fell right to my right foot. I was about eight yards out but off balance and had to stretch slightly to reach the ball, so didn't catch it as cleanly as I would like. The ball went down into the turf and ballooned up off my marker, Osgood and then Dempsey, who'd moved to block my effort, leaving the rest of the defence and Bonetti, who was scrambling back towards goal, wrong-footed. I fell to the turf and watched as, in one of those slow-motion moment life brings at times, the ball fell perfectly for Terry Conroy, who was doing what all good wingers do by making a late run into the box. He was about eight yards out when he connected, unusually for Terry as he himself freely admits, with his head. If it had been John Ritchie – or indeed myself – I'd have known it was going straight into the back of the net, but with TC you never knew. But what I did know was that this was a glorious chance. 'Don't miss it, Terry!' raced through my mind.

His curly ginger locks flew in the general direction of the ball, sending it in another arc, up and over the despairing Bonetti's dive to nestle into the very bottom corner of the goal. We'd scored! Stoke City led at Wembley after just five minutes.

I leapt up and jumped on TC just after Jimmy Greenhoff clambered onto him. Somehow, with us on board Terry still managed to pump his little legs to jump up and down in a frenzy! I think after the initial ecstasy a sense of disbelief permeated through the team, a mark of our inexperience in big finals. TC, for example, froze solid after he scored that goal. He freely admits that for the next 15 minutes or so he could do little more than stare at the huge scoreboards at either end of the ground on which were now proudly displayed the words 'Stoke City 1 Chelsea 0; Conroy 5'. He was just dazzled by the enormity of what happened. It was too much for him to take in and he was drawn to the scoreboard like a moth to a flame. As a group it affected us too, although not as starkly as that. It took Jackie Marsh to – literally – shake Terry out of his daze and bring him back to reality.

Chelsea were forced into a reorganisation after injury to their right-back Paddy Mulligan. Ron Harris was forced over to cover that position as Chelsea's substitute was forward Tommy Baldwin. That allowed us to make inroads down their flanks. Meanwhile the Blues were beginning to put the early shock of conceding behind them and causing us problems with their own attacks. Charlie Cooke, Chelsea's impish Scottish winger, was proving a problem, so Pej chopped him down and took a card for his trouble. I remember Bluto bowling Chris Garland over too and getting a ticking off from referee Norman Burtenshaw. For my part I had my hands full with Peter Osgood. After about 20 minutes, as we got up from a tackle which had left us both on the floor,

Ossie stamped on me on my ankle, which swelled up and remained painful for the rest of the game. It didn't bother me really, but I gained a small amount of revenge by heading the back of his head in a challenge on the half-way line. We had a battle royal, which Osgood finished the half on top in after scoring a goal to bring Chelsea back into the game. The Blues had been keeping possession and launching a series of attacks as we held out for half-time. But just before the whistle a ball into the box evaded me and found Osgood, lurking at the far post where he'd moved to try to get the jump on little Jackie Marsh. Osgood tried to bring the ball down on his knee but his control was so woeful it bounced off him by about six feet leaving all three of us off balance, so much so that I fell backwards and Ossie ended up prone on the turf about 10 yards out. Fortunately for Chelsea, Ossie's dreadful control led to the ball falling to David Webb right on the penalty spot. Now Webby was a great defender and scored plenty of goals with his head, but was never the best shot. He totally scuffed this effort, which if he'd hit properly I'd have blocked. Instead it fell perfectly for Osgood, still lying on the floor, to fling a foot at and somehow hook the ball past Banksy and into the net.

I couldn't believe that we'd conceded another flukey goal in such an important game. It was a weird goal, with the ball pinging round the box before falling so beautifully for a player lying on his back to score. It was really quite odd. To concede just before the break was sickening and the atmosphere in the dressing room reflected that. We were all looking at each other saying, "how did they score?" But we got ourselves together and Gordon was great, making sure that we knew he would be telling us where to go if he saw potential problems. It's a major plus within a dressing room if you've got people involved in sorting their own problems out as long as they don't go over the top and don't start f'ing and blinding too much. It has to be cool and collected otherwise people fall out and that can be counter-productive.

The second half was an absorbing encounter with both sides creating half chances, but on 73 minutes we fashioned a goal which would win the cup. Terry beat Chopper on the right flank, got to the bye-line and chipped a cross to the back post, perfectly picking out John Ritchie, who had hung back beyond his marker. Ritchie's downward header found Jimmy Greenhoff about 15 yards out but in tons of space. Jimmy, who by this stage was actually carrying a shoulder injury he'd picked up earlier in the half, volleyed the ball perfectly towards goal and Peter Bonetti pulled off a wonderful diving save, low to his left, but he couldn't hold on to the ball. With the Chelsea defence having pulled this way and that by the precision of our move, when he parried the ball out it fell into a space about six yards out. Peter Dobing and George Eastham, the two old men of our side, rushed in to score, and George just beat Peter to prod it into the net. He was 36 years-old and is still the oldest man ever to score in a Wembley final, yes older even than Teddy Sheringham! That goal was a fitting end to his career. George was just a little wisp of a fellow, but he had speed, finesse, craft and an eye for a killer pass. He could find space in a phone box and I consider myself fortunate to have played with him.

We knew then that the next 15 minutes or so would be all about us repelling Chelsea's attacks. They were a very good side and we had to defend and defend. Pressure built, but Banksy was brilliant, both in terms of making saves and also telling us what was going on around us as the ball bounced around our box in a succession of frantic scrambles. I remember one save Gordon pulled off from an Osgood header when the ball looked destined for the corner, but Banksy flew across to tip the ball around the post.

We survived, but there was one problem that we couldn't have anticipated. Jackie Marsh wore contact lenses – he was one of the first players who tried them – but somehow he lost one! We were defending a corner. I was marking Ossie and Jackie was on the post just behind me. Suddenly I hear him shouting, "Den, Den!"

Trying not to be distracted from Osgood I replied, "I've got my man, Jack – what's up?"

"I've lost my lens. I can't see!" he told me.

We were defending a corner at Wembley and Jackie had lost his flaming lens!

Lenses were thick things then and he had to scrabble around on the turf near the post to find it. Jack had to leave the pitch, but we defended the corner OK and were coping reasonably well, even after Jackie returned fully sighted, when all of a sudden Mike Bernard had a total rush of blood to the head. He pulled a long ball out of the air on the edge of the centre circle just inside our half, but he was facing his own goal and thought he'd send a long pass back for Gordon to pick and waste some more time. There was no way I was expecting Bernie to pass it that way. He should have turned and played the ball forwards. As it turned out he played the perfect through pass for Tommy Baldwin, the Chelsea substitute, to run onto. I was loitering on the edge of our penalty area, making sure none of the Chelsea forward could cause us any trouble, but here we were creating it ourselves! The ball Mike played arced perfectly around me, leaving Baldwin clean through on goal. I couldn't catch him and had to watch another of those slow-motion moments as Banksy raced out to close Baldwin down. He covered an incredible amount of ground in double quick time and by the time Baldwin prodded the ball goalwards, Gordon was almost on him, right on the edge of the box. The ball flicked off Banks's legs and bounced just wide of the goal. It was a truly great save, borne out of concentration and superb anticipation of what was happening right at the death of a frantic game. That was yet another reason why Banksy was the best. He didn't just pull off the spectacular saves, he could make the vital, messy ones too.

That incident affected Mike greatly. After the final whistle, despite being a strong, tough guy, he was in tears as he realised how close he had come to costing us the game. Can you imagine him having to live with that? But Banksy had got him out of jail again as he did most of us at times.

Then, suddenly, the final whistle sounded. We've done it. We've won!

It's amazing how a moment like that affects you. It's just total emotion and it's then that you realise just exactly what football is, what football means to people. Especially to yourself. Reaching a pinnacle like that is quite something and the enormity of it hit me.

But it didn't stop me celebrating to the full. We collected our winners' tankard and watched as Peter Dobing lifted the first major trophy in the club's history. It felt as if the entire stadium was filled with red and white and the lap of honour seemed to last forever. They were truly wonderful moments. Red and white people, banners, flags and shirts filled my sense. We paraded the cup and I managed to grab one of the handles to show it off to my people. I didn't want the cheering to end. This was what football was about for me. It was a wonderful, incredible half hour or so and we milked every last second of it. To win the League Cup is one of my major lifetime achievements. I could and arguably should have had more, but unfortunately I didn't.

That night we had a gala dinner to celebrate, with plenty of alcohol flowing. It was a great occasion, if slightly formal. I remember that John Ritchie actually wasn't very happy during that meal because he hadn't scored. At the time I thought that he was being a bit moody, but when you look at it now it is a massive thing to have scored in that game. At the time we thought, 'what the hell is he grumbling about?' as the rest of us were just happy that we'd won. But I understand a bit more now about how goalscorers' minds work.

It was a heck of a bash. There were bottles of everything, wine, champagne, you name it. I am a beer drinker. At the time I wasn't really a wine drinker, and that night I really fancied a pint, but could I get one? No. I could not. Somebody finally managed to find me a half of bitter. It was Saturday night and I had one half! Around half past ten, most of the other young lads decided to continue the celebration of our victory to the full out on the town. My ankle had swollen up and without the alcoholic, or other, anaesthetic, to numb the pain it was killing me. I just couldn't accompany them. So while the likes of TC, Jackie and Pej hit London, by eleven o'clock I was tucked up in bed, where I did manage to order a pint – of milk. Most of the older players stayed around the hotel and George Eastham, the old campaigner who had been through so much in his career, pulled rank, snaffled the trophy and took it to his room with a large cigar, and his wife to celebrate his winning goal.

In retrospect I'm glad it worked out like that because Sunday was fantastic. I haven't a clue whose idea it was to do the journey back but whoever it was is a genius. We had boarded a train at Euston to head back to the Potteries, and the journey had gone smoothly, but as we approached Barlaston. The train slowed down and eventually ground to a halt at this tiny local station about five miles south of the city. We were really worried that something had gone wrong and we wouldn't get back to Stoke station in time for the open-topped bus tour we all expected, so we began to stick our heads out of the windows of the carriages. At first we thought there must be a problem, there must have been a hell of an accident up here. For as far as we could see all the roads were packed with cars, with many parked up banks, on drives or were strewn across pavements as if they had been abandoned. It was just solid. 'What the hell's going on here?' I thought.

It soon became apparent that what we thought was some kind of horrendous carnage was in fact what felt like half the people of Stoke-on-Trent waiting for us even this far south.

We disembarked and got onto this old bus which the club had hired to meet us at Barlaston and take us around the city to eventually arrive at the Town Hall in Stoke. Normally that journey would take you 20 minutes. This day it took us at least two hours. The entire route was jam-packed with supporters, sometimes 20 or 30 deep alongside the road. The atmosphere was incredible as the city celebrated arguably the biggest achievement in its history. It was just absolutely mental. And for someone like me to have been part of it was extremely moving.

From Barlaston we slowly progressed to the southern edge of the city and my own home area of Meir. The reception there brought tears to my eyes and a huge lump into my throat. When we drove past my parents' house, where I was born, at the top of Ryder Road, where it joins Sandon Road, it struck me what an incredible thing football is. There was such a strong connection between these few young fellers who kicked a ball around for a living and these thousands of people who struggled to make ends meet, scrapped around for a living and who were now filled with such unconfined joy.

For myself and Alan Bloor, who like me had grown up right here, it meant so much. For that part of the journey Bluto and I stood at the front of the bus holding the cup aloft for everyone to see. Every so often we would catch a glimpse of someone we knew from the estate, waving and cheering. As we drove through Meir I spotted Kate's Mum and Dad and the kids amongst the throng, and then my Mum and Dad at Ryder Road. It all got a bit too much for us and before we knew it there we were, two big, tough centre-halves, bawling our eyes out. Thank goodness the likes of Tommy Smith, Norman Hunter and Chopper Harris didn't find out about that!

There were people everywhere – up lampposts, hanging out of top floor windows of houses and pubs – it was just a sea of people for miles along the route through Fenton (where Jackie Marsh went through the same homecoming experience as I had in Meir), Longton and Hanley. But I know it got to Gordon Banks too. Even though he didn't come from the Potteries he'd been at the club and in the area long enough to know what these success-starved people – in pretty much any walk of life or by any criteria you care to mention as don't forget pits were already closing, pot banks shutting down and unemployment was rising towards the mid-Seventies – felt about their football club finally winning a trophy.

I think the abiding feeling for me is one of belonging. You obviously still get cavalcades to celebrate success these days but so few players play for their hometown clubs. There are very good reasons for that but it just makes that bit of difference in my mind. There's also the fatigue of success to take into account. When you win as many trophies as Chelsea, Manchester United and Arsenal do a single League Cup success doesn't mean anything. But, much like Portsmouth's 2008 FA Cup win will be, Stoke's 1972 League Cup victory now stands as a major pinnacle in a golden era, and something that is still reminisced over now in countless Potteries pubs over a pint of Titanic from the local brewery.

As we drove, occasionally we could hear the strains of We'll Be With You emerging from sections of the crowd and we'd join in. It's still sung at the Britannia Stadium today and is a fantastic reminder every time I hear it of that wonderful day.

Eventually we reached Stoke itself and arrived at the King's Hall where the Mayor was waiting with a Civic reception. The day blurs into a haze of champagne and tears of pride from that point, but it was just such a fabulous, great day.

That 1971/72 season was arguably the best in Stoke City's history, as not only did we win the League Cup, but thanks to a simultaneous run in the FA Cup we reached a second successive semi-final. The Potteries was on top of the footballing world. We were on for a domestic cup double, a feat which had not yet been achieved since the League Cup's inception.

To achieve that we now had to get past Manchester United in the sixth round. When the draw came out we were delighted because we'd already disposed of United in the League Cup. We weren't even intimidated by being drawn away from home, as we knew we should have won the game at Old Trafford in the League Cup, so the tie held no fears for us. We proved that too, by taking the lead when Greenhoff fired in a shot, which Stepney parried, but Jimmy reached the rebound first and turned it in. After that United threw everything at us and we defended brilliantly. We should have nicked another, but Micky Bernard missed a great chance. We were within seven minutes of a famous victory at United when George Best pounced to lash home and force yet another replay. It was massive for us and I think sometimes psychological things go on in players minds all the time. If you can go through each barrier and emerge the other side a stronger, more determined person you are becoming a really top class player – if you can handle George Best and Bobby Charlton you think to yourself "I can defend anybody in the world." It's good for you.

That was the first times I felt we came off the Old Trafford pitch the better side. We were very disappointed because we had controlled the entire game. We were right at our peak and the replay, two and a half weeks after the League Cup final victory, attracted a passionate crowd of over 49,000 to the Victoria Ground, the second largest crowd ever to pack into the stadium. This was the game I referred to earlier on when I hurt my back and didn't expect to play because I could barely stand up when I arrived at the ground. Besty scored that incredible individual goal, and I netted the equaliser. It was one of my classics from a yard out in a melee, heading home George Eastham's corner.

I love big crowds. I love big occasions. I loved the Cup and playing at the likes of United, Arsenal, Liverpool. As did George. It suited my nature, so for me to score that goal, when I should have been sitting in the stands with my bad back, was fantastic. I knew I'd get the better of Best sooner or later!

Terry Conroy scored the winner in extra-time, after Banksy had pulled off a couple of superb reaction saves to keep us in it. That game was one of the great nights at the Victoria Ground and we had emerged victorious and into the last four for the second successive season.

Sometimes fate deals you a hand which you take one look at, smile and really revel in – and when we heard that we had drawn Arsenal in the last four once again, the opportunity for revenge left us jigging around the dressing room with delight. We were on a massive high. 'This time,' we thought, 'it's going to be different.'

Since lifting the League Cup our league form had suffered quite a bit and we only won once more that season. But we felt unbeatable in cup games and so meeting Arsenal at Villa Park held absolutely no fears for us. We were simply out to right the wrongs of the previous season.

Villa Park was bursting at the seams with a sell out 56,570 crowd. We didn't get off to the flying start we had the previous season, but we did play well in a tight first half. Just after the break Geordie Armstrong opened the scoring for Arsenal as he latched onto a weak clearance by Alan Bloor to lash home.

Arsenal's goalkeeper was that Scottish international from Chesterfield Bob Wilson. I was determined to do everything I could to win the game, so soon after they went ahead I took to challenging him for some high balls to unsettle him and make him think twice about coming out to collect crosses. I figured Bob being confined to his line would leave the likes of me and John Ritchie able to win the ball more in the air and cause Arsenal further problems.

The game was very intense because of all the history between us and there were a lot of very hard, but fair challenges going in. As I went up for a corner with Wilson and, as he clung onto the ball with his fingertips above my head, I clattered into his outstretched arm, sending him sprawling on the turf. Little did I know that he had damaged his knee badly in landing. I want to make the point here that the injury he received was not a direct result of my challenge, but to be fair if I hadn't have hit him he wouldn't have damaged his knee.

Of course in those days teams were only allowed one substitute and Arsenal's that day was Ray Kennedy, an attacking player, so Wilson had to struggle on between the posts. Almost immediately he had to have his left knee strapped up and then each time the ball came near him he somehow managed to cling on to it, often falling over as he tried to hobble around the area, almost immobilised as it had locked rigid.

Our pecker was up. We could smell blood and we poured forward, carving out chance after chance. First, as Wilson lay prone in the area after falling over trying to clear the ball and not being able to get up because of his knee, Jackie Marsh won the ball in the right and Peter Dobing lashed in a left-footed shot which crashed against the far post. Worse still Jimmy Greenhoff sliced the rebound wide form 15 yards. We were inches away from equalising. We kept pressing forwards and somehow Wilson stopped one attack by throwing himself into a goalmouth melee and ending up sitting on the ball. Chance after chance went begging and the Arsenal goal lead a charmed life. The ball would not go in – not least because peg-leg Wilson seemed to be having the game of his life.

Just when it seemed as if we would have no luck at all, Eastham fired in a cross from the right wing to the near post. I had stayed forward from a previous attack and stole in. I knew I couldn't quite reach the ball as it dropped, but got myself in there to create whatever problem I could. To be honest I thought that this particular attack was one of the most innocuous we put together. We'd wasted far better chances, but on this occasion Peter Simpson made a total hash of clearing the cross, allowing the ball to skew wildly off his left foot and flash past the helpless Wilson into the back of the net. We were level.

Once again a crazy goal had changed the course of a cup semi-final between us. This time it was in our favour and things seemed to going totally our way when Wilson gave up the ghost, leaving Arsenal with ten men. What was more they chose to put their centre-forward John Radford into goal as Wilson's replacement. I have no idea what Radford's goalkeeping pedigree was, but we now really fancied our chances. If we scored again we couldn't see the Gunners coming back at us as their team pattern had been upset so badly. We thought they were in disarray and so piled forward looking for that vital second goal, which we were probably half expecting to get handed to us on a plate by this first time keeper. Everything we hit, however, seemed to arrow straight at John Radford. He had a blinder, making better saves than I thought we'd ever seen Bob Wilson make! Twice he pulled off low fingertip stops from headers from corners, both from me, one of which I really felt would beat him when I connected. Somehow he got to it.

On the one occasion Radford was beaten Dobing hit the post from distance. It just wasn't our day and incredibly Arsenal somehow clung on for a replay, which was scheduled for Goodison Park, the venue for the previous season's second match.

This time we dealt with our disappointment far better and began the game still on top. Jimmy scored a penalty, after being flattened himself by Frank McLintock. The Gunners got back into the match when Arsenal won a spot-kick of their own, which Charlie George put away. To continue the theme over these matches of contentious decisions, the Gunners penalty was given for an off the ball push by Peter Dobing on George Armstrong. To be honest I didn't see it, but then I don't think anyone but referee Walker did. The Arsenal players were surprised to be given the pen, although they accepted the chance to get back on level terms.

With 15 minutes to go John Radford completed his personal fairy tale in this semi-final by scoring the winning goal again. I might have thought it was a fitting end given his heroics in the first match had it not been for the utterly ludicrous nature of what happened. At Goodison Park there were white-coated ice-cream or peanut sellers walking around the track selling stuff to the crowd. Fair enough, you think, but how could they cause Arsenal to score the winning goal in an FA Cup semi-final? Well, quite incredibly, both sides were paying the fourth of these matches playing in change strips. Now ours was all white and with ten minutes to go linesman Bob Matthewson committed the all-time cock-up in Stoke City's history by mistaking one of those sellers for one of our defenders and allowing Charlie George, who was clearly yards offside, to run onto a pass, race through and cut it back for Radford to fire past Banksy. We were stunned. We'd stopped because George was at least ten yards behind our defence and so we'd just assumed he would be hauled back. I was utterly taken aback that this could happen. It was farcical, ridiculous and shocking to the point of being numbing. But the goal stood. We'd got barely any time to claw the deficit back and Arsenal held on. We'd lost to a goal that should never had stood. If the events of Hillsborough had taken us from the heights of anticipation to the depths of despair then that decision really took the biscuit.

When I next saw that linesman I felt compelled to ask him to explain himself and he owned up and apologised for his mistake. He had indeed mistaken the seller on the far side of the pitch for one of us. I was so taken aback I couldn't bite his head off. It was too ridiculous to take in.

Because of that the Stoke City Official Supporters Club put a hat round, collected some money together and had a statue of a horse's backside made, which was awarded to the linesman. I can't sum our feelings up any better than that. It was not just offside, it was miles offside. Looking back now it sounds a funny story and to give him his due Matthewson did apologise, but it was no consolation.

Over those two years the catalogue of events in the four games was quite incredible. It got to the stage, though, that my wife Kate didn't like me mentioning Arsenal at all. The name is still banned in her company and if it does get slipped in she warns whoever lets it past their lips, "now don't swear in this house". At the time I didn't know it, but over a decade later I would get a little bit of my own back on the Gunners as manager of York.

Kate saw how down I was after both those defeats. Semi-finals are massive, and we had been so close. To lose in the final would have been bad enough, but to lose in the semi-finals for a second consecutive year was devastating. No-one remembers teams that fail to reach Wembley. Many would see reach two successive semi-finals as success. But that isn't my mentality. To my mind losing at that stage simply means you just weren't quite good enough. I think that having just experienced that Wembley buzz and the winning feeling, it made it particularly hard to bear. I was desperate to walk out in front of 100,000 people again.

The strange thing about those two semi-final defeats was that neither was our last match in the competition. At that time the FA were experimenting with a third versus fourth place play-off between the two losing semi-finalists. The previous season, on the night before the final, we had comeback form 0-2 down to win 3-2 against Everton at Selhurst Park before a distinctly underwhelming crowd of just 5,031.

In 1972 the play-off against Birmingham City was played as a pre-season friendly that August at the Hawthorns. We drew 0-0 and lost the first penalty shoot-out that Stoke City had ever taken part in 4-3. It was a strange one because even though we lost we still got a tankard, which I've got at home somewhere. It's not among my more prized possessions and the FA wisely scrapped the match because nobody was interested. From our point of view we simply didn't care because we'd been knocked out of the competition. I think the fans were the same. They were deflated as well.

I'm fortunate in that I've been able to win things ever since I played as a kid. I've still got trophies and medals I won as an 11 year-old and if you've won something you've got to recognise it. But for finishing third in the FA Cup in 1971 we received this teeny plastic thing. I've still got that, but it means little to me, or, I'm sure, any other members of our team. What we cared about as players was turning this cup form into something more tangible in the league. It's one thing to win a trophy and reach a couple of semi-finals over the course of two seasons, it's quite another to bring sustained success to a football club such as Liverpool, Leeds, Manchester United and Arsenal have all achieved for periods in the game during my lifetime. We believed that the 1972 League Cup triumph could be the start of something big for Stoke, a club which had never truly delivered on its status as one of the 12 founder members of the Football League until that wonderful Wembley moment. Now we believed that we could go and compete with the best.

Chapter Nine

WALKING ON WATER

Stoke City were now trophy winners, a force to be reckoned with, and Tony Waddington had plans to develop the squad with the kind of signings that would make the football world sit up. In the summer of 1972 he began that process by capturing the £70,000 signature of one of the biggest names in the game, Geoff Hurst, the England striker who had famously netted a hat-trick on that Wembley day in 1966 to secure the World Cup triumph.

That signing meant a lot to me both in terms of Stoke making a statement of intent, and on a more personal level. When he first arrived Geoff told the press that said that there were two reasons why he'd joined Stoke. The first, in reference to the famous penalty save at Upton Park, was so he didn't have to take penalties against Gordon Banks, and the second was so he didn't have to play against me. I took that as a huge compliment, coming from such a high profile player.

Geoff was by now 30 years old and coming towards the end of his time as a truly top class striker, although he was still an excellent target man and good finisher. His England career had just come to an end as he had been superseded by the likes of Rodney Marsh, Malcolm Macdonald, Mike Channon and Joe Royle. So he wasn't at his peak, and he was also beginning to look at what to do outside the game. He bought a pub called the Sheet Anchor at Baldwin's Gate not far away from where we lived and so he had one eye on that throughout his three years at Stoke. He still scored 30 goals in 108 games for the club, so he hadn't come to the club simply for the money. His presence and experience were important to us, but it was the fact that Stoke City were dealing with top class names that was the most vital component of his signing.

The only player to leave, which came as something of a surprise to me, was midfielder Micky Bernard. He joined Everton for £125,000 as Waddo believed the young Josh Mahoney had matured enough to take over in midfield. Josh was more of an attacking player, always looking to drive forward, and, in the nicest possible way, he wasn't as nasty as Mick. Mick could really dig into the tackle and win battles in the middle of the pitch, while Josh wanted to play football. I think, despite the show of strength in signing Geoff Hurst, the club still needed to balance the books. Micky insists they should have named one of the Victoria Ground stands after him because the money from his signing kept the club going. It certainly paid for the arrival of Hursty. Whether it was a financial reason or a footballing one, I feel that we rally missed Bernie when he left. He was the extra layer of protection for our back four, and his departure left us exposed.

The 1972/73 season kicked off with a massive wave of optimism surrounding the club, not least from within our squad. But despite an opening victory over Crystal Palace, after nine games we'd drawn three of our four home matches and lost all our five away games. We were 20th in the league, just one place above the relegation zone. We knew this wasn't a realistic reflection of our true ability, and in the next game it all clicked together as we thrashed Manchester City 5-1. Our form remained very in and out, though, and frustration began to build within the squad. This wasn't how we had expected the season to go.

It all came to a head at Anfield on 21 October. Liverpool, as I've said, was never a happy hunting ground for Stoke City, even in our glory years, but on this particular day we played superbly. Jimmy Greenhoff gave us a deserved half-time lead with a header. But then, halfway through the second half, the trouble started. Referee Roger Kirkpatrick penalised Gordon Banks, who was in possession of the ball and taking plenty of time a goalkeepers since time immemorial have, for taking too many steps under the Laws of the Game. Banksy was livid. He had taken no more steps than he took every week of his career, so why had the ref awarded Liverpool an indirect free-kick? Once the hullabaloo had died down Emlyn Hughes plunged the knife deeper by belting in the equaliser off the underside of the bar.

At least we were still holding onto a point in the face of a typical Liverpool onslaught as they attacked the Kop goal. We were giving as good as we got in an intense last few minutes when our world exploded in more ways than one. Further controversy reigned as the referee seemed to us to change the established interpretation of the Laws of the Game, which he had early stuck to so adhesively, when he waved play on after both Eric Skeels and Jackie Marsh had fouled Steve Heighway with the Liverpool man heading for our penalty area. Kirkpatrick, though, chose to bring back play when Heighway's subsequent pass to Keegan resulted in Liverpool losing the ball.

I was incensed, after all he'd waved play on and Liverpool had then totally independently lost the ball. We hadn't tackled or intervened, Heighway had played a bad pass, and yet Kirkpatrick had brought the play back for a much earlier free-kick. It just wasn't something that was done then. The whole team was livid, but none more so than Gordon Banks, still fuming at the earlier incident. Banksy raced out of his area to have a go at the referee. He was usually the utmost professional and so it was surprising and perhaps indicative of how we were feeling about our season that he protested sp strongly about the award of the free-kick right on the edge of the box. It got worse. As we fumed, Liverpool took a quick free-kick ad Ian Callaghan rammed home the ball to win the game. It was an exceptionally controversial last minute goal and prompted Banksy to completely lose his rag. He hared after the referee, strongly making his point that he'd acted outside the Laws of the Game. I knew how Gordon felt. We'd lost and felt utterly robbed. Gordon, despite Ray Clemence trying to calm him down, stalked Kirkpatrick off the field haranguing him as he did so. Banksy freely admits now that he had lost his cool for just about the only time in his career. It would prove to be very costly.

The next morning Gordon went into the Victoria Ground for some treatment on an injury. Every Sunday morning, being the ultimate professional, he used to go in early, have a shower, warm down and relax, get a massage or do a bit extra while everybody else was still lying in bed. This particular morning he was still seething at the manner of the previous day's defeat. His mind was racing all over the place as he drove home and somehow he ended up having a horrendous accident on a renowned tricky bend as an oncoming car cut the corner, causing Gordon to roll his vehicle, smash into a wall shattering the windscreen, cutting his face to ribbons. He ended up having to be cut out of the car. Normally he used to take his son Robert with him. Thank heavens Robert wasn't in the car that day.

The BBC broke into their news broadcasts to bring news of Banksy's accident to the nation. It was devastating to hear it. What annoyed me when it first happened was that the first newspapers made it sound as though he'd been out on the town Saturday night and was coming back late Sunday morning, when the truth could not have been more starkly different.

Our house at Ashley Heath used to back onto Gordon's and Kate went straight round to see if Ursula, Gordon's wife, needed anything. His room at the hospital was inundated with cards, telegrams and flowers as well-wishers from around the globe sent messages of support to a man who was still at the top of his sport, but now appeared to have had his career cruelly cut short. Gordon's eye was badly damaged and it soon became apparent that he probably wouldn't play top flight football again. It was devastating for him, as it was for us. For the greatest goalkeeper in the world to be so cruelly denied a good proportion of his career was a truly horrendous thing. Banksy was as fit as a flea. He would have gone on playing forever – at least till he was 40. Now he was finished at 32, although, typically, he attempted numerous comebacks.

Banksy's loss hit us badly. It was a major, major, blow – it's silly to say it in many ways, but I don't think the club has ever recovered from that. At the time certainly morale was very low and it affected our already up and down form. 1972/73 limped along when we'd expected it to be a glorious rise. A week and a half after Gordon's accident we were knocked out of our defence of the League Cup by Second Division Notts County. We had a tough Christmas programme looming against Derby, Manchester City and Arsenal and things were looking bleak. We couldn't understand how we could go from the heights of March and April, just six months previously, to playing so poorly.

Gordon's replacement was England Under 23 international John Farmer. He'd been an England basketball player and had not taken up football until late in life. He was an educated man and a magnificent athlete – we used to call him Garth because he was so big. He was a lovely fellow, who looked as though he was going to be an outstanding keeper. John was what might be called today a great shot-stopper. His handling was fantastic, and he was difficult to beat one-on-one or from distance, but he lacked the command of Gordon, and it took as a good while to get used to him as a back four. That certainly contributed to our lack of results.

It got to the stage that we needed to get a grip and get ourselves back together again, set aside all the disappointments we'd been through and allowed us to go out and perform the way we knew we could over Christmas. Derby were swept aside 4-0, while we picked up good draws away at Maine Road and home to Arsenal. We were doing much better, but unfortunately so were the other teams around us. Leicester had gone on a fantastic run and were now safely in mid-table, helped by a 2-0 win over us at Filbert street in March, which was the fourth in a run of games in which we picked up a single point. We were back in the quagmire again, just two points of the bottom of the table, back down in 20th place. It is situations like this that the mental strength of a team is really tested. We had that in spades. The other element of course is ability. Without those two attributes you will never survive in the top flight of English football. With a solid defence, decent midfield and Geoff Hurst and John Ritchie up front we were really in a false position for our ability, but other factors had contributed to our miserable season.

We pulled ourselves out of our melancholy to win six out of our last eight matches to finish 14th, eight points off the relegation zone, which featured Crystal Palace and West Brom, who we beat 2-0 in a massive four-pointer at the Vic at the end of March to really kick-start our survival bid.

******

1973/74 didn't start any better, however. We didn't win a league match until our ninth game. It was such a relief to finally come off the pitch with two points and that 2-0 victory over West Ham in late September. Our form remained distinctly average, however, and by the turn of the year we were languishing in 17th, only three positions above the newly-extended relegation zone, which for the first time would see three clubs demoted to the Second Division. It wasn't lack of effort, or lack of belief, there was just something missing. Worryingly, this malaise which had affected the squad and the club had now lasted almost two years. In this day and age you have to wonder whether Tony Waddington would be given almost two years to build on a major trophy win, but the Stoke directors at that time were a very settled bunch and understood the need for continuity. We never got the sense that Waddo's job was under pressure during that time. Still he knew that he had to cast his net far and wide to pull a rabbit out of the hat.

He needed a signing that would galvanise the club from its lethargy, and like all truly great managers he found one.

In keeping with the talismanic arrivals of Banks and Hurst, Waddo continued his pursuit of one of the biggest names in English football by persuading Chelsea's skilful midfield general Alan Hudson, the self-styled King of the Kings Road, to join the club. He joined Stoke in mid-January 1974 and brought the place to life with his cocky arrogance and brand of flowing, attacking football, which gelled the entire team together, giving us a focal point around which to base our game. He was the catalyst, Waddo the ring master and before we knew it Stoke City were back as a competitive force.

We were in 17th position on the day he signed, but Huddy's arrival galvanised the team. He sparkled on his debut against Liverpool giving what Bill Shankly described as "the best debut performance I have ever seen", and destroyed his former team-mates Chelsea in the next match, earning the penalty kick which Geoff Hurst rammed home to earn victory. That set us off on a run which saw us lose just twice more before the end of the season as we swept all before us, winning seven of our last ten games to finish fifth.

Huddy was a truly great footballer who should have played 100 times for England. He had everything – incredible skill, vision, a change of pace, a drop of the shoulder to earn vital inches to play a pass, the light-footed ability to skim over the treacherous surface of the Victoria Ground, supreme fitness and athletic prowess despite his playboy aura, and the charisma to match that sublime blend of abilities. I first discovered this when he left me for dead in our first training session together. He turned me inside and then out, leaving me on my back side that first day and I thought to myself, 'if you can do that son, you've got to be in my team.' There weren't many people who could leave me swishing at the air.

I'd be the first to admit that genius as he was, Huddy is also a legend in his own mind, but there's nothing wrong with that kind of swagger and belief if it's backed up with the kind of talent which Alan Hudson possessed.

But the effect Huddy had on the team was not only seen up front. The defence began to tighten up too. In the last nine games of that 1973/74 season we conceded just two goals. I think that was in large part due to the fact when Huddy was playing we tended kept the ball a lot. He did not like the other side to have possession at all and he hated giving it away. We controlled long periods of games and cut out the kinds of errors which surrendered possession. Every player responded to this, and confidence bred throughout the squad. Huddy also knitted the disparate elements of our team together by providing the link between defence and attack. He picked the ball up deep, played one twos through the midfield, and then into the front men. And what's more he could keep that kind of incredible workrate up for 90 minutes.

Perhaps the most iconic game during that phenomenal run we put together was the visit of Leeds United on 23 February 1974. Don Revie's Leeds side was at the zenith of its powers. They had put together an incredible unbeaten run form the start of the season. It had now reached 29 matches and the press was full of stories about them going unbeaten to the end of the season. Every team they faced had to endure a barrage of stories about how Leeds would steamroller them aside. When it came to our turn to host Leeds the routine was set; sacrificial lambs to the slaughter would roll over and allow Leeds to progress serenely on to the title unbeaten.

I was a great admirer of Leeds United and the way they played football under Don Revie because I've always had a desire to be very organised and to play with people who want to do it that way. Leeds were THE side during that period. They were a great team. People talk about them being nasty, but they could play. The balance of the side was so good. They had two good attacking fall backs, Bremner and Giles in midfield, Eddie Gray on the wing, and Clarke and Jones up front. They were fabulous, although the funny thing is that ultimately they didn't win enough trophies considering they were so good.

I had great times against Leeds as a player. I'd scored one of my favourite goals up there to earn us a 1-1 draw in October 1973. I'd played the ball out of defence and carried on going forward because it was quite late on and we were a goal behind. TC crossed to the far post and I outjumped goalkeeper David Harvey to home, so I relished the opportunity to put the kybosh on this incredible unbeaten run of theirs.

I think every football fan of that generation remembers that game against Leeds. It was such an incredible game. It began terribly for us. Early on I lunged into little Billy Bremner, letting him know I wasn't going to be taken lightly. Billy fell to the floor as if he'd been shot, but as I was telling referee Homewood just what a little sod Bremner was, up jumped the Scot to place the ball down for the free-kick on the edge of the area and smack his shot past John Farmer, who was starting to line up the wall, and into the goal. Cheeky blighter! He'd well and truly done me. My protests fell on deaf ears. And I promise you they were vehement.

While we were still licking our wounds at being so 'professionally' mugged, Allan Clarke shrugged off the attentions of Alan Dodd, a young central defender, to slot the ball home to make it 0-2. Surely the game was over wasn't it? Surely the press were right. But they weren't. Any doubters were put right by our fantastic fightback, begun when Mike Pejic smashed home a free-kick from the edge of the area. And he didn't even have to revert to deception. He fair lashed the ball into the net off the post with his left foot. As Leeds raised question marks in their mind about their ability to hang on, Huddy grabbed the game by the scruff of the neck, pulling the strings from midfield, notching the equalising goal himself when Ritchie nodded down a cross from new signing Jimmy Robertson, who had joined us from Ipswich for £80,000, at the far post. Huddy dug the ball out of the clinging mud on the Victoria Ground pitch to slot home from six yards out.

2-2 at half-time, the second half became a tremendous end to end match. John Ritchie scored, but the goal was ruled out for reasons I'm still not sure of, then, with about 25 minutes remaining, Roberston swung a corner deep into the Leeds box. I was lurking, as I always did, and got my head to the ball about 1 yards out, directing it back towards the near post. It found Geoff Hurst, who realised that all attention had switched off me, and so nodded it back into my path. My momentum had carried me forward, and with the entire Leeds defence flat-footed with Geoff's quick thinking, I leapt to hurl myself bodily at the ball. propelling it and myself full-length into the Boothen End net.

That goal proved to be the winner in a pulsating contest which ended Leeds' fantastic run at 29 games. It was a mark which would be levelled by Liverpool's electric start to the 1987/88 season, and only bettered by Arsenal's Invincibles of 2003/04 who went through the entire Premiership season unbeaten. The reaction from around the world to that goal winning that game made me understand what a phenomenon football is. I'm pretty good at geography, but I got letters and photographs to be signed from places in the world I'd never heard of in South America, Africa, and Asia – in they came in bundles. I had never realised just what world news a game like that was. At the time I was playing all it was to me was a football match. Of course now we are used to the Premier League making global superstars of players. Back then it was only televised summer tournaments such as the World Cup which could do that, so it was a real eye opener to become so famous in so many places by scoring that header.

It was that year when, following the retirement of Jack Charlton, warhorse central defender and England World Cup winner, I learned that Leeds had made Stoke a world record offer for a defender of £250,000 for me. Waddo refused to sell. Times were very different then. Not only in that we were one of Leeds' main rivals and so I would never have countenanced joining them, but also that moving clubs would not have made me any significantly richer. Not like it does today. I also didn't want to go. I was convinced Stoke City would win the league title with me in the team.

Our next home game had something of a tale about it too, although for very different reasons. As I've said before John Ritchie was a tough, bluff character who didn't take any prisoners and so when Southampton's recent signing from Chelsea Peter Osgood did a newspaper story about how Big John was not very good with his head. That was a red rag to a bull as far as John was concerned. He had an absolutely blinding second half, scoring a hat-trick, the crowning glory of which was an absolutely sublime moment of footballing retribution. Having already scored twice to put us 3-1 ahead, Ritchie rounded off the scoring by racing onto a through ball, taking it past goalkeeper Eric Martin, stopping it on the line, kneeling down and heading the ball into the net. The message was clear . . . who can't score goals with his head Ossie?!

Believing we could now win the league, we began the new 1974/75 season with a bang, giving Brian Clough's Leeds a 3-0 hiding at the Vic with Huddy at the hub of everything. Victories at Queen's Park Rangers and newly-promoted Carlisle were similarly orchestrated, leaving us in fourth place by mid-September and with pretty much our entire team at the top of our game. That was the kind of effect Hudson had on us. It wasn't a single-handed effort by any means, more that he was the last spoke in the wheel which now ran smoothly, gathering speed as we raced towards the top of the First Division table.

If he had a fault on the pitch it was that Huddy was one of the most one-footed players I ever played with. Alan would not know what to do with his left leg besides stand on it, but he didn't have to worry about what his left leg was doing because his right was so busy weaving magic. I remember a game in February 1975 against Manchester City on an absolute quagmire of a playing surface at the Vic when he tore City's defence to pieces, scoring once and making the other three goals in a 4-0 white-wash. That win saw us leap to third place in the table and Huddy's performance on an absolute mud bath prompted a group of fans to come to the next home game a couple of weeks after that when we next played at home there was a banner that appeared – "Alan Hudson walks on water" because it had just been an absolute virtuoso display.

Those fans were absolutely right. At times Huddy would float and glide around the pitch. He calls football 'The Working Man's Ballet' and in many ways that is an apt description, especially when applied to Hudson's own approach to playing. His whole rationale was to use every blade of grass on the pitch and every player in the team to keep the ball, work opponents out and the strike. He loaned you the ball did Huddy. He gave it to you saying 'you can have it as long as you give it me back' and we were all, especially the likes of Jimmy Greenhoff, Terry Conroy and Josh Mahoney, soon on the same wavelength. It was a wonderful time. We didn't think we could get beat. Everybody was buzzing. It's great to go out there thinking you are the best or believing that you are going to win. There is nothing better. Everybody is relaxed, everybody is smiling. That's when football is simply the best way to make a living. Everybody loves one another. You are all best of mates. It's always the same if you are winning. When you are winning everybody loves you.

We had first hit the top of the table in late November 1974 when I lashed in a loose ball in the box four minutes from time against Leicester. During that autumn I weighed in with some vital goals, none more crucial than that right-foot volley in a crowded penalty area four minutes from time to hand us a 1-0 victory.

The following Saturday we won 3-0 at Birmingham, with Jimmy Greenhoff scoring probably the best volley I have ever seen. A long ball forward dropped over his right shoulder out on the edge of the box, towards the touchline. Much like Holland's Marco van Basten in the Euro 88 final, Jimmy swivelled and lashed the sweetest strike imaginable into the corner of the net. Thankfully it was preserved for eternity by ATV who were filming that game. It was one hell of a goal.

That was the first time Stoke had sat atop the First Division in 37 years. It was a very tight division, with eight teams vying for the title over the next couple of months before the likes of Jack Charlton's Middlesbrough and Harry Haslam's Sheffield United fell by the wayside. It was nip and tuck with the lead changing hands constantly. In February, two weeks after that hammering of Manchester City we hit the top again thanks to a 2-0 win at Tottenham and a 2-2 draw at home to Wolves. That game saw the team display tremendous fighting spirit to claw back a two goal deficit inside the final five minutes. When you are on a run like that you think you are going to win every match. You certainly don't think you're ever going to lose. It's great. We were on a real roll and realised we had a realistic chance of challenging for the title. The excitement built within both the squad and fans as we were finally fulfilling the undoubted potential we'd show in those cup runs previously.

Any successful side has to overcome adversity somewhere along the way. In September 1974 we played in a bruising encounter at Ipswich Town. Our matches against Bobby Robson's side were always eventful and always tough. Kevin Beattie and Allan Hunter were two extremely physical defenders, much like me and Bluto. It was a midweek game at Portman Road and we were comfortable at 0-0. Just after half-time Beattie crunched into a tackle on John Ritchie, who had been causing their defence real problems. The challenge left John crumpled in a heap clutching a badly broken leg, complicated by Beattie falling on him. At 33 years old it would prove to be the end of the line for Big John, who finished his career as Stoke's record goalscorer, a mantle he still retains.

In my career I've been lucky enough to manage plenty of players with that goalscorer's instinct. John was one of the best, if not the best I ever came across. He was a big old fashioned centre forward, similar to Alan Shearer. Like The King of the Geordies, John could score every kind of goal. Left foot, right foot, head, on the run, tap-ins. Rockets from outside the box. He was the complete centre-forward. John also had a similar temperament to Alan. He was a right miserable bugger when he hadn't scored and we always viewed that as a good thing. John was desperate to score and he thrived on it. He needed goals, he wanted the headlines that came with them and we needed him to score them for us. We missed him terribly when he had gone.

Personally I didn't actually think Beattie's tackle was a foul. It was a hard tackle, but it wasn't illegal. John's leg was loose and the situation was compounded by Beattie falling on top of John. But John was adamant he'd been illegally clattered and that Beattie was to blame. I don't think he could handle his career ending that way. It must have been terribly difficult, not least because it was so unexpected. Fortunately John went on to become a very successful businessman in his own right, running a pottery company in Stoke-on-Trent.

It was frustrating in the extreme for us that our main goalscorer was taken out of the equation. If we were to challenge seriously for honours we would have to overcome this huge setback. We couldn't cope in the immediate aftermath, letting in three goals in 16 minutes as we reshuffled. Then Alan Dodd was shown a second yellow card for handball and was dismissed. Geoff Salmons' late goal was no consolation.

Richie's wasn't the first serious injury we had to cope with. The previous season our captain Peter Dobing had been forced to end his career after having his leg broken by a

Mr Holbrook and the Sandon Road Junior school team. That's me front and centre, holding the ball.

The Sandon Road team show off the Longton U11 cup in front of a proud Headmaster.

CITY OF STOKE-ON-TRENT EDUCATION COMMITTEE

SCHOOL LEAVING CERTIFICATE

NAME OF SCHOLAR ...... DENNIS SMITH .

SCHOOL ...... Queensberry County Secondary, Longton.

FORM ..... 4.A.   DATE OF BIRTH ... 19.11.47.

ATTENDANCE: (a) REGULARITY Excellent (b) PUNCTUALITY - Excellent

SCHOLASTIC ATTAINMENTS

RELIGIOUS KNOWLEDGE	V.Good.	HOMECRAFT	
		NEEDLEWORK	
ENGLISH	Good.	WOODWORK	V.Good.
MATHEMATICS	V.Good.	METALWORK	
SCIENCE	V.Good.	TECHNICAL DRAWING	V.Good.
HISTORY	V.Good.	ART AND CRAFTS	V.Good.
GEOGRAPHY	V.Good.	PHYSICAL EDUCATION	Excellent.
MUSIC			

Deputy Head Prefect. Member of School Cricket, Boxing, Athletics, and Cross-Country Teams. Member of City Football Team.

.... HEAD TEACHER

.... CHIEF EDUCATION OFFICER

DATE ...... December 19th, 1962.

My school leaving certificate. I was 15 and F. Good at pretty much everything! Except, of course, P.E.

The City of Stoke-on-Trent Boys team coached by Dennis Wilshaw which won the second of back-to-back English Schools' Shields in May 1963. Front row second from left full-back Jackie Marsh, who I would room with for years at Stoke, third from left midfield powerhouse Bill Bentley, who played for Stoke and Port Vale but never truly fulfilled his potential, second from right darting winger John Worsdale, who would make his Stoke City debut on the same day as me at Arsenal five years later. I am on the right-hand end of the middle row.

As teenagers my mates and I sampled the delights of Butlins at Minehead. Clockwise from bottom left, Trevor Doughty, Chris Boumford, Alan Merry, Reg, Billy Bath and myself.

...lfilled my dream by signing professional terms in
...66 after three years as an amateur at Stoke,
...rking as a plumber's mate and on a shoe
...duction line in the process.

...e world's greatest player, Pelé,
...ted Stoke in 1968, although my
...ndchildren refuse to believe I
...yed against him. Here's the proof,
...hough the evidence suggests I
...n't mark him closely enough. Pelé
...red twice and Edu (top) the other as
...ntos won the friendly 3-2, although I still claim my goal just
...ore half-time should have stood.

I was given an early
lesson by Mick Jones,
left, star centre-
forward of Don Revie's
Leeds side, when he
scored a hat-trick at
the Vic in March
1969. I was young and
I'd been ill before the
game but was
desperate to play –
maybe I shouldn't
have!

The red mist descends for Peter Dobing after just a
few minutes of our home game against Roma in the Anglo-
Italian Cup. Peter's punch had left irritating Roma defender
Giacomo Losi, no. 6, on the floor crying like a child. When
he got up I finished the job off.

Left, simply the greatest goalkeeper the world has ever seen,
Gordon Banks made our back four so much more effective
because of his organisation, communication and the fact
that he could save pretty much anything.

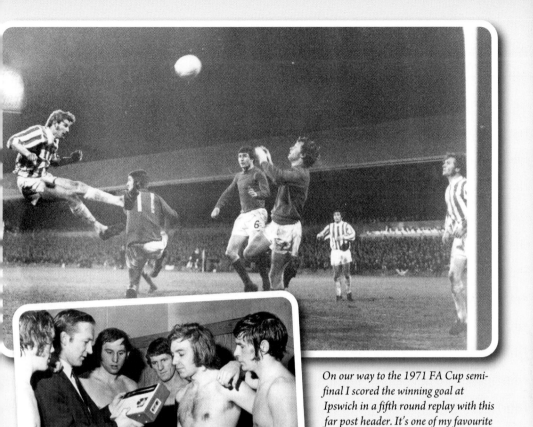

On our way to the 1971 FA Cup semi-final I scored the winning goal at Ipswich in a fifth round replay with this far post header. It's one of my favourite goals and pictures.

Captain Peter Dobing tunes into the FA Cup draw to hear that we have just been pulled out of the hat with Arsenal in the semi-finals.

That season I was playing in cup matches with a broken ankle, which would be set in plaster during the week to recuperate. I would then play with the aid of a cortisone injection.

Running out at Hillsborough to play the first FA Cup semi-final Stoke had competed in for over 70 years. I scored, but that doesn't taint the feeling that we should have won.

Jimmy Greenhoff races on to a through ball but fires his shot over Arsenal's bar in the 1971 FA Cup semi-final. We were leading 2-0 at the time and a third goal would have killed the game off. As it was Arsenal scored twice, including a late penalty that should never have been, to take us to a replay.

Big John Ritchie was Stoke's wonderfully gifted centre-forward who would not take no for an answer. He still holds the club's career goalscoring record and here is pictured celebrating yet another of those 171 strikes with winger Harry Burrows.

Ritchie climbs above the entire Everton defence to power in a header.

The genius that was Tony Waddington, our manager and the man who built Stoke City into one of the best teams in the country.

Jimmy Greenhoff was a complex character. When he was on top of the world there was no-one better, but when he got down on himself he could let his head go down. On occasions I thought he was as good as any forward player I ever saw, some of the stuff he played was both magical and sublime.

Greenhoff hits the back of the net, this time the fifth goal in a 5-1 rout of Manchester City, which completed the first hat-trick of his Stoke career.

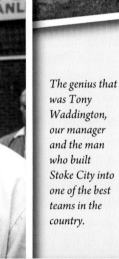

West Ham goalkeeper Bobby Ferguson collects a cross in the League Cup semi-final second leg at Old Trafford in 1972. Bobby was knocked unconscious during this game and his stand-in Bobby Moore saved a penalty, but we still squeaked into the final 3-2 on the night.

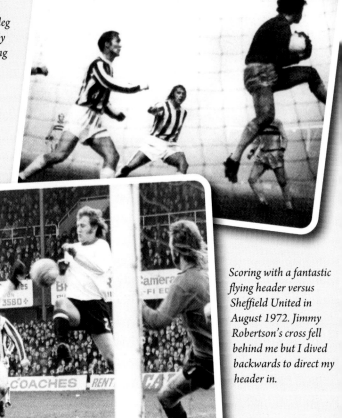

Scoring with a fantastic flying header versus Sheffield United in August 1972. Jimmy Robertson's cross fell behind me but I dived backwards to direct my header in.

WAGs 1972-style. The Stoke City wives and girlfriends gather to get ready to cheer on their team at Wembley in the League Cup. My wife Kate is standing, extreme left.

Walking out at Wembley and seeing the sea of faces behind the goal at the far end of the ground was an incredible experience.

Above, my early shot loops up off Peter Osgood, on ground, for Terry Conroy to head home the opening goal in the 1972 League Cup final, left, sparking wild jubilation at having having taken such an early lead. Osgood scored just before half-time to equalise, but George Eastham's late goal clinched the Cup for us.

Soaking up the euphoria after our fantastic Wembley win.

The throng which awaited us when we arrived at Barlaston station, above, was incredible. It felt like every single person in the Potteries was out on the streets waiting to cheer us. And, left, when Bluto Bloor and I held the cup up high for the residents of our home patch, Meir, to see it was an incredibly emotional moment.

Right, drinking out of the Watney Cup after beating Hull 2-0 in the final thanks to two Jimmy Greenhoff goals. As this was the last final of this slightly odd pre-season tournament that makes Stoke the defending champions!

Above, challenging Arsenal keeper Bob Wilson, who was trying to punch me, in the FA Cup semi-final at Villa Park in 1972. The elbow was merely for self-preservation! Bob damaged his knee badly in landing after this challenge, but somehow we could not beat him and only drew the game.

Alan Bloor rises to get in a header against Kaiserslautern in our first foray into European competition. We won the home leg 3-1, but were hammered away 0-4.

From left to right, Jimmy Robertson, George Eastham, Terry Conroy, Geoff Hurst and myself. The sideboards are exemplary.

Controversy during the 3-3 draw at Queens' Park Rangers in August 1973 as our keeper John Farmer is adjudged to have moved and Terry Venables is allowed a second chance to score from the penalty spot. I'm giving the linesman the evil eye.

The Guinness Book of Records called me the most injured man in football. Roger Davies of Derby will tell you this was a mere flesh wound.

Geoff Hurst talks tactics with manager Tony Waddington. When Geoff joined the club he said he was delighted he'd no longer have to take penalties against Gordon Banks and be kicked around by me!

Liverpool striker John Toshack was a tough opponent, although here I'm getting the better of him to clear.

Alan Hudson walked on water for Stoke fans after arriving with a bang in January 1974. We finished fifth in the league in the next two seasons and should have won the title in 1975, but injuries intervened.

Relaxing at the Cannes Harbour yacht club with the Stoke squad. A supporter owned a perfume factory in the south of France, so we popped over at his expense and beat Monaco 2-0. We sailed on his yacht round to Monaco – a hard, hard pre-season!

I was lucky enough to be asked to model for a boutique called Regalia. They even let me keep the clothes, although checks never really suited me!

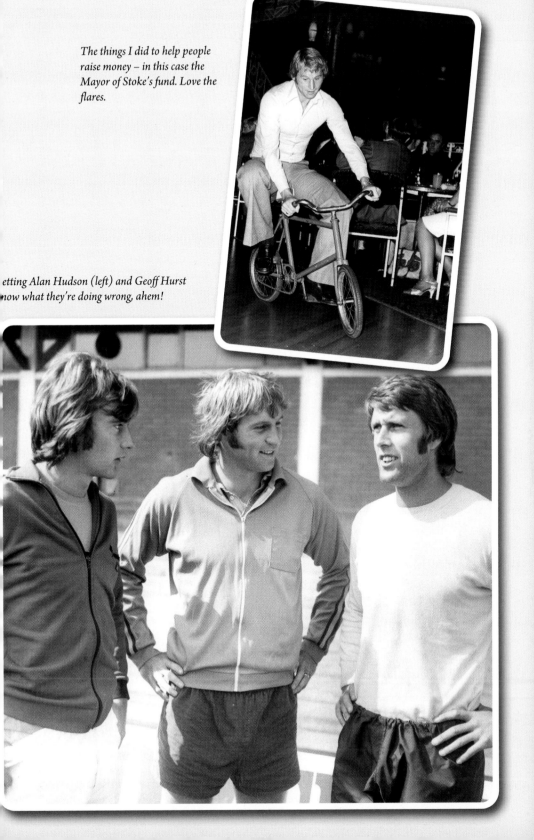

The things I did to help people raise money – in this case the Mayor of Stoke's fund. Love the flares.

...etting Alan Hudson (left) and Geoff Hurst ...now what they're doing wrong, ahem!

Another flying header – this time the goal which beat Leeds to end their incredible unbeaten run of 29 games in February 1974.

A fantastic little cartoon which my son Paul found and had framed for me. It refers to my predilection for getting injured and the dark days of the strikes and power shortages in the mid-1970s.

● "Before the cuts I had more hot dinners than Denis Smith's had broken bones."

Signing the best goalkeeper in the country should have given us a great opportunity of winning the league championship in 1974/75, but unfortunately Peter Shilton did not have a great three years at Stoke. We got on well particularly as training partners, but Shilts had an unhappy time at the Vic.

My badly broken leg and consequent ligament problems were all my own fault. As I recuperate, here I am, clockwise from bottom right, getting to grips with a wheelchair, being comforted by Bandit the dog, named after Clive Eaton, a lad I managed in the Sunday League, pumping weights to get fit again and showing Josh Mahoney how to use a medicine ball. My knee never bent properly after this injury and it finished me as a top class player. I would have to exist on my wits from here on in.

Signing autographs at an open day.

The date 2 January 1976 is one of the most important, and gloomiest, in Stoke's history. The storms which brought down the roofing of the Butler Street Stand cost it millions of pounds and left the club needing to sell its best players to raise money to rebuild the stand. It was an unmitigated disaster.

Being made captain of my hometown club was a proud day. I used to talk and organise anyway, so Waddo made me skipper and told me to do it and keep talking.

Playing in the Second Division was something of a comedown after years in the top flight. Here I am rising unchallenged against Swansea to clear with the help of goalkeeper Roger Jones.

Even at age 30 I was turning my thoughts to a managerial career, here helping coach Tony Lacey with some local kids . . .

. . . and here managing my first Sunday League side, Taylor & Tunnicliffe.

Defending against Blackburn Rovers, supported by Geoff Scott (no. 3) and player-coach Howard Kendall. We lost this game 1-2, but the defeat spurred us on to far greater heights and we eventually won promotion on the final day of the 1978/79 season.

Two of the young stars who helped get Stoke promoted and then established the club in the big time again. Right, Garth Crooks earned a big money move to Tottenham, while left, Adrian 'Inchy' Heath secured a transfer to Everton. Both won plenty of silverware.

eing captain meant a lot of work in the
mmunity and I loved meeting supporters and doing
e media work necessary. Top, I'm presenting a local newspaper prize winner
th a season ticket with help from, from left, chairman Percy Axon, secretary Mike Potts, the winner,
d the editor of the Sentinel. Bottom left, presenting a young fan with a 'Alan Durban's red and white Army' T-shirt.
ttom right, helping Viv Busby get to grips with Miss Royal Doulton.

We won promotion to the top flight in 1979 with an extremely well organised team.

Above left, Viv Busby, background, Garth Crooks and Howard Kendall help me celebrate a goal.

Right, My centre-half partner Mike Doyle and I applaud the fantastic supporters who travelled in their thousands to see us clinch the third promotion spot in a tense game at Meadow Lane in which we beat Notts County thanks to Paul Richardson's late goal.

...n the prowl against Brighton and Hove Albion after gaining promotion back to the top flight. The head band was ...t for advertising, merely protecting my forehead from yet more cuts I had picked up.

...his header hit the back of the net to make it 2-2 against Everton at the Vic, unfortunately a Sammy Irvine own goal ...n the game for the visitors. Strikers Garth Crooks and Adrian 'Inchy' Heath take notes on how it's done!

DENNIS SMITH TESTIMONIAL MATCH

Admit to
REFRESHMENT ROOM B
AT HALF TIME

WEDNESDAY, 16th APRIL

- -

DENNIS SMITH TESTIMONIAL MATCH

Admit to
REFRESHMENT ROOM B
AT FULL TIME

WEDNESDAY, 16th APRIL

acing page, top to bottom,
unning out between the two invitation teams for my testimonial at
e Victoria Ground in 1980 with my son Paul in background; a ticket for the match; thanking the
ns for their incredible support. This page top, thanking legendary goalkeepers Peter Shilton and Gordon Banks for
eir help in turning out; bottom, chatting with former captain Peter Dobing and legendary former Stoke manager
ony Waddington.

Above: Little & Large
were fantastic when the
provided the
entertainment at my
testimonial dinner at
Jolly's nightclub.
Right, hitting the deck
in a pro-celebrity
Boxing match during
my testimonial seaso
I'd enjoyed attending
the monthly evening
Pat Brogan
organised and so I
had one for my
testimonial.

When I broke my arm at Burnley, I was so frustrated I had a plate in it and no plaster, but in my comeback game against Manchester City a player fell on the limb snapping the plate and bone again under his weight and I was out for another three months.

Above, imbuing my first two children Paul, right, and Becky with ball skills from a very young age. Right, celebrating becoming manager of York City with my third child, Tom.

Chaired off the Victoria Ground pitch for one last time after our 3-0 victory over West Bromwich Albion secured Stoke's safety in the First Division. It was a fantastic way to say 'farewell'.

EVENING SENTINEL, W:

Smith for York

DENIS SMITH was today appointed the first player-manager of Fourth Division York City, but is expected to play for Stoke City on Saturday at Manchester United.

Stoke Manager Richie Barker said only minutes after today's announcement in York about the new appointment that Smith still figures in his team plans up to the end of

Above left: My new assistant Viv Busby and I raise our hats to the prospect of good times ahead at York City. Above centre: Becoming player-manager at York, with new signing Chris Evans, left, (as I write assistant manager at Bolton Wanderers), and Viv. Above right: The first of several Manager of the Month awards which our meteoric rise up the league brought.

Left: The local Stoke newspaper announces my departure to Bootham Crescent.

Coming off the pitch alongside former colleague Jimmy Greenhoff who was then in charge of Port Vale. As you can see we've lost. I wasn't happy.

The 1983/84 York City squad which became the first ever to notch up over 100 points, featuring, back row third from left, Ricky Sbragia, fourth from left, John Byrne, fourth from right, Keith Walwyn, front row third from left Malcolm Crosby and fourth from left goalkeeper Roger Jones.

Showing off the Division Four trophy on the open-top bus tour of York

City gain a place in history

By Sports Editor Malcolm Huntington

YORK CITY wrote their names into the history books in the season which ended on Saturday by not only winning the Fourth Division title for the first time but also becoming the first club to reach 100 league points.

Whatever happens in the future, no-one can ever take those 'firsts' from them.

Yes, it's been a marvellous season and one that must go down as the most entertaining since I started to report City first team affairs in August, 1968.

Many people will argue that the feat of the 1954-55 team in reaching the FA Cup semi-final and that of the 1973-74 side when they swept into the Second Division in 1973-74 were better achievements. I wouldn't disagree.

However, for pure joy and entertainment at a highly consistent level, nothing can match 1983-84 and I salute manager Denis Smith, coach Viv Busby and the players for giving so much pleasure to so many.

I am often asked at the start of a season how I think City will fare and I always say, 'ask me again when the team has played 12 matches and I can see what pattern is emerging'.

Outstanding

This season it was easier, for when City won

Champions!

101 points

96 goals

York Evening Post sports editor Malcolm Huntington reports our record-breaking season.

Making my point to defender Ricky Sbragia

After knocking out Arsenal from the FA Cup we drew Liverpool at home. The frost nearly claimed the tie, but our innovative groundsman covered the Bootham Crescent pitch with straw, volunteers cleared it all away making the pitch playable and, left, I convinced referee Peter Willis that the game should go ahead. We drew 1-1 and could have beaten the treble winners.

dreadful challenge by Ipswich's Mick Mills. Later, on Boxing Day 1974, winger Jimmy Robertson broke his leg in the first minute of our game at Coventry and did not play again that season. For a club like ours these were major difficulties to have to cope with. To cap it all they were to either creative players, or goalscorers. It stretched the squad to the limit.

There would be more injury problems later in the season, but those broken legs weren't the only setbacks of the early autumn of 1974. Thanks to our tremendous run of form and fifth-placed finish we had qualified for the UEFA Cup. In the first round we drew one of Europe's most feared teams, Ajax. I had always wanted to test myself against the best. That was my raison d'etre for playing top flight football. Pure and simple. Ajax had invented 'total football' and dominated Europe. They were the best. As winners of the European Cup for three successive seasons from 1971 to 1973, and providers of the vast majority of the Dutch side which had reached the 1974 World Cup final, I relished the prospect of facing them. Johan Cruyff and Johann Neeskens may have been sold to Barcelona in the summer, but with Ruud Krol, Johnny Rep, Piet Schrijvers, Arnold Muhren and Arie Haan in their team they were as good as any side around.

The 1972 League Cup win had seen us enter the UEFA Cup the following season. Drawn against German side Kaiserslautern, we won 3-1 in the first leg at the Vic, but were completely taken apart 4-0 in the return, so I was determined we would learn from that experience. But the build up to this huge game was upset by news of an incident involving our star player. There was a huge social scene around the club back then, as I think is common knowledge. Most of the lads loved a drink or two, as did the manager, and on the plus side it really did help bond a lot of the team together. I liked a drink with the best of them, but only at the right time. During the week leading up to the Ajax first leg, on his way home Alan crashed his car, badly damaging his hand. He played against the Dutch, but with his limb in plaster and groggy under the influence of painkillers. He didn't disgrace himself, but Huddy wasn't the dominant influence he was capable of being.

We really wanted a two goal lead to take to Amsterdam if possible, but knew it would be very tough. We fielded the same back six in both legs against Ajax as had played in the ignominious defeat in Kaiserslautern – Farmer, Marsh, Pejic, myself, Bloor and Mahoney as the defensive midfielder – so we had plenty to make up for. It was a tight game, although we struggled to win the ball off Ajax's midfield and late in the first half Ruud Krol smashed a 30 yard shot beyond John Farmer to give the Dutch the lead. Krol was Huddy's man and Alan knows that he should have closed him down, but he was just those few vital seconds off his game that night because of his car crash. That also meant we didn't create much at all in the first hour of the match.

Finally, with fifteen minutes to go, we managed to get a foothold in the game. From a free-kick Mike Pejic shot with his left foot, but it was touched against the post by Schrijvers. I had been up in the penalty area in case the ball was crossed and had followed in after the ball. I lunged in to prod it over line, leaving my marker Dusvaba sprawled on the ground in the process. I had scored against Ajax.

There was no time to glory in that achievement. We had to win the game. We put them under some pressure with crosses into the box and plenty more set pieces, and I should have had a hat-trick with the crosses we put in to be honest. Ajax didn't like that approach to the game and we unsettled them a bit, but essentially they were in control that night, although we felt we now knew enough about them to give them a good game over in Holland.

I was fairly battered and bruised after that match and had to have three stitches in a cut just below my eye which I'd done lunging in to score the goal, but I had loved the competitive nature of the game and the cut and thrust of European competition. It was football at the highest level.

At the time it was rare for British players to go abroad. Those that had experienced mixed fortunes. Denis Law and John Charles were huge heroes in Italy, for example, but the likes of Jimmy Greaves had failed. It wasn't until Kevin Keegan made the move to Hamburg in 1977 where he ended up becoming European Footballer of the Year two season in succession that it began to be a serious option to consider. I think if the opportunity had arisen I would have considered it simply from the point of view of learning new things, both on the pitch and off it, but it never did.

Alan Hudson was back firing on all cylinders for the second leg against Ajax in Amsterdam. We were not intimidated at all by playing Europe's biggest name in their own backyard and took the game to them from the off. We kept them quite quiet overall, and only really allowed them a couple of sniffs at goal. Farmer palmed away a Haan volley and saved point blank from Mulder. At the other end we had plenty of chances, but none of them would go in. Haslegrave brought a fine save from Schrijvers with a 15 yard shot and then Greenhoff swerved a 20-yarder just past the post. Huddy, Sammy and Josh were getting the upper hand in midfield. As it became obvious that one goal would steal the game, Schrijvers had to scramble back onto his line to tip over a Greenhoff chip. Then, after he had come on as a substitute, Terry Conroy got to the byline and curled a cross against the bar. We were so close, but nothing had quite dropped for us in their box.

Then, right at the death, came the moment that so nearly won us the game. As we pressed forward and Ajax looked to defend their away goal lead, the ball bobbled around their penalty area before falling to our other substitute, Jimmy Robertson. He was six yards out and only the keeper to beat. The ball fell really nicely to him on the half volley, but he slipped slightly as he struck it and didn't get a full contact. His point blank shot hit the flailing Schrijvers on the left boot and ricocheted to safety. We were inches from scoring. Only that outstretched boot saved the mighty Ajax from defeat.

Shortly after that, amidst some last minute scrambles in the penalty area, TC shot over from eight yards with only the keeper to beat. When the final whistle sounded it was agonising. I felt that we had done so well that, although I was obviously disappointed that we had gone out of the competition, we had proved a massive point that we could compete at the highest level. It was a shame that all most Stoke fans ever saw of the game was some very short TV highlights, which didn't do us justice at all as they just showed three or four missed chances, rather than the domination of the game we'd had. I prefer to remember what Brian Clough, recently sacked as Leeds manager and who travelled with us to the away tie as an observer said to us after the game, "it deserved to be the final. It was that good."

Would we have won if Huddy hadn't had a few pints, hadn't had that crash? Who knows. Huddy now often claims that we'd have beaten Ajax in the first leg if he hadn't had that car smash, but they were so good that night, so much in control, that I'm not sure that even a fully fit and firing Hudson would have made that much difference.

Drinking was an integral part of being a footballer in the 1960s and 70s. It served the twin function of relaxing players and allowing them to bond in each others' company. There have been far too many examples of footballers tumbling off the rails, and suffering badly after falling pray to the demon drink. Now I don't think that Huddy ever went that far, but his lifestyle did lead to several incidents I remember. Don't get me wrong, Alan Hudson was a joy to play with when he was sober. In fact I'd go so far as to say that there are very few people who are capable of playing as well as Huddy did when he had a few drinks.

There was a culture of boozing as we were a very sociable club, something Tony Waddington used at times to attract people such as Huddy to come up north. His main partner in crime was new signing Geoff Salmons, a £160,000 capture from Sheffield United. Sammy was a cultured left-sided midfielder who effectively replaced the retired George Eastham, but his capacity for drink matched the sweetness of his left peg. I realised I couldn't have done my job and drunk what they did. It was the kind of culture that bred George Best and later Paul Gascoigne as extreme examples of an endemic disease amongst footballers. I just looked on in total amazement.

Tony Waddington didn't have rules as such. He thought the lads going out together and having a few drinks wasn't a problem and most of the time it wasn't. His attitude was 'as long as you turn up on Saturday and play and play well, what's the problem?' Roy Vernon once told me that "the problem with this club is there are no rules." Waddo's attitude left a lot of leeway to hang yourself. So Huddy did. That incident before the Ajax game was just the first of many. In fact in many ways Huddy was lucky. A session like that later cost midfielder Sammy Irvine, who was part of our 1979 promotion side, his career. Sammy had been out on a session with Huddy and Sammy and was driving home when he crashed his car. He was never able to get back fit enough to play again. It's a crying shame when those sort of things happen.

Essentially I don't think there is any harm in players having social drinks. But as a manager, having seen where it can lead and how it can affect players on the pitch, I have enforced strict rules on booze. No drinking after Wednesday night or for two days before any game. It's a very difficult rule to enforce because you never know what they might drink about their own house and unless they come in stinking of it you can't do anything about it – they do say don't make rules you can't enforce.

The thing about Huddy was that as well as being a big drinker, he's always been a big talker, so after any little misdemeanour he'd come in telling us all about it the next morning at training. It might be a night out on the town, or an all night session with a couple of the other lads. He wasn't boasting, just sharing the joke. But Waddo always heard what was going on. He never stepped in to stop it, though. In many ways he loved being a part of it himself as he felt it created a strong bond between us all, but when it created problems it frustrated me intensely.

Around that time sponsored cars were just coming in, but Huddy spoilt all that for us because his vehicles would regularly be found abandoned in hedges, in the middle of the road, all over the place. The sponsors were understandably perturbed by this and because of that nobody else could get one because Huddy, being the big star of the team, had been the first one to get one.

Whenever we were on tour or I was away with the lads I had a rule, I wouldn't have a drink until at least 7 o'clock. But some of the lads started at lunchtime on their days off. I decided to try alternative pursuits instead, so I'd go swimming or I'd read. I'm an avid reader of books. It may sound boring but I couldn't see the point of all the daytime drinking because by the evening they didn't know what they were doing half the time. At least I could enjoy the evening.

There was a famous incident in August 1975 when we were due to play Arsenal. On the Thursday morning Waddo let Huddy and his big drinking buddy Geoff Salmons, skip off to the big smoke, where of course Huddy hailed from, with a promise from them to arrive at the ground in plenty of time on the Saturday morning. So off they went, taking in a race meeting on the way on the Thursday afternoon, before spending that night and all day Friday out on the town. By the time they pitched up at Highbury they were totally wasted. Absolutely whacked. Huddy couldn't even bend down to do up his boots in the dressing room to go out and warm up.

I went berserk, hauling Alan up against the wall in the dressing room, yelling, "what's going on? This is my living, it's my mortgage your playing with." I was livid and told Waddo, "I ain't playing with them." I found it amazing that Waddo hadn't hauled that Huddy and Sammy over the coals. Waddo hated that kind of confrontation and said he'd handle it, telling me to calm down. I remember being so frustrated that I felt Huddy was pissing my mortgage up the wall, but Waddo just wanted to take the sting out of it instead of disciplining the offenders.

So what happens? Huddy only goes out and scores, just before half-time! After he'd found the net, Huddy came up to me and said, "Den. I've scored. Now it's your job to keep them out"!

We won that game 1-0. We barely glimpsed Huddy after his goal, but we won the game!

I still think Huddy was a fantastic footballer and so will never decry what he was good, but I would regularly be crying at the other things he did which infuriated me, but that was because he and I were so different. He would tell me that I was wrong, but fair play to him nowadays he tells me, "Den, you were our Tony Adams." So any fall outs were purely temporary as we both admire each other's abilities. But ultimately I feel I maximised my potential, whereas he had an abundance of talent and, I think, he wasted it. Huddy disagrees. But if you ever get the chance to see a video of his international debut against West Germany in which he played Gunther Netzer off the park and took the World Champions to pieces you'll see what I mean. He could have been a world figure. The fact he wasn't is down to the way he conducted himself off the field. The point is that you don't know what he did after that game at Wembley. He quite possibly had two days on the piss to celebrate his dazzling performance or something. The thing is it was just a part of him. You can's separate Huddy the player, and his vivacious and audacious skill, from Huddy the person. I think he wasted his talent, he doesn't. Huddy and I will have to agree to differ on that one.

Huddy may have been the mega star in our team, but that suqad was packed with personalities and pin-ups. We'd had Gordon Banks and Geoff Hurst, and numbered Josh Mahoney, Terry Conroy, Jackie Marsh and Geoff Salmons among our high profile players. I was lucky enough to be approached to be one of the first to be asked to do some modelling for a local clothes retailer called Regalia, who were based in Hanley. It was the boutique that everybody went to for the trendy, in-gear at that time, although this being the 1970s the pictures tell a different story! I used to have some weird dress sense at the time – six inch lapels and 12 inch flares. It was great fun. They did give me the clothes, which was a bit of an incentive to do the shots, and that led to me turning up at one of the PFA awards dinners, which is always a black tie do, in a white suit, with a brown dress shirt with ruffles and the James Bond dickie bow and everything. Yes, I did get fearful stick!

Aside from just drinking there were plenty of other social activities we'd get involved in. One of these was the Stoke City cricket team. It featured the bowling of Geoff Hurst, who'd once played a county cricket match for his home county of Essex, Tony Allen and Peter Dobing, and myself, who were all decent players. We would get together to play in benefit games, most often against Lancashire, whose team would feature the likes of Clive Lloyd, David Lloyd, Faroukh Engineer, John Lever, and 'Flat' Jack Simmons. They would always be great social occasions, raising money for a good cause and I really enjoyed them.

Around this time I was being mooted in the press as a potential England player. I thought it was not before time, but then I always was a confident lad! I attended several get togethers, including the infamous one early in the Don Revie era when about forty top pros were brought together for a week of what turned out to be drinking and moaning about how they weren't earning enough money for playing for their country. Even the manager sat us down and talked about how much he'd get us all as bonuses for playing, scoring, keeping clean sheets or qualifying. Everything revolved around the money. Perhaps it was no surprise when Revie bailed out to work in Saudi Arabia for a pot full of cash. I thought 'I don't want to listen to this'. I just wanted to play for England. The desire burned inside me. It was a massive ambition I'd held ever since I'd begun playing football seriously.

I was certainly at the pinnacle of my personal career, in the form of my life, playing in a team heading the First Division table for periods of a topsy-turvy season. Waddo's gamble all those seasons ago on the raw youngster who he had so many misgivings about had come off. It had now got to the stage where other clubs were coming in for me, making huge offers to prise me away from Stoke. I now know that Manchester United, Leeds, Nottingham Forest and Ajax, after my performance against them in that pulsating UEFA Cup tie, made formal approaches for me. I also believe that an Italian club made an offer for me, but I don't know which one. I now know that the offer Leeds made for me would have been a world record fee for a defender of £250,000. That would have made me more expensive than Huddy!

Brian Clough, who had just joined Nottingham Forest, an unfashionable club he would take to double European glory, also wanted me. He loved me. Cloughie used to regale me with this one particular story about how much he rated me. He had brought his son Nigel, who would go on to stardom himself, to watch the youth team as I was making my comeback following a major knee injury in 1975. I put in a dominant performance, as you might expect at that level, although this was my first game back after several months out, and scored a hat-trick to boot. All the way home Cloughie raved on to Nigel about me, and he was that impressed he got done for speeding because he totally lost his concentration!

Cloughie was a one off, incredible. He had a simple mantra, not dissimilar to Waddo's – sign good players. The thing about Cloughie was that often people didn't realise the players he signed were good players until he bought them. Garry Birtles, Peter Davenport, John Robertson, Kenny Burns and Larry Lloyd, for example all won the European Cup with Forest, but all failed elsewhere. Clough could judge a footballer and, crucially, see how he might or might not fit into his team. Anybody can see Rooney or Ronaldo is a great talent, it's being able to look in other places where people aren't expecting to see something that marks out a truly great manager. Look at Arsene Wenger these days. He has made a career out of producing rabbits from hats – Thierry Henry being just one example, but there are many more.

I loved Cloughie too, and had done ever since I first got to know him when he'd accompanied us on that trip to Holland to play Ajax. I asked him to speak at my testimonial dinner in 1981 and he came along with Peter Shilton, who he'd signed from

Stoke three seasons earlier. Word had got around that Clough was speaking and so I had people queuing up outside trying to buy tickets. It was a black tie do and all these folk turned up with dinner jackets on not knowing whether they'd get in! Brian was very good at supporting people in that way, much like Sir Alex Ferguson is today. Cloughie didn't charge me a penny for that dinner and he said some of the nicest things ever about me.

Tony Waddington's answer to all of these flattering enquiries from major clubs was to just tell them all in no uncertain terms to "get lost." I was never any the wiser until long after the event. That was how it was then. I was a Stoke City player. They owned me and I could not make any decisions as to my own future. That all changed with the Bosman ruling as we know. But as it happens I was very happy with that situation. At that time I thought I was in absolutely the right place. I was a hero in my home town, performing out of my skin in a side challenging for honours. I was the first name on Waddo's team sheet. What more could I want? Money didn't come into it. The wages were not so disparate as they are today when one of the big four clubs can simply buy internationals, paying them extortionate wages, to keep them on the bench or in the reserves so that other clubs don't have them to play against them. Money has never held a strong pull for me, I've never asked for a new contract as a player, for example, the club simply improved my terms on what seemed like a reasonable and equitable basis, so I was happy because I was playing in a successful team. As a manager I've never been that bothered about the money as long I get paid a reasonable return. I wouldn't have taken the jobs I did if I was motivated by cash. It was the desire to succeed, or to change the fortunes of a club that drew me in. That's just how I am. And anyway, we were challenging for the big prize by now – the League Championship. Footballers through time have fought tooth and nail over the course of nine months to lift the ultimate accolade in the game. Nothing can beat winning the league, it marks you out as the best. It is the Olympics, it is the Ashes, it is the Formula 1 world title, the heavyweight boxing crown. Win it and you have proved you are the best. I was sure that we could achieve that.

Some of the rebuffed clubs tried the less formal approach too. I was invited to Bobby Charlton's testimonial dinner in Manchester. I had no idea why I'd had the call to ask if I'd like to attend, but it soon became apparent as various United directors and then Bobby himself plied me with drinks and asked me if I was happy at Stoke or how much I envied United's wonderful Old Trafford stadium. In fact I saw United's European Cup-winning midfielder Paddy Crerand recently and he said to me, "Den, if only you had signed. We'd have won more European trophies with you."

Now technically I suppose that 'invitation' was what would today be called 'tapping up'. I didn't think any more of it. It was done in the classiest of ways, and was just a gentle nudge in the ribs to politely enquire as to whether I might be interested. I wasn't. In the modern era agents have changed all of that. Now they do actively foment dissent on occasions. Not all of them by any means. There are in fact a lot of very good, honourable agents and they do perform a very necessary service. But there are quite a few dishonourable exceptions.

I also felt that the international recognition which had been so long in coming my way was now just around the corner. We'd made the breakthrough as a club when Mike Pejic was called into the England team to play the Home International tournament in 1974, becoming the first Stoke City outfield player to be capped by England since Tony Allen in 1959. I was called into several of Alf Ramsey's last squads, but never made the final group of players for the games, as Alf felt I got injured too often for him to justify giving me a chance. I could see his point, but I was missing out to the likes of Steve Whitworth, Jeff Blockley and Larry Lloyd, which irked me no end. Personally I thought only Derby County's majestic Roy McFarland was better than me. What a defensive pairing we would have made. For the record Roy, who also played for a less fashionable club, only won 28 England caps, so to say that the selection process at that time was all over the place would be putting it mildly. I'm not saying that if I'd been in the team it would have all been different, but I do think that my situation was a symptom of the wider malaise of inconsistent selection and managers picking favourites. It was also an era when you got picked because of who you played for, with Liverpool and Manchester United players receiving preference, even though United were relegated in 1973!

I would never win an England cap, something which does hurt me still. But I've learned to live with it. It does get dragged up occasionally and led to one funny incident when I was manager of Wrexham towards the end of the 2005/06 season. At that time I had on my team a massive centre-half called Dennis Lawrence. Dennis, bless him, is a wonderful man, with a brilliant attitude and winning smile. He proved to be a huge inspiration in so many ways to the people of Wrexham, Swansea, to whom I sold him shortly afterwards for £100,000 to pay the bills at the Racecourse Ground, and Trinidad & Tobago, his home island in the Caribbean. In November 2005, Dennis scored the goal that won his national side a play-off against Bahrain to qualify them for the following summer's World Cup in Germany, where they would eventually play against England and famously draw against Sweden. The goal was an absolute belter of a header from 16 yards which rocketed into the net. Dennis became a hero and the focus of a lot of media attention overnight.

Shortly afterwards we were playing at Carlisle when Dennis, who was renowned for his inability to find his forward with clearances, whacked a long ball, but sliced it horribly into the stand. The home fans hooted with derision and the Carlisle assistant manager Dennis Booth, who was standing in their technical area next to me shouted across, "Den. How come he's going to a World Cup when you never played for England?!" I had to laugh. As I've said before, football is many things, but it is almost never fair.

******

Perhaps the clinching thing for me which convinced me that Stoke City were set to be a force to be reckoned with in the next decade was the signing of England international goalkeeper Peter Shilton in October 1974. Now Banks was gone Shilton was simply the best in the business, as he would go on to prove over a career which lasted another 22 seasons and saw him win a record 125 caps, including being an integral part of the team which reached the semi-final of the Italia 90 World Cup.

Waddo paid Leicester City a world record fee for a goalkeeper of £325,000 and within a fortnight, on the back of three clean sheets and that 2-2 draw at home to Wolves, we were on top of the First Division. We had sent a message to the football world. Stoke City meant business.

As ever in football, the signing of a huge star like Shilton meant the end for a lesser name, but arguably no less a talent. Since the loss of Gordon Banks, Waddo had stuck for a couple of years with England Under 23 goalkeeper John Farmer. John was a very talented goalkeeper, but he was prone, much like David James in the modern era, to make the occasional blunder. There would be two or three a season, and the problem with making such mistakes as a goalkeeper was that they almost inevitably lost us a vital goal.

Eventually I think what destroyed John was an incident right on full-time in our game against Chelsea in October 1974. I remember he was having a bad time with crosses that day. Ian Hutchinson was slinging balls in for Chelsea's huge centre-half Mickey Droy to come in and plough right into John, hurting him in the process. That eventually caused farmer to stop coming for crosses or drop some because he had half an eye on where Droy was in case he got hurt again. Right at the death, John came for a cross and dropped it. Chelsea scored a late equaliser to make the final score 3-3 and Waddo, fuming at another in this series of errors by John, decided he had to act. That goal cost a vital point, which would have seen us climb into third place. If we had true ambition to win the championship we could not afford any more such incidents. It was a defining moment for John. Waddo moved to bring in a new goalkeeper.

It was a cruel, but necessary choice in my opinion. Given the opportunity any of us would swap a club goalkeeper for the one lauded as the best in the country, if not the world. Farmer, once he'd taken in the enormity of what had happened simply chose to retire from football. He was 27 and went into a career in sales for Walkers Crisps, doing extremely well, as I would expect for such a bright, educated man.

The problem for us was that John's replacement did not fit in well to our team at all. Great goalkeeper though Peter Shilton undoubtedly was, his three years at Stoke were probably the worst of his career. Perhaps we'd been spoilt with all those years playing with Gordon Banks, who not only organised us superbly from the edge of his box, but would be ready to deal with through balls. Shilton, as he would later prove in a Wembley up final when he cost Nottingham Forest the 1980 League Cup by clattering into central defender David Needham to leave Wolves' Andy Gray a tap in, was not good at hovering up through balls.

We just couldn't get an understanding at all. As a ball came over the top, I would be thinking 'why is he back on his line?' Other times I would think the ball was mine only to find Shilton had come out to collect and I'd be in danger of running into him.

Shilts was more of a line keeper and shot stopper. He hated being beaten, even in training. I feel that was one of the reasons behind his longevity in international football, because the game was different and there are never so many crosses. He was a great one-on-one, brilliant the best I've ever seen but as far as reading the game and all-round play Banksy, in my opinion – and I am one of very few people who played for a sustained period directly in front of both men – was far, far better.

I also feel Peter's obsession with training was not such a positive attribute as many make it out to be. Sure it prolonged his career until he was into his forties, but I thought he trained too much. We'd have arguments about it. He'd be for staying after training to practice catching crosses and wanting someone to stay with him to continually pump balls into the box. We wanted to relax and conserve energy.

In fact I know that when he joined Nottingham Forest Cloughie put a stop to his over-training.

Clough had realised that it was at the root of his lack of form, focussed him and Shilts went on to help Forest win back-to-back European Cups. Now that is management.

Shilton may have been a tremendous pro, but he had this obsessive side to his nature that also led to his significant and well-documented gambling habit. I think his gambling was a bit like his playing, it was an obsession. We would be on the coach to and from a game and the usual card school would be in operation at the back of the bus. Shilts would hit a losing streak and get a huge cob on him. I never played, but I used to try to point out to him how he was losing, but he'd insist "I'm alright".

"But they are taking money off you left, right and centre," I'd say.

"No, no, no – I'm winning."

He wasn't.

Eventually some of the lads like Terry Conroy stopped him playing because he was losing too much to them. He didn't want to be helped at that stage, though. Fortunately Shilts is over that now.

It's my belief that Waddo made a mistake with Shilts. He overreacted to that one particular match in which John Farmer made a couple of mistakes. I'm not saying John was the best out there, Shilton would prove to be that in time, but Shilts was not the right man for our club and our team. He knows it himself. His form dipped and he lost his place in the England team to Liverpool's Ray Clemence. In fact Peter played just three times for England during his three years at Stoke. By the end he was in the international and club wilderness and in his autobiography he describes his time at the club as his 'lost years'.

The real tragedy was that the Shilton signing changed the balance of the squad. Waddo had gone out there and spent the entire £325,000 he had at his disposal on Shilts when, given the talent we'd already lost to injury that season – Robertson and Ritchie – we could really have done with a striker. £325,000 was a lot of money in those days. We needed another striker. We needed a John Richards or somebody to score goals.

And I firmly believe if Waddo had spent the money on a goalscorer instead of Peter Shilton we would have won the league that season.

As it was Stoke entered the New Year of 1975 in fifth place in the league, a point behind leaders Ipswich Town. We went out of the FA Cup in the third round, losing 0-2 to Liverpool, so in time honoured fashion could concentrate on the league, except this time we were in with a chance of winning it. By mid-February, via that magnificent 4-0 victory over Manchester City, we were back on top of the table thanks to a 2-2 draw with Wolves. But that rousing late comeback to earn a point came at a cost. Left-back Mike Pejic broke his leg in a fierce challenge with Wolves striker Steve Kindon. The injury curse had struck again. Now we'd lost three major players through broken legs during the season and a fourth was only just around the corner.

Our next home game was against title rivals Ipswich. It proved to be a dreadful day for the club and myself personally. The team slumped to second home defeat of the season and I suffered a fifth broken leg of my career. This time I had no-one to blame but myself. The game was poised at 1-2 to the visitors when Ipswich's Mick Lambert was sent clear to race through on goal. Mick was quick. I was faced with a choice of letting him race ahead to take Shilton on, or bringing him down. I lunged and tripped him up. It was a fairly cynical 'professional foul' if I'm brutally honest. But I would argue necessary in the context of the game. We were chasing an equaliser and could not afford to go two goals behind with only a dozen minutes left. I certainly did not hurt Lambert. In fact quite the opposite. As referee Gow hared over to give me what I can only assume would have been a red card, although the automatic dismissal for that kind of offence was still a way off, I told him that it was a waste of time him getting his cards out because I'd have to go off anyway. One glance down at my right knee told me that I'd buggered my leg. I hobbled off. Ultimately it didn't help the team either. Our substitute had already been used so we were down to ten men. Ipswich hung on to win a vital game 2-1.

The problem for me was that not only did I break the bone, but the massive trauma to the knee damaged the cartilage badly and even when I was back playing again I had continual problems. In November 1975 I had to have an operation to remove it, which was a major and new procedure at that time. Nowadays it's keyhole surgery, but then it meant going under general anaesthetic and leaving a huge scar across my knee.

To cap it all, on the day of the operation, which took place in Coventry because the surgeon there had some experience of this kind of injury, my mum died. They didn't want me to leave the hospital, but of course I had to. I was desperate to get home and be with everyone. All seven siblings were gathering to support dad. But I had this bloody plaster on covering my entire leg and because of the lack of time spent convalescing my knee blew up inside the cast, effectively knackering my chances of a complete recovery. When I went back in for a check up after the funeral they sent me home saying it was alright –it wasn't. Not really.

That injury was the worst I ever suffered. It signalled the end of my period at the top of my game. The biggest killer as far as I was concerned was that it finally did for my chances of winning a much coveted England cap. Ironically the man I thought was my biggest rival for one of the central defensive places in the England side, Roy McFarland, also got badly injured around the same time. His problem was a ruptured Achilles. Neither of us would be the same again. From that point until the end of my playing career in 1982 I played at half pace, having to some extent to nurse my knee though games as it never bent properly again. If I'm honest I was only really top class until 1975. After that I played 80% with my head, with my knowledge and reading of the game allowing me to beat opponents, willing my body to keep up. I was finished as a truly top class performer.

The succession of injuries threatened to derail our championship ambitions. There was a big question mark over who would provide the goals to push us back to the top of the table as none of the three remaining strikers – Hurst, Greenhoff and Ian Moores – were that prolific, but to give the lads credit we stuck in there right until the end. A lot of that was due to the return of Terry Conroy, the impish Irish winger, from similar knee injury problems to my own. TC had by this stage got no cartilages left, something he, like many pro players of that era, is paying for now he's entering his sixties. But as the team entered the run in to the season still in with a shout of the title, his return galvanised the entire club. He went on a fantastic scoring spree, netting 13 goals in 16 games, including a hat-trick in the 5-2 hammering of doomed Carlisle. He wasn't a natural goalscorer, Terry, but with fresh legs and pressed into service up front alongside Jimmy, he added a new dimension and a lot of pace to the team.

During the run in my role was to keep spirits up and minds on the job. I'd be in the dressing room before the game talking to the players who'd be going out there. I tried to take on the job of keeping everybody bubbling, but focussed. I suppose it was he beginnings of my managerial career in the sense of dealing with a dressing room packed with nerves, tension and anticipation. I discovered that I'm good in that situation, but all the time I was wishing I was going out there. It was so frustrating not to be involved. You sit in the stands kicking every ball, heading away every cross. It's probably worse to be in that position rather than out there on the pitch involved in the action, but as a manager it's what you have to get used to.

My replacement was a young centre-half called Alan Dodd. Doddy was a very different personality again. He was very quiet and obviously at that stage lacked experience, although he would eventually play 416 games in his Stoke career. He was an unbelievable athlete. Even today he runs marathons for fun. But the problem with Doddy was that he didn't know how good he was. He had to be pushed and coerced into even thinking about it. He had barely any sense of desire to win. He was almost entirely opposite in personality to me. He was, however, a fabulously skilful player who read the game wonderfully well and played the ball out from the back superbly. He just didn't really believe in himself. It was a way of making a living for Doddy. It just so happened he was a very talented footballer. He would probably have been far just as happy being a builder or plasterer. You never felt that Doddy thought that playing the game was that important – whereas I had the burning passion to play football and to win. I was also the talker in the back four, and I think that was another element which cost Stoke in that run in.

Mike Pejic's replacement was a young left-back called Danny Bowers, who was thrown into the mix alongside Doddy and did OK. Danny never went on to have a long career, and was probably pitched into the heat of a title battle before he was ready. But needs must in times of injury crisis. He certainly didn't let anyone down, although the team missed Pej's experience, tenacity and over-lapping runs down the wing.

On Easter Monday 1975, a couple of weeks after a last minute Jimmy Greenhoff goal had given a massive boost of a win at title rivals Derby, the side faced a massive game against Liverpool at the Vic. 46,000 packed into the ground to delight in a virtuoso performance by Terry Conroy, who scored both goals in a 2-0 victory. This was a fantastic result, which put us right back in the mix for the title again.

TC netted a penalty after Josh Mahoney was felled by Phil Thompson, and then was sent clean through to beat Ray Clemence at the second attempt. The Liverpool defenders just were not quick enough to catch him. Terry had a winning combination of brains and pace, which gives any defender a huge problem. If players are merely quick you can catch them offside, but TC had a footballing brain and to ally with that pace and at the top level that's frightening. He had two or three seasons when he was unplayable before the damage to his knees began to affect his form.

Terry was also a strong character. He's a funny lad – a pain in the backside really! Full of pranks. Some days your socks would go missing after training or your shoelaces would be tied together. He loved getting up to mischief. He's just natural funny. He loved taking the Mick and to be honest that was good because I was too serious. Sometimes I would get a bit too intense and Terry helped me to relax a little bit. You need people like TC to take the edge off tense situations, which is something Waddo understood. He knew the kind of blend of personalities you need to make a good team. On the field Terry was just the same. He caused opponents all kinds of problems with his skill, pace and vivacious, irrepressible spirit.

The Saturday after that fantastic win over Bob Paisley's team, we thrashed Chelsea 3-0, Terry scoring twice more. He was in a rich vein of scoring form and that win took us level on points with three other teams – Liverpool, Everton and Derby – at the top of the table. Ipswich were a point behind, with a game in hand, and the best goal average. It was all to play for.

Our last three fixtures were away at Sheffield United and then Burnley, with a visit by Newcastle sandwiched in between. The team had scored five goals without reply in defeating Liverpool and Chelsea in the last two games and everyone was buzzing. Even with the injuries we thought we were in with hell of a chance. The title, in the most open and exciting top flight season in living memory, was well and truly on.

But then the wheels came off. We lost at Sheffield United when Shilton miscalculated on one of those through balls and upended Bill Dearden to concede a penalty and Anthony Field scored a brilliant individual goal to send the team crashing to a 0-2 defeat. We were still in with a chance, but needed to win both our last two matches. Just when we really needed the side to rise to the challenge, the boys could not find it within them to raise their game. Both the games ended goalless. We really should have been beating 15th placed Newcastle at home at that stage. Somehow we finished fifth, while Derby won the title, finishing four points ahead of us. We had a better goal average, so two more wins would have won us the title. In fact if we'd won those last three matches we'd have won the league by a clear point. Instead we picked up just the two draws and failed to score a goal. That decision to invest in Peter Shilton and not a striker had come home to roost.

It's interesting actually when you look at the results. The team only kept three clean sheets after I was injured. Could that have made a difference? We conceded the last goals of the games to draw at both West Ham and Arsenal just before those fantastic Easter victories, for example. In many ways wondering what might have been is irrelevant, but I can't help thinking that the defence needed me to get in there and pull people together to keep it tight when necessary. Bluto was never good at that, Doddy definitely wouldn't do it, Danny was a kid and Jackie, at right-back, wasn't the type either. My job was to organise and do the talking, because that's what I'm good at. So in the end the reason we didn't win the league championship could come down to me making that rash tackle.

As it was we finished a season of great promise totally empty-handed. Another point would have seen us into Europe, so we didn't even have a UEFA Cup spot to act as any kind of consolation. After riding all the blows which had come our way since lifting the League Cup, and coming so close to the Championship, to miss out on the run in to the season was agony to watch – particularly from my seat in the stands. We had failed. As a group of players we had not had the mental strength or the ability when it came to the crunch. Had we been Champions how might life have been different then? Success breeds success and attracts bigger players, bigger names, more attention in the media and would have lifted Stoke City onto a new level, one which the club has never been able to attain.

Instead, the following winter, as the team purred along nicely in the chasing bunch as the 1975/76 season unfolded, a further twist of fate, this time causing irreparable damage, literally blew the club apart.

Chapter Ten

BLOW THE
HOUSE DOWN

Despite the fact we hadn't invested in any major signings by the start of 1975/76, our squad was easily good enough to compete for the title again. But I remember speaking to Waddo at that time and telling him that in my opinion we needed a striker to really make the difference. He just looked at me and said "I haven't got any more money". He'd blown his budget on signing Peter Shilton and it hadn't come off. In fact I'm sure from his reaction that he'd over spent.

I'd worked so hard over the summer of 1975 to get fully fit again and I was delighted to be back in contention for a first team spot come the first game of a new season against West Ham, but I knew I wasn't quite the same player because of the injury and everything had gone on. I was also under pressure to play earlier than I should have done. Waddo wanted me to play and so I did. But my knee blew up, leading to the cartilage operation and I soon discovered that had cost me vital mobility and pace. I was never as good after 1976 as I had been before that.

Even then, following a run of three wins in four games, by November 1975 we'd fought our way into seventh place in the division, just three points off top spot. We were helped by the inspirational return of Jimmy Robertson, who'd been out for almost a year with a broken leg. On his return against Everton he came on after 65 minutes with us 1-2 down and changed the game, causing endless problems for the opposing defence with his speed and close skill, scoring an equaliser on 80 minutes and then creating the winner for Ian Moores just 60 seconds later.

The following week we visited second placed Queen's Park Rangers and another five goal thriller ensued. We fancied our chances as we'd already won five games away from home, which was an outstanding record and we feared no-one at this stage. We gave it a real good go. This time, though, it was us who let in a late goal, with David Webb poking home in a goalmouth scramble in injury time. That was gutting as we felt we'd got a good chance to get right into the shake up by Christmas. As it was we were eighth at the turn of the year. I felt we were set for a good go at the UEFA Cup places if all went well, and was looking forward to the FA Cup. But I was reckoning without a twist of fate which was as unpredictable as it was devastating.

In the early hours of 2 January 1976 a storm whirled around the Potteries, causing minor damage around the city. The Victoria Ground did not escape so lightly. When we turned up for training we discovered that the roof of the Butler Street stand, which ran the length of the pitch opposite the main Boothen Stand, had crashed down, causing countless thousands of pounds worth of damage. The roof was, I think, a good 60 years old or so, certainly pre-war. It was one of those old barrel-shaped constructions like a Dutch bran, but now it was lying in shards across the pitch and the terracing. Of course we thought it was a really bad thing to have happened, but we didn't realise quite how disastrous until little whispers began emerging from the offices into the dressing room that there was a major problem on the horizon.

First we had to get over the small matter of not having a ground to play on as rebuilding work began. Port Vale loaned us their Vale Park pitch for the one and only time that Stoke have played a home game on enemy territory. We beat Middlesbrough 1-0, but all that was a sideshow to the soap opera which was unfolding behind the scenes. The board had revealed to manager Tony Waddington that the stand which had been all but demolished by the gale was not insured. That meant in order to rebuild it money had to be raised. Waddo's overspending was really coming home to roost in the cruellest fashion. The cost of the construction of the new Butler Street stand would have to be covered by sales of players. Disappointingly all that came out to us in the media. We were never sat down and told. We discovered what was going on in dribs and drabs. Soon it became obvious that a fire sale would ensue.

First to be sold were Sean Haslegrave for £35,000 to Nottingham Forest and then Ian Moores to Tottenham for £75,000. To give him credit Waddo was at least trying to keep his crown jewels. But over £250,000 needed to be raised, plus the scenario was affecting our form as everyone was worried about how the club was coping. Huddy and Pej both slapped in transfer requests and crowds were regularly dipping below the 20,000 mark, something that was exacerbated by falling gates because of the problem of terrace violence and other options for entertainment on a Saturday opening up.

As a player you don't often get involved with the financial side of the club. Your focus is purely on playing football. It's part of being cocooned in the world of playing the game. Nothing else should matter, so you don't concern yourself with it. That is until it creates problems for you. Within a couple of weeks in November 1976 Waddo was forced to sell Jimmy Greenhoff, for £120,000 to Manchester United, and Alan Hudson, for £200,000 to Arsenal.

Jimmy's sale was pivotal to the downfall of the club, in my opinion. He had been the fulcrum of all that was good and exciting at Stoke City for eight years and he still had two or three more years at the top in him. It hurt all the more that he scored in that season's FA Cup final as Manchester United defeated Liverpool 2-1 at Wembley. Jimmy never wanted to leave Stoke. He loved it at the club and cried when he was told by Waddo that he had to go. Waddo cried too.

I'll tell you a story about Jimmy which illustrates what a good player he was within our team. I was often complemented throughout this stage of my career for my ability to play the ball out of defence and find one of our players – mostly Jimmy. Meanwhile over at Manchester United there was a Scottish international central defender called Gordon McQueen. They used to say he passed water. When Jimmy Greenhoff left Stoke and joined United suddenly I couldn't pass the ball and McQueen was brilliant. That was Jimmy, he was always available for the ball into feet. He made your life easy as he was super targetman and you could get it in to him no matter what. We had something of a telepathic relationship. I knew where he was going to be, I didn't have to look. He would really back in to his marker, receive the ball and either play a quick pass to get us going forward or win another free kick. It's sad that people never saw what he was capable of doing on the international stage.

Waddo knew he was being forced to sell his best players and when he parted company with Alan Hudson, who had been like a son to him in his four years at the club, it was obvious that not only had the heart had been ripped out of the side, but it had been ripped out of our manager. The sales began a spiral, which pulled the side down from the Christmas high to a run of one win in ten after the turn of the year and a further sequence of one win in 15 games to the end of the season. Mike Pejic was also sold, for £150,000 to Everton in February, leaving Jackie Marsh having to cover on the wrong side of the defence, while Alan Dodd plugged the gap Marsh left on the right. Before I knew it, Josh Mahoney was off too, sold to help Jack Charlton's resurgence at Middlesbrough. Also leaving was Jimmy Robertson, who had paid the price for the repeated injuries which had finally caught up with him. Jimmy joined Walsall as his career wound down.

I began to think I would soon have nobody to play with. It was obvious then that we'd got a problem.

Waddo tried to plug the gaps as best he could, but with no money at all being available to strengthen he was forced to blood youngsters such as Brian Bithell, John Ruggiero and Danny Bowers. To replace Alan Hudson, a young lad called Paul Johnson came in. Stoke at that time actually had two players on the books called Paul Johnson, so this one, who played in central midfield, differentiated himself from the left-back, by calling himself 'PA' – his initials. We had a different way of telling them apart. 'PA' was known to us by the nickname 'Tubby', or in moments requiring less etiquette, 'Fatty'. He was a chunky lad. Paul was interesting because, although he was a strong little feller and could pass the ball very nicely. His problem was that despite being a reserve teamer he thought he was a great player. I'd say he was a very confident lad. In fact he was full of himself. He would be constantly saying to Waddo, "I should be in the team, I should be in" – badgering him to play.

So the situation saw Paul given his debut against Ipswich in February 1977 and for the first half hour he didn't touch the ball. He was watching the game pass him by and saying, "what's going on, Den?" He thought he could do it all in training, but once he got into a proper game against an Ipswich team that could move the ball around, he couldn't get anywhere near anybody for half an hour. He just couldn't believe it. He'd been controlling reserve team games at a stroll, but the real thing was too much for him.

Unfortunately we had too many of these inexperienced players coming into the side all at once. Midfielder John Ruggiero was a young lad who had some pace and wasn't bad but not top class. Striker John Tudor was not bad in the end as a target man – but he was no Jimmy Greenhoff – and that was the level of quality we were trying to replace.

Then there was Steve Waddington – the manager's son. Little Waddo was a strong lad, both mentally and physically. You have got to be strong-minded to be at a football club at which your dad is the manager. Steve was. Waddo put himself about for a little lad and had a good shot on him, but again, really he wasn't good enough. Without being rude to Steve, he shouldn't have been in the side. I don't blame Tony for that, though. Steve wasn't in because he was his dad's son. He was in because we had no-one else.

Alan Suddick, who arrived from Newcastle as the last throw of the dice as we sought a way of scoring some goals, was towards the end of his career. He was a forward who could find the net, but you needed to be playing well to have Suddy in your team. He was like Tony Currie – he was comfortable on the ball and could produce some lovely tricks, but ultimately he was a luxury. He, like many of those players, was not the kind you would choose for a relegation scrap, which was what faced us now.

Perhaps surprisingly, through all this we had Peter Shilton in goal for the entire season. However, he was not playing well and was very unhappy with both his form and the overall situation. It affected everyone, mainly the defence. Because things weren't going well he just worked harder and harder. And the harder he worked the worse he got. He got himself uptight and wound up about it. It became obvious that he needed a change because he wasn't doing anyone any favours, but until someone came in with a good offer for him the board weren't prepared to sell. As that didn't happen before the transfer deadline we were stuck with each other until the end of the season. You'd have thought that having one of the two best goalkeepers this country has ever produced behind you during the run in would help, but it didn't.

Not surprisingly the supporters weren't very happy at all as they saw their team ripped to shreds and results turn for the worse, and there were a number of regrettable incidents at games and on the terraces. I can understand why they were angry. The spine had been taken out of the team – Banks, Ritchie, Hudson, Greenhoff, Dobing, Eastham, Pejic, Mahoney, Robertson and Bernard all gone. No team could cope with that loss of quality and experience. We certainly couldn't. The players that were brought in weren't good enough, the directors were culpable for the lack of insurance for the stand which led to the fire sale and frankly the place was in disarray.

The whole situation was bad enough, but what happened next beggared belief. I remember I was at home one evening in mid-March when the phone rang, It was Tony Waddington ringing from his office at the Victoria Ground. He'd been at an emergency board meeting, called following the 1-0 home defeat by Leicester. I listened in disbelief as he said to me, "Denis, the board have called me in and told me they want me to go."

"What!" I couldn't believe what I was hearing. I was shocked the board were effectively blaming the manager for everything that had gone on.

Waddo sounded really cut up and said to me, "They want me to leave. What do you think?"

I replied, "It's simple. If you go, we'll go down. You have got to stay. Convince them that you have got to stay. Don't you resign. If it's got to happen then make them sack you."

I thought the board wouldn't want to sack him because Tony was a legend and dismissing him would make them look so bad. But they did. And they made out he'd resigned too. It was a shocking way for the board to treat the manager who had brought so much success and glory to the club.

I have no idea if it was simply another cost-cutting exercise or if the board were just scared about the possibility of relegation and wanted to freshen things up. Either way they appointed our coach George Eastham to replace Tony.

Early in the season I had been in and out of the team as I tried to fully recover from my knee problem. Each time I was rushed back in, playing before I was truly 100% ready. I would do anything for the cause, but perhaps that wasn't the cute way of approaching this particular problem. I played solidly from November because I knew we were in trouble and was persuaded to get out onto the pitch probably two months before I should have done. I came back too early. Waddo was pushing and I was wanting to play, so it was a dual thing and I can't blame anybody for the way I was. If I thought I could play I would be saying to Waddo, "I'm alright now". I was constantly being injected with cortisone to get me through games, but it was the done thing then. Everybody did it. I didn't think it was going to cause me any harm. Now my knees bear the scars of those days and I suffer as so many of my fellow former professionals do on a daily basis. But I will never complain. Agreeing to have those injections was a decision I made back then and you have got to live with that. At least I didn't have to go down the pit.

Our survival all depended on how we fared over the final eight games but we lost a vital away game to Birmingham thanks to two goals in the last ten minutes, and only drew with Bristol City and Spurs, two of the others deep in the relegation mire, at home. Those results just weren't good enough. Looking back the issue was compounded by the fact that we didn't think we were in that much trouble. On 12 April, after beating Leeds 2-1 at home, we were still 14th. But there was a massive scrap going on in the bottom half of the table. In 12th place, Birmingham had 31 points, we had 30, while five clubs had 27 points including QPR, Sunderland, West Ham, Coventry and Tottenham, who were 21st, and Bristol City were bottom with 25 points. Just six points covered 12 teams. We were so used to looking up the table after the years of success we didn't even consider the possibility that we might get dragged into the battle to stay up. Now panic was setting in across the club and we were getting more and more desperate.

I wasn't happy on a personal level either. Firstly there had been the frustration of sitting on the sidelines for so long because of my knee injury and watching as it all went wrong on the pitch, and then, when I got back, I knew I wasn't the same player. I had to learn to cope with my knee and my lack of mobility contributed to Stoke's slide down the table. It left me hugely frustrated. It all came to a head four games before the end of the season when we lost 2-5 at Coventry, and I got sent off. It wasn't a straight red, I was dismissed for two bookable offences, the second a bad foul on winger Tommy Hutchison. Simply put, I wasn't used to losing 2-5 at Highfield Road. In fact we were 0-4 down before half an hour was up. We'd been such a good team and now we were getting hammered at the likes of Coventry. I was not a happy bunny. That sending off was indicative of everything that was going on and none of it was particularly pleasant. There is no doubt I deserved that one.

Part of the frustration was with our new manager. George was never the right man in my opinion. Everybody liked him and he had obviously been a great player, but he was a quiet lad and as a manager he tinkered and messed with the team too much. George, after all, was a coach not a manager, and he'd got coach's ideas and got to the stage where he was changing the team for the sake of it, without a true understanding of what difference he was actually making with all his tinkering, especially with undermining the confidence of the players who didn't know what decision he might make next. It was change this, change that, change the other and in the end I am certain it was a bad decision by the Board to sack Waddo. I admit we wouldn't have been great if he'd stayed, but I fully believe we'd have kept ourselves up. He would have helped us, given us confidence and given us a pattern. As it was the player sales and change of manager that killed us.

Even after all this mayhem with two games to go we still hadn't dropped into the relegation zone yet. In fact we just needed to pick up two more points and we'd be safe. However our last two matches were both away and we'd just completed our home programme with a 3-3 draw against Manchester United in a game we should have won. The next game was against West Brom at the Hawthorns. It was Johnny Giles's last game as a player and George selected a young lad called Dennis Thorley, who was really a centre-half, to go man to man in midfield with Giles, who was one of the wiliest, most experienced players of that, or any other, era. Giles had Thorley for breakfast and got 10 out of 10 in most of the following day's papers as we lost an early lead to go down 1-3. I have no idea what George thought he was doing. Giles absolutely took the poor kid to pieces. Those sort of decisions are coach's decisions. They seem good on paper, but an experienced manager like Waddo would never have done that.

To add insult to injury Brian Bithell was sent off in that game at West Brom and we were now in the bottom three for the first time. We had 33 points, and above us there were five other teams on 34 points. Unfortunately we had the worst goal difference, so we knew we had to win our last game at Aston Villa to have any chance of survival. Even then we needed two of the other clubs to fail to win. But we were in with a decent chance, despite everything that had gone on. Villa were a tough proposition, with players such as Andy Gray and Brian Little in their side. Because the season had gone on so long, that game was played on a Monday night in mid-May.

We went down to a 0-1 defeat after Alan Dodd pushed Andy Gray over and the big Scottish striker tucked away the penalty. We had been relegated two years after almost winning the league.

It's an odd phase of my Stoke career for me. Because I missed so much of the season I often think that it wasn't me that got relegated. I might say that 'they' went down, meaning the players that were in the side while I was in the side. I kid myself that I didn't play that season. But I did play enough games – 30 in fact – and I always believe that in football you win together and you lose together. It is absolutely a team game.

It felt as if it had all happened in the blink of an eye. Somehow, from 7th place in November, we had lost many of our best players, then our manager, suffered a nightmare run and found ourselves out of the top flight. I felt less devastated than non-plussed by what had gone on. I just couldn't quite square it all. It was enormously frustrating and it is only now, when I think back to what went on, that I fully understand the tornado that literally and figuratively had pulled the club apart. If the loss of Gordon Banks was a major blow, then the storm which demolished the Butler Street stand was the straw that broke the camel's back. It arguably cost Stoke City 25 years of development.

The worst thing in the world had happened as far as I was concerned. I didn't want to finish my career getting beat. I have tremendous pride in my achievements and that relegation looms as a huge blip. I was angry and frustrated because the problems went so much deeper than merely losing a few games of football on the pitch. The place was just in total disarray. To all intents and purposes my beloved Stoke City were broken.

Chapter Eleven

THAT'S
ENTERTAINMENT

I was bored out of my skull. Simply, Division Two was crap.

Dropping down a division brought me up against some very poor forwards and I have got to be honest, the standard just wasn't what I was used to. Even with my knee injury restricting my performance I felt so comfortable on the pitch that I didn't think any opposing forwards would give me problems.

In fact I was so bored I used to make things more interesting for myself by telling the forwards I was playing against how they could improve. As the ball was played into them I would stand a little bit off them and shout to them which way they could turn and where they were going wrong in trying to beat me. I think most of them thought I was taking the Mickey, but I wasn't. I actually wanted them to give me a game, to make it harder for me, so I wouldn't die of boredom.

At that level forwards tend to do a standard thing – the ball is played up to them, they hold it up, play it off and then look to make a run. It got so repetitive that I wanted to freshen things up. So there I'd be saying things like, "you're too far away from me" or, if I got too tight to them, "you could have turned me there".

I'd been so used to how top class forwards would challenge me through speed, skill and thought, and I loved the cut and thrust of that skirmish. If you were marking them too tight they would spin you and leave you for dead. If you were too far away from them they'd turn and come at you, getting you on your heels. If you were the right distance off them they'd bring the ball down and try to play a one-two or move the ball out wide. It was a battle of wits played out over a matter of inches. In Division Two the pace was slower, my mind was not tested and I was bored, bored, bored.

Despite that I still never wanted to leave. While the likes of Peter Shilton and Geoff Salmons followed all those other stars out of the Vic, I was determined to stay to help right the wrong of relegation. You might think it weird that Shilton had stayed so long when he would surely have been one of the most marketable assets with which to raise the much-needed cash to rebuild the stadium. In actual fact Shilts's stock had fallen so low at that stage that nobody seemed to want him. He began the 1977/78 season in Division Two with us, playing three games before joining Brian Clough's revolution at Nottingham Forest for £270,000. Peter's spell at Stoke was nothing short of a disaster – for him and the club. He'd arrived thinking, "I can win something here", and helped us reach the top of the First Division within a couple of weeks, but then nothing had ever come of it. It was a dreadful disappointment all round.

What's weird is the change of scene when he moved to Forest. Suddenly he won everything in sight – League title, League Cups, and of course two European Cups – but I can tell you the story there. On his first day the squad did some light training and then Clough came over and said, "that's it lads. I'll see you all Thursday". Shilts, ever wanting to be seen as the dedicated, top professional, asked, "can I come in tomorrow gaffer?"

"What for?" replies Clough.

"I want to do a bit of work on crosses," Shilts says.

"What do you want to do that for?"

"Well, you won't be too happy if I dropped any."

Clough replied tartly, "Son, I don't pay £270 grand for you to go around dropping them. Go home."

I fully believe that was what Peter needed. He came to understand that Clough had total faith in his ability, that he could relax a bit, that he didn't have to prove himself to be the best every day in training, because Clough knew he was the best. It was brilliant man-management and perhaps indicates that Tony Waddington, who had been unable to find a way to relax Peter, had failed with this master goalkeeper. Shilts didn't need to work so hard because he was that good. What he did crave was someone that believed in him and Cloughie gave him that – through his usual fashion of tough love! It worked.

Shilton's departure meant we'd lost almost all of the team which had come so close to the league title just two years previously – bar me. My central defensive partner Alan Bloor had retired due to injury, while Terry Conroy and Jackie Marsh were still around, but Terry's knees had gone and he would shortly move on to try his luck in Hong Kong with a club named Bulova. Jackie had one last hurrah in him as part of the side that was rebuilt to win promotion back to the top flight.

The one ray of light who'd broken into the team in that depressing relegation season was young striker Garth Crooks. From the minute Garth walked through the door as a youth he looked a player. He'd got the lot – great touch, good movement, a strong left foot, good pace, was quick and sharp and had an eye for goal. His first touch was sublime. It always took him where he wanted to go to either open himself up to get his shot away or to go past people. He had a super attitude and a super nature. Garth and I got on great. I loved him as a player and a person and I still do.

For me Garth should have done more in his career in the game, especially when he got his move to Tottenham. He went down to London and, although he won back-to-back FA Cups in 1981 and 1982, he was on the fringes of the team that won the UEFA Cup in 1984, being an unused substitute in both legs of the final. He also missed out on selection for England's 1982 World Cup squad, which I felt was a crying shame. Manager Ron Greenwood did the usual thing of taking all his favourites including the injured Trevor Brooking and Kevin Keegan, who both played just a few minutes in a last desperate attempt to stay in the tournament. Garth had the kind of spark that could have unlocked the massed defences of the Spanish and Germans in those games, but he was not selected. Instead he worked for the BBC during the competition and that started a new career for him. He got an agent for the radio DJing he began to do, and over the next few years his football – as he went on to play for Manchester United, West Brom and Charlton – began to take second place to his media work.

Now, of course, he presents BBC football's TV coverage, so perhaps he was right to concentrate on that. I thought he was definitely good enough to play for England. But he enjoys being eloquent, asking those long and involved questions that he's famous for, and, for those of us who have known him since he was a kid at Stoke, it's fair to say he's had elocution lessons as well!

Garth was actually the second black player to play for Stoke City. Just after the War a lad called Roy Brown, whose brother Dougie would become Mayor of Stoke, made a few appearances, but Garth was the first of the modern era and he was playing at a time when grounds were hostile environments. It was an unpleasant, difficult time for a young black lad to be coming through. Garth knew he was going to get stick and he didn't enjoy it, but I kept telling him that they were only shouting things at him because they were afraid of him. He had real talent and they wanted to put him off. It was actually as much as football thing as it was racist. He needed to let that abuse fuel his passion to play the game and ram the words back down those obnoxious supporters' throats – and he did.

The bigots were fighting a losing battle that the likes of Cyrille Regis, Laurie Cunningham and Brendan Batson at West Brom, John Barnes and Luther Blissett at Watford and Garth at our place were winning. Their talent and durability meant that sooner or later the monkey chants and the bananas being thrown reduced, until suddenly they weren't there any more. It took a decade or more, but British football was much the better for the acceptance of these gifted players.

We began the 1977/78 season badly, winning just four of the first 14 games as we struggled to shake off the impact of the previous season's devastating relegation and the new players bedded into the squad. We improved a little, settling into mid-table, which after the horrendous previous season, was at least some sort of security, but it had become obvious to all of us that George Eastham was not cut out for management. George wasn't a natural man-manager. He was given a reasonable length of time to arrest the slide and at least we didn't keep plummeting, but we weren't playing well under him. At the turn of the year we lost in the league to Orient and Southampton without creating a single chance and then ignominiously 2-3 at home in the FA Cup fourth round to Northern Premier League Blyth Spartans. I suppose that I was lucky in some senses because I was injured and missed that game, just as I had been the previous season when we'd been knocked out of the League Cup by Fourth Division club Lincoln City. That result – made worse by being on TV that night as one of the great Cup upsets – spelt the end for George, who resigned after the game.

To be fair he'd brought in some players such as Alec Lindsay, Paul Richardson, David Gregory and most importantly Howard Kendall from Birmingham after relegation, but they would vary in their success at the club. Gregory, a striker, was quick and had a decent career in the game after moving on from the club. Alec had a big problem. He'd been a good left-back during his career at Liverpool where he'd won trophies galore, but by the time he signed for us he'd given up to be honest, and would be stopping for beef burgers on the way in to training in the morning. You got the feeling Alec wasn't really interested. He didn't last long.

Richo was a good honest player – what I would call a championship player. He was strong and worked hard. He was a decent passer of the ball, but he would need to have a look to see a pass – I'd been playing with George Eastham and George never looked – he played it, creating openings with that extra split-second of guile and disguise. There is a difference. Richo would stop it and look and then play. It used to frustrate me actually. But Paul did a very good job at that level.

Generally we got on great, but there was one occasion when we fell out big time. We were 2-0 up against Brighton at home and we'd allowed them to get back to 2-2. So Paul started having a go at us at the back. He was blaming us for the two goals. He wouldn't stop. When we got off the pitch and back to the dressing room. Once we'd closed that door I just lost it because it was actually him who had cost us. So I got him and pinned him against the wall in the dressing room – the lads had to pull me off him. Now that's not me. It is incredibly rare that I react like that. Richo obviously touched a nerve. He told me afterwards, "Den, your eyes changed like Damon's in The Omen, it was horrible." We still talk about it when I see him now.

Howard Kendall was coming to the end of his career as well, but H was always focussed on coaching and management as his future. He joined Stoke as player-coach and proved to be a natural, and a winner. As a midfielder he was up there with the players I'd been used to, possessing the kind of qualities of the Dobings, the Hudsons, and the Greenhoffs of this world. He was in that class and he got every drop out of himself, pushing himself to the limit. I remember he was a cut above the quality of players in the Second Division because he could anticipate what was going to happen. For example it sometimes put me off when I was jumping for a header because he would make a run, expecting me to win the ball. No-one else was working at that level. He read the game superbly. Howard could also make a tackle and then see a pass to get us moving forward. He did like his booze though, with his favourite tipple being Champagne!

H and I lived fairly close to one another and we would stop at the Mainwaring Arms pub on the way home, sit down with a pint and go over what we had done in training, what we should be doing and how we should be moving. We did nothing but talk football. It might be tactics or team selection, the forthcoming opposition or what we would do when we had our own clubs to manage. Two major managerial careers were planned during those chats. We both believed in good movement and mobility in our offensive players, coupled with solid defence.

This coaching job would prove to be the start of great things for Howard, who would go on to manage Blackburn, where he won promotion to the Second Division and just missed out on elevation to the top flight, then moved to Everton where he won two league titles and the European Cup Winners' Cup. He then tried his luck in Spain with Athletic Bilbao, saved Manchester City from relegation in 1990 and having further spells with Sheffield United and Everton, twice. He remains the last English manager to win a European trophy.

Following the debacle against Blyth Spartans, the board acted swiftly to bring in a thrusting young manager named Alan Durban from Shrewsbury Town. Durban had been a battling midfielder in the successful Derby side, which had won promotion to the First Division in 1969 and the League title in 1972. He had captained the Welsh international team too before joining Shrewsbury Town as player-manager in 1974. He'd done well at Gay Meadow, winning promotion from Division Four in his first full season and had established them in the upper half of the Third Division by the time he was persuaded to join Stoke.

Durbs was an organiser and something of a disciplinarian. I loved that in him. He sorted things out very quickly. He pulled us back together, creating a settled team for the first time in two years. He'd got a totally different attitude to management to George. He handled the players well and he was much more in your face when he needed to be. He made you believe what he was doing was the right thing and that gave us all confidence. I have got a lot of time for him.

One of the first things Durban did was to scour the lower leagues for a player to complement our attacking talent and bring the best out of Garth Crooks. He signed Brendan O'Callaghan for £50,000 from Doncaster Rovers. Bren wasn't a big goalscorer himself, but he proved to be the link that allowed our attack to function at its best as we improved as a team. Bren was 6 feet 4 inches tall, wonderful in the air, a great target man, and very intelligent with how he used the ball. He had a decent touch and a good appreciation on what was going on around him. He was brilliant at getting near post flick ons, or touches on to through balls to play others in.

As the old maxim says: it's better to be a lucky manager than a good manager. Durban certainly began to prove himself in the former category when he brought Big Bren on as a substitute during a home match against Hull. There were around 20 minutes left and the visitors had successfully numbed our attack. Bren was on the bench, having arrived from Doncaster a few days earlier, and Durban brought him on just as we had won a corner in front of the Boothen End. It was a brilliant move. O'Callaghan rose at the near post to beat keeper Eddie Blackburn and score with his first touch, just 11 seconds after running onto the Victoria Ground pitch.

Somehow that moment, coming so soon after Durban's arrival and courtesy of his first signing, signified a turning around of Stoke's fortunes. When Bren signed I have to admit my heart had sunk. I had my doubts about the quality that Durban was bringing in. I remember saying to myself, 'who plays for Doncaster?' and 'where are we going?' Then this big lad trots on, the ball comes across and he powers it home. I thought, 'Yes – he'll do!'

That goal made Bren something of a cult figure, as did his role in City's rise from that point. He had a big bushy moustache, an enormous physique and, perhaps a bit like me, lived and breathed the club. He was a fabulous ambassador, always out attending fans' events or community projects. He remains popular today around the Potteries.

Alan won four of his first six games in charge and by the end of the season we'd finished 7th, so were the form team going into the new season. We just needed to find more consistency on the road as we had a tendency to lose 0-1 away from home, but we worked on the tightness of our defensive unit so that in the new campaign we set a club record for fewest goals conceded in a season of 31. That best ever defensive record for a season in the club's history is something which I am proud to have been a part of, albeit in Division Two. We just didn't think we were going to let a goal in. We'd get in front and then didn't think we were going to get beaten.

Durban had a particular way of playing, which allowed this to be possible. You might call it long ball percentage football. The press certainly did. We would play the ball into Big Bren as soon as we could to allow him to bring Garth into play. It was fast and it was direct, but it was also effective. Equally, because we were pressing teams back, winning the ball high up the pitch, we had less to deal with in defence. Consequently we were able to set the record, feeling pretty comfortable through almost all the season.

It helped that we also had a settled defence, staffed by quality players. Over the summer of 1978 Durban had brought in a top quality central defensive partner for me in Mike Doyle from Manchester City. Mike had been part of the City halcyon days of the late 1960s, winning the FA Cup and league title. He'd also won five England caps. After 448 games for Manchester City he was looking for a new challenge as manager Tony Book revamped his team.

Mike had had an equally tough upbringing as the son of a policeman in Manchester and consequently was a hard, tough man. He was voted as Manchester City's hardest player in the clubs official magazine. Because of that reputation and before we got to know each other I thought that Mike was going to be a bit like me, both as a player and a personality, but he wasn't. He sat off me, allowing me to go and deal with the ball. It was a real good, solid partnership.

The only thing was Mike used to love a moan. He was a pain in the backside in truth. He'd just be complaining, whingeing and all the lads were moaning back "don't pick him again. We all think he's a right prat." But of course, Mike was one of the first names on the teamsheet and I thought Durbs dealt with him really well.

Mike's arrival allowed Durban to redeploy Alan Dodd as a right-back. Doddy's versatility was truly frightening. He could and did play anywhere he was told. He was a manager's dream in that sense. Doddy was decent in midfield, a great full-back, solid centre-half and he could run for fun. In many ways the game was too easy for him because of his combination of athleticism and ability to read the play. The problem is Alan is so relaxed it's untrue. Alan Hudson always says that the missing link with Doddy was that he didn't have the desire burning within him to make the most of his talent. He wasn't a leader either. He would just do what he was told, and do it incredibly well. That was his mentality.

On the left-hand side of defence Geoff Scott came in. He'd actually been signed by George Eastham, but hadn't been given a run in the side. Durban gave him the opportunity, which Geoff took with both hands. He looked a hell of a good player with such a great build for a full-back. He was a tall and chunky, with huge thighs, great pace and a good left foot. He was a bit like Forest and England legend Stuart Pearce, but wasn't quite up to Psycho's high playing standards.

Behind us was a very solid goalkeeper indeed in Roger Jones. I thought he was outstanding and could have played for England had he not picked up a knee injury whilst at Newcastle, from where Tony Waddington had signed him. Roger had understudied Peter Shilton and then taken over early in the 1977/78 season. I rated him so highly that when I moved into management I took him to York and he played for me as we rose up the divisions. He was voted as York's best ever goalkeeper by fans there and has subsequently carved out a career in coaching. That all started when I brought him to Sunderland with me as a goalkeeping coach. His knowledge of the game is brilliant. If I'm honest I'm not sure he's top notch at communicating that, which is a shame, but as a goalkeeper and coach he was outstanding.

The other player who turned up was Viv Busby. Viv was reaching the end of his career when he signed for Stoke under George Eastham. He'd played in the Fulham side which reached the 1975 FA Cup final and joined us from a season with Norwich City. Buzzer was quick, he had a good leap and a good touch, although he was forever bloody injured. He used to get hamstring strains all the time so he was never better than a squad player at Stoke, filling in as a striker when needed because of injuries. I remember Viv could put his elbows on the ground during the stretches as we warmed up, but despite his supple nature his hamstrings would go. You have many lads who can barely touch their knees, but who never have hamstring problems! It was tough on Viv, but that's the way it was. His scoring record was sparse, but he had a great knowledge of the game and a wonderful personality. I thought straight away that he was great with the young players. He had a lot of influence around the dressing room, and that was something which stayed with me.

We had a settled team throughout most of 1978/79. The only major addition coming when Durban paid £150,000 for pacy striker Paul Randall from Bristol Rovers. His arrival meant that Garth Crooks was moved to play slightly wider on the left, using his pace and whipped left foot to provide service for Randall and O'Callaghan.

On the right was little Sammy Irvine. Sammy had followed Alan Durban from Shrewsbury and he was a brilliant little lad. He was very quick and sharp, with energy to burn, and wasn't afraid to get stuck in to win the ball back. He was a bubbly character in the dressing room and was full of energy. He was always liable to produce a goal from nothing. I remember Sammy used to drive Roger Jones crackers in training because, where people would normally draw their foot back to strike the ball he would just run in and toepoke it past him. Sammy was a good little player.

With the likes of Sammy, Garth, Scotty and Bren, Durban had built a side packed with youth, but blended in with the experience of myself, Howard, Roger Jones and Mike Doyle. It worked brilliantly. Our defence was impregnable and we were always likely to nick a goal. We simply won 1-0 pretty much every week. We were heavily criticised for our approach to the game, but we didn't care. It was effective. Durban would famously say a year or so later, after a 1-0 victory at Highbury when journalists complained about the style of football, "If you want entertainment then get some clowns."

Whatever your feeling about the brand of football we played, it launched us up the table and we were in the promotion places pretty much for the whole campaign aside from a couple of weeks in March 1978 when we lost consecutive home games to Sunderland and Blackburn. That blip spurred us on to win four of the next seven games as we went unbeaten to the end of the season. That run left us going into the final game knowing that a win would give us promotion.

The final fixture of the 1978/79 season was at Meadow Lane, and there was very little on it for opponents Notts County, who were guaranteed to finish 6th no matter what the score. The ground was packed to the rafters with Stokies willing the team on, but there was a lot of tension around. We had the lion's share of possession and created all the chances in a fairly drab first half. For some reason we just couldn't fashion a clear cut opening. We'd had very few blank scoresheets in our great run since Christmas. Three of those, however, had been in goalless draws against opponents who had kept it as tight as the Magpies were doing this day.

We were in such a great position because one of our promotion rivals, Sunderland, had lost at home to Cardiff in midweek, leaving us with this opportunity to go straight up with a win, but the minutes ticked by without us fashioning a good chance. We couldn't see County scoring, but then we couldn't see us scoring. We were getting desperate by now. There were ten minutes left, five, then three. Every time the ball thrown in to their box, into the mix, I thought it must drop for us, but it didn't. We knew we needed to win. It was just absolute mayhem.

With two minutes remaining I took it upon myself to go and assist up front – trying to get onto something or cause enough havoc to create an opportunity. Crosses rained in, the clock ticked round to full-time and the referee told us there were just two minutes to be added on.

Frome one of those crosses came the crucial breakthrough. I'm not sure who crossed the ball actually, but Brendan O'Callaghan knocked it back for Paul Richardson to throw himself bodily at it about four yards out and just bundle it over the line.

That was it. We'd scored the vital goal that meant promotion. Pandemonium erupted around Meadow Lane as all the Stoke fans went absolutely berserk. The release of the tension build up of the day was just too much for them. They were on the pitch, hugging each other, going crazy. The game was still going on!

I told the ref he would need another ball if it came anywhere near me because it would be going over the stand. We were determined to hold on, and to be honest County had nothing left. That was it then. The final whistle blew sparking a massive celebration with what I reckon was about 10,000 Stokies rushing all over the pitch. We were all mobbed, chaired off the pitch and cheered into the dressing rooms and back out onto the coach. It was a truly fantastic day.

When we reached the Victoria Ground the Board greeted us and said "take it to the Boardroom lads" and there was champagne to celebrate. But normally in those circumstances we would have expected new contracts, or an envelope containing some cash or a holiday. Do you know what they gave us for getting promotion instead? Have a guess. A tie. A club tie! That's what we got. I know what you're thinking – surely you had one of those anyway? … that just says it all.

We began the first season back up in the top flight really well. Garth Crooks was on fire, scoring four goals in the first three games. Crooksy really made an impact that season, scoring 15 goals to earn his £650,000 move to Spurs the following summer.

Durban was still developing the team with judicious signings. signed right-back Ray Evans for £100,000 from Tottenham and the club's first overseas player, Dutch midfielder Loek Ursem from AZ67 Alkmaar for £58,000. He moved on Viv Busby and Roger Jones, and released Howard Kendall to begin his stellar managerial career at Blackburn.

Stoke were blessed at that time with a fantastic crop of kids coming through the ranks. One of those, Adrian 'Inchy' Heath, took Howard's midfield spot and began to show the verve and flair which would mark him out as one of the top players in the country. Also emerging at that time were midfielder Paul Bracewell, striker Lee Chapman and defender Steve Bould. All four would make a huge impact in the game, win heaps of medals and top honours in their careers – sadly none of them with Stoke. Just imagine what a team Stoke would have had if the club had been able to cling on to such a huge amount of talent.

Brace was one of the most two-footed players I ever came across. I didn't know which his best foot was. And I'm not sure any fan would be able to tell you. He was that good. Brace was almost mechanical or metronomic in the way he played, keeping possession, spreading play, winning the ball back, supporting his defence, spraying passes to runners, you name it he could do it. He took responsibility no matter what the score was. Whatever mess you were in Brace was always there trying to get you out of it. He was brilliant – I loved him to bits, both playing with him and then when I had him in my squad as a manager. I remember when I wanted to sign him at Sunderland, but he failed his medical. So I insisted the club sign him anyway. Forget the insurance or anything like that. I just wanted him in my dressing room giving the younger players' confidence and on the pitch retaining possession. He was different class on both counts.

Basically, though, by then he was knackered, even though his career would last another ten years! His knee was shot to pieces. He was so unlucky with that injury because he had forced himself into the England team readying itself for the 1986 World Cup in Mexico by dint of his effervescent performances for Howard Kendall's all-conquering Everton side. I was so pleased that team had both Brace and Inchy Heath in it under Howard's guidance. It felt like a little bit of Stoke had won the league!

Lee Chapman was always a confident lad. He was tall and bustling, but had the great knack for a striker of being in the right place at the right time. He often scored goals which went in off strange parts of his body, but he was also a player who worked incredibly hard to improve himself. He developed tremendous skill which went on view as his career developed through spells with Nottingham Forest and Leeds United.

Another player who broke into the team who had been around the Vic for a while was goalkeeper Peter Fox. Foxy would go on to become a total legend at Stoke. He played over 400 games and became a true fans' favourite. He arguably should have been given an England chance, but ultimately he was just that tiny bit short for a goalkeeper at 5 feet 10 inches. But I thought he was a wonderful shot-stopper, brilliant in one-on-ones and good at coming for crosses. I changed next to him in the dressing room and we often talked about things outside football, such as working with the fans and in the community. Foxy was someone who preferred to follow my lead in joining the Round Table rather than go drinking. He was a kindred spirit, and I feel it's no surprise that he has gone on to become a highly skilled goalkeeping coach working across the midlands and north.

With all these talents blending in to the team we stabilised in the division. Later Durban returned to his former club Shrewsbury to pick up winger Paul Maguire for £262,000. Paul should have signed for Everton, but he had failed his medical because of a bad back. So Durbs, knowing what a talented player Paul was, moved to bring him in swiftly. There are certain players you can give a ball to when they are being marked tightly and Paul was one. He loved it. He could feel them and turn them. He had got great feet. He was a free-kick and corner expert and from his deliveries and corners we developed a fantastic near post corner routine whereby Big Bren would flick balls on for runners to latch on to. It was devastating and brought us bundles of goals.

Paul was a really good player but he did prove to be a bit fragile. He did have some trouble with his back which held him back. It became very frustrating for him because no=one could isolate what it was and he only found out what it was after he left.

Paul wasn't the only one to suffer through injury. Halfway through that first season after promotion I did my knee again. By now I was 33, a ripe old age for a centre-half and I knew that my powers of recuperation were not going to be as strong.

The problem was that this injury came on top of other major problems. I smashed my arm twice in 1980. The first occasion was at Burnley. I remember a corner came over and I jumped up to flick it on at the near post. I was sandwiched between two players and as I came down with my hand breaking my fall they both landed on me, crushing my forearm. I had to have a plate in it, which meant I could get back playing quicker. This wasn't too much of a problem – until we played Manchester City at Maine Road. In a goalmouth scramble the ball was whacked towards goal. I threw myself at it to just get something, anything in the way, putting my arms up to protect my face as I fell. The ball crashed into my forearm exactly where the plate was, snapping it inside my arm where the screws had gone in and to cap it all a City player fell on it for good measure. So now I had broken bones being held together by a broken metal plate. More surgery, and I was then stuck in plaster for 12 weeks.

To cover my absence throughout the 1980/81 season, Alan Durban asked Big Bren to drop back and play in central defence alongside Mike Doyle. Bren adapted superbly to the position, calling on all his experience as a centre-forward to understand what he had to do to make life uncomfortable for his opponents. The partnership blossomed and I began to wonder if I would be needed when I returned, although I always knew that Bren really wanted to play up front.

In the end my playing career wasn't ended by the injuries. In fact I did get back into the side at the start of the 1981/82 campaign. My career was ended by a watershed event for Stoke City that happened in the summer of 1981. Manager Alan Durban left to join Sunderland after receiving an offer which was too good to turn down. Effectively the club had let him reach the end of the contract, so he had a choice of accepting Stoke's new deal or taking the fantastic package on offer at Roker Park. As I would later find, the draw of such a huge club proved too much for Durbs to resist. Sunderland's fortunes seem almost constantly to need reviving, but in 1981 they languished low in the First Division table. Durbs at that stage was a young, up and coming manager who was looking for the big stage. I think he had realised there would never be any money at

Stoke to match his ambitions, while Sunderland were waving wads of it at him as befits a club known for years as the 'Bank of England'.

For my money Alan Durban's major strength was that he understood players and would deal directly with you, telling you where you were going right or wrong. He worked you hard, selected the right players and he got results. What he didn't do was get involved in day-to-day coaching. He was interested in motivating the players and left the coaching to his extremely capable deputy Richie Barker, and a couple of the senior pros – one of them being me.

The problem I now had was that, straight after Drubs' rather sudden departure, the Stoke board saw fit to promote Richie to the manager's chair. There is a world of difference between a manager and a coach and there are not many people out there who don't know that. Seemingly the Stoke board were among that minority. Suddenly it was like having a foreman in overall charge. The big problem for me was that this foreman was afraid I was after his job.

I had to learn to live with the fact that my face no longer fitted at the club I had given my life to. It's a very harsh reality in football when years of service, of laying your body on the line for a team are 'rewarded' by being told you are no longer wanted. It's very very tough, but there comes a point in every pro's career that you have to think about what lies ahead after playing.

Thankfully I'd known for years.

Chapter Twelve

THERE ARE GOOD MILLIONAIRES AND THERE ARE BAD MILLIONAIRES

I had always wanted to be a manager after I had been a successful footballer.

I'd begun my apprenticeship to become a manager aged 15 when, as I was recuperating from the first of my two broken legs that year, I'd taken over the Queensbury school team after the teacher who had been running it left that Christmas and wasn't replaced until the following September, and we won the cup for southern Stoke-on-Trent schools. Queensbury had regularly won at boxing and athletics, in fact everything but football, so when I got the boys together and organised them, changing the playing style to be a bit like Wimbledon, we managed to take on all comers and win the final on the ground of our main rivals, Meir Square school. To our opponents we must have appeared like the Bash Street Kids, rough and ready and happy to put in a few tasty tackles and, when we were leading with five minutes remaining, resorting to launching a few balls as far from the pitch as possible so they had to be fetched by our opponents.

That victory also gave me my first experience of managerial sour grapes. They really didn't like losing – especially to us. I remember this school teacher from Meir having a right go at me and I just said to him, "look, we've beaten you. Get lost."

That experience also taught me some of the early lessons which would stand me in good stead throughout my managerial career. I remember when I first took over the school team there was a very talented lad a year younger playing in the City of Stoke-on-Trent team coached by Dennis Wilshaw. I dropped this player from my school team,

162

which caused a lot of protests from various people, and the next time I saw Dennis he took me aside and asked me what the hell I was doing? My answer was simple, the lad was selfish with the ball. He just played for himself. He didn't pass when I wanted him to, preferring to dribble, and he would often lose the ball. He wouldn't adhere to my system, so I left him out which was a hell of a thing to do as a 15 year old to a 14 year old with a lot of obvious ability. I also told Dennis that the lad I'd bought in gave a hell of a lot more to the side and that was better for the team. He came to watch the final and saw the lad I picked score twice as we won 3-0. No-one said anything after that.

Your best team's not always made up of your best players and often people can't understand that. An obvious example is how Alf Ramsey left out Jimmy Greaves in favour of Geoff Hurst in the 1966 World Cup. Greaves is head and shoulders a better goalscorer than Hurst, but Geoff fitted that England team far better. Was Alf right to leave out England's greatest goalgrabber? Hurst scored a hat-trick in the final, plus the winner in the quarter-final against Argentina. You can't argue with that.

So I was seeing it even then – what would make a team better, what is the balance we need, how do we beat today's opponents?

I wanted to keep involved with youth and local football once I'd established myself in the Stoke City first team. I tried to go into schools around southern Stoke-on-Trent to help with their teams sometimes begging the sports masters to let me help. Often they wouldn't let me in because I was a footballer and so not 'academic' which was hilarious when you think about it, so I turned to Sunday morning football with a team called Taylor and Tunnicliffe. It was real lowest rung of the ladder stuff, not changing rooms, cadging kits from all over the place, but I loved it. I was building a breadth of experience at low levels of dealing with players and situations, and learning that I really enjoyed the responsibility and also that players responded to me. I also needed to be competitive in life, and didn't want to lose that element of my day to day existence. Ultimately I realised I just enjoy being moaned at by players and fans!

I remember there was this player in that team called Clive Eaton, a feller affectionately nicknamed 'Bandit'. He was a stocky striker, who had a good amount of pace and knew where the back of the net was, especially good in the air for his size. I thought he was good enough to be considered by Stoke, so I asked Tony Waddington to go along and watch him, but Waddo thought his join up play wasn't that good, although he took him on because I insisted his finishing was excellent.

Bandit was good, so good in fact that Geoff Hurst commented he reminded him of Jimmy Greaves. One of Clive's first games was Bury away in the reserves. I knew they'd won 3-0, so when they got back to the Vic I grabbed hold of Alan A'Court, who had been in charge of the team, and said, "Come on," I said. "What did you think?"

Alan said, "Denis, he can't bring players into the game and doesn't join in much." Generally he wasn't very complimentary.

"But did he score?" I asked.

"Yes, he got all three," came the reply.

I was flabbergasted. Scoring goals is the Holy Grail of football.

Bandit eventually decided to emigrate to Australia. I remember his leaving party, which was held in a pub called The Old 'ut, in Longton. It was held on the same night as another do I had to attend for Stoke City at Jolly's, the nightclub made famous by the coverage of darts which was broadcast from there throughout the 1970s and early 80s, so I decided that Kate and I would say farewell to Clive and then go on to the club bash. Because the second event was black tie, we arrived at The Hut dressed to the nines, feeling more than a little out of place amidst a throng of Potters and bikers. I squeezed my way to the bar and asked for a Campari and Soda. The barman looked me up and down, taking in my sartorial elegance, and said flatly, "Look Youth, we've got beer and whisky, what dos't want?"

I liked Bandit so much both a a bloke and a player that we named our lovely bounding dog after him.

******

The next step in my managerial grounding came along in 1980 after I had smashed my arm and was out for a several weeks as the bone knitted together. Because the first team were on an end of season tour around the Caribbean and I couldn't go as I had my arm in plaster I was asked to take the Under 20s to Haarlem in Holland to play in the prestigious and very competitive early summer youth tournament there. I was delighted to do it because I knew I was realistically coming towards the end of my playing career. The team that was given to me had some good players in it, including one lanky youth called Steve Bould. I was told that Bouldy was a centre-forward, but I took one look at him and, despite him having a good physique, decent pace and good awareness, I knew he'd never make it in the game as a striker. So I turned him into a centre half.

I taught Steve to think and move like a centre-half, not to allow his man to get across in front of him to have a strike at goal at the near post. Once he began to cut out that dangerous ball into the area we knew the only place the opposition could play it was towards the back stick, so defending became very easy. It was a lesson which stayed with him throughout his career. Steve was also so comfortable on the ball for such a big man. Fortunately for me Bouldy had grown up with me as his hero so he listened to every word I said and was happy to put my ideas into practice. Before we knew it Steve had turned into a quality defender, happy to put his foot in, great in the air, and, thanks to his time as a striker, well-versed in what his opponent was trying to do to him.

If I'm honest that move also partly came about because as coach of this team I was looking at what I hadn't got and I hadn't got a centre half, and I hadn't got a goalkeeper, so I borrowed a young lad called Mark Harrison from Port Vale, who would impress enough on the trip to join Stoke the following summer, and converted Bouldy to plug the gaps.

Obviously I was delighted to see Steve move on to Arsenal and have such a wonderful career in the game. I don't want to claim all the credit for the famous Arsenal back four of Bould, Adams, Dixon and Winterburn, but I like to think I helped Steve become the dominant player that he did! Once he'd listened to what I had to say Steve went out on the pitch and did it all for himself and it was a delight to see him win so much silverware.

The strange thing was when Steve broke into Stoke's first team he was played at right-back by manager Richie Barker. I just couldn't see that at all. He was far too tall to be a full-back, he didn't like having the restriction of having the touchline immediately next to him, and he wasn't able to make the forward runs that full-backs are asked to. It was a bad managerial call and it wasn't until he reverted to centre-half in 1986 under new manager Mick Mills that Steve really began to shine.

The rest of the squad I took to Haarlem wasn't too shabby either. We had Paul Bracewell and Adrian Heath in midfield, plus Lee Chapman up front. At that stage I didn't realise how good Chappie was. He looked all arms and legs, but when I began working with him I realised how good his touch was. His real strength lay in the fact that round the box he hit the target 99 times out of a 100. That was a brilliant ratio.

I taught Lee how to back in to defenders and use his elbows to ward off people. I taught him every trick I knew in fact. How to put his foot on his marker's foot as the cross comes over so he can't get the jump on him and how to nudge a defender off balance to give himself that split second to get free to score a header. I'm pleased to say Lee learnt well and went on to star for Cloughie's late-eighties Forest side and Howard Wilkinson's successful Sheffield Wednesday and Leeds teams.

I had a decent, talented side, which was good because it was a very strong competition. We did well, reaching the semi-finals where we lost on penalties to eventual winners Haarlem, who had the likes of Ruud Gullit in their side. We then won the third/fourth play-off on penalties against a Celtic team that boasted a cocky youth called Charlie Nicholas in their team, and defender David Moyes, who has gone on to become a long-serving and successful Everton manager.

That experience of helping those young players coming through was invaluable for me and for them. They all had glittering futures ahead of them.

I thought I'd had my future mapped out for some time. My original ambition was simple – to manage Stoke City and follow that up by moving on to the England job. It was that clear cut in my mind. I knew I could be a success as a manager and that would put me in with a shout of the top job in football. That was my goal.

The problem was my route into management, and even coaching, at Stoke was firmly blocked. Manager Richie Barker had a big problem with me being so open about my ambition to progress into management from senior pro. To put it bluntly, he thought I was after his job and because he was in the position of power, he did everything he could to stop me. All too often with managers, egos get in the way.

Stoke City's 1981/82 season had not gone well. I'd played 15 or so games early on as I came back from my cartilage injury and multiple broken arm, but by the time injury forced me out again we were sitting precariously just above the drop zone in 18th position. We lacked both goals and the finesse to break down defences.

I was frustrated both because my injuries were affecting my performance and also as I felt the management were not getting the best out of the players they had available. Richie was into his coaching manuals and he'd decided he wanted to adopt more of a direct style. I wasn't happy with this given the midfield talent we had available in Bracewell, Heath and Maguire. The rest of the squad were unhappy too. I was approached by a deputation to ask me, as captain of the team, to talk to Richie because the players weren't happy with the system. But when I did approach Richie he thought it was just me getting on his case. It all came to a head when I had this argument with Richie and Wally Gould, his coach. They wanted myself and Dave Watson to drop deep because they were worried about us two oldies coping with the pace of Ian McParland. I thought they were wrong.

"We'll be just giving them room to play in," I told them, mindful of Notts County's midfield revelling in the open spaces we'd allow them. "We've got to squeeze them."

Richie insisted. I was proved right. They absolutely mauled us, winning 4-0.

On the coach on the way home afterwards I spoke to Richie again, insisting, "look, we can't play like that."

Perhaps my timing was wrong because he was still smarting, but he simply replied, "I'm a good coach".

Nothing else. Just, "I'm a good coach".

"I'm not saying you're not a good coach, but you are a manager now and there is a difference," I told him.

That's half the problem. Coaches want to tend to change things, to tinker, to prove their credibility. Managers want to win games. I think the perfect example as I say, Joe Mercer and Malcolm Allison. As a pair they were great. Allison was disastrous on his own, but he was a great coach. That applied to Richie too. He was far better as a coach.

It wasn't a major fall out by any means, but it made Richie more mindful of the possible threat I posed to his job if, as I thought might happen, I was forced to retire through injury at the end of the season.

A solution presented itself when an offer came up for me to go on loan to Fourth Division strugglers York. It came at the perfect time for me. I needed get out of Stoke City. I needed to play somewhere else and test myself. So I thought I'd go and see what happened. Obviously Richie was quite happy for me to disappear from the scene and give him some respite. So up I went up to York and, pardon the pun, I have never seen such a shambles in my life. It was unbelievable. When I arrived I found lads sitting out against the wall sunning themselves. That, apparently, was training.

I said, "what are they doing?"

"Oh, they are injured," replied the club official who was showing me round.

"What?" I couldn't quite believe what I was hearing.

"All the senior pros are not playing because they are claiming on the injury insurance."

It was incredible, unbelievable, but it was true. The claim on the insurance was taking precedence over the fortunes of the football club.

Where are you going? It was a total shambles. There is no other way of describing them. They had no coaching, just running. How were the players supposed to improve either individually or as a unit?

We lost our first game 1-3 at home to Hull. It was a big local derby with nearly 5,000 people in Bootham Crescent, which gave me a taste of what could happen at this little club. I very soon learnt why they were languishing down in 19th position in the league. As an early centre came over, I was marking my centre-forward, a big bull of a lad called Billy Whitehurst. The cross just dropped down to the goalkeeper Mike Astbury, who dropped it right at the striker's feet. He couldn't miss. 0-1 and Hull hadn't even created a chance. It didn't get much better in that game. We had a lot of improving to do.

The next week I went into the gym one of the days when the coach insisted that everyone do running. I had refused to join in and instead went over to the little gym in the corner so I went in. There was a game going on amongst the young players and I singled out one of the kids who could really play. So I went to see the acting manager, a guy called Barry Swallow. Barry had been a player himself and now was a club director who was acting as manager following the departure of Kevin Randall, who had only lasted a few months.

I told Barry, "that kid in the gym, he can play. He's the only one I've seen since I've been here. If I was you I'd keep him."

Barry said, "oh that's John Byrne. He's good, but he's allergic to grass". A footballer allergic to grass – it could only happen to me! It turned out John had got asthma and the grass gave him problems with breathing, so we got medicines sorted out for him and he did alright after that, scoring four goals during the run in to the season.

Gradually I exerted my influence on the team, organising the defence on and off the pitch. They had been crying out for an older head like me. We improved. From my arrival in mid-March we arrested the slide of 11 matches without a win. It took a while to get any consistency, though, and when I missed a game through injury they took a fearful 0-5 hammering at Northampton Town, but after a 3-1 home victory at Scunthorpe, we did OK. I really enjoyed working with the youngsters and helping along the other pros to coach them into good habits and develop their skills. I felt they responded well to me in that month too.

******

Meanwhile, Stoke City were another team in need of help.

"There is no crisis," Richie Barker had insisted publicly after the team had gone nine games without a win from February 1982 to drop to 21st position following a 0-2 defeat at Ipswich in mid-April.

Behind the scenes, Richie was panicking. He called me back from my loan spell and as soon as I arrived at the Vic he pulled me in to his office and told me, "just go out there and play and talk and tell people where to go and what to do." He was acknowledging the fact that he needed my help and my organisational skills. At last he'd appreciated me.

I was a bit worried about our chances of avoiding the drop because I was playing alongside Dave Watson, the former Sunderland and Manchester City centre-half. Despite the fact he'd won over 60 caps for England, he didn't always follow instructions. We'd been told to mark zonally, but he insisted on marking players tightly while everyone else marked space. That created gaps which opponents were exploiting. Richie was at his wits end with him and wanted me to sort him out. Them all out, in fact.

I made my second 'debut' for Stoke against old rivals Wolves and, despite going an early goal behind, we won a vital game against fellow relegation strugglers 2-1. Much of that was thanks to two wonderful saves by Peter Fox. I often think Stokies underestimate what a top keeper Foxy was. He was taken for granted quite a bit because everyone just expected him to keep producing brilliant saves and clean sheets. His contribution to that run in was crucial.

Our results picked up, especially thanks to a vital 1-0 victory over Aston Villa in early May that lifted us to 17th position. A draw and a defeat in our next two games meant that the season came to a head with a couple of matches which had been held over until after the end of the regular season. In those days matches were allowed to be played late even if they were vital to the outcome of relegation or championships. It wouldn't be allowed now, of course.

The scenario was that there was one relegation spot remaining, with Wolves and Middlesbrough already doomed, and three teams – West Brom, Leeds and Stoke – involved in the shake up. First West Brom defeated Leeds 2-0 at the Hawthorns on 18 May. That left the Baggies safe, but us a point adrift of Leeds, who had now completed their programme. Our final match was at home to the Albion just two days later. Everything was set up for me to enjoy one last glorious moment in the red and white of Stoke City.

It was a big, big game because we went into it knowing we had to win. Anything less would send us back down to Division Two. Because of the three-way nature of the match, there were a lot of Leeds fans in attendance that night to watch as their fortunes turned form bad to worse. Dave Watson bundled home from close range within half an hour to put us ahead. As Albion's weary men tired we scored twice more. Lee Chapman and Brendan O'Callaghan heading home the vital goals to keep us safe and condemn Leeds to relegation.

The crowd, once again, swept onto the pitch and carried us off shoulder high. It was a very emotional moment for me because I knew this was it. My final game for Stoke, in front of these wonderful fans who had given me everything, just as I had given them. This was the end of the line for me as a Stoke player. I knew that I would be given a free transfer. I milked the moment on those wonderful fans' shoulders. It meant a lot to me to go out on this fantastic high. OK, I'd been used to challenging for honours, but keeping my club in the top division was still very important to me. It was a great, great day and a fantastic way to say goodbye.

I knew my knees were shot. You know you can't go on forever at the top level. Having said that my penultimate First Division game was at Manchester United – Tony Waddington was there and he said he thought I was the best player on the pitch, but that was because I was using my head. That day a young lad from Northern Ireland called Norman Whiteside scored two as we lost 2-0. After the match Waddo was asking me, "what are you retiring for?" Unfortunately for me Richie Barker wasn't the same – he must have felt some kind of threat. He didn't want me around me anymore. Which in many ways is understandable.

Leaving my beloved Stoke City was terrible. It hurt me deeply. I didn't want to eat. Ever since I had known, my life, everything was Stoke. If they'd offered me the assistant manager or coach role I would have stayed. Ironically five years later, after the club had been ignominiously relegated from Division One in 1985, they came chasing me. For about three years Stoke had been playing long ball football, first under Barker and then under Bill Asprey. There were a lot of teams doing it at that time. I'm just not happy with it, I didn't think it was the Stoke way and I didn't think it suited the players the club had got. Under present manager Mick Mills the club had stabilised, but in the summer of 1987 local businessman Maurice Neild rang me to tell me how the club were planning to bring me back to manage the team. He told me, "we were coming out to see you. You were in Magaluf with York, but Chairman Frank Edwards had a heart attack and we didn't get there."

At that stage if it had happened I'd have snapped their hand off, but I soon changed my mind about ever coming back to Stoke. As I've got older I've got more sensible and realised that sooner or later things would probably have gone wrong and I'd have probably have had to leave and not been in love with Stoke City the way I still am. That's how much it matters to me. I didn't want to have that sullied.

Football management is a combination of a myriad of factors, many of which you can't control – certainly not as much as you could as a player when you can actually influence things out on the pitch. You cannot be a fan. You have to be dispassionate, clinical, and care only about the result. Results keep you in work, and I've been lucky enough to stay employed as a football manager for well over 20 years, so I can't have done badly.

It's for those reasons that I decided early on in my managerial career that I would never come back to Stoke to manage. It would create too many problems being a fan and a local lad. It might seem like everyone's dream, but my dream was to play for the club, not manage it. Management is too fickle, too short term to ever risk damaging how Stoke fans felt about me. I hope that doesn't let anyone down or disappoint anyone, but that was how I felt and so I always steered a course away from the club I love.

My last hurrah as a Stoke player was to go on tour with the first team to Morocco in June 1982. We played the Tunisian national team and I scored my last goal for the club in a 1-1 draw. In truth even that episode was tainted with the kind of organisational ineptitude which had become virulent at the club following the stand roof incident. In fact I only went on the trip because I had to. The club were going to stop paying me in May, even though I was contracted through to July. By going to north Africa I ensured I'd get fully paid up. It wasn't exactly the way I'd planned to end my Stoke City career.

I knew I wanted to go into coaching, take my badges. Even at that stage I was still open to staying at Stoke and I believe that if Alan Durban had stayed as manager I probably would have done. With Richie clearly not happy with the prospect of being forced to give me a coaching role, I knew the time had come for me to spread my wings.

Before I knew it, in June 1982, I was presented with an opportunity to put all that preparation into practice. York City, the club at which I'd been on loan, approached me to apply to become their manager. I jumped at the chance,

In many ways going to York didn't actually make a great deal of sense. It was a long way away for a start. The club had all the things I'd thought about: potential, underutilised players, good board and the added advantage of me having spent some time there to get to know the club. The most important thing the club had got was a good board, which had surprised me during my month up there.

The Chairman was a wonderful guy called Michael Sinclair. He was a local businessman, very honest, very straight. A true gentleman, and there aren't many of them around when you're talking football Chairman. I'd got on well with him during my loan spell and I think he understood my abilities and ambition. Michael rang me to ask, "have you written in?"

I replied, "well you know me and what I can do."

Michael, being Michael, said, "oh no we have got to do it through proper channels."

I think I was a shoe in, but I still had to go through the full application and interview process. I went up for a chat and they'd had about four people through in the two hours before me. My interview went on for over two hours with me doing most of the talking, telling them what I could do and how I was going to do it. I clinched it by telling them – setting a silly precedent which I adhered to for far too much of my career for my own good – that if we didn't finish in the top 10 next season they could sack me. It sounds like a grand gesture now, but I said it because I believed that I could turn what I'd seen – and they were right down towards the bottom when I arrived, having applied for re-election seven years out of the previous ten – into a force in Division Four.

Fortunately you could do that then by bringing in top class professionals who had either suffered from injury, or were over the hill and losing their pace, but who could still do a fantastic job at a lower level on free transfers. Most importantly these players needed and wanted to carry on playing. Obviously in the modern era there are very few examples of such high profile players playing on lower down the leagues. I can only really think of the likes of Peter Beardsley and Teddy Sheringham in recent years. Back in 1982 I was able to bring in Roger Jones from Derby, and defenders Alan Hay from Bristol City, Ricky Sbragia from Blackpool and Chris Evans from Stoke, a young full-back who had joined the Potters from Arsenal but had never made a first team appearance for either club. With the addition of myself I had changed the whole back line and goalkeeper.

It had been pretty obvious from the mess which had existed at the start of my loan spell that I didn't think I could do anything with many of the existing players, so out went goalkeeper Eddie Blackburn (who had let in 90 goals the previous season), Mick Laverick, Mike Czuczman, Roy Kay, Eddie Flood, David King and Derek Craig.

Such a cull wouldn't be possible without upsetting a few people. One of the good things about being in the dressing room as a player is that it disguises you from everybody else. It had revealed to me some of the attitudes that existed amongst some of these players. When I realised for example that Czuczman had been offered a contract before I'd arrived I insisted I didn't want him. I felt he wasn't up to the mark. The board replied, "he's been offered a contract". So I went to the PFA and spoke to them about him. They agreed I could offer him the minimum wage of £30 per week because there was nothing in the contract that said how much he would be paid. He wasn't very happy with that and eventually moved on. It was harsh but necessary. I couldn't carry any passengers.

The other man I brought in was my old colleague from Stoke Viv Busby. Viv was signed as a player, but his primary function was as my number two. I would be playing regularly as a centre-half as my priority was shoring up the defence, so I wanted a pair of eyes on the bench.

Given that our managerial partnership would last a decade or so, I think people assume we were great friends from our Stoke days, but that wasn't really the case. It was more the fact that I knew Viv wanted to get into coaching full-time and I had seen how keen he was previously. He loved to talk about football and every time I went to lower level games Viv always seemed to be there too. I also remembered Viv's good work with the Stoke youngsters. He'd moved on to play under Howard Kendall at Blackburn. He was only 33, but I tempted him to join me.

York is a beautiful place, but the major thing that I found different– especially having lived in Stoke, where the city is football nuts – is that it's not a hotbed of football. In fact when I first went there the Rugby League side were getting more through the gates than the football club. I didn't even know what the hell League was, because they play Rugby Union not Rugby League in the Potteries!

Viv and I saw that we had got the makings of a team that could compete, and we believed, because we were young and a bit naïve, that we could turn this club with average gates of 2,000 into a very good team, despite there being just no money to spend on players. The club had a well-run Board, who were always as supportive as they could be. On top of that they were really nice people – people that you would invite into your house and who would reciprocate. It was important to me that I was working with people who I thought were respectable. That didn't change the fact that financially it was hard because I was earning around half the money that I had as a player and I'd still got my wife and kids down in Stoke with a house to run there and I had got to pay rent in York. I remember Viv and I looking for places together to keep the cost down. We first found a house on the grounds of a farm called 'Miserables', which we discovered in short order summed the place up nicely. Almost as soon as we moved in I got some sort of rash and we found the house was infested with fleas and I'd been covered with bites.

So we left that place and the club got us a city centre flat. This may sound as if it was extremely glamorous, well-located, plush residence, but the reality was starkly different. The flat was over the top of a laundrette. The good thing about that was that the laundry below kept it warm upstairs to a degree. Once that residual warmth had worn off of an evening, however, Viv and I used to sit in sleeping bags with bobble hats on so as not to freeze to death. It was that cold – and this was September!

In a strange kind of way that circumstance helped us do our jobs better. Instead of staying in the ice-cold flat, we found it warmer to go out and scout at games to check out players. When we did stay in, one of the very early managerial choices I was faced with was whether Viv and I should put another 50p in the electric meter, or pop down to the pub next door and buy a pint of John Smiths which was on special promotion. The pint won more often than not. Times have changed since 1982.

Despite the hardships, I had a ball right from the off. Everything about having my own club to manage was exciting and new. Dealing with the media was one aspect of the job that I hadn't really considered and I managed to get myself in trouble with the York Tourist Board soon after I arrived because I was happy to crack a few one-liners and felt that I could talk to anyone. I soon learnt to think before I spoke. On this occasion I was asked for my first impressions of the city by the local newspaper and told them, "for one thing if it wasn't for the tourists, the traffic would be great". That managed to be reported as 'Smith slams traffic chaos city', or something like that. The Tourist Board were not happy!

In fact the media around York were fantastic to work with right through my time there. BBC Radio York had only been instituted in about 1982, so was still very much in its infancy. I remember a young John Champion, now heard commentating on football for ITV and Setanta, coming through the ranks there. For the written press I mostly dealt with Yorkshire Evening Post sports editor Malcolm Huntington. Malcolm was very much the gentleman. He loved his tennis and he was an umpire at Wimbledon. He suited York down to the ground. All I would have to do in terms of media work is a piece with Malcolm each day for the radio and something in the morning ready for the evening paper. A couple of phone calls to the Yorkshire Post if there was a really big story on the go or when we were doing well would complete my tasks on that score. It was a great way to learn when to talk, who to and what about.

I remember being called both 'Dirty Den' and the 'Democratic Dictator' in newspaper interviews as reporters tried to characterise me to the Yorkshire public. That was interesting because I think they hadn't had such strong-minded people in charge of the club before. Certainly they hadn't had anyone with the kind of top flight background I boasted. I was a big focal point during the next few seasons.

It's my belief that natural leaders of men are very hard to find. I believe I was and remain one of those. That was what I was good at in the dressing room and on the pitch. Even as a player people used to say to me, "will you shut up?" I'd reply, "you do what I'm telling you and then I'll shut up." I think that's what you've got to do. As a manager it's no different except your head's on the chopping block!

I now thought I'd got a good, if small, squad, which was prepared well for the season, but, for example, when I first arrived there was this habit that the training kit used to be dumped in the middle of the room and you just picked it up as you came in for training. It was first come first served sort of thing. I wasn't happy with that. I felt everyone should have their own kit. So I found the kitman, who was this feller called John Simpson, and he showed me all this brand new kit still in its packets. They'd been keeping them aside until the kit they were using had worn out. It had been sitting there unused for years, which was ridiculous. So I took it all out and gave it to the lads. But then I made them take it home themselves and wash it because until then John's wife was having to do it.

John was also the club physio, but he wasn't trained. He was just someone who helped out because he loved York City and did pretty much every job going. I remember him working on Roger Jones's thigh, kneeding it like bread! Then he'd just put heat on any muscle that was stretched. After that first treatment Roger said, "he isn't coming near me again!" So I brought in a properly trained physio called Gerry Delahunt.

We also used to train at the York mental hospital just up the road from Bootham Crescent. They had a pitch on their grounds which we were allowed to use for a song, but there was one problem. We would be working on positioning for corners and free-kicks and while I was organising things and talking the players through what I wanted them to do, some of the patients would just walk across and pick the ball up – and we couldn't afford to be losing any. What could we do? You couldn't shout at them. If anything we were told not to talk to the patients, but often we were forced to ask these people really politely, "can we have our ball back please?!" It was what you might call interesting.

Those sort of things needed to be changed, of course, but it all cost money – and every penny I spent on these peripheral matters was a penny less I could spend on the squad.

I had been delighted with the reaction of the players who I'd retained to my arrival. I thought I had a great nucleus to bring those experienced heads in alongside. Derek Hood, Brian Pollard, Gary Ford, Malcolm Crosby, John Byrne and Keith Walwyn all seemed delighted that I had was the new broom which was sweeping Bootham Crescent clean. Their attitudes would become key to our success.

We didn't make the best start, winning only two of our first 12 games, but we remained positive and it all clicked together in our home game against Hartlepool at the end of October. We won 5-1 with goals from five different scorers, which really pleased me. The confidence oozed through the team after that, but at this stage they only truly believed in themselves when they were playing at home. Our next two games at Bootham Crescent finished in 4-0 and 6-1 victories over Aldershot and Mansfield respectively. But away form home it was a totally different story. We just could not win. There was some sort of mental barrier across the players' minds which told them they were great at home, but rubbish away and we worked really hard on that side of things to convince them that it didn't matter where they played. They were one of the best sides in this division.

The breakthrough finally came at Torquay in January, where a 3-1 win set us off on a run of 23 games in which we lost only four times. That was promotion form and on top of that we were cracking in goals left, right and centre.

Right from the first day I had walked into the club I knew I had a fantastic strike partnership. I've already mentioned John Byrne, and I paired him up with the colossus that was Keith Walwyn. Keith was big. But his power, pace and incredible ability to leap higher than anyone I've ever seen from a standing start were negated by a total lack of belief in himself. In training sessions he often couldn't kick the ball between the corner flags during shooting practice. But in games he was capable of volleying fantastic goals from 30 yards. His awesome aerial power also meant that we played the ball out to the wing as much as possible allowing Brian Pollard and Gary Ford to whip balls into the box for Keith to win, and Byrnie to sweep up the bits and pieces.

Keith was a lovely big man, but I realised he basically needed teaching from scratch again because he had lost all belief. The raw materials we had to work with were super. I tried various techniques including sometimes having a go at him in training or in the dressing room when I felt he needed shaking up. The other lads couldn't believe it because apparently no-one had ever been brave enough to have a pop at Keith before. They had been intimidated by his physique. That didn't scare me, although everybody else in the dressing room apparently said to Buzzer, "what's the gaffer doing with Keith? Nobody talks to him like that." I laid into Keith a couple of times, judging the level of what I said to get a response, and Keith proved what a great man he was by responding

174

and producing out there on the pitch. He netted his first hat-trick in that 6-1 hammering of Mansfield and cut a swathe through the division in the second half of the season. I always think it's amazing what people will believe if you tell them it often enough and we banged on to these players about how good they were. Keith was a prime example of ho it worked. He started believing and reaped the rewards.

For me that first season was all about giving the players the belief that we could do on the pitch in matches what we talked about in training. I remember in one of my early games I hit a long diagonal ball out to the right wing, putting Gary Ford in behind the full-back to send over a peach of a cross for Big Keith to head a goal. Fordy said, "can you do that all the time?"

"Of course," I replied. "Can you?"

"Fantastic. Keep them coming." He'd just never seen anybody with the ability to do that before. My long passes made his crossing easier and consequently we were more dangerous on the break. It was a formula which saw Keith score 21 goals and John Byrne 12 over the season.

Pretty much everyone bought into the ethos I was espousing, which I reinforced by using a sports psychologist, something which was unheard of in the professional game at that time. None bought into it more than Fordy, who had a good eye for goal too. He scored 11, while on the other flank Brian Pollard was also amongst the goals. Brian wasn't quite as enthusiastic as my new, more professional work ethic. He'd enjoyed the lax regime previously and really didn't appreciate it when I singled him out for some extra pre-season work. Polly was an idle little sod, so I made him partner up with me on the hill work we did which is probably the most despised of all training routines. He hated me for that, but more because I was challenging him to improve for his own sake and that of the team. He had been lazy up until now, but I wouldn't allow him to be. I knew what Brian was capable of. The previous season he'd scored just five goals. This time round he finished as second highest scorer with 17. Need I say more.

As well as more goals being scored, my new defence tightened things up at the back. My centre-half partner was Ricky Sbragia. I'd seen Ricky play at Walsall and Blackpool. He lacked pace but he had a good physique. His problem was that he would go diving in to tackles, kicking people all over the place, giving away free-kicks in dangerous places.

I took in what he was up to for a few games and then said, "what are you doing?"

Ricky replied, "well they told me at Blackpool I'm not that good a player, so to get stuck in."

"Is kicking people your game?" I asked.

"Not really," he replied. "I like to read the play and clean up the loose ends."

"I'll do the kicking and you do the reading," I told him and he was brilliant after that once he had got out of the habit of thinking he had to go and win the ball. It shows how players can be ruined by coaching because Ricky was a big, strong lad, but he had been taught as if he was a bludgeoning centre-half and he wasn't. He was a good reader of the game and good on the ball. Our relationship had similarities to that between myself and Alan Bloor.

In our last 11 games we conceded only eight goals, a record I was really proud of and wanted to improve upon the following campaign. That first season we finished seventh, only four points off Scunthorpe, who edged into the final promotion spot. I was reasonably happy, not least because we had finished above tenth so my job was safe. We'd also conceded just 58 goals, compared to 91 the previous year, and only 19 of those were at home. At the other end of the pitch we were banging in the goals from every area of the team. Even I scored four, the same number as Viv, which was very pleasing.

We'd also woken up the local public to what was going on at Bootham Crescent. The attendance at our first home game was 1,737. By the end of the season, our last home gate was 4,814, while the crowd for the local derby against Hull on Easter Monday was an enormous 9,909.

We'd won 15 of our last 24 games. That was promotion form. The total shambles of the previous season had disappeared and I was determined we would carry that forward. Through hard work, and bloody-mindedness, plus a lot of fun, we'd hit upon a winning formula. The new season was where we had to make it pay.

Travelling all over the world with Stoke had allowed me to discover that I wanted to spread my wings outside the normal gambit of the professional footballer – drinking, girls, gambling. Much as I love a pint here and there, and I'm told I can hold the drink pretty well too, I have never over-indulged. As a player, when I was with the lads I was very much a social party animal, but my wider interests lay in looking at businessmen and how they managed their lives, careers and businesses. At Stoke I had joined the Round Table. I hoped to pick up tips which would stand me in good stead. It also got me used to public speaking. That experience helped me to realise that there was another whole world out there besides football. I also learned that the people I met had different problems and different aspirations.

I became chairman of the charity fundraising committee and learned how to make decisions. My committee meetings used to be great because I had mine in my house. Where other people would sit down and discuss things in detail, I'd say, "right lads this is what we're doing" and they'd simply reply "yes, let's get moving". I supported Muscular Dystrophy. We used to do all sorts of things to raise money. We'd have charity football games, charity boat races down the canal, Santa Claus at Christmas going round on his sleigh – somebody was always coming up with some idea.

I remember one family for whom we raised enough money to buy a bus for their three handicapped sons. They were great lads. We played cards with them. They used to love taking money off me. They had got a great sense of humour. Their mum and dad had to get up in the night every two hours to turn them over so they could breathe. If you imagine that as an integral part of your life and couple it with knowing that the lads were going to die by the time they were in their early twenties because the disease is degenerative then try telling me you have a hard life. That van made a crucial difference to their day-to-day existence and I took so much out of that experience, not least in it bringing me a greater perspective.

In many ways that was another foundation for my managerial career. Apparently a lot of people find making decisions difficult. I discovered I don't. I'm positive about what I want to do which tends, if you are on a committee such as that, to swing decisions your way. I also thought doing that work helped broaden my horizons further and helped me in my career as a manager with all the other aspects of the job outside pure footballing matters that are so important. It also gave me plenty of fresh ideas when it came to analysing the performance of players. Just little things, like when I was at West Brom I insisted that I be bought a computer on which I kept the records of all my own players and was also able to analyse those I was interested in putting bids in for. That was as late as 1997, so you can see how backward a big club like West Brom had been. Really it was all brought in because of the innovation of Arsène Wenger and I thought it was vital to keep up with progress. Now, of course, Pro-zone and video analysis of players is standard.

For me, having been a manager for 25 years now, I want players who give me total commitment, because that means they fulfil their potential. Attitude is so important. That's what really makes the difference between what division players can play in. Talent is just one aspect of being a footballer. If you've got all the talent in the world and don't work at your game you won't make it as far as you should do. It's about desire and passion and that's something that's relatively rare these days. It's certainly what sets many so-called talented lower division players apart. I like to think that I gave my all in every game I played. Some matches I played better than others, of course, but it was never due to a lack of application. That was something I felt I had got across well in that first season in full-time football management.

Now, nearly 30 years later, I've learned that in the modern era there are good millionaires and there are bad millionaires sitting in dressing rooms up and down the country. The question of how you motivate rich players who maybe don't care, are arrogant, have an oversized ego, love an excuse or adopt the wrong metal approach is one of the modern games great conundrums for managers. At the top of the game the attitudes can sicken even the strongest stomach because of the huge amounts of money which swill around the game. Down at the level at which I ended up operating for the last decade of my career there are no millionaires, but the attitudes still prevail. For me Mums and Dads make or break footballers with their examples of behaviour and dedication. At the basic level they can make sure their kids are out there on the street playing the game and learning the core skills in an unstructured, uncoached environment. That's key for me. Coaching shouldn't come into the equation until much later.

Part of the problem, of course, is the value society now places upon footballers, who could feature in glossy magazine or on television. There is a status that is conferred on a young, fit, athletic lad who can go out at night and tell the girls he's a footballer. It's cool, hip, trendy, chic. It's also a load of old tosh if that player does not perform next time he goes out in front of his paying public. Balancing that conundrum is such an important part of modern football management.

Having built up some momentum in the second half of that first season, it was vital we carried it on to the following 1983/84 season. Essentially we kept the same team as I felt they had proved how good they were in that fantastic run. I just added a couple of players after convincing the board that with a slightly larger squad to deal with injuries we could have a serious chance of promotion. I've talked about how it was vital I got the players believing in both themselves and me, well it was vital that the board did so too. They gave me the budget to sign another of my former team-mates, Sean Haslegrave, from Crewe. Sean always had great energy and at this level buzzed around the field, winning the ball and distributing it well. He was strong for a little guy and was really, alongside Malcolm Crosby in central midfield, the engine room of the team.

I had realised that my own career was to all intents and purposes over. My knees were no good any more and I'd done my bit by passing over my experience to my defence, so was happy to move to the sidelines. I brought in John MacPhail on a free transfer from Sheffield United to replace me, although I still made the occasional appearance in emergencies. I'd also realised that when you are a manager you are going out two or three nights a week watching games, so to play as well is not ideal.

The story of how I came to sign John is worth retelling. I was on the lookout for the right man to replace me, but it had to be on a free transfer so I could spend any money on the wage package. I'd heard that John was available and that he was unfortunate not to be in the Blades' team. I checked the fixtures and, bingo, a plan formed in my mind. I picked up the phone and rang Kate, my wife.

"Hi darling," I said. "Put something nice on and phone the babysitter. I'm coming down tonight to take you out."

She was delighted, but not quite so happy when she learned our destination for the evening was The Hawthorns to watch West Brom reserves take on Sheffield United, starring John MacPhail. To give Kate her due, she has always backed me 100% and she enjoys watching any game of football, plus she knew we'd be going for our customary post-match meal anyway. On this occasion she had her eyes on my transfer target and turned to me and said, "Denis, are you sure you mean the number 5? You must be joking." Never one to mince her words, Kate!

To be fair to her, that night she was right. John was hopeless. He spent the entire evening following the number 9 he was marking everywhere. Even when the striker went into the left-back position he followed, leaving a gaping hole in his defence for the opposition to exploit. But what I saw again was the raw material I could work with.

John was such a good athlete, big, strong and good in the air. He had a most unusual way of heading the ball as he used to get in front of the centre-forwards if they tried to back into him and upset his balance. Initially I thought, 'I'll get that out of him,' but as I watched him I found that it worked for John and he would cut out a lot of dangerous balls.

When I met him to discuss the possibility of him joining us, he impressed me straight away by saying, "what do you need me for because I ain't going to take your place?" He was sharp enough to know there must have been something going on. He didn't know about my knees. So he signed – yet another free transfer – and the next season I didn't play a game. He played them all.

Monty, as we all used to call him, was a leader. He always seemed very erect and very proud. He is a good-looking lad, sharp, well-dressed and full of himself. He was a hugely positive influence in the dressing room. If I tell you he's a car salesman up in the north east now, then you'll understand what a suave presence and magnetic persona he always had. He also dovetailed perfectly with Ricky Sbragia and the partnership blossomed. They really were super together, complementing each other beautifully.

Even with those two additions the squad was tiny compared to most other clubs. I'd opted for quality over quantity and thankfully we didn't pick up any major injuries. The few other squad players were Derek Hood, Brian Chippendale, right-back Steve Senior and young local lad Alan Pearce.

I'll tell you a good story about Stevie Senior. After he'd played a couple of games I realised he was missing or misjudging high balls in the air. It was particularly bad from kicks from the goalkeeper's hand. It was so bad that I had begun to think that he had an eye problem. Instead of pulling him up in front of the entire squad and making a big issue out of it I decided that everyone would have to have their eyes tested. That way we could discover what his problem was surreptitiously. So I sent them all along to the opticians thinking that we'd get to the bottom of what the problem was. When they got back I sauntered over to Steve and said, "how did it go?"

"Yes, fine," he replied. "But we've got a big problem."

"What's that?"

"Our goalkeeper is blind in one eye."

What! I pulled Roger Jones in.

"Jonesy, can you see out of both eyes?"

"No boss."

"Why didn't you bloody tell me?"

"I didn't think it was that important," he said.

I couldn't believe it. One of his eyes was about as useful as Hattie Jacques's ballet shoes. Mind you, it didn't bother Roger. His performance levels never dropped for us all season. I often wonder how good would he have been if he could see properly! Unbelievable.

I never did manage to get to the bottom of Steve Senior's problem, so I came to the unavoidable conclusion that he just couldn't bloody judge the ball in the air.

To say that we stormed to the Fourth Division title is something of an understatement. We started with a 2-0 win at Stockport and had win after win after win. 31 in all in the 46 games. It wasn't all plain sailing. We had the occasional slip up. I remember one match at Hereford. We lost 2-1. Roger Jones came out of his box to clear a couple of through balls, but mis-kicked both and left them on a plate for Hereford to bag the two goals which clinched victory. If only he'd had two good eyes!

In truth we were streets ahead of the rest of the division. Our two forwards scored over 50 goals between them. John Byrne netted 27, while Big Keith Walwyn hit 25. Byrnie was awesome that season. He took his play to another level, another dimension. When I first arrived at York I used to fine him 50p every time he didn't pass when he should do. I got fed up with the number of occasions when he'd dribble to the byline, beat three or four players and then try to score from a ridiculous angle. The fines worked. He started to think about what he was doing, and looked for his strike partner or incoming midfielders around the penalty spot and he laid on hatfuls of goals for us. He also had such a good touch. I wasn't surprised when he went on to play in the World Cup with the Republic of Ireland in 1990.

Alan Pearce came in to replace the occasionally injured Brian Pollard partway through the season. Pearce looked as though he was going to be quite a player. He was strong, quick, scored goals, had two good feet, a blistering shot – the kid had got the lot. But again finances come into it, we weren't paying him enough really. I only had the budget to pay him £80 a week, which wasn't much considering he was in the first team and he was scoring goals. It didn't really give him the money to live the right way. That's one of the things that I learnt from that scenario. I should have looked after him better – to make sure he was being professional off the field as well as on. Alan didn't help himself, though. His lifestyle frustrated me. So much so that I let it get to me one particular matchday. Pearce went down injured behind one of the goals. I was on the bench that day, so I walked round to where he was being treated and had a word with him. Kate was sitting in the stand and as I went over she turned to Pearce's girlfriend and said, "oh isn't that nice. Denis is seeing how Alan is."

What she didn't know was that I had gone over there to vent my spleen. At that precise moment I was saying something along the lines of, "get your arse back on that pitch". It worked, he got back up and he went on and played.

We were only headed for a week in the entire season, when back-to-back defeats and a draw at Reading saw us slip behind Bristol City by a point. We were irresistible, though, and won seven of the next eight games to forge back ahead. March 1984 was a huge month for us. We played six league games and won five of them, drawing the other. We also won the next game on 1 April too as I was awarded the Manager of the Month for the first time. Next up was the visit of Doncaster. It was our 38th game of the league season and third-placed Rovers drew a crowd of over 11,000 to Bootham Crescent. There were people in the rafters of the stands, on the pylons, crammed into every nook and cranny. The 1-1 draw left us just two wins from promotion, which was sealed by a 4-1 hammering of Halifax in which John Byrne scored a hat-trick and Keith Walwyn netted the other.

We beat Tranmere at Prenton Park in the next game and then clinched the title with a 2-0 victory over Hartlepool thanks to two Keith Walwyn goals. Then to cap it all we topped the 100 point mark with a 3-0 win over Bury. We finished with 101 points, 16 ahead of our nearest challengers Doncaster, having scored 96 goals and conceded just 39. It was a phenomenal achievement.

The celebrations around winning the title in May 1984 were truly memorable. I think it's fair to say York had not seen anything like it since the Viking invasion! We were feted with an open-top bus tour around York. The city was chock-a-block with people and we were all having a ball. There was a Civic reception. No-one could really believe what was happening as they hadn't understood the revolution which we'd started the season before. We had won the league after starting the season with about 2,500 fans at the first home game and ended it with over 8,000 crammed into that tiny little ground and with the entire city out cheering and waving flags and scarves.

The club was on this massive roll. We were flying. Myself and Viv thought we were going to keep doing this all the time.

What I think is interesting is how many of that team have gone on to have coaching careers in the game. For example, as I write, Roger Jones is at Swindon, Chris Evans is now the assistant manager at Bolton under Gary Megson, Malcolm Crosby, is currently assistant manager at Middlesbrough having worked for me at Sunderland, West Brom and Oxford, and Jim Smith at Derby amongst others, Ricky Sbragia is now at Sunderland, having been Sam Allardyce's coach at Bolton and also at Manchester United. Sean Haslegrave is the coach of the English Colleges national team. It's not a bad record for a club of that sort of standard. Neither was our record that season. Winning promotion with the first ever 100 point haul – and scoring 96 goals into the bargain – was not bad football from a bunch of free transfer nobodies managed by a novice.

Chapter Thirteen

THE MINSTER MEN

As a manager I have always been in favour of the lads getting together for a few drinks and having a bonding session. It's great for team spirit and it's amazing how players use the time to talk things through. People think players simply go out, get hammered and talk about girls, but often they sit down over a quiet beer and talk through how they can improve playing together, discussing tactics and details such as the timings of runs and passes. That's always been my experience as a player and through the first twenty-odd years of my managerial career. In the last decade the culture has changed. Now it's about being seen. It's also harder for them to go out without being pestered from pillar to post. But often they like that anyway!

At York, as at all my clubs, drinking was banned for three days before a game. Just occasionally exceptional circumstances cropped up which required special permission. I remember this one occasion a couple of the lads came to me and asked if they would be allowed to have a couple of drinks.

"It's Wednesday…" I said.

"I know boss," came the reply. "But it's Sean Haslegrave's birthday."

I said, "oh fine great, you go and have a few drinks, but keep it sensible."

Off they went.

It was only then that I realised it had been Sean's birthday about three months earlier. He generally had about three birthdays a year, although I mostly let it ride if I thought the lads needed to get together. Sean was great at knowing when the team needed a 'gathering' and they never abused the privilege.

Sometimes people totally underestimate the amount players are able to drink because they are so fit. Their metabolism is different to your average person's because of their fitness regime. If they go out on a session they'll absolutely floor most people. I remember the end of season trip to Magaluf after we'd won the Division Four title we took along our part-time youth team coach Ian Hope, who for his day job was a police sergeant. He thought he could take the boys on. I told him simply, "don't drink with the lads".

But he insisted, "I'll be alright. Eight pints of lager, no problem".

The next morning I was walking along the beach front and I came across Ian sitting out cradling a beer in his hands, looking pretty rough. He saw me coming, raised the drink in my direction and mumbled something like, "Denish, you told me about them, you warned me, I didn't listen."

Success such as ours at lower levels meant the eyes of the football world began to look in our direction, casting covetous glances over our better players. So it was that soon after winning the Division Four championship I had to bid a fond farewell to one of my two goalscorers who had propelled us to that success.

Early in September 1984 we lost to QPR over a two-legged second round League Cup tie. It was a fairly comprehensive 8-3 scoreline over the two matches, but John Byrne must have impressed because straight afterwards we received a bid for his services from Rangers manager Alan Mullery. The initial offer was about £50,000, but I didn't think it was nearly enough. I was trying to chat with Alan on the phone to negotiate the price up, but was getting nowhere, so I thought I'd try something. I knew chairman Jim Gregory would be sitting in the corner of the room nodding his consent to what Alan was saying and so I asked Alan to, "just put Jim on." Knowing what Jim was like I thought he would be desperate to get his hands on Byrnie, as he was the kind of person who, when he had set his heart on something, would persist until he got it. Within a few minutes I'd got him up to £100,000. That was a lot of money at that stage for a Third Division player, given that it was only four years since the first million pound deal for Trevor Francis.

I always believed that was a good transfer for York City. John was obviously ready to move on and you have to be totally realistic at that level. Keeping hold of such a talented player was going to be nigh on impossible once First Division clubs started sniffing around.

It was, though, the first occasion in my career that I had to sell one of my best players. It wouldn't be the last, but then that is the story of every manager's career. On this occasion it wasn't against my will and I understood the need for the club to cash in on one of its finest assets to develop further. I found the York board easy to deal with and so knew exactly where they were coming from and we were all singing from the same hymn book over John's deal.

It would turn out, however, not to be the last time the paths of John Byrne and Denis Smith crossed in our careers.

The money Byrne's sale brought in allowed me to invest during the season in Dale Banton, a striker from Aldershot, who at that time were a decent side, with him slotting in the goals. He'd scored 47 in 106 games, which was a very good record in the Fourth Division. I actually paid a club record £50,000 for Dale at a time when we had been previously restricting ourselves to free transfers. I thought he was well worth it. I'd played against him and rated him highly and he didn't let me down.

There's a great story about Dale's signing. When I first joined York, one of my early games was at Aldershot's Recreation Ground. I was marking Dale and we were leading 1-0 going in to injury time. We won a corner after the ninety minutes were up, so I didn't bother going forward to attack it, preferring to stay tight to Dale so we didn't concede a late equaliser. As I sauntered next to him on the half-way line I ventured the opinion that, "if that ball comes anywhere near me and you, both it and you will be going in the stand, son. I would advise you to not even think about going for it, just pretend the game is over."

Dale looked at me, slightly worried, I think, by this, but the game finished before the ball came our way. I never thought any more about it.

Next time I saw Dale was the day I signed him for York. After we'd done all the paperwork the Chairman said he'd show him around. When I came across them again they were sitting at the front of the main stand and I discovered that Dale had told the Chairman about the bodily harm I had threatened him with the previous season! Now Michael Sinclair was one of the most proper, correct people you will ever come across and Dale has only gone and told him the story. Little bugger! Michael came across and asked me "Denis, you didn't say that to this young boy did you?"

"No, Mr Chairman, he's winding you up," I said, affecting a hurt expression. Dale regretted it at training the next day.

Banton had a great first season, netting 12 goals in 30 games to finish as our second highest scorer. He would eventually score 49 goals in 138 games for York over four seasons.

Before Dale arrived I bade farewell to another member of our title-winning side. Despite the fact that he'd worked his socks off as I'd pushed him to throughout the campaign, I'd come to the conclusion that Brian Pollard was just too much like hard work to keep motivated and fit. I released him at the end of the championship season, but eventually I came to realise that I was wrong. I thought I could do better by spending Brian's wage money on a young lad called Gary Nicholson from Mansfield Town, who'd begun his career at Newcastle. Nicholson didn't cut the mustard. It was the wrong move.

At times during a managerial career you make decisions about players. That is your job – who to retain, who to sign, who to release. I've only ever had three players that I really felt I should have kept hold of. Polly was one of them without question. You should be capable of retaining differing personalities and abilities within a squad, particularly at lower levels, especially when they are blessed with experience, skills and abilities that are otherwise difficult to find and they can score you goals or win you matches.

During our Championship-winning season we'd finally managed to move Kate and the family up from the Potteries after having a terrible time selling the house in Ashley. It took over a year to sell. Our third child, Tom, had arrived in 1978, completing our wonderful threesome, but it was a very traumatic move for Paul, who was 14 and did not want to leave his friends. We bought a lovely house on the outskirts of the city and thoroughly enjoyed living in such a vibrant place. It was the first of several moves, as I always thought it was very important to live in the immediate area of every club I managed. You need to get a feel for a place, what the fans are thinking and saying, how they like their teams to play and how you should react to that. That doesn't mean to say I always listened! But it's important to imbue yourself in the culture of a new area, especially if you feel it's something that needs changing as I was achieving at York. Football had now taken over from Rugby League to become the pre-eminent sport in a city which was hardly a hotbed of sporting achievement until we'd turned up.

In 1984/85 as we established ourselves in Division Three, doing pretty well in the league. We were not beaten until 6 October when we lost at home to Bristol City. We were top at that point as we continued our red hot form of the previous season. The following month we thrashed Gillingham 7-1, with new signing Keith Houchen bagging a hat-trick, then either side of Christmas we scored four goals in victories at both Preston and Cambridge.

But the story of the season for us was our incredible FA Cup run. Much like the Stoke City team I'd been a part of, York were ideally suited to playing one off, high octane games. We were set up to be a great Cup team because of our spirit and ability to conjour goals out of any situation. We were also still on a high. We beat non-league side Blue Star 2-0 at home in the first round, then drew Hartlepool away from home. Back then Hartlepool was a hell of a place to go. The dressing room was just a wooden shack you could seen into from outside and in it was this stove which was supposed to heat the place. The bath was about the size of a coffee table, built in bricks and not tiled. It was terrible. When we'd been storming to promotion the previous campaign a lot of my team talks had centred around the idea of winning so we never had to come back to such dumps as Hartlepool. "Just think about going up and we won't have to come back to places like this," I'd said over and over again.

Then who did we draw – bloody Hartlepool! When that came out of the hat the lads piped up straight away, "boss, you said we wouldn't have to come back places like this!"

Thankfully we won easily as MacPhail and Houchen scored.

As a smaller club you are hoping to come out of the hat during the third round draw with one of the big boys, but we drew Walsall, also of Division Three, who had a good cup fighting pedigree themselves, having reached the League Cup semi-finals only to lose to Liverpool the pervious season. We disposed of them fairly easily 3-0, thanks to goals from 17 year-old Martin Butler, who had graduated through the reserves and was making his first start for the club after a couple of run outs as a substitute, Walwyn and Hay.

Once you make it past the third round there is such a good chance of being paired with one of the bigger clubs that really what you are praying for is that you come out at home. Luckily for us we did, and the unfortunate First Division club to face us at

Bootham Crescent would be Arsenal. Their side was packed with great players, from John Lukic in goal, right through the likes of England full-backs Kenny Sansom and Viv Anderson, centre-half David O'Leary, midfield general Brian Talbot, and strikers Charlie Nicholas, Tony Woodcock and Paul Mariner. It was almost offensive how many big name players they had. They oozed quality and class and back then there was no such thing as squad rotation. Every single one of them played. Their team cost over £4.5 million, while ours had been assembled for just £20,000. But the great thing about the previous two years' growth within our squad, both in terms of experience and belief, was that no-one was frightened. The only emotion we experienced were delight at the draw and determination to seize our chance. We knew we could beat Arsenal because everybody believed it, it was ridiculous really when you think about it. York beat Arsenal? No chance.

The BBC, sensing an upset, had dispatched John Motson, king of the cup shock, to commentate on the game. He arrived in the city the afternoon beforehand and came and had a chat with me as he wasn't too conversant with our squad. I invited Motty along for our regular pre-match night out with the directors of the club. It had become something which we'd done regularly over the promotion campaign and solidified the bond between myself and the board members. Every Friday a couple of directors, the secretary, myself and Viv would have a couple of beers and chat about what was going on. That night Motty joined us and we had a rare old time with me spending most of the night telling John that the BBC covering a York City match just showed how far we had come.

The 26 January 1985 dawned frosty and cold. Hay had been strewn across the snow-covered pitch to ward off frost to make sure our game was played. Volunteers helped clear the ground, fork it over and ensured that the match went ahead when so many were called off that particular day. It was indeed a classic upset scenario. I would imagine that Arsenal, used to their underfloor heated, marble dressing rooms at Highbury, turned up at our little, snow covered ground and thought to themselves, "what the hell is going on here?" But that's what the FA Cup is about. That's why it is such a great competition. It is blessed with this romance which it will always retain for me.

The day remained phenomenally cold, freezing the surface of the pitch once again as the game progressed and dark drew in. Over 10,000 were crammed into the ground. They made a hell of a racket. The atmosphere was as electric as any of those glory nights I'd experienced with Stoke. This, however, was very different. We were total underdogs. No-one gave us a cat in hell's chance.

Of course the conditions played their part in making it a level playing field, but the biggest influence they had was to cause problems of keeping control of the ball. That affected both sides equally as I felt we couldn't truly get going up front. It totally negated Arsenal's attack. We were strong defensively, too, and I can honestly say I was never really worried that we were being put under too much heavy pressure. John MacPhail's commanding presence kept the Gunners at bay while at the other end Butler was a livewire. However our strikers were having trouble breaking through a well-marshalled offside trap.

The first serious chance came our way when Butler capitalised on Kenny Sansom's initial mistake to charge down Tommy Caton's clearance. As he raced onto the loose ball and towards the Arsenal penalty area, he squared for Gary Ford, who shot across the face of the goal. We came close again when, just before half-time, Alan Pearce headed into the side-netting.In the second half we really began to get on top as our powerful running suited the conditions more and Arsenal looked as if they just wanted to get us back to Highbury for a replay. At one point I thought we'd scored when Big Keith ran onto a long punt forward to lob over the advancing Lukic only to see Caton somehow effect a brilliant clearance off the line. Butler and then Pearce fired narrowly over. The chances were coming, but we hadn't taken one and now time was running out.Right at the death the decisive moment arrived. Keith Houchen broke into the box in an attempt to reach a pass and was hauled down from behind by Steve Williams for what I and 10,000 others thought was an obvious penalty. Referee Shaw agreed. Fair play to Keith, he picked himself up and stuck the spot-kick into the net, beating Lukic comfortably despite the incredible tension. Ninety minutes were up, so that took a lot of bottle.

The FA Cup was made for Keith. Just two years later, after we'd sold him to Scunthorpe United and he'd then moved on to First Division Coventry City, he would make himself a household name by scoring a wonderful diving header in their 3-2 victory over Spurs in the final. He was one of those players who just popped up in the right place at the right time in big games. Sometimes in humdrum matches he could go missing. People would then get on his back, but I always felt he could get you a goal at any stage in any game. All good goalscorers make you feel like that. Keith was one of them.

He'd arrived for a £15,000 fee some eight months earlier. The fees for Keith and Dale was the only money I spent in the two years I was managing in the Third Division. I knew Keith from Hartlepool where he'd been top scorer in four consecutive seasons. He'd gone down to Orient but hated it because they just took the Mickey out of his accent. So I brought him in as cover to sit on the bench and come on and play at the front or midfield and he did the job beautifully. Often he would come on as a substitute to take advantage of tiring legs and he scored a lot of late goals.

The goal came so late that there was absolutely no way back for Arsenal. At the final whistle, ecstatic City fans invaded the pitch, jigging with delight. It was a wonderful moment. This was Arsenal we'd dumped out of the Cup. They'd won the thing just six years previously, been beaten finalists the following season, and had never been relegated from the top flight in goodness knows how many years. Little York City had dumped them out of the Cup in one of the great upsets. Clubs like Arsenal usually overcome the problems their players had been faced with that day. They didn't deal with the situation at all well and result has gone down as one of those wonderful upsets along on a par with Colchester knocking out Leeds in 1971 and Barnsley beating Chelsea in 2008. Don Howe was very complimentary. He had no excuses and just complimented me on how we had played. Don was always a gentleman. He knew we had claimed York's biggest scalp ever in any cup competition and wasn't going to spoil our moment as others might have chosen to do.

As reward for that fabulous victory, and a huge amount of press coverage across the nationals and local media, in the next round we were drawn at home to League and European champions Liverpool. No bigger prize could possibly have come our way. The place was buzzing like you would never believe. York had never played Liverpool before and now Dalglish, Rush, Hansen, Wark and Grobbelaar would all be coming to Bootham Crescent.

Once again the conditions were freezing, the pitch almost unplayable, and referee Peter Willis had to be convinced whilst walking around it that the game would be able to be finished. But he gave the go ahead and once again we launched into a match against improbable opposition thinking we could win. It's funny, at that stage the team had so much in belief of their own ability they didn't think it was possible for them to lose. Even to arguably the best Liverpool team of all time.

Again the First Division side didn't really put us under that much pressure. Obviously the pitch might played its part, but we were a passing team too, so it should have affected us as much as Liverpool. I just thought we just played better on the day, which is very nice to look back on.

Even so Liverpool took the lead early in the second half with a clinical finish from Ian Rush. Rushie was a master goalscorer. A real one off. He had pace, power, and could find the net in every possible manner – left foot, right foot, head, knee, nose, backside. He didn't care, he just lived for goals. But I was very proud of the way we responded to that setback, which was actually the first FA Cup goal we'd conceded that season. We didn't crumble. Inspired by a capacity 13,500 crowd we fought back and created a couple of decent chances. But unlike Rushie we weren't clinical enough in front of goal, something which really demarcates the cream from the rest. But my team would not lie down and with five minutes remaining Ricky Sbragia smashed the ball home in a goalmouth scramble to a tumultuous reception. It was Bootham Crescent bedlam! York 1 Liverpool 1. Incredible. Those players who had seen off Arsenal and now held the European Champions deserve every possible credit for what they had managed to do. What an achievement it was to get a club like York to be on a par with Liverpool; okay, maybe not in the league, but at least for one day. It reinforces my point about the quality of the players I had.

The thing that was different about the replay was that it was at Anfield. Now I'd never won there as a player, and this was my first crack at it in management, but I knew what the place could do to footballers with less than iron wills, especially on the kind of electric nights which seem to generate a life of their own in that cauldron of a stadium. On this occasion it got to us. No question. At times we were chasing shadows, although the clinical nature of Liverpool's finishing beggared belief. They had eight shots on target in the entire game and seven went in. Seven out of eight is phenomenal, different class. We just couldn't compete with that. The 7-0 defeat was tough to take after all the euphoria. No-one had ever taken one of my teams to pieces before, but I think their pride had been massively hurt. They had taken a lot of jibes in the press and they had a point to prove. They were frighteningly good. That was the first time we appreciated the gap between the top of Division One and where we had reached in Division Three.

One of the things that really hurt us in that game was that Liverpool had extra runners from midfield joining the attack late. They were irresistible, particularly in the second half when they scored five goals and especially John Wark, who bagged himself a hat-trick, while Ronnie Whelan scored twice. It was interesting that five of their goals came from that source. The others came from full-back Phil Neal and late substitute Paul Walsh. Neither Kenny Dalglish or Ian Rush scored that night. That gave me food for thought.

As fate would have it, the following season offered an opportunity to get our revenge. We reached the fifth round again, this time by defeating four non-league sides – Morecambe, after a replay, Whitby, Wycombe and Altrincham. When we were paired with Liverpool once again, at Bootham Crescent, we really felt we had a chance of knocking them out. We weren't worried by what they'd done to us at Anfield. We had a far stronger mentality than that. We thought back to how close we'd taken them in the first game and how they must have felt when the tie came out of the hat. They must have all sighed and thought, 'not them again'. What was remarkable in many ways was that after the last three years of success we were actually expecting to knock Liverpool out this second time around.

Not only did we give them a game, this time we really should have won. We should have beaten Liverpool. To this day it irks me that we didn't. The scenario was the same again. Freezing cold day, questionable playing surface, Match of the Day in attendance. But this time we got our noses in front when Gary Ford scored. The crowd went ballistic once again and we were absolutely flying. We played superbly and held on as Liverpool mounted wave after wave of attacks. We repelled all borders all the way up to 90 minutes, but on the brink of victory we were undone by a dodgy penalty. We were just going into injury time when referee Peter Willis saw a hand make contact with the ball as the it bobbled around our box and he blew for a spot-kick. I couldn't believe it. We'd been so close. I was thinking, 'this can't be happening'. I never did really find out exactly what the referee thought he saw. Suffice to say he was pretty much alone in spotting the offence.

Jan Molby tucked the penalty away in what was now about the third minute of injury time to rescue another 1-1 draw for Liverpool. It was sickening.

When you come round after a setback like that you realise that financially there are at least £40,000 worth of reasons why the Chairman is doing cartwheels. The club benefited hugely, although the incentive of a home quarter-final, which popped out of the draw on the Monday lunchtime, was far greater than any money which may accrue as far as I was concerned.

We had to pick ourselves up and enter Anfield once again. The great thing was I didn't have to pick to many heads up. As the team was largely the same we wanted to put right what had happened the previous season. We thought we could give them a game this time. Mindful of how they had destroyed us in that replay, I employed defensive midfield players who were detailed to track the midfield runners. Despite the fact that John Wark did score, I felt we'd done a job on him when he was substituted. His goal had given Liverpool a half-time lead, but in the second half we really got stuck in. I had brought a lad called Tony Canham in to plug the gap which I'd left myself by releasing Brian Pollard and the failure of his immediate replacement Gary Nicholson. I'd picked Tony up from Harrogate Railway, a tiny club, then not even the best team in Harrogate. It had come about because Tony had played pre-season with our reserves and scored a hat-trick, including possibly one of the best goals I've ever seen. Picking the ball up on the half-way line, he beat everyone before slotting home coolly. I signed him on the strength of that as he looked a natural. He could go past people on both sides. Those long, mazy runs would become his signature as he made an immediate impact on his debut by scoring the winning goal before going on to make a record 347 appearances and score 57 goals in over a decade at Bootham Crescent.

Tony was a real lad. I don't think he came from the best of background as he had plenty of tattoos at a time when they really weren't a fashion accessory. Until I signed him I don't think anyone had taken him seriously. They certainly hadn't at Leeds where he'd been an apprentice, but he could play. He was quick and had two great feet. It's fair to say he went on to become a club legend. For Tony to score at Anfield to make it 1-1 halfway through the second half was a dream come true as this was his first full season as a pro.

For the next 15 minutes we played Liverpool off the park and then we scored what we thought was the winning goal. I say we thought it was because for some reason it was disallowed. I've no idea why and neither has anyone else who I've ever spoken to who was at Anfield that night, on either side of the fence. On 77 minutes the ball was played through for Big Keith who raced between Alan Hansen and Mark Lawrenson to score. I remember looking across at their bench as the ball hit the back of the net and without any shadow of a doubt they thought they were out.

But for some reason the referee gave Liverpool a free-kick. It wasn't offside as the linesman hadn't raised his flag, there was no foul to speak of. I couldn't fathom it. For the second time against Liverpool we felt as if we'd had a victory stolen away from us. Nobody to this day – not even Craig Johnston who was playing in the game and refers to it in his book – has a clue why a free-kick was given to them cancelling out the goal.

The game went into extra-time and Liverpool called on their experience and extra reserves of energy and class to score twice to seal a 3-1 win. When we conceded the second goal I decided to go for broke and so replaced Sean Haslegrave, who had been responsible for snuffing out the threat of Liverpool's midfield with Keith Houchen to try and nick an equaliser. That probably cost us the third goal as we were pushing forward without defensive cover looking for that vital breakthrough. At the final whistle, Kenny Dalglish went over to Andy Leaning, shook him warmly by the hand and admitted that City had been robbed over the two games and I remember Alan Hansen later going on record as saying that match was Liverpool's toughest on their way to lifting the cup that season. Coming that close to producing arguably the greatest upset in the tournament's history is testament to how good that team was. It's something I'm immensely proud of.

Just to show, though, that the FA Cup is a great leveller, the following season we got beat by a non-league side – Caernarfon Town, 1-2 at home.

There is one great story that I remember from that halcyon period which involves the York fans. During these big cup ties the opposing players would often come in and complain that they'd been pelted by Rowntree's Fruit Pastilles. Often it was the wide players or those who took the corners who would moan about it most. The Rowntree factory, of course, was just up the road from our ground, and many of our supporters would have worked there. I can only think that they were using the free stock they'd be given as part of their jobs to give the likes of Ian Rush and Kenny Dalglish a very special local welcome to Bootham Crescent!

In fact I remember Viv Anderson saying after the Arsenal game that he'd only realised after the game that the ones being thrown at him throughout the 90 minutes were all green! Perhaps there was a special staff offer on. Against Liverpool the supporters raised the stakes to something more substantial. Gary Gillespie came off the pitch and whinged on and on about being hit by a Yorkie bar! For me that just sums up the joie de vivre around the club at the time – brilliant.

******

Although I said we were a Cup fighting team, we actually did pretty well in Division Three too during those two seasons. In 84/5 we finished eighth, but 18 points off the promotion spots. The following season we came far closer to winning promotion. We finished seventh and made Bootham Crescent a fortress, only losing three games at home, one fewer than champions Reading. I really felt as if we were building something at this stage.

Those early years at York were packed with exciting times and exciting players, many of whom were either at the zenith of their careers, or at the start of a life in football that would take them to the top of the game. One such player was a young pup that caught my eye in training named Marco Gabbiadini.

I have always loved goalscorers, both as a manager and as a player. I want those type of people, it's selfish because I want them for myself. It's based on something fairly simple – if you don't stick the ball in the net you've got nothing.

Marco was an unbelievable goalscorer. He had a mental capacity to put everything behind him and just concentrate on the here and now which marks a truly great striker out from the average. He would miss five chances and then score one and you couldn't really talk about those he'd missed because he'd forgotten them. He'd just blanked them out. All that mattered to him was the next opportunity. That mindset also meant that he never thought that scoring once in a game was enough. He was always looking out for the second or third goal. He regularly scored multiple times in a game, particularly at Sunderland, where I took him. A lot of strikers, especially at lower levels, will either let their heads drop when a couple of chances go begging, or score early on and think their day's work is done. Marco was never like that. It's a very important aspect of a goal scorer.

Marco had come through the youth system and made his first team debut at 17 as a substitute towards the end of the 1984/85 season. He was so physically developed that he was a man at 16. Broad chest, thick thighs and a fantastic turn of pace, Marco could strike the ball well, jump and head too, and, importantly for a kid, he wasn't frightened. I was more than happy to try him in the first team and see what happened. In my opinion if you are good enough or old enough. I've always liked to give youth its chance.

In his first full season, 1985/86, he scored on the opening day and then netted three more goals as I gradually introduced him into the side. The following campaign he bagged nine goals, including one spell of four goals in six games, but picked up an injury in March which kept him out for the rest of the season.

That injury was part of a general loss of momentum that occurred around that time. In the summer of 1986 I was forced to sell John MacPhail to Bristol City for just £15,000. It annoyed me that John should be sold, especially as Bristol were actually one of our major promotion rivals at that time. On top of that Alan Hay and Sean Haslegrave were nearing the end of their careers, as Roger Jones had done, while youngsters Martin Butler and Simon Mills did not kick on and fulfil their potential. It felt as if the bubble had burst.

Despite a bright start to the campaign 1986/87 did not go well. We struggled and eventually finished 20th, just one place above safety, although 18 goals from Keith Walwyn kept our heads above water. We were never really in that much trouble, though the tension did rise somewhat during a poor run in April. A vital 2-1 victory on 2 May over fellow strugglers Bolton, who would eventually be relegated through the newly-instituted play-off system, meant we were safe, so we played out the last two game in relative comfort.

The highlight of the season another cup triumph. In the League Cup second round first leg we managed a 1-0 home victory over Chelsea thanks to a Tony Canham goal.

We went down 0-3 in the return, but that electric night came on the back of four wins in the first six league games, which had left us in second place. It seemed at that point as if it was going to be business as usual, but a run of one win in 14 games put the lie to that as the lack of the right personnel began to hurt us.

The season showed me all too starkly that I had taken York City as far as I could. Unless something major changed on the funding front we simply couldn't rise any further. We'd hit the ceiling. I'd got the squad doing so well and the Board were stupid to expect me to keep achieving at that level, let alone win promotion, with no more money. Instead of investing in the team the cash we generated all went into improving the facilities at Bootham Crescent. When I first joined the offices were portakabins out in the car park. With the profits of the player sales and the cup runs the club built new offices, board room and changing rooms. It's beautiful now, but it meant that the budget I had to spend on my squad stayed pretty much the same despite the fact we'd moved up from 19th place in Division Four to seventh in Division Three in just three seasons. The problem was it meant I had to keep the player situation very tight. Towards the end of the 1986/87 season the Board told me to let a few of the players go. We were struggling and they were worried that maintaining even the size of squad we had meant we were jeopardizing the club's future. I didn't mind a couple of the names they mentioned, but I balked at the last one on the list, goalkeeper Andy Leaning. I'd signed Andy from the Rowntree's factory team. He'd become our regular first choice, displacing Mike Astbury who had succeeded Roger Jones, and I thought that at 24 he was a fantastic future prospect. Now the board wanted me to replace Andy with the younger, less experienced, cheaper Neil Smallwood to see out the season and then bring a more experienced keeper over the summer.

I had a big argument with the board over that. They were telling me, "you've got to release him, you've got to release him".

I retorted, "it's my team, I put it together and Andy's really good, outstanding."

"Well, he's got to go."

"No. No way."

When you have an argument like that there is only ever one winner. It broke my heart to do it, but I set about finding a club to take talented goalkeeper Leaning off my hands. I felt I owed that to him because he was such a talented player. I tried John McGrath up at Preston and then phoned Harry Bassett, who was manager Sheffield United. I was telling them how good my goalkeeper was and why they should take him. Pleading with them to sign him. It was bizarre. Harry signed Andy and he never looked back. He's still coaching for Sheffield United even now.

Ultimately I felt that the board were now influencing football decisions. In forcing me to release Andy Leaning they were questioning my judgement and that's what they paid me for. They had never interfered up till now, but once they were trying to tell me about the players that was it for me. That situation crystallised the problem which had been forming over the last year or so. Fun though it had been, I knew I too would have to move on.

I had all this in my mind at the end of the 1986/87 season when we went on our end of season jaunt to Magaluf in Majorca. This would have been the same summer that I was approached by Stoke City had chairman Frank Edwards not had a heart attack. While we were there it was mentioned to me by one of the club's Vice Presidents who was on the trip, Stewart Watson, that Sunderland might be interested in me as their new manager.

I told him not to be ridiculous. Sunderland had had a bad season, but then so had we. But when I got back home a newspaper reporter from the north east got in touch with me and asked if I would be interested. Interested? Who wouldn't be? Though Sunderland may have suffered relegation to the Third Division for the first – and so far only – time in their history, they were still a massive club as far as I was concerned.

Before I knew it I was being shown around Roker Park. I fell in love with the place immediately. It was one of those old-style football grounds, much like Stoke's Victoria Ground, which had an atmosphere all of its own. It was almost as if I could feel the history of players such as Len Shackleton, Charlie Buchan and Charlie Hurley pulling me inexorably in.

York's board had given me permission to interview for the vacant position. I have to say that they were fantastic all the way through the process of me moving on. They understood my frustration at what had gone on during the previous season and were realistic to know that they couldn't keep hold of me once they reined in the spending.

There was one sticking point, though. York wanted compensation as I was still under contract. Sunderland insisted they were not going to pay. It just wasn't the done thing to pay a 'transfer fee' for a manager in mid-80s. I'd already been offered and accepted the job by this stage and couldn't believe that this situation could lead to me missing out on something which I had now set my heart on. It was ridiculous. York were insisting on receiving £20,000, but I was technically contracted to the club and so they held all the cards. I could only think of one of my own to play. I negotiated with the York board to get the sum they were demanding down to £10,000. They eventually agreed, but Sunderland chairman Bob Murray still refused. I was at my wit's end. This was beginning to feel quite petty.

Then a thought struck me – something that could settle this without either club losing face – as long as they would both play ball. I approached both sides and put my proposal to them. Both thought it highly unusual, but both liked it. So it was agreed. York released me to become manager of Sunderland.

The proposal? Well, it was a tad unusual to say the least. Sunderland would pay York £10,000 now. At the end of the 1987/88 season a further £10,000 would change hands to make up the £20,000 York had been looking for from the start. The only thing was that if I got Sunderland promoted from the Third Division at the first time of asking the club would pay that extra £10,000. However if I failed to win promotion I would have to pay the whole amount out of my own pocket.

No-one can say I didn't have the confidence to back myself.

The scariest part of that deal? Not the thought of dragging a once-proud club up by its bootstraps with a demotivated squad of players who clearly weren't good enough to play in the Second Division. Not even the thought of winning over some of the most passionate, but longest-suffering supporters in football. Or even doing all this on a budget not that much larger than I'd been used to working with at York.

No. The scariest part of that deal without question was selling the idea to Kate.

Chapter Fourteen

ROKER ROAR

Over the summer of 1987 I worked on winning Kate round to my way of thinking. It wasn't easy. Look at it from her point of view. Somehow I'd got myself into a situation in which I was moving from little York City to a massive club like Sunderland for a lesser deal. For example I'd lost my right to a club car, which at York had been sponsored by the local garage. I was on about the same money, around £40,000, and had this £10,000 noose around my neck! Try selling that to any partner you care to mention and it's a tough ask.

It didn't seem so important to me that I'd gambled £10,000 of my own money on my family's future, I'd walked into the stadium and imagined it full. I was utterly sold on it. I'd stood in the middle of the Roker park pitch in the empty stadium and thought to myself, 'I've got to be able to get Sunderland out of this. If I can't get a club like them out of this mess I don't deserve the job anyway, I deserve to be fined.'

Despite at first not really understanding my desire to take the post because we had such a good life in York, and her obvious misgivings over the £10,000, Kate finally came round. She reacted in the way she always does to my hare-brained ideas, by doing the immensely sensible and practical step of increasing our mortgage by £10,000 just in case I failed and had to cough up the readies.

Joining Sunderland also meant another house move. A lot of players and managers don't move with each transfer, but each time I moved I tended to think, "I might be here for life with any luck." In this game you just don't know. So I wanted my family with me. It was difficult moving the kids about. I remember when we left Stoke Paul, then aged 14, was distraught, but he'd settled in famously. Now we were moving them all again. At that point Paul was 18 and off to University, Becky 16 and would go to college in Durham, while Tom was 9. We sold the house in York very easily. Each time I moved club Kate would remain behind to sell the old place and then move up to buy the new one. Pretty much the next time I would see her she'd have the new house up and running and a meal on the table. In fact when I moved up to Sunderland she did exactly that.

We'd actually just done up the house in York, so when I moved up north I said to her, "Look I want a totally finished house. Four nice bedrooms, a couple of bathrooms, not too bothered about the location, but it has got to be finished."

Sunderland trained at the Durham University facility at Shincliffe overlooking the city during the week and I remember this one morning I received a phone call in my office from Kate.

"Denis, I've found a house."

"Great, where?" I asked.

"Near Durham, overlooking the cathedral."

"Perfect. I'll come and have a look." On the way over I was thinking this place would be great for getting to training and was imagining a really nice, cosy home, ready to move into.

How wrong I was. When I arrived at the address I discovered as Kate' perfect house was actually a pair of semi-detatched houses that had been knocked through into one. There were no internal walls downstairs, so we had one put in. The plumbing worked, but it was pretty much a shell on the ground floor.

I took one look and said, "Kate, forget it." I got in the car and went back to work.

When I arrived back at our hotel, the Royal County in central Durham, that evening she opened the door with a smile on her face, saying, "I bought the house".

I couldn't believe it!

I remember my first night at home in three months as I'd been out every night working. I walked in and settled into the nice big kitchen complete with a big aga and Kate had the meal on the table as always. Halfway through the meal Kate piped up, "Denis, I've got something to tell you."

Already on my guard after being hoodwinked into buying precisely the type of property I hadn't wanted, I said, "what's that?"

"The plasterers are coming in half an hour."

My first night in and she'd organised for the work to start!

I took one look at her and said, "right, I'm going down the pub." Once the plasterers had arrived and been briefed Kate joined me for a great evening in our new local. She's great.

It took over six months to get the place sorted out, but it was wonderful when it was finished with the sun setting down behind the cathedral and the castle.

Thinking about it, the rebuilding of the house mirrored what was going on at Sunderland AFC. The club was at its lowest ebb, having been ignominiously relegated to the Third Division for the first time in its history. It was the equivalent of having Leeds and Nottingham Forest down in the same division in recent seasons. Of course I'd joined York with the club pretty much rock bottom and managed to turn things around, but this situation presented a very different challenge. The first major difference was that funds existed to rebuild the side. It was a good job as I soon realised I had a much harder job on my hands at Sunderland AFC than I could possibly have thought. It wasn't just that there was a surfeit of average, under-motivated players who needed to shape up or face being shipped out, there was a far deeper problem permeating the entire staff of the club – not just the players. There was a total lack of belief at the club, in fact I would go so far as to say the place was entirely imbued with fear.

Everybody – the fans, the press, the Board – connected with Sunderland was in a terrible frame of mind in the summer of 1987. They had got into this mindset that they were going to go down again. This was Sunderland and quite frankly they shouldn't have ever been there. But I realised I had to convince the players, the press, the tea lady and everybody that the club shouldn't be there. "We're too good to be in Division Three," I would insist. It was important to change that mentality as soon as I could.

The previous year Bob Murray had taken over as the new Chairman, replacing motor magnate Tom Cowie, who had been responsible for bringing in Lawrie McMenemy the previous season as the highest paid manager in football. Bob was an accountant by trade and had made his fortune out of the growth and sale of the Spring Ram Kitchen Company. He was young and ambitious, but it had all gone belly up and Sunderland had endured a dreadful season with no continuity of management, selection or players. That was what had led to relegation. Now Bob wanted me as manager because he had seen me out and about scouting at just about every game going. Obviously my record at York was impressive in terms of working in difficult circumstances and I had been operating at the level Sunderland now found themselves at so I knew the division.

I found it really interesting as someone coming in fresh to the situation that when I talked to people around the place everybody was telling me how hopeless the players were. I thought the squad was actually very good, especially at the level at which we found ourselves. If you think about it there were some top professionals there, people like Eric Gates, George Burley, Frank Gray, Iain Hesford and Mark Proctor. These were quality players. Some had been in the relegated side, some not. I had to sort it all out and discover why this talented group had underachieved so badly.

It was incredible that the club were down in Division Three. When you thought about the size of Sunderland football club and its history, but that didn't matter at all. When you find yourselves in a situation like that you have to deal with the present. Roker Park may have been an inspirational place when it was packed to the rafters with raucous Rokerites, but when I rolled up on the north east coast the whole club and city were wallowing in endless, morose negativity. Had I bitten off more than I could chew?

I still remember my speech to the players the first day I walked into the dressing room for pre-season training. I simply said, "Right you must think I'm a total nutter to come to this club in this division. I don't think I am a total nutter, so with the players in this room we are going to enjoy winning promotion. Let's get down to work." I thought they had got to the stage where they didn't realise what good players they were. They needed to be told.

Thankfully I wasn't trying to undo all this on my own. I had negotiated within the deal to take Viv Busby along with me to Roker Park. Through all the glory at Bootham Crescent Viv had been my absolute right-hand man. He was the perfect assistant, a real foil to my intensity and strategic planning, he worked brilliantly with the players on a daily basis to improve both their skill and, vitally, mentally.

Alongside Viv I brought in Malcolm Crosby, who had been a midfielder at York, but who had recently been coaching in Kuwait. To complete the York connection I brought in Roger Jones as goalkeeping coach. We were a great team and set about changing the entire culture of Sunderland around, but with all that we had to deal with it's perhaps no surprise that we made a bad start. An opening day victory at Brentford was followed by just two more wins in the next eight games. After a dismal home defeat by Chester City on 26 September we sat 12th in Division Three, the lowest league position in the club's proud history.

Football is the be all and end all of life in the north east. In many ways winning the people of Sunderland around was as crucial as convincing the players that they were up to the task. The great thing about it was I could just walk around for a few minutes and come across someone who wanted to talk about football and how I could revive their team. I would tell them, "I believe in this football team, and if I believe it you should too." It began to take effect once we'd started to win a few games.

Everyone has their own opinion up there. I'd be walking about and there would be a 9 year-old kicking a ball against the wall and he'd say, "Mr Smith, I think you should drop so-and-so a little bit deeper and push what's-his-name on a little bit." Then I'd go into the paper shop and there would be a 90 year-old lady serving and she'd say, "have you tried playing this player alongside that one in the middle of the park." It really is that kind of obsessive, knowledgeable place. I found that rather than criticise and tell you that you are crap, the fans all had suggestions of how you could improve the team. That's the great thing about the north east football supporter. I loved them because they have got a real burning passion.

The local press was a totally different level to that which I'd experienced at homely York. I used to have one meeting with the locals in the morning and anther one at lunchtime. It was tricky because you had to have different stories for each one because the morning one was for the evening papers and the lunchtime ones for the morning. It was all-consuming.

Because of the traumas of relegation some of the local journalists had voiced heavy criticism of the manager and chairman and got themselves banned. With me everyone started from scratch, so I reinstated them all and they appreciated it. I'd got off on the right foot with them, which was vital if I was to get my positivity across to supporters through the media.

Because of the profile of the club in the region, the TV, radio and press commitments were far more arduous and time consuming than I'd been used to. Thankfully I had a brilliant secretary called Moira. Occasionally I would get into the office and find that about five appointments had been rubbed out in my diary.

I'd say, "what's going on here?"

And Moira would reply, "Kate rang. She'd like to see you."

Every morning she'd come in and put a cup of tea in front of me and the papers – not even say good morning and walk out. Then about 20 minutes later she would come in with another cup and say "morning". She kept me sane at times.

I wasn't despondent as many of the fans were who had gone beyond the end of their tethers. I knew we were moving things in the right direction. I'd had time to assess the players both over the summer and also in the first few games of the campaign. The first thing that had become obvious was that the defence, which had conceded 71 goals during the previous regular season and then six in the two play-off semi-final games against Gillingham, needed remodelling. So once again I returned to my York connections and brought in centre-half John MacPhail, who had endured an average season at Bristol City. He hadn't settled down in the south west and was delighted to join forces with me once again. He repaid me in spades, scoring 16 goals that season, ten of them penalties, as well as commanding the defence and captaining the side. He was brilliant and became a real hero with the fans, who loved his strut.

Alongside Monty I played Gary Bennett who became a total legend in his 11 seasons at Sunderland. He'd laid the ground work a couple of years earlier, just after he'd joined the club, thanks to a famous incident which the fans still talk about now over 20 years later when he picked up the tigerish Coventry striker David Speedie by his neck and dumped him into the Clock Stand paddock during a League Cup tie. It had earned him a red card and cult status on Wearside. Benno was an incredibly popular player, although he did have his moments when the red mist would descend and he'd either give the ball away hopelessly or commit a rash challenge to get carded or give away a penalty. At this level, though, Gary was an imposing barrier for opposition strikers to try to get past. Paired with the steadying influence of Monty the duo made a frightening centre of defence.

Another Sunderland legend was at left-back. Reuben Agboola had come up from the south coast when Lawrie McMenemy had joined the club. Reuben was an experienced top flight defender and an uncompromising tackler. For some reason instead of helping Sunderland battle relegation the previous season Agboola had been loaned out to Charlton as Frank Gray and Alan Kennedy had shared the duties. I couldn't understand why that would be. He was first choice for me right from the start.

I had to change the goalkeeper too. Steve Hardwick played the first few games, but I soon lost faith in him and brought in a real character in Iain Hesford, who had been heavily criticised during the relegation season. Iain had a fairly obvious weight problem – he was a big lad, in fact he was huge – and the Chairman was desperate to get a new keeper in, but I thought Iain had something to offer still. He was a great character and as long as he kept goal well I wasn't bothered what size he was.

To a large extent Iain fitted the profile of the people I wanted to get into my team. I had decided that as well as skilled footballers I wanted characters around to lift the place. I added to this quota by signing someone who I had always thought was a proper right-back. The position had been a hug problem following the injury to George Burley the previous season, but I knew about this young lad from Sunderland who had been playing at Wimbledon called John Kay. I phoned Harry Bassett up and chatted to him about John. Harry confirmed what I thought, the lad was a bit crackers, down to the fact that he'd left Arsenal for Wimbledon in order to be closer to his north east roots!

I could offer him something slightly closer than south west London and so agreed a deal with Harry and John proved to be a super signing. He was fantastic to have around the place, and being a Sunderland lad he was desperate to play well for the club. He was full on commitment on the pitch too. The Sunderland fans christened John as 'The Red and White Tractor' because of his no nonsense approach to tackling. He had more than just agricultural challenges in his armoury however. Standing on the touchline as I did I could often hear John talking to his winger throughout the games and some of the things he used to say were hilarious. Often he'd be telling them about the clandestine meeting he'd had with their wife the night before! He would be constantly talking. He just couldn't stop, but he had got a lovely way about him and did a great job. He was one of two ever presents that season.

One man who wasn't too happy with me for that was former Ipswich defender George Burley. He was only 31, but I thought after the previous season's problems that George's knees had gone. I was, after all, an expert in disguising injuries, so I thought I could spot some tell-tale signs. Although he had a great attitude to training and his quality as an attacking player was great, I just thought he could be defensively suspect. It didn't turn into too much of an issue as he was injured for much of the season and I released him the following summer to join Gillingham. I have to say George's attitude was fantastic throughout and I am not surprised he has gone on to have such a good managerial career at Ayr, Colchester, Ipswich, Derby, Hearts, Southampton and eventually in charge of Scotland.

In midfield I gave youngster Gordon Armstrong the opportunity to stamp his class on the division. Gordon had got a great left foot and was wonderful from dead balls. We scored a lot of goals from corners and free-kicks throughout the season. He was also superb in the air. Gordon ran everything, especially in terms of feeding the balls into the forward, and ended up playing 600 games or more. Alongside Gordon were youngsters Paul Lemon, on the right hand side, and Gary Owers, while 21 year-old Paul Atkinson also made a fair few appearances throughout the season. Atky had a big problem, though, or rather I had a big problem with him. Yes, he could pass the ball, in fact he had the talent to do pretty much anything, but his lifestyle was horrendous.

I remember one particular away trip to Brighton when it came to a head. We all sat down for a meal the night before the game and I remember seeing him sit and eat less than half. I said to him, "come on lad, eat up."

"I've had enough, gaffer," he replied. "I don't want any more."

But then, while I was sitting in reception later on reading the paper in my usual fashion and seeing exactly what's going on, I spotted a big plate of burger and chips heading upstairs. I stopped the waiter and said, "I'll take that."

As I took it up to Paul's room I took in the full horror of what he had ordered. It wasn't just a beef burger and chips as I'd suspected. He'd also rung down for chocolate, crisps, coke, the lot. Needless to say when I knocked on the door he was acutely embarrassed, but the cussing I gave him didn't change anything. That was hugely frustrating because the lad had got great left foot. I tried and tried I just couldn't convince him. From his performances I knew he was eating regularly like that. Even back in the late-eighties diet was beginning to be taken seriously amongst the football community and it was obvious that Atkinson could not keep away from the kind of rubbish that he loved to cram down his throat. He wasn't able to work back quickly enough to warrant his place in the team and so I took the decision to move him on. It was tremendously disappointing, but sometimes players do not want to help themselves. I sold him to Port Vale.

To balance all that youthful exuberance I began the season with Mark Proctor in the engine room. Mark had begun his career at Nottingham Forest and was a quality passer of the ball. He'd made 117 appearances for Sunderland, but when a bid came in I allowed him to move on to Sheffield Wednesday, generating £275,000 from his sale. I replaced him from within the squad with Steve Doyle, a highly experienced defensive midfielder, who'd spent far too long the previous season filling in at right-back. Doyle was perfectly suited to the kind of midfield dogfights which playing in the Third Division brings. He'd spent almost his entire career at that level playing for the likes of Huddersfield and Preston.

The team was taking shape. I knew we had the makings of a top side in this division, so I was not yet as worried as many of the fans, who still thought we could slip down the table just as quickly as we could rise up. They were mentally shot after the terror of relegation via the new play-off system at the hands of Gillingham and finding themselves midway down the division after nine games was causing deep concern.

Having sized up my options in attack, and decided that the likes of Dave Buchanan, Dave Swindlehurst and Terry Curran were not for me, a few weeks into the season I returned one last time to my old club York to sign young striker Marco Gabbiadini. I'd handed him his league debut and been excited by his potential but since my departure he had not been performing to it under new manager Bobby Saxton.

Gabbers made his debut in that defeat by Chester. But the following Tuesday he scored both goals as we won 2-0 at Fulham to really kick-start our season. The nickname

'Magic' Marco was coined that night amongst the fans who I could sense were filled with excitement at the prospect of what Gabbiadini could do in this division. They were right. He scored twice in each of the next two games as well as we won six matches in a row to rise to the top of the table by defeating York City 4-2 towards the end of October. It was a very relieving victory for myself and Marco as we were perfectly set up for a fall since we'd both swapped sides.

The following home game, against Southend United, was for me, the perfect crystallisation of what I had been trying to establish in training with the players. After starting the season with Keith Bertschin, the former Norwich and Stoke striker, as my first choice centre-forward, I had lost him to a bad ankle injury in that victory at Fulham. I had imagined Bertschin and Gabbiadini forming a devastating attacking partnership, but now had to come up with an alternative. Luckily for me I had a ready-made one already at the club. Eric Gates had been a top class professional in the halcyon days at Bobby Robson's Ipswich, winning both the FA Cup and UEFA Cup. He'd moved back up to his native north east to help out Sunderland in 1984, but had been underused in their fight against relegation as McMenemy put his faith in striker Dave Swindlehurst, who'd scored just six goals.

I called Eric over after training the day after the victory at Fulham and asked him how he felt about playing up front with Marco. He replied, "Gaffer, if you can get the ball into my feet in this division, with Marco's pace we can destroy teams. I was fed up last year because I was being asked to run onto balls over the top myself. I'm 32 for god's sake. I can't do that. It was never my game."

"Let's do it then," I told him. And we did. The midfield were told to get it into Gates at every opportunity and the play revolved around him turning and looking for a pass to Marco who would be on the shoulder of the last defender where I'd told him in no uncertain terms I expected to find him at every waking moment. Gatesy was absolutely magnificent, an absolute joy to work with and he proved to be the fulcrum around which our scintillating play revolved. His first touch and appreciation of what was going on around him was superb. He'd got great big calves on him and he took some fearful kicks on them throughout his career, not least that season as teams realised what a huge influence he was on us. Eric was cute, though. He just used to read them coming in and ride the challenges.

Ultimately football is not that complicated. If you've got somebody with a talent then you use it. Play to his strengths not his weaknesses. Gates flourished because we did just that. Playing with Eric made Marco into a breathtaking goalscorer as he cut a swathe through defences up and down the country with his lightning acceleration. He went on to score 21 goals, a total Eric matched.

We took the field against Southend on the back of a poor 1-2 defeat at Notts County. I'd had a bit of a go at the players after that game as I felt they had thought it was going to be easy and had consequently lost. The team responded. They were irresistible that day as our new team pattern stretched the Southend defence to breaking point as Eric pulled one centre-half forward as he dropped short to receive the ball, while Marco span and set off the other way dragging the other one in his wake. We cut huge holes in them and took full advantage. Eric Gates scored four, Paul Atkinson two and Marco one as we hammered the Shrimpers out of sight by 7-0. It was a scoreline that made the rest of the division quake in their boots. The Sunderland giant was really stirring.

That 7-0 victory was the first game in a 15 match unbeaten run in the league. By the end of it we were on top of the table, two points ahead of Notts County and with Wigan and Walsall a further five points back. The chasing pack were already out of sight. We were playing beautifully, with goals coming from all over the team.

Then came our wobble. Of the next ten games we won just two, drawing five and losing three times. Draws against Wigan and Notts County left us in second place, between those two sides, but with a game in hand.

In that run we had a couple of really bad results. We lost back-to-back games at Bristol Rovers and Aldershot and received some terrible stick, especially for the 0-4 hammering we'd suffered against Rovers. Fans and press were questioning if we had the balls to cross the finishing line. Everybody had long faces and you could see that people were reverting back to their old lack of self esteem. You would think the world had collapsed. So then we had to start building people up all over again – players, staff, press and supporters alike.

Our next fixture had special resonance though. We travelled the short distance to York to return to Bootham Crescent for the first time since my departure the previous summer had led to something of an exodus. Now all of us were putting our reputations on the line in a stadium and on a pitch which we all knew was made for upsets.

This game at York caused problems. I was worried because I knew how many of our supporters would try to make the short trip down to try to get in. They'd still got fences up at this point – although they were the ones which had been installed when I was there and I knew they had releases on so you could drop the fences forward. I had been conscious for years that fences could cause potentially grave problems akin to those we'd seen at Bradford and Heysel where supporters could not get out of crowded areas, and would sadly take so many lives at Hillsborough just over a year later.

The only thing was that York chairman Michael Sinclair wasn't happy at some of my comments as he maintained I'd 'whipped up a frenzy' and that I was intent on causing trouble. But I didn't see it that way. I merely thought they wouldn't be able to cope with all of our fans, which might lead to some kind of incident.

Obviously because I was coming back with Sunderland, along with Marco, Viv and Malcolm, there was a certain amount of tension surrounding the game. Among the 9,000 crowd there were people intent on causing trouble and I remember some of them getting onto the pitch and threatening me. There didn't seem to be anything more than straight anger, though, so I chose not to react.

It was a white hot atmosphere and a goal from Dale Banton meant we got beat 2-1. I just told the press afterwards, "I told you I'd put together a good side at York."

In that run of games there was one fixture which stands out in my mind, not for what happened on the pitch, but rather off it. It was 12 March 1988 and our visit to Wigan's Springfield Park. The ground was a real ramshackle old-style stadium with grass banking behind the goal which the visiting fans were asked to populate. That day it rained solidly all afternoon and turned the banking into a total mudbath. During half-time in the 2-2 draw, which staved off Wigan's potential challenge to our promotion spot, our fans had an absolute ball slipping and sliding down the banking. It's stuck in my mind ever since because the whole thing has been preserved for posterity by someone with a camera in the crowd who sent it in to Sky TV's Soccer AM show. The producers put it on one of their compilation videos and it's now a massively viewed item on YouTube. It was such a good example of football supporters getting up to high jinks that harmed absolutely no-one. It is hilarious viewing, especially the last guy who does a forward somersault on his way down the hillside.

Towards the end of the season, feeling we needed one more kick towards promotion, on transfer deadline day I brought in winger Colin Pascoe from Swansea City. Colin could play anywhere, wide or in the middle and had a good turn of pace, adding to our attacking threat. I knew he would offer us a lot in the vital last few weeks of the season and I was determined to get him. The only problem was I was in Sunderland, he was in Swansea and the forms had to get to Lytham St Annes near Blackpool by 5pm. Fax confirmations were not allowed in those days so there was nothing for it, I had to drive all the way to Swansea's Vetch Field, get the forms signed, shake Colin's hand and then belt along the M4 and up the M5 and M6 to Lancashire. I made it with a couple of minutes to go.

Colin made his debut two days later in a tense 1-0 win at Grimsby, which took us back to the top of the table and sparked a fantastic run of seven wins from the last eight games. It was nip and tuck as ourselves, Notts County and Walsall battled it out for the two promotion spots. Every game counted. We won comfortably 4-1 at Southend, but then lost a tight match at Bristol City by a single goal. It was all still in the balance.

We recovered our composure to record a fabulous 4-0 victory over Mansfield which left us just one win away from promotion because our two rivals were facing each other on the same day as our visit to mid-table Port Vale. John Rudge's men provided a stiff test, but Eric Gates scored the vital winning goal and the three or so thousand travelling fans among the 7,500 crowd went ballistic. We were back up into the Second Division at the first time of asking.

I had known all along that the players I had were far too good for this league. They should, as I had said all along, never been there. In the end as manager you try anything you want, but if you haven't got the raw material to work with you don't stand a chance. At times managers get far too much credit or criticism for what they do tactically or in training. In the end if you've got good players, you are going to get more good results no matter how good you are as a manager.

Our first home game of the season had seen a perfectly respectable crowd of 13,000 turn up to cheer us on. Our last home game of the campaign, which had become a major promotion party, was somewhat different. There were nearly 30,000 inside Roker to celebrate our fantastic season. It was the culmination of a year's work for me. Ever since I'd shown Kate around the ground and stood on the pitch with her and told her to imagine it full I had been striving, along with all my players and coaching staff, in every waking moment to bring the club success. To have nearly 30,000 inside the stadium for the final home game, a 3-1 victory over Northampton on the May bank holiday Monday was fantastic – a joy. That victory also clinched the title for us, which was very special indeed and one of my greatest memories in football is being chaired by my players around Roker Park that evening as the massive crowd rose to acclaim our achievement.

The official celebrations of our promotion were fantastic, and on a different level again to those we'd experienced at York. We had a splendid Civic reception and a much more raucous club party. We were entitled to it. We'd won promotion at the first time of asking. It was a glorious victory, one which signalled a sea-change in the fortunes of Sunderland AFC, and one of my proudest achievements.

I'd have to admit that there was a certain amount of relief mixed in amongst the euphoria of the celebrations as we paraded the Third Division trophy around Roker Park and then the city. It wouldn't be me putting my hand in my pocket to pay York City that extra £10,000. I'd say it was one of the best fees that Sunderland and chairman Bob Murray had ever spent. I never did establish if Bob would have made me pay that money to York if we'd failed, although I suspect that even if we had not won promotion he would not have insisted that I do so. We simply never needed to discuss it because the team had performed so superbly.

******

Any promotion-winning manager will tell you that as soon as the final whistle goes on the game that clinches elevation to a higher division the planning begins for the new challenge. That planning can be upset by a number of variables along the way, but the most difficult to overcome are injuries. Missing key players for any length of time is always tricky for any club, not least because it costs money to get in replacements, however temporary.

So it really didn't help our cause when right-back John Kay broke his leg against Shrewsbury early in the season. I was forced to utilise Frank Gray as cover before handing the job to Gary Bennett. Paul Lemon also picked up an early injury which restricted him to just 12 appearances that season. The changes upset our rhythm and we started badly, not helped by some poor form amongst other key members of the side such as Bennett and Gates. We didn't record a win until 1 October when we defeated Oldham 3-2 at Roker to haul ourselves off the bottom of the nascent table. Particularly worrying was our lack of goals. We were missing a battering ram of a centre-forward, so I opted to bring one in who has since become a legendary character at Sunderland – and indeed at every other of his nine Football League clubs.

Billy was big. He was built like Giant Haystacks the wrestler, had almost permanently black eyes from scrapes with bouncers at clubs around the north and a particular fondness for curry. To say he was a man's man would be understating it.

His move to Sunderland came by chance as I met him when his club Reading were on a pre-season tour of the north east and were using the facilities at Durham to train. I walked into the showers and saw him there. Despite being covered from head to foot in bruises, Billy was instantly recognisable.

"Bloody hell, Billy. What have you been up to?"

"Oh, last night I got turned over by a couple of bouncers".

To be honest that's when I knew I could get him because I was fairly certain Reading would want to get rid of him after such an incident! I was certain, though, that I could handle him because I knew Billy respected me fully as I had once battered him whilst playing for York against Hull. In 1982 I'd cracked him a few times early in the game to let him know I would not take any messing from him and their manager Chris Chilton told me afterwards that Billy had spent the whole of the half-time break moaning about me.

When Billy turned up for training after signing I sat him down and said, "look Billy, I sorted you out once and if you step out of line I'll sort you out again."

"Yes gaffer, no problem," came the reply.

The tales of Billy are many and varied, but almost always revolve around drinking and getting into trouble of one sort or another. Around the same time as Billy arrived, September 1988, cricketer Ian Botham had moved to the north east to play with Durham as the county had just achieved full county status. I asked him to come in and be around the dressing rooms at the training ground to pep the boys up and boost morale during his close season. Botham liked his football and had played for Scunthorpe earlier in the 1980s, although that was for publicity purposes as much as anything. Both thought he was a footballer, but he wasn't really. But he was a hell of a cricketer and an incredible competitor. He was doing those Shredded Wheat adverts at the time and we would test him by betting him whether he could do 50 press ups one-handed.

"You can't do that," I'd say.

"Yes I can," he'd say, taking up the challenge, and he'd be off. More often than not he would refuse to be beaten. Beefy's a strong man and would take anybody on at anything – no-one could beat him at Table Tennis, for example. Botham thinks he can control the world and that's a great, positive attitude to have. His enthusiasm was unbelievable and infectious. He was brilliant to have around the place.

It didn't always go down too well with some of the Sunderland board of directors. They were worried about Botham's reputation for socialising, but when you work with him you realise what an ultimate sporting professional he is. Sure he had got a social life, why not?

Ian did have an incredible capacity for drink and he and Billy drinking together on the town was a frightening sight. You had to be a very brave man to go out drinking with them. They'd be having competitions, races, whatever. I didn't mind lads going out drinking as long as they didn't cause any trouble and are always polite. If somebody asked them to leave a club or bar because they were being boisterous they knew they had to leave. They all had to live within the rules. If they got into trouble out at night then they would be in trouble with me the following day. I'd whack them with a heavy fine and, if the problem persisted, I'd get rid of them.

Sometimes being a footballer with a social life can lead to problems being created where there really are none. I remember one Monday morning taking a phone call from an irate supporter.

"Gary Bennett was out drinking last night," said the fan.

I was already thinking, 'Oh Christ, what has he done?' but I said, politely, "Okay, was he drunk?"

"Oh no, he wasn't drunk," came the reply.

"So what's the problem then? Was he abusive to you? Has he been rude to your wife?" I was waiting for the crunch to come. There had to be something.

"Oh no no, he was just drinking," the caller responded.

"So?" I was losing patience now.

"Well, you got beat Saturday."

I was flabbergasted. "When you've had a bad week at work don't you like going out drinking at the weekend?" I offered, ending the call.

Having Billy and Beefy around certainly made for a lot of official bonding sessions, and some impromptu ones besides. Every so often a couple of the lads would tell me before training, "Gaffer, Billy's been out drinking again last night".

My answer would be to single Billy out in warm up and tell him that if anyone beat him in the run he'd be fined. But Billy had this ability to run distances easily. For such a big man he was a good mover and on the field of play he used to terrify full-backs and his work rate was incredible.

Whitehurst's introduction at least helped alleviate our poor start. He scored the winning goal against Leeds in early October and then later in the month netted again in a 4-0 victory over Swindon. By the time he'd scored his third and final goal for the club in his 17 games at Roker we had risen to eighth place.

We went flat then, though, and it was becoming increasingly obvious that change was needed at the other end of the pitch. Iain Hesford had begun to make more mistakes than I could countenance at this level and after a 1-3 defeat at Leicester in December which dropped us back down to 16th, I thought it was time for a change. Iain's chances had run out and the limitations his lifestyle and consequent size placed upon him were beginning to tell. Wonderful character though he was, I knew the end had come for him at Roker.

I used Hesford and Whitehurst as carrots to entice Hull City to let me have 30 year-old Tony Norman, their outstanding goalkeeper. The deal we put together was worth around £500,000 all told, a club record. Now you can call it great management if you like – you certainly won't hear me complaining – but we won five of our next six matches once I'd taken the decision to drop Hesford. The first two were with reserve keeper Tim Carter, who I'd signed from Bristol Rovers, between the sticks and the remainder with Norman in goal. The first game in that run was a very pleasing 4-1 victory at Plymouth Argyle, while we also scored four in defeating Portsmouth at Roker Park on 31 December. Tony made an immediate impact, conceding just one goal in his first four games as we flirted with the play-off zone for a few weeks around the turn of the year.

Tony was an unbelievable athlete. Considering he was a keeper he could put quite a shift on. Over 100 metres he was good, but he was actually better over 400 metres. He murdered everybody at the club bar Gary Bennett. Sometimes when you analyse why really good players haven't got to the absolute top in the game you discover particular character traits that have betrayed them slightly. If anything with Tony it was because he was such a nice quiet retiring sort of fellow. If he had been somebody who had pushed himself and told people, "look I'm good enough" and had been calculating enough to have moved on from Hull earlier and then moved on again, he could perhaps have played at a much bigger club and played more games for Wales than the five he did because of the dominance of Everton's Neville Southall. He certainly had the ability to do so as he proved in over 220 games for Sunderland.

Tony was a great signing and provided a solid foundation for the next few seasons between the posts. Having a good goalkeeper the higher up you go is probably as vital as having a top notch goalscorer. Goals stopped can equal those scored.

Overall we weren't strong enough that season to maintain a challenge for the play-offs, and eventually finished 11th, slap bang in the middle of the table after a season of ups and downs, which ended with a run of just two defeats in 11 games.

Towards the end of that season came the moment which I had been dreaming about all my life. I was to manage a team at Stoke City's Victoria Ground. Obviously it didn't quite fit in with the childhood fantasy because it was the visitors I was in charge of, plotting the downfall of my boyhood heroes and the team I had served for 20 odd years as a player. The 14 March 1989 was a massive day for me. Going back to my hometown club was so important to me. With my brothers and sisters and everybody else in attendance I was desperate to win. Pride was at stake. I needed to win this game.

Unfortunately for me Mick Mills's Stoke side played well and earned a 2-0 victory, with winger Peter Beagrie the star. I was devastated, but I would have my revenge the following season when, in November, we visited the Vic again and came away with a 2-0 victory ourselves. It wasn't just myself who enjoyed a winning return to Stoke that day. In the summer of 1989 I had signed my former Stoke colleague Paul Bracewell, who had become a star at Everton under Howard Kendall's tutelage. Brace hammered in an unstoppable goal from 25 yards to set us on the way to a 2-0 victory. It took some doing for Brace to score from that kind of distance.

Marco Gabbiadini scored the clinching second in that game, which saw us rise to fifth place. He had now become an established goalscorer in this division. He'd netted his first hat-trick against Ipswich towards the end of the previous season. Now he was well on the way to topping 20 goals for the season as the team grew in confidence and belief throughout. The improvement was fuelled by a couple of signings that strengthened the side and added quality and verve to the ranks.

Bracewell arrived back on Wearside after an injury ravaged couple of years. In fact he actually failed his medical because his ankle was knackered. When I got the result I went and saw the specialist and asked, "besides his ankle, what's he like?"

"Absolutely 100% on everything else," was the answer.

So I asked Brace, "can you play with that?"

And Brace says "yes, I've got no qualms."

Brace is as honest as the day is born, so I signed him. It may have been a risk then, but it was a calculated one and he didn't let me down. He was an important influence on the pitch and in the dressing room. He went on forever, including playing for Newcastle and then re-signing again for Sunderland for a third time after that. All the way through he was rubbing off his magic on the rest of the squad. He'd won so much at Everton that he could only be a great presence.

Paul was at the hub of our solidity as we battled towards the play-off places at the end of that 1989/90 season. He raised the rest of the squad's standards. One of his great strengths throughout his career was that he was always available for a pass. If you were in trouble Brace was always there to get you out of it. He'd got a lovely sense of humour too. When we walked in to the Wembley dressing room he declared "usual peg Mr Bracewell?" It brought a smile to everyone's lips and relaxed us. Only he and I had experience of playing big games at Wembley, although it was famously not a happy place for him. In his career he played in four losing FA Cup finals, plus a play-off final.

In the summer of 1989 I signed Portsmouth left-back Paul Hardyman for £130,000. Paul was an important signing. He had played for England's under 21s and was a solid defender with a do-or-die attitude. He would never admit defeat, which was a quality I admired in him. These two signings meshed the elements of the team that the previous season had finished in mid-table and turned it into a force to be reckoned with.

The first half of the season progressed well and we reached Christmas in third position, beating Oxford at home on Boxing Day 1-0 to consolidate. But January 1990 was not a good month for us. We lost two games and drew one in the middle of a run of seven games without a win. We dropped to seventh, out of the play-off zone, and had to dig deep. Two goals from Thomas Hauser, a big German striker I had brought in from

Old Boys Berne, defeated Brighton and arrested the slide. We then hit a purple patch of form, with four wins in a row following the defeat of West Ham in a seven goal thriller at Roker. Completing the double over Stoke with a 2-1 win left us in fifth position with seven games to go. Around this time I was experiencing managing one of the most enigmatic personalities in my career.

Far too many people have never heard of Kieron Brady. He had the talent of a Gascoigne or a Best, and the wayward nature to match. He was that good – and bad. Sunderland fans who watched his few, brief, electric appearances for the club still talk about the left winger's dazzling skill, turn of pace and eye for goal even today. That lad had more talent than anybody I ever managed. I'll give you an example of what I mean. He was in digs on the seafront at Sunderland and he would take a ball from the ground and walk along, keeping it up as he went, whilst talking to whoever he was walking with, not missing a beat. He'd walk across a couple of roads, through the park, over a mile, without dropping it. You would sometimes see him standing watching practice games with a ball nestled on the back of his head.

We knew he had skill, but we soon realised he had the audacity to execute equally sublime manouevres in match situations. I attended a youth team game at York and as we kicked off Brady was the player receiving the ball from the players on the centre spot. I couldn't quite believe what happened next, but happen it did. The ball came back to Brady and Kieron just flicked it up, inside our half and volleyed it at pace over the head of the opposing keeper, who was off his line, but hardly culpable for conceding a goal to this piece of pure genius.

That told me this kid had got the lot. Skill, nerve, the ability to produce sublime genius – I find it difficult to put into words how much talent Kieron had. He could pass quickly and accurately with both feet, was quick, strong, and scored goals. I got him into the first team as quickly as I could, despite the fact that he was only 17. On his second full appearance he scored against West Ham in that thrilling 4-3 victory and then netted again in the next game to defeat Bradford City at Valley Parade. He scored three times in eight games as a lot of people got very excited about this raw talent we had on our hands. The word soon got around about how good he could be. More scouts than usual attended youth and reserve team games to watch, while fans were already talking Brady up to be the next Jim Baxter, the last true maverick talent Sunderland supporters had had the pleasure of watching.

But then the wheels came off. That Easter we lost at home to Hull and then travelled to Oxford for a vital game on the Monday as we clung on to the final play-off place under strong challenge from both West Ham and Wolves. The problem was that after the match against Hull on the Saturday Kieron had a mate down from Scotland. At the time he was living in the seafront digs which were run by Malcolm Crosby with his wife Carol. Kieron asked if he and his pal could go out for a meal. Crosser gave his permission saying, "so long as you are in by 11 o'clock. Don't go and do anything stupid."

Kieron rolled in at 4am. He'd had a few to drink and so was not in training on the Sunday, and wasn't able to travel down to Oxford with us ready to play on Easter Monday. Now I had a problem. Kieron had been outstanding on the Saturday and the fans were chomping at the bit to see him weave his unfettered magic once again. So when the team was announced for the game at the Manor Ground and his name had been replaced by that of Reuben Agboola boos and jeers rained down from the travelling supporters. I was getting absolutely slaughtered for leaving him out.

After the match, which I should point out here we won 1-0 anyway, I decided not to give the press the truth as to why he'd been left out. Instead I said that I'd chosen to omit Kieron. "He's a young kid of 17," I said. "And he needs a rest." But I was vilified for it.

Kieron won three Republic of Ireland Under 21 caps as his star continued to rise, but he could not make the transition from playboy football fledgling to full-blown star because of his inability to keep his place in the side due to continued misdemeanours. It's a sad waste when that happens.

That was Kieron – frightening ability but he'd got no responsibility. His brain was wired differently to anyone else I ever managed and that caused nothing but problems. Someone of that unbelievable talent should have gone on to be somebody you talked about as one of the greats. Instead he disappeared from view after I'd gone, mainly due to a debilitating muscular injury. I didn't know what happened to the lad for years until he pitched up helping the FA's Show Racism The Card campaign in the north east a few years ago.

That 0-1 home defeat by struggling Hull and the Brady episode didn't help the tension that was mounting amongst fans desperate to clamber back into the top flight as quickly as possible. The defeat bumped us back down to sixth place, just a point ahead of both West Ham and Wolves. The close fought 1-0 win at Oxford, thanks to a goal by Magic Marco, proved vital, but not as much as the victory in our next away game, at Molineux, where a rare Paul Hardyman strike handed us all three points and left us five points ahead of Wanderers and West Ham with just two games left. We finished the job by notching another away win, this time at Port Vale, again thanks to a Hardyman goal. Paul weighed in with seven goals that campaign, a fantastic return for a full-back. He loved to roam forward and unleash shots. He was a clean striker of the ball which meant he also took our penalties. That was a duty which would unwittingly create Hardyman something of a folk legend during our play-off semi-final first leg against Sunderland's sworn enemy Newcastle United.

It was one of those twists of footballing fate which saw the two north east rivals paired together in the play-offs. Newcastle had chased Leeds and Sheffield United all the way to the line, but been pipped to the two automatic spots. They'd had a much better season than us, although the fact that both league games had ended in draws perhaps suggested we were more evenly match than the bookies, press and Newcastle fans chose to believe.

The first leg was at Roker and we created more than enough chances to earn a lead, but we just couldn't take one. Then, right at the death, we were awarded a penalty. Paul Hardyman took the kick, but Newcastle keeper John Burridge saved. Typical of Paul, he followed up his kick and, losing his head for a moment tried to slot Burridge into the back of the Fulwell End net in an attempt to kick the ball out of his grasp. It was obvious frustration, but it was also very reckless. Needless to say mass pandemonium ensued, both on and off pitch. A red card for Hardyman being the obvious result. Because it was violent conduct Paul would miss our next two games, ruling him out of the rest of the season.

But in a funny kind of way the chaos of the end of that game helped us. The Newcastle players thought they'd already won the tie, when in fact all they'd done was secure a goalless away leg. I remember them singing in celebration as they went down the tunnel at Roker Park. I told my players then that Newcastle were playing into our hands. We'd finished the season by winning six out of our last seven away games and I fancied us strongly to do a job on the Toon in their own backyard. In a match that was being hyped as the most important game in both clubs' history everybody else thought it was a foregone conclusion. The whole atmosphere in the north east was that there was no point in Sunderland even turning up – the newspapers, the fans, you could feel it. If I'd allowed our players to think that way, to listen to all the doom and gloom, then it would have been curtains. But I couldn't and I didn't. We built them up to understand that it was possible to win at St James' Park and we were quite happy for everybody to think that we should be written off.

That second leg was a tumultuous affair in more ways than one. It was a hot, passionate evening of the kind that can only be found in a Tyne-Tees derby and what a cracking match the players served up. After nine minutes Mark McGhee hit the post with a left foot volley, but then Eric Gates popped up at the near post to slot home a right wing cross to give us the lead 1-0. In a pulsating game both sides had shots cleared off the line with the keepers well beaten. Try as they might Newcastle tried to get back on to level terms, but we defended well. After countless goalmouth scrambles, five minutes from the end Marco and Eric swapped a sublime one two and Gabbers struck the ball left-footed inside the far post to give us an unassailable 2-0 lead.

At least we thought we couldn't lose, but we reckoned without the Machiavellian thoughts of a large number of Newcastle fans, who tried to take over by rushing onto the pitch, forcing referee George Courtney to take the teams off the field before the game could be restarted. The Toon army seemed to think the game would be abandoned if they stayed on the pitch. But we knew from the off that there was never any doubt that the match would not be played to a finish. As we waited for the police to clear the pitch George Courtney told us, "don't worry, if we have to clear the stadium entirely we are going to finish this." I think we needed a strong referee like George, this was Newcastle against Sunderland in the play-off semi-final after all.

So we went back out after spending over 20 minutes off the pitch in the end and played out the final five minutes without too much trouble. In fact I think the pitch invasion had taken the steam out of the Newcastle players' efforts. Sitting around for that time allowed them to realise that there was no way back for them. When the final whistle sounded we had won 2-0 to complete a memorable victory.

To celebrate everybody went out into Sunderland. The place was in uproar. There was no question of me or any of the players buying a drink. I think I got home something like 6 o'clock the next morning. It still didn't seem quite real, but unbelievably and as unlikely as it seemed Sunderland were at Wembley. The play-off finals would all be played there for the first time, whereas before they had been played on the same home and away basis that the semi-finals remained on. Our opponents would be Swindon Town, under the management of Argentinian midfield legend Osvaldo Ardiles. The Robins had defeated Blackburn 4-2 on aggregate in their semi-final and were heavy favourites with the bookies and pundits alike. Their team was a combination of solid defence, passing football and flair, which Ardiles had moulded into a tremendous unit. We were going to have our work out to emerge victorious.

The city of Sunderland was alight with two weeks' worth of anticipation in the build up to the final. The supporters crowded the training ground over at Durham desperate to get a glimpse of their heroes. It was wonderful but overpowering, so to take the players' minds off all of that we found what we thought was a secret training ground away from it all. That lasted about a couple of days before word leaked out. So instead we went away for a week to Minorca.

The final was played on the late May bank holiday Monday as the climax of the big weekend of finals which has now become traditional. It was a fabulous occasion, with over 72,000 fans inside Wembley to watch us, at least one season ahead of schedule by my reckoning, attempt to win this one off match to gain promotion to the top flight. Talk about an all or nothing game. It's become known as the biggest single game in football, with around £50 million riding on it in the modern era. Back then the stakes weren't quite that high, but they were still the biggest they had ever been in one match.

I have to be honest and up front about Swindon. Throughout the season the whisper going round football circles was that everybody was wondering how they were outbidding bigger clubs to sign top players, it just didn't add up. They had David Kerslake, Fraser Digby from Manchester United, Jon Gittens from Southampton and Duncan Shearer up front. I certainly couldn't compete financially and I found myself thinking that really shouldn't be right when it comes to assessing the relative strengths of Sunderland and Swindon Town. But I had no idea about exactly what had been going on. That would only come to light later.

On the pitch, the players Swindon had got certainly did a job on us. We'd planned for the game with Eric Gates and Marco playing up front as usual, but Colin

Calderwood, who would shortly join Spurs, went straight through the back of Gabbers. Marco was hurt. Far more than any fan knew. He carried on, but effectively Calderwood had put out our number one weapon. Nowadays he'd be risking a possible sending off, but from their point of view it was brilliant. They'd cracked our dangerman.

As well as that we just couldn't get going on an incredibly hot day. I'm still not sure what it was but we seemed just that bit off the pace. Our approach was dictated in part by the fact that Swindon under Ossie had been playing good football all season. Our plan had been to close them down and get in their faces but the heat prevented us from getting tight enough. Swindon were quicker in thought, quicker to the ball and eventually the pressure they built up told when, just before half-time, Alan McLoughlin shot from the edge of the area, the ball taking a slight deflection off Dave Bennett, before nestling in the corner of the net beyond the dive of Tony Norman.

We didn't improve in the second half and didn't create anything resembling a decent chance. In truth it was a poor, poor final. Being brutally honest we didn't deserve to win. Swindon were better than us and only the heroic performance of our back four and especially Tony Norman kept the deficit to 1-0..

I couldn't complain about it afterwards, but I'm sure our tactical approach was a mistake. I couldn't communicate that to the players, though. I remember going round picking the lads up saying, "don't worry, we've done well to get here, we'll be here again."

For such a grand occasion and after such a great run it was a dreadfully disappointing way for our season to end.

Except of course that wasn't the end of the story. Our fairytale had been well and truly cut off in its prime at Wembley, but the harsh reality of football as a business was about to intervene on our behalf. On 7 June, while my players were all off enjoying well-deserved holidays, I was in the Sunderland shopping centre doing some sort of presentation – I can remember wearing a collar and club tie – when before I knew what on earth was going on the press just descended! It was difficult to make sense of what I was being told in all the frenetic activity and scenes of celebrations that were beginning to break out, but I managed to sift through to the essence of it which was that Swindon had infringed a lot of regulations and thus had been demoted two divisions (which would later be revised to one). On top of that the League had decided that Sunderland would replace them in the top flight the following season.

If I'm honest I didn't think we were good enough yet. In our second season in Division Two we'd finished 6th not 3rd and I'd thought that was a fair reflection of our ability. I was already readying myself for a tilt at cracking the top four in the new campaign, but this news threw me totally off kilter. We were up! I was absolutely delighted. I could only imagine how many of the players heard the news.

One of the questions I was asked was how I felt for Swindon Town. My reaction was that, while I obviously felt very sorry for the players who had been unwittingly caught up amidst all the shenanigans which had gone on, I felt no remorse or sorrow for the club who had clearly been proved to have been bending the rules and quite rightly had been penalised.

The other obvious question is 'were we lucky?' In the cold light of day I suppose we were in the sense that the Football League decided to promote the defeated side from the play-off final rather than the third placed side in the division, Newcastle United. But I am not a big believer in luck. You earn everything in life and especially in the game of football.

That week or so in which we went from the total devastation of a poor performance in the biggest match of most of our lives to being a top flight team was such an incredible, bewildering period. From the start point, just three years earlier, of joining a club on its knees and at the lowest point in its history, somehow – and it didn't actually matter how – I had won promotion into the big time. I was now where I felt I belonged and was hot property as a young manager. As far as I was concerned it was England here I come.

Chapter Fifteen

STABBED IN THE BACK

I still rate it my biggest achievement in football that I turned Sunderland round from a club in deep depression to one that believed had a future at the top table of English football. To rise through the divisions in just three seasons and beat Newcastle in the play-offs and then earn promotion to the top flight was a fantastic achievement. Truthfully both Newcastle and Swindon were in a far better state than we were at that stage to cope with going into the First Division, in terms of infra-structure and playing staff. We could have done with another season developing in Division Two, but you don't turn promotion down.

What you can do, though, is take full advantage. Looking back I don't feel that I was given a fair crack of the whip at what would prove to be my only top flight season. I was not given enough money to spend on enough quality players to keep us up. In short I don't feel chairman Bob Murray backed me sufficiently financially.

At our first board meeting after we'd confirmed as replacing Swindon in the First Division, I asked, "what money have you got to strengthen?"

At that meeting my budget for transfer fees was set at £500,000 but I was not given an increase in wage budget. So if I wanted to bring anyone in I would have to prune my existing squad first.

Try as I might I just couldn't get the support from chairman and board I felt would be essential to be able to compete. I will maintain to my dying day that had chairman Bob Murray allowed me to spend the money I wanted – and I'm not talking silly money – we would have established ourselves in the First Division.

Bob was an accountant by trade and I think he wanted to make sure everything was straight. I do know that he now regrets not having invested at that point. I was on at him constantly to give me more to spend because I knew he was dicing with the prospect of a season-long relegation struggle. I could not, though, make him budge.

Of course the point here is that it would not have been the First Division we'd have been playing in thanks to the advent of the Premier League two seasons later. Had

Sunderland been involved in its foundation I truly believe we would have been up there with the likes of Everton and Aston Villa as permanent fixtures in the top flight of English football. As it was we became also rans all too quickly because Bob failed to realise how the landscape of football was changing.

I first got wind of the sea change which was about to occur when I attended a reserve team game at St James' Park. I was talking with Newcastle's chairman Sir John Hall and he was telling me about his plans for his club over the next couple of years. Because I was a First Division manager and carried the league handbook printed inside my head, I piped up, " but you can't do that, John".

"Why," the Newcastle owner asked.

"Because it's against the rules."

Then, in an immortal line which will stay with me forever in terms of the symbolism it now has, Sir John said, "then we'll change the rules". That is basically what they did, ripping up the template the Football League had provided for over 100 years and starting again, fuelling the revolution with a massive injection of money from Rupert Murdoch's Sky empire.

Football was reinvented that year and Sir John's comment always stayed with me. It shows the kind of people who were beginning to shape the future in which we live today. These were powerful men who would not take no for an answer. I liked the way they did that, banding together to scrap one aged organisation and starting a new, fresh one of their own.

Everything changed when the Premier League took over. In my lifetime Manchester United, Liverpool and Tottenham Hotspur have all been relegated from the top flight of English football. That would be impossible now. These multi-million pound businesses have got themselves into a position where they simply cannot be dislodged from their relative positions of comfort and power.

The governance of football across the UK, Europe and globally has become a massive issue for so many reasons. I think the current UEFA President Michel Platini is brilliant. He approaches everything he tries to do from the point of view of sporting ideals, rather than business, but whether he can get though all the reforms he desires is another matter.

There is so much self-interest involved in football now that it is almost impossible to change the status quo which keeps the big clubs at the top of the game, raking in money through the big competitions and the huge sponsorship deals which also mean they attract the best players.

If Platini can just tweak things a little to redress the balance towards making the playing field more level it will help retain the impression among the paying public, who consume football either through their TV or inside the stadia, that the possibility of any club rising up to achieve is still alive. If we lose that ideal and football becomes a completely closed shop, as the big clubs no doubt desire, then it may lead down a path to ruination. Platini knows that. I sincerely hope he can succeed.

I should really have had an inkling from what Sir John Hall said to me that everything was about to change, but when you are just about to enter your first season as a top flight manager you do not have time to sit back and consider the wider context of anything. All your focus is on your own team, your own job.

I'm sure Sunderland Chairman Bob Murray was similarly unaware of the revolution being planed amongst England's elite. If he did know then why did he not spend more money in the summer of 1990? The situation I was faced with meant all I could do was bring in players to effectively replace two men who were nearing the end of their careers and moving on.

The manner of our promotion had meant that we had even fewer weeks than any club who goes up through the play-offs in a normal season, which leaves three fewer weeks to plan for the new season and begin work on bringing in new players. Even then you are aware you have the possibility of a top flight season ahead. We had thought that defeat in the play-off final meant we were a Second Division club still, so we were starting from a position of weakness. The restrictive budget position didn't help and meant I had to make some tough decisions.

I'd decided to release Eric Gates on a free transfer because I thought he would not be up to the rigours of a season in the top flight at the age of 35. I realise now that I got that one wrong. Eric was one of just three players in my managerial career who I feel I should have kept for one more season. He joined Carlisle and had a good season with the Cumbrians before deciding to retire a year later.

Unfortunately another player I now know I let go too early was our captain, centre-half John MacPhail. Monty was a different case to Gates. After appearing in our opening game, he was offered the opportunity to join Hartlepool United as player-coach, where he helped them to promotion from Division Four at the first time of asking, playing over 40 games. It's ridiculous to admit this, but as well as the attraction of beginning the path towards a coaching or managerial career, part of the attraction of joining Hartlepool was they were also paying John more money than he'd been earning at Roker.

There was a footballing reason in my mind when I agreed to Monty's request to leave. I had come to believe that he was losing some of his pace, so I thought I had got to deal with that potential fatal weakness at the top level and so felt the opportunity well-timed because of this.

I took it as a compliment that Monty's back four at Hartlepool played exactly as mine had always done. He'd obviously taken in everything I'd been espousing. It really hit home later in the season when I popped down to watch Hartlepool play and all I could hear was Monty bellowing out instructions from the back. I knew we missed that at Sunderland. His leadership qualities can not be underestimated. Gary Bennett was never that kind of voice. Monty was also a great physical presence, a great athlete, and would take on board everything you said and demand a high standard of performance from his team-mates. I loved him because he was like my sergeant-major on the pitch. He would ensure that players did what I wanted, regimentally.

Given the way the season unfolded I think that both MacPhail's and Gates's experience would have benefited the team and could have made that vital difference in what would prove to be a very close run campaign. But because my hands were tied by the budget I was forced into these decisions which I now regret. At the time they were the only option financially as I felt I needed new blood and some more recent top flight experience, albeit on a lower wage spend.

As a straight replacement for Monty I brought in 26 year-old Kevin Ball from Portsmouth for £350,000. Although I will maintain until my dying day that I should have kept hold of Monty, there is no denying that Kevin has become a Sunderland legend. In some ways Kevin has been two or three signings in one. I bought him as a centre-half, but he ended up proving to be worth his weight in gold as a defensive midfielder. Now he is a fabulous coach, who has also acted as caretaker-manager as big names have come and gone.

From the moment he signed Bally was brilliant in training, on the pitch and a fantastic presence in the dressing room. For a lad of 5'9" Kevin stood proud. He was a gritty competitor who got stuck in, mostly fairly, although he developed a reputation amongst the supporters, who deified him as a hardman who would die for the cause. Kevin would never say die and in his time took on the likes of Vinnie jones, Dennis Wise, John Fashanu and various referees He was a man after my own heart. Anybody can talk a good game but Kevin could play and he could battle. Kevin developed into a wonderfully destructive defensive midfielder. As Chelsea have proved with Claude Makelele, you need people like that. Bally became known as 'the hatchet' and was the kind of player that opposing managers loved to hate. Terry Venables once said of Kevin that "he has the touch of a blacksmith." I always felt that sort of statement was a backhanded compliment because what Venables was actually doing was challenging Kevin to stop playing his natural game, which was so effective and challenge him to play like Ronaldo or Ginola. Kevin wasn't so naïve as to get suckered into those kind of mind games.

To replace Eric Gates I brought in Peter Davenport from Middlesbrough. Peter had been a superb, crafty forward under Brian Clough at Nottingham Forest, but had lost his way following a million pound move to Manchester United. Peter had disappeared from the scene while at Ayresome Park, but I had always rated his ability and thought he would respond well to being given another chance. I have to admit, though, that it didn't really work out. The problem was that once we'd signed him I didn't have the budget to sign anyone else.

To effectively only be given the budget to replace the two players I'd lost was not good enough. Bob Murray accepts that was a mistake now. More than that it was a big error that would eventually destabilise the club and my career, sending both into a wilderness from which neither would recover for some years.

If we'd have realised the opportunity in 1990 that was there for us to push on then Sunderland could have been amongst the top five or six teams in the country, but we didn't. Now I look back and wonder what might have been if I'd been given enough money to bring in the two or three players that I felt were necessary to give us a great chance of survival.

Bob Murray did go on to spend megabucks not too much later, giving new manager Peter Reid a vast transfer fund with which he signed Kevin Phillips, Niall Quinn, who proved to be massive success and earned them promotion back to the top flight in 1999 and established them in the top half of the table. But then came the millions squandered on the likes of Tore Andre Flo, Emerson Thome and Don Hutchison. In fact during that spell Bob spent far too much money, which surprised me. It came at a point that Sunderland had finished in 7th position in the Premiership in two consecutive seasons in 2000 and 2001, and he gave Reid an absolute fortune to try and break into the top echelon. It backfired. It was a huge risk and arguably consigned the club to a prolonged period of bouncing up and down between the top two divisions before Niall Quinn's consortium bought Bob out and stabilised them in the top flight by handing new manager Roy Keane about £40 million a season to spend on strengthening the squad. I would have loved to have managed Sunderland at this time with the money available to spend on players. Playing the transfer market was always enjoyable and with the World market now I think it would have suited me.

The sense of anticipation from everyone involved at Sunderland was so great that over 30,000 turned up to watch our first home game following promotion. The visitors were Tottenham Hotspur, Gazza, Lineker and Mabbutt and all. The emotional occasion saw excited supporters allowed the five years of torment which had followed the dismal relegations in 1985 and 1987 to slip away from their shoulders. It was a heady evening for everyone at the football club, except one man – me.

A few hours before the kick-off of this massive game I had received a phone call to inform me that my father had died. It was a devastating piece of news, a massive event in my life. Dad had spent much of the time since my mother's death 15 years earlier following my career, often coming to games. We had become as close to each other as at any time in our lives and so this news was extremely tough to take. The split emotions of preparing for our first home game in the top flight and coping with this news were extremely difficult for me to handle, but deep down I knew that Dad would have expected me to do my duty. It was how he and Mum brought us all up. When it comes down to it you've got to deal with personal crises and disappointments and set them aside when you are involved in football. It's your job and supporters expect your complete attention on giving of your best.

I got us through the game, from which we emerged with a point and a solid performance against a very good Spurs side who would go on to lift the FA Cup that season. As soon as I had completed my post-match press duties I got into the car and drove down to Stoke to be with the rest of the family. I at least had the consolation of knowing that Dad had enjoyed a good, long life and that he had seen me succeed in reaching the very top level of the game as a manager to match my achievement as a player.

Despite the lack of preparation time, new players and budget we started the 1990/91 season half decently. In our second home game we defeated FA Cup holders Manchester United 2-1 thanks to goals by Owers and Bennett. Marco Gabbiadini ran both himself and the United centre-halves, Bruce and Pallister, ragged before I had to substitute him through sheer exhaustion. It was a thoroughly good display, but one of few top class performances we managed to produce. A 2-0 victory at Sheffield United in late November secured by two goals by 'Marco Goalo' as he ad also now become known, saw us rise to a season's highest position of 14th, but we only picked up one point in six games to the turn of the year after that. It was a run which plunged us into the relegation zone and the midst of a dogfight for survival, which was as deadly as it was predictable.

As I had no budget remaining to work with I decided to examine other ways of improving the performance of my team, one of which was to focus on the mentality of my players. As a manager I have always looked at new ideas, whether they be psychological or physical. In football there is a decent chance that whatever you did last year could be out of date by the time pre-season training resumes. So this campaign I decided to operate a system whereby I had each player in each week to talk through what they'd done, how I thought they played and where I would like to see improvement. I prepared copious notes and let everyone know that one of the reasons I was doing this was so that the whole squad would feel that I was focussing on them, rather than on those high achievers or players with problems who traditionally crowd manager's offices across the country. I had picked up the idea from a local businessman who had suggested it because he felt it work in his own company because it kept morale high and allowed staff to feel wanted and cared for. I don't think it was a huge success, perhaps because I over-concentrated on preparing the players mentally, but I think you've got to try these things.

I always kept my coaching qualifications up to scratch because again I felt you could glean things form attending them. I don't believe that merely having the qualification proves you can do the job. Management is all about understanding people and so when it came to practical application I always preferred men with personality and character than those with bits of paper telling me they could coach. Viv Busby and Malcolm Crosby were both such men and they were incredibly loyal too.

Despite all this the reason Sunderland struggled that season came down to a far simpler thing – we didn't have enough good players.

The kind of signing I would have loved to make was the one Alex Ferguson secured, Danish international goalkeeper Peter Schmeichel. The big Dane was arguably Fergie's best signing as he pieced together the side that began its domination of silverware in English football. It's well documented that it could have all been so different for Sir Alex. Most notably the run to the FA Cup final of 1990 which began with Mark Robins' header at Nottingham Forest that is often cited as the goal and moment which saved Alex's job and altered United's destiny.

That is true, but there were other moments when it could have all gone wrong for Fergie, including one which involved me. I took my side to Old Trafford in January 1991. United were totally out of the running for the title, sitting in fifth place, eleven points behind leaders Liverpool having played a game more. At one point the previous month a 2-2 draw at Coventry had seen them drop down to ninth position. All was not rosy in the Old Trafford garden.

Because of the size of our squad I was forced to play young defender Paul Williams in that game against some fresh-faced kid called Lee Sharpe, who played wide left and ran Williams ragged. It was harsh on Paul. I had to substitute him in the end and it would be the only appearance he made in the first team all season. The problem with having such a small squad was that injuries bared the threads.

Tactically I got that game wrong, we squeezed up thinking Sharpe was quick and would destroy us by running on to through balls, but we weren't quick enough and got caught. The offside trap was sprung. Mark Hughes scored twice and Brian McClair once as United secured a comfortable 3-0 victory, but over a post-match glass of wine Fergie confided in me that it was quite likely he could have been sacked had he not won. I was amazed. Not seven months earlier this manager had lifted one of the two major trophies in a season's worth of English domestic football. The club may have won FA Cup the previous season, but all that had served to do was increase the pressure on him to win the league, a prize which had eluded this massive club for a quarter of a century. Thankfully for the club he was given another two seasons before he would bring home their first title since before my first team debut for Stoke. I'm sure winning the Cup Winners' Cup in 1991 played a big part in him being given that time, and look how the board's loyalty has been rewarded since.

Incidentally I have shared a few glasses of Claret, Alex's favourite tipple, with the great man and have always felt the experience was not the post-match relaxation that the media paints it to be – two managers, after the fray, having a chinwag. Far from it. That glass of wine is Fergie's way of luring you into his den so he can assess you, probe you and discover your strengths and weaknesses for the next time he faces up to you. His mind is at work as he kicks around the incidents in the game and dissects his team, yours and just about anyone else's.

I had a different pressure on me, the pressure that comes with fighting against the drop. It was the first time I had experienced relative failure. Much as clubs get on a roll, as success breeds success as I had experienced at both York and Sunderland, failure also brings systemic problems and a lack of belief amongst all levels of staff. You can smell the fear and then the negativity as people seek someone else to blame, to save their own skin.

To give them their due my small squad did me proud. Gary Owers was ever present, Tony Norman and Gary Bennett played all but one game, while Paul Bracewell, Armstrong. Davenport, Gabbiadini, Hardyman, Pascoe and Ball all played regularly.

At this higher level I wouldn't play Gary Bennett at centre-back unless I had to because I didn't trust him and there was too much at stake. He'd got pace, was good in the air and decent on the ball, but he would make mistakes. Making them out near the touchline lessened the impact of them on the team. It wasn't that he did not prove to be a total professional, he was just prone to the odd howler and I didn't want to take the risk. I had a simple method of trying to improve Gary. I'd basically say "you ain't gong to play unless you improve your concentration". Gary was forever picking the ball up and going on runs, which is great so long as somebody filled the holes in but often they wouldn't.

In December 1990 we were leading 3-2 at Tottenham in the 90th minute when Benno charged down the right wing looking to cross the ball into their box rather than running it down to the corner flag. Needless to say Spurs nicked the ball, went straight up the pitch and Gary Lineker scored to make it 3-3. I remember cracking on to Benno for doing it. Even when I'd thought I had got him under control, when things were going well, he would lose his head.

The only other option for defensive cover I had was a local youngster called Richard Ord. Richard had played for England under 21s. He was a good centre-half, who took things in and it looked as though he was going to come through to be a top player, but he was perhaps too young to be thrown in there at that stage. The problem was there was nobody else. It's interesting to note that in all his 14 appearances that season in which he filled in across the back four, Richard played in just one victory. That's when it comes home to me that I should have kept John MacPhail. Instead of Ord playing those games, Monty should have been in there talking, shoring up, keeping it tight.

Despite the problem, we stuck together, battled hard and scrambled points as and where we could. That United defeat aside, from the turn of the year we lost just one of six games, including victories over Southampton, Chelsea and Nottingham Forest.

My squad was effectively only 15 senior players, plus young pups such as Kieron Brady, David Rush and Tommy Mooney. Rush in all honesty was not good enough at that level, but he was fantastic in lower divisions and I would later sign him for Oxford United where he did a great job for me. Some Sunderland supporters thought Rush let his talent go to his head when he declared 'he would never play for Sunderland again' after impressing top flight clubs in the 1992 cup run. That did not go down well and it would not be until I came in for him two years later that he moved on.

At the beginning of Feburary the board relented and allowed me to spend £225,000 on bringing in one player. The problem was attracting someone to the relegation battle

Our fantastic FA Cup runs in 1985 and 1986 brought me yet more whisky!

Making my point at half-time in the York dressing room. Note the hat and coat – we played Liverpool in sub-zero temperatures.

FINAL

Get your Summer Shoes and Sandals from

Goodsons
THE SHOEMEN

TONTINE SQ.
HANLEY
(Open 6 days)
Telephone 25035

30 HIGH ST.,
CONGLETON
(Closed Wed. aln.)
Telephone 279096

14p

The Tri-Star jet nose down off the runway.

'My flight of fear' —Smith

Denis Smith—
"frightening experience"

FORMER Stoke City ironman Denis Smith today relived the horror of the Tri-Star jet crash at Leeds-Bradford airport.

And he revealed how his York City players helped people to safety after they plunged down escape chutes when the plane ground to a halt 50 yards off the runway with its tail in the air.

"The lads were fairly close to the exits and did a great job when they had got down from the plane by helping the older passengers and children at the end of the chutes," said the York manager.

"It was a very frightening experience—we were right under one of the big engines which was still ticking over—our fear was that it might blow up."

The party of 25 York players and staff were among the 416 passengers and crew on the British Airtours flight from Palma Majorca. They had just completed an end-of-season holiday.

By CHRIS STONE

The jet ploughed off the end of the runway, lost its nose wheel and stopped in soft earth.

Weather

Weather forecast for North Staffordshire and South Cheshire as supplied by the Manchester Weather Centre.

Mainly dry with sunny spells. Maximum 15C, 59F. Clear and cold overnight with ground frost in a few sheltered parts around dawn. Minimum 3C, 37F. Light and mainly westerly winds.

Outlook: Fine with near normal daytime temperatures, but still chilly at night.

Lighting-up time: 9.49 p.m. to 4.22 a.m.

© Crown Copyright 1986. All rights reserved.

Statement by N.G.A. '82

National Graphical Association '82 members working at Staffordshire

For once I wasn't in hospital because of a serious injury or major operation. This visit was to promote the 'Give Blood' campaign for the Blood Transfusion Service.

One of the more frightening episodes in my career as York's Tristar plane went off the end of runway in landing at Leeds Bradford airport.

Welcoming John MacPhail to Bootham Crescent. Monty would prove to be a mainstay of both my successful York and Sunderland teams.

In the summer of 1987 I was persuaded by Sunderland chairman Bob Murray, between Viv Busby and I, to take up the challenge of reviving the fallen club's fortunes.

Viv and I moved from York to Sunderland together and galvanized the side to win promotion from the Third Division at the first time of asking. Viv was a magnificent assistant.

Eric Gates was the pigeon-fancying doyen of Sunderland when I arrived. His career had an Indian summer as he and Marco Gabbiadini cut a swathe through defences, combining perfectly to notch 21 goals each in our Third Division title-winning campaign.

YOU DON'T MESS WITH DIRTY DEN!

By STEVEN HOWARD

WHEN Denis Smith walks on to the pitch at Roker, the grass almost snaps to attention.

Apprentices lounging over brooms scurry into action — a fevered look in their eyes.

"I don't normally have problems with players," says the Sunderland boss.

That is a bit like Mike Tyson admitting he does not get mugged on the subway.

In 10 years as a buccaneering Stoke centre-half, Smith had his nose smashed five times, suffered five broken legs and had enough stitches in his face to knit Frank Bruno a sweater or two.

In just five months at Roker Park, Smith has pumped new life into the corpse Lawrie McMenemy and Bob Stokoe left behind in the Third Division for the first time in its history.

EXCLUSIVE
The man who's making Roker roar

Promises

They now stand at the top of the division.

Smith, 40 this week, does not want to deride his predecessor but says: "The fans here were fed up with promises. They had heard enough about 'next season this, next

I'm a positive character.

"And there is no excuse for this club not to do well this season."

When Smith arrived, the popular opinion was of a bankrupt club, riddled with boardroom dissent, paying old sweats a fortune to see out fat contracts in the reserves.

Smith says: "I sold Mark Procter to Sheffield Wednesday for £250,000 and we are averaging

The scrutiny I received up in the north east took various different forms, from being compared to an infamous, and murdered, EastEnders character, above, to having songs written about me by local kids (right).

CHESTER TOWN FOOTBALL CLUB

HONORARY DITTY

Denis Smith is a jolly good bloke
He came up to Roker from Stoke,
Its our under 12s dream
To be picked for his team
And play Luton again for a joke!!

A big thank you to Denis we say
For presenting our medals this way
In return please do savour
This wine of full flavour
With best wishes from all here today.

Top left, being chaired off the pitch by Reuben Agboola, Gordon Armstrong and Marco Gabbiadini after clinching promotion and the title with a 3-1 victory over Northampton Town in May 1988.
Top right, Posing with the trophy with my Dad, centre, and brother Graham.
Bottom left, 'Magic' Marco Gabbiadini, who scored 21 goals in 37 games during the glorious 1987/88 Division Three promotion season. The best £80,000 Sunderland ever spent.
Bottom right, my lovely, and very understanding
wife, Kate, celebrating with the spoils.

Receiving the 1988 Manager of the Season award given by Hennessy.

I always enjoyed big charity events such as this match played at Gateshead stadium with stars like Steve Cram, Linford Christie, Dave Regis, Daley Thompson, Denis Waterman, Ian Rush, Frank Bruno and Steve Coppell turning out to help.

Newcastle's Paul Stimson, left, chases the ball alongside Paul Atkinson, right, in a goalless Tyne-Wear derby in February 1990. The meeting of the two north east giants is always a hotly passionate affair. We would eventually defeat the Toon in the play-off semi-final, thanks to a famous 2-0 victory at St James' Park in the second leg.

I had known Paul Bracewell since we played together at Stoke. His influence on the team both in the dressing room, where he brought experience and a lovely sense of humour, and on the pitch where his passing, calmness, leadership and two-footed play was top class, went a long way to helping us secure promotion in 1990.

Showing off another Manager of the Month award to the Roker faithful. The crowd inside the old ground made one hell of a racket. It was an intimidating place for visiting teams to come and generated an incredible atmosphere.

My Sunderland coaching team. From left to right, Malcolm Crosby, Viv Busby, Myself, Steve Smelt, physio, Roger Jones, goalkeeping coach and Jim Morrow

Marco Gabbiadini tries to take on Swindon's Colin Calderwood during the 1990 play-off final at Wembley. The Scotsman crocked Gabbers early on and gave himself a quiet afternoon. We didn't play well and missed Marco's pace as he really couldn't run after Calderwood's tackle. However Swindon's financial shenanigans put paid to their promotion and saw us elevated instead.

The whole town came alive after we made it into the top flight, albeit through the back door. It was great driving across the Wear bridge every morning throughout the summer of 1990 with this banner singing our praises!

ROKER SPURRED TO GREATER HEIGHTS

Young makes Murton bow

MIDFIELDER Kevin Young makes his Murton debut at Durham City in the Northern League First Division tonight.

His international clearance has arrived. He was playing for Utrecht.

Andy Wetherall is still injured for Murton, but City manager Charlie Gott has a full squad available.

Dean Gibb comes in for Seaham Red Star at home to Blue Star, following the injury to David Robinson.

Promoted Peterlee visit Shildon with an unchanged side, but John Graham returns to boost the squad. Washington visit Hebburn in Division Two (6.30).

In the League Cup preliminary round last night, Langley Park won 3-0 at Chester-le-Street.

Langley scored through John Nicholson, Kevin Berry (penalty), and Joe Calvert. Chester's Colin Howey missed a penalty.

In Division Two, Easington beat Evenwood 3-1. Dave Bellwood (2) and Dave Howard struck. Tony Hodgson replied.

Boro walk tightrope

MIDDLESBROUGH face a League Cup exit at Tranmere for the second time in three years.

SUNDERLAND confounded their critics to hold highly-rated Tottenham to a goalless draw.

They earned a deserved first point of the season.

If Sunderland's first half finishing had matched their attractive and non-stop approach work then an emotional Denis Smith would have had the consolation of an initial First Division win for the loss of his father.

"That was a good performance," said the Roker manager. "It was for my dad. He died this afternoon.

Smith has had no bigger critic than his father throughout his career both as player and manager. But he would have been proud to witness Sunderland's transformation.

Unfortunate to miss out on a point at Norwich, Sunderland took the game by the scruff of the neck in the opening period to frighten the life out of the North London aristocrats.

FASCINATING

But they paid the penalty for squandering three good chances in as many minutes midway through the first half. That let the visitors gradually gain control and assert their undoubted skills upon a fascinating and entertaining match.

Sunderland 0 Tottenham 0

By GEOFF STOREY

should have led to Gary Owers scoring in 23 minutes. Owers stormed clear only for giant goalkeeper Erik Thorstvedt to turn his shot behind.

Gabbiadini then burst into the area, beating Steve Sedgley for pace, and took the ball wide of Thorstvedt, who was saved by a deflection. From the resultant Hardyman corner, Kevin Ball's point-blank header hit Paul Allen on the line.

A delicate chip from Peter Davenport in 31 minutes floated just outside the far post and two minutes later Gabbiadini had the ball in the net only for John Kay to be penalised for blatant hand ball.

Paul Gascoigne, a big disappointment on his return to the North East, was just wide with a 25-yard free kick to end the first half.

There was more purpose about Tottenham's play after the break. Stewart immediately set up a great chance for Lineker, whose close range header failed to seriously test Tony Norman.

Gascoigne again failed to direct a free kick from a dangerous position on target and then David Howells brought Norman to his knees with a mis-hit shot.

Sunderland sent on Tony Cullen for the injured Hardyman in 55 minutes with

Ferguson tips Leeds to shine

LEEDS will stay in Division One and perform with style, insists Manchester United manager Alex Ferguson.

Ferguson was impressed by Leeds in their 0-0 draw last night.

"They're not just a long ball side," he explained. "They play a mix in their game with Gary McAllister, David Batty and Gordon Strachan.

"I think they played in a certain way to get out of the Second Division. Now there's perhaps another way to stay in the first division.

"They were revved up tonight and they had a magnificent win on Saturday at Everton. You cannot be saying they will go down. I don't they'll have any problem."

Kenny Dalglish was delighted with Liverpool's 2-0 win over Nottingham Forest.

After seeing Ian Rush and Peter Beardsley kill off Forest, the Anfield manager said: "We played very well. There were a lot of things that were very pleasing to watch. Given a little bit of luck they could have won more convincingly."

Dennis Wise, Chelsea's £1.6m summer signing and Crystal Palace midfielder Andy Gray were sent off after an 11th minute brawl.

The opening home match of our First Division season against Spurs was an emotional occasion, not least because that afternoon I learnt of the death of my father.

I used Billy Whitehurst and Iain Hesford as bargaining chips to secure the signature of Welsh international goalkeeper Tony Norman from Hull City. He would prove to be a magnificent servant for Sunderland, playing nearly 200 games for the club.

Dave Bennett will always be a legend at Sunderland, but I couldn't trust him to not make mistakes at the very highest level, so I moved him to right-back. Here he sees off the dangerous Paul Merson of Arsenal.

In the summer of 1991, after that agony of last day relegation from the First Division Bob Murray persuaded me to stay at Sunderland rather than rejoin my hometown club Stoke City by telling me he'd never sack me. Less than six months later he had. Here, above, Stoke's greatest son Sir Stanley Matthews endeavours to persuade me that I should return to the club, while, left, I contemplate my future after another defeat and right, some of the headlines my departure made.

I will never understand why chairman Bob Murray let me sign John Byrne for £225,000 from Brighton and then sacked me a few weeks later. I feel vindicated that it was John who scored in every round of that season's FA Cup to help Sunderland to Wembley, although he couldn't manage it in the final as they lost 0-2 to Liverpool. I ended up signing John three times, which just shows how highly I rated him.

The saddest aspect of my departure from Sunderland was the ending of my professional relationship with Viv Busby who had been my trusted and very capable assistant for nearly a decade. We do still talk, but the events which led to him leaving Roker Park in 1991 have soiled our personal relationship.

Bob Murray's failure to pay the severance package we'd agreed meant I jumped at the first opportunity I got, to manage Second Division Bristol City.

weet dreamer

team beat odds again

ut a Sunderland team
nd optimism at Wem-
ve left the famous old
ling embarrassed by
nance.

hey can do themselves
g the FA Cup against all

hat they WILL win. But I
y CAN. What is for sure is
ill play better than they
990 promotion play-offs
on.
wful that sweltering May
only an outstanding per-
goalkeeper Tony Norman

DENIS SMITH'S
THE ROKER PA

TONY NORMAN:
him from Hull in Dec
1988 for £200,000 p
own goalkeeper lai
ford and striker Billy
hurst. The last time
was at Wembley wit
derland — two years ago in the
tion play-offs against Swindon —
brilliant in a 1-0 defeat. A lovely
quiet and reliable. The kind of m
would like your daughter to marr

JOHN KAY: If you
the trenches you wou
this man alongside. H
hard as nails, con
fearless. He cost me f
from Wimbledon ar
given Sunderland fiv
of great service. Can be very funny
pitch — he once told a Liverpool
won't name: "Walt Disney could n
drawn your face." Players on bot
fell about laughing.

PAUL HARDYMA
thought his days at
Park were numbered
bought Anton Roga
Celtic. He wanted to

I couldn't stay in the country to watch Malcolm Crosby lead my team out at Wembley for the 1992 FA Cup final, but the boys had my total backing in bringing yet more success to Sunderland. They had done fantastically well to get there, but I will always maintain I should have been given more time after spending the money from the £1.7 million sale of Marco Gabbiadini to Crystal Palace. However, I was dismissed a month later before I could bed the three new signings in.

I had an abundance of goalscorers in my short time at Bristol City, Jackie Dziekanowski, left, and Andy Cole, right, who I signed from Arsenal's reserve team, being the best of them. They were a very hard combination for defenders to stop. I left over the board's refusal to allow me to sell Andy to Newcastle, but within a month he had joined the Magpies and went on to become one of the best goalscorers in Premier League history.

*Joining First Division
Oxford United meant
working with Chairman,
Robin Herd, founder of
the March Formula 1
racing team, and some
great perks!*

Oxford managers new and old. Myself and Jim Smith, on this occasion bringing his Portsmouth team to the Manor for a Division One game.

Celebrating Joey Beauchamp's vital winning goal against Notts County along with John Clinkard, our physio, on the final day of the 1993/94 season. We thought the victory would keep us up. Sadly away wins for both Birmingham and West Brom saw us relegated. What a player Joey should have been, especially after his dream move to West Ham, but his homesickness for the Cotswolds brought him back to Oxford in the blink of an eye.

Had I taken on Steve McClaren at Oxford when he was looking to start out in coaching then his career may have developed very differently. Instead he joined Jim Smith at Derby, became Alex Ferguson's assistant and manager of Middlesbrough before being appointed as England coach.

Top right, Paul Moody, and right, David Rush celebrate goals in the sweet 2-0 win at my former employers Bristol City, which was the first of four consecutive victories that would see us sneak into the second promotion spot at the end of the 1995/96 season.

In the aftermath of winning promotion back into the First Division thanks to a wonderful run in to the end of the 1995/96 season culminating in the clinching 4-0 home win over Peterborough, amidst the mayhem of on-pitch celebrations one fan stuck this accoutrement on my head. It became a bit of a symbol of that success and Oxford fans still ask me if I've got it even today!

Matty Elliott soars to head the winning goal in a 3-2 Division One victory over Manchester City at Maine Road. I rate Matty as probably my best ever signing.

In the fourth round of the 1996/97 League Cup we drew with Premier League Southampton, whose manager Graeme Souness was really not happy at all when Paul Moody scored a 90th minute equalizer to earn us a replay.

I sold Jim Magilton (in background, far left) to Alan Ball at Southampton for £600,000 after the gritty midfielder scored the goal that beat Premier League Leeds at Elland Road in the FA Cup in 1993. Knowing him as I did we were able to nullify his threat, although Southampton scraped through the replay at the Manor Ground with a 3-2 victory. It hasn't surprised me to see Jim making a good start to life as a manager at Ipswich.

Alex Dyer was a fast raiding left winger, and a really bubbly lad, who I converted to a defender during his three seasons at Oxford.

I paid £100,000 to nab towering central defender Darren Purse from Leyton Orient in 1996, where he'd been captain of the team at 17, something which impressed his qualities upon me. Darren was my kind of centre-half, competitive and solid. He was sold after my departure to Birmingham City for £700,000. I was actually trying to buy him for my new club West Bromwich Albion at that time, and Darren would eventually end up signing for them in 2004 and then join Cardiff City where he starred in their FA Cup exploits of 2008.

Phil Gilchrist tackles Shaun Newton of Charlton in a game where we ran a team who would win promotion to the Premier League close, losing 2-3.

Joey Beauchamp celebrates scoring the third goal in our 3-0 victory over Wolves in September 1997.

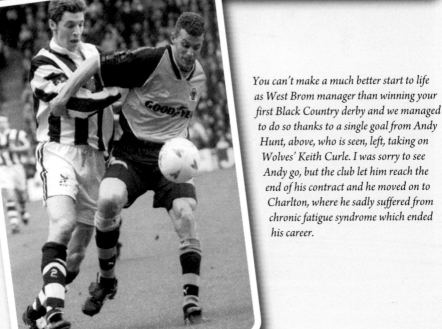

You can't make a much better start to life as West Brom manager than winning your first Black Country derby and we managed to do so thanks to a single goal from Andy Hunt, above, who is seen, left, taking on Wolves' Keith Curle. I was sorry to see Andy go, but the club let him reach the end of his contract and he moved on to Charlton, where he sadly suffered from chronic fatigue syndrome which ended his career.

Left: Looking stressed at another defeat. Our form in my first few months in charge of Albion was nothing to write home about. In fact we won just two of our last 16 games, although we finished a comfortable 10th. I thought the side needed major surgery and so opted to deal with things head on.

Right: Dutch midfield star Richard Sneekes was one of the most intelligent men I ever managed. If anything he was possibly too intelligent, and too questioning, to carry out instructions on the pitch. He has gone on to become a very successful restaurateur and is still extremely popular with Albion supporters.

We opened the 1998/99 season well and this 2-0 victory over Norwich City saw us sitting in third position. But just two days later we crashed 1-5 at Grimsby Town and the knives began to come out. Here my big summer defensive signing Matt Carbon, who cost £800,000 from Derby County sees off the challenge of Norwich's youthful Craig Bellamy. Matt started very well, was a very pacy player, but didn't fulfil his promise.

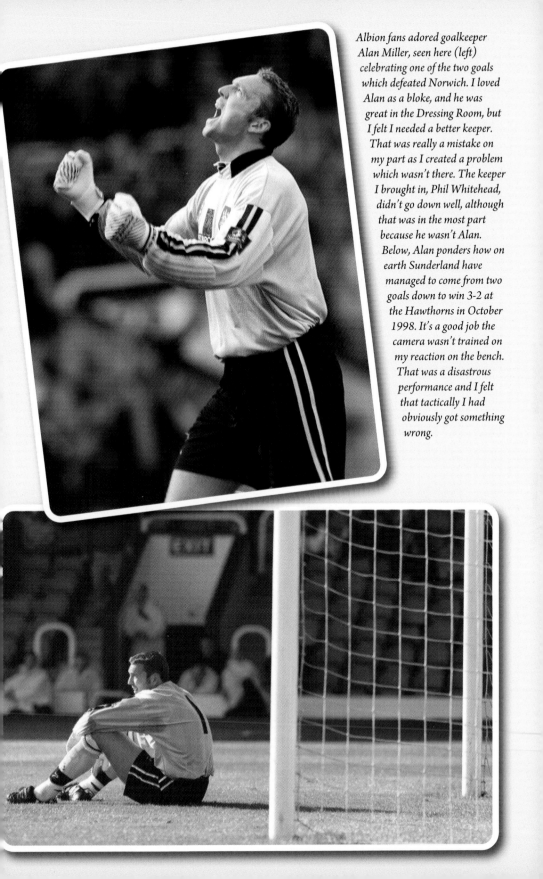

Albion fans adored goalkeeper Alan Miller, seen here (left) celebrating one of the two goals which defeated Norwich. I loved Alan as a bloke, and he was great in the Dressing Room, but I felt I needed a better keeper. That was really a mistake on my part as I created a problem which wasn't there. The keeper I brought in, Phil Whitehead, didn't go down well, although that was in the most part because he wasn't Alan. Below, Alan ponders how on earth Sunderland have managed to come from two goals down to win 3-2 at the Hawthorns in October 1998. It's a good job the camera wasn't trained on my reaction on the bench. That was a disastrous performance and I felt that tactically I had obviously got something wrong.

The one bright spark of the 1998/99 season was the form of my wonderful goalscorer Lee Hughes. I had spotted him from day one at the club, stuck him in the first team, where previously he'd only been a substitute, and watched as he banged in an incredible 25 goals by Christmas, finishing as England's leading scorer with 31 goals that season. He was a brilliant goalscorer, frightening defenders with his pace and willingness to stick on their shoulders, and at 22 Lee had the world at his feet. But he let it go to his head, got into all sorts of bother and ended up going to jail for a devastating incident. Thankfully all that happened after I'd gone.

Right: Stylish young midfielder Enzo Maresca, who I picked up for a song rather luckily while he was over from Italy and his agent was touting him around.

Left: Matt Carbon, right, and David Johnson, left holding ball, try to break up a scrap between Manuel Thetis and Sean Flynn (no.4) in a tetchy game between Albion and Ipswich. Both the offenders were dismissed, but the incident was symptomatic of our frustration at our poor form. To be honest Flynn was always causing trouble.

riker Mickey Evans, who suffered terrible injury problems during my time at the Albion, leaps into the arms of lbion physio Nick Worth as our bench celebrate us opening the scoring against Wolves in April 1999. The game ded 1-1.

My return to Oxford was short and not particularly sweet. I had been asked to return by Mickey Lewis who was doing every conceivable job including manager, coach, scout and kitman on his own, but I found new chairman Firoz Kassam a tremendously difficult man to get on with. The club was in a total mess.

My older sister Beryl taught me to wolf whistle and it's been a key skill in my managerial career. Now my secret's out, taught to whistle by a girl…!

Martin Aldridge's untimely death in a car accident was a dreadful shock. The fact that my first game back at Oxford in February 2000 fell just a week afterwards and was against Martin's then team Blackpool made for an extremely sombre and moving occasion. Here he battles with Southampton's Ulrich van Gobbel

Darren Ferguson, son of Sir Alex, curls a beauty of a free-kick around the Tranmere wall. Darren would become a major player in my team, and developed into a leader of men, so it is no surprise to me that he is following in his father's footsteps by being successful in his first managerial job at Peterborough. Darren has the drive and temperament to be a top manager.

My first game in charge at the Racecourse Ground was a 1-0 victory over promotion favourites QPR. Michael Blackwood scored the only goal, centre, while, bottom, I endeared myself to the Wrexham faithful by getting into trouble with referee Michael Ryan as we clung on for victory in the last few moments when the ball was thrown on from crowd and I headed it back to them to waste precious seconds.

Then, when I got home, I was in trouble with Kate because I'd just had a plate put in my neck and I'd forgotten all about it!

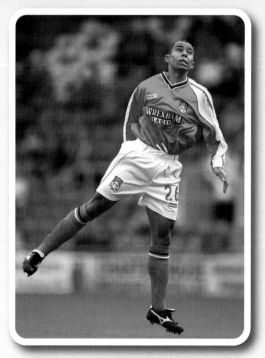

Jim Whitley would be a mainstay of my Wrexham midfield from my arrival in 2001 until 2006 when we had to let him go aged 31. Jim did a good job for me, but he picked up so many injuries through his all-action style. Perhaps surprisingly he is now an artist and sells paintings for a living. Jim also does a great Frank Sinatra cabaret act.

The frustration of relegation is evident as I endeavour to find out what on earth is going on with my defence as we slump to a crucial 0-1 home defeat to Chesterfield in March 2002.

Former soldier Marius Rovde arrived from Ayr United on a free transfer. The big Norwegian goalkeeper proved to be a real character, who loved being in the English league.

Top, Lee Trundle escapes the clutches of Everton's Scott Gemmill as we take on the Toffees in a League Cup tie in October 2002. Lee, who began with us as a semi-pro, coming to professional football relatively late in life, was magnificent for me, although he could be a handful at times. The problem with him has always been his application, but there is no doubt he has wonderful skill. He was capable of doing special things which get you off your seat.

Bottom, my assistant at Wrexham Kevin Russell issues instructions while Everton manager David Moyes contemplates extra-time. Fortunately for him, David had some kid called Wayne Rooney on the bench who came on to score two late goals and announce his arrival to the footballing world. Two weeks later Wayne would become the youngest goalscorer in Premier League history by scoring the winner against Arsenal.

The ecstasy on my face is obvious as somehow my Wrexham team have won promotion from Division Three to Division Two, despite huge financial problems which would eventually lead to administration. If ever a group of professionals in all areas of a club needed commending for performing way beyond expectations then this season was it.'

Clearly delighted to be awarded Manager of the Season in Division Three for 2002/03, I also had the pleasure of being able to see Sir Stanley Matthews' FA Cup winner's medal from the legendary 1953 FA Cup final, which had just been sold at auction to renowned Stoke fan Nick Hancock.

Above, Andy Morrell, on the right with flag, starred in our promotion-winning side of 2002/03, scoring 35 league goals. Here he celebrates promotion with strike partner Lee Jones following our 5-0 thrashing of Cambridge in our last home game of the season.

Left, tricky winger Carlos Edwards, along with fellow Trinidadians Dennis Lawrence and Hector Sam, starred in the 2006 World Cup finals for Trinidad & Tobago. Not bad for a team from Division Three.

Shaun Pejic was selected in my Wrexham team on his own merits, rather than my friendship with his Uncle Mike from my Stoke playing days or the fact his father Mel was Wrexham's physiotherapist.

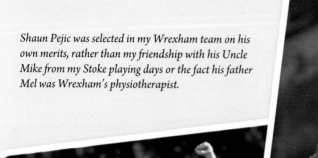

Above, Juan Ugarte, left, and Andy Holt, celebrate our opening goal in the 2005 LDV Vans trophy victory over Southend at the Millennium Stadium. Right, parading the trophy was a great feeling. To win a first major competition in the club's history was a fabulous achievement and it was brilliant to reward our loyal and long-suffering supporters with some silverware to celebrate, especially as the final was played at their national stadium.

I'd known about Ben Foster since Stoke City signed him from non-league Racing Warwick and took him on loan in 2005 to give him experience and help our battle against relegation. We lost that, but ended up winning the LDV Vans trophy and during the final Sir Alex Ferguson, attending to watch his son Darren captain our team, spotted Ben's ability and eventually paid Stoke £1 million for him. Strangely Ben never played for Stoke and, as I write, has only made one appearance for United, but he could be the future of English goalkeeping.

The unexplained death of Tim Carter was a source of tremendous sorrow to me. I brought him to Wearside where he would eventually become a goalkeeping coach under the Roy Keane regime and I have no idea why he would want to end his life the way he did. Death has been something I have had to deal with over the years, from the sudden collapse of Stoke team-mate Paul Shardlow on the training ground in 1968 to Martin Aldridge's car smash and Keith Walwyn's heart condition.

The stress and strain of managing a club in administration clearly show in this photograph.

With my sons Tom, left, and Paul on the morning of my 1,000th game as a manager in 2004.

My brothers and sisters on the occasion of my 50th birthday. From left, Graham, Susan, myself, Beryl, Mick, Joyce and Ron.

we were clearly facing. I needed to get this one right and make the money tell in the right area of the team. At the time I had a need to plug a gap at right-back because of an injury to John Kay, but try as I might I couldn't find one at all. Instead I moved Gary Owers from midfield to full-back and spent the money on securing the signature of Republic of Ireland under 21 international Brian Mooney from Third Division Preston North End. Every time I had seen him play he had played extremely well and looked really fast, with an ability to go past people, hurting defences. But I have to admit I got this one wrong. John McGrath stitched me up. Mooney was a bad signing. I'd go so far as to say a disaster. He seemed to be carrying an injury and that affected his pace and mobility. In short he was a disaster.

We used to have these Meet The Manager events in pubs around the area and I remember a few weeks after Brian had joined us and he had not done very well at all I attended one and had to field an inevitable barrage of questions about our new signing and his lack of form. They were all having a right go at Mooney, and me for signing him. It was getting very heated.

So I said "come on, calm down. Right, let's have a vote on it, anybody who thinks he was a bad buy put your hand up". Up went every hand in the pub – including mine! And that was it – the criticism killed dead as supporters fell about laughing. They appreciated my honesty and everyone accepted that. Possibly that was why I got on with the fans, I would go out and talk to them. Even when things were going wrong I would turn up and talk.

By late April we had dropped into the bottom three on the back of a run of one win in seven games. We were struggling badly and had just four games left to save our skins. The first of those was against fellow strugglers Luton. If ever there was a six pointer this was it. In that season, 1990/91, the division was being adjusted from 20 teams back up to 22 as the administrators confused everyone before settling on the 20 team set up we have now. Consequently only two clubs were to be relegated. We now sat 19th, five points behind Luton, but with a game in hand. We had to win this match at Kenilworth Road. Gordon Armstrong and Graham Rodger made it 1-1 at half-time, but Colin Pascoe scored the winning goal to give us a vital lifeline with a 2-1 victory. The great escape was on.

We had two home games against Wimbledon and Arsenal in which to make up the ground on Luton if we were to go into the last game of the season ahead of them and with our fate in our own hands. Both matches were extremely tense, nervous affairs. Over 24,000 willed us on to beat the Dons, but we couldn't find a goal and drew 0-0. Arsenal also held us to a goalless draw at Roker, securing a vital point for them in their quest for the league title, live on television in a game played after we'd learned that Everton had beaten Luton to keep our hopes alive.

Those two points meant we entered the final match, away at Manchester City, level on points and goal difference with Luton but needing to better their result because they had scored more goals than us. We'd missed a fabulous opportunity to save ourselves in those two home matches, but it was not a case of an individual failing, or making a mistake which cost us. It was the whole scenario.

Now our entire season had come down to this one, nailbiting day. Our problem was that Luton were at home to already relegated Derby, although the Rams had shown some signs of life in winning their first game in 20 against Southampton in their penultimate match.

We had to better their result or margin of victory to stay up, and we had to do it without our talismanic captain Kevin Ball who was suspended for this last game, Richard Ord deputising.

Sunderland's fans had been fantastic all season and when we walked out at Maine Road for that decisive game it felt as if the whole of Wearside had followed us to Greater Manchester. Well over 10,000 had made the journey south. The backing they gave the team was incredible and the players responded by putting on probably our best performance of the season. In an incredible first half both sides scored twice. We put together some fantastic moves and from one of them Marco Gabbiadini scored a classic flying header for our first, and at that point I thought we could pull off the impossible. Gary Bennett netted a rare goal to make it 2-2, but we still displayed some of our usual defensive frailties to concede, exacerbated by Ball's absence.

Throughout the second half the fans chanted my name all the way through it and as the game wore on and we swarmed all over the Blues seeking that vital goal. It wouldn't come and instead City scored a third goal on the break. Once that goal went in we could not get back on level terms.

The irony was that, of the three goals we conceded, two were scored by Niall Quinn, who is now Chief Executive of the club. I will forever remain convinced that if Bob Murray had invested properly at the start of the season history would have been totally different and Sunderland would have established themselves in the top half of the Premier League right from the start. That would probably have meant that Niall and his consortium would never have had the opportunity to buy the club.

It was a hell of a game, played in a raw, passionate atmosphere. But ultimately we weren't quite good enough and the 2-3 defeat sent us down as Luton won 2-0 against Derby. It really was an incredible afternoon. I can remember both sets of fans at the end climbing the fences in the Kippax to swap shirts, scarves and hats. The Sunderland fans sung their tear-soaked hearts out as the players walked round the pitch clapping us. The outstanding reaction of the supporters made that one of the most emotional days of my life.

Relegation hit me hard. It was the first time it had happened to me in my managerial career, so it was a huge blow. Until now I had only ever been on the up. I regret not being able to keep Sunderland in the First Division that year. If I had done so, I think I would have been there for a lot more enjoyable seasons.

******

That summer, as I grappled with the disappointment of that final day defeat and demotion to the Second Division, I was faced with one of the biggest dilemmas I've ever had in my life. Happy though I was at Sunderland and determined as I was to right the wrong I felt we'd done the club and those wonderful fans, I was almost torn in half by a phone call I received from Chairman Peter Coates offering me the opportunity to manage my beloved Stoke City. The club had suffered a disastrous season under manager Alan Ball and finished in the lowest league position of their history in mid-table in Division Three. I would be taking the reins in almost exactly the same circumstances as I had at Sunderland. Mr Coates also offered me more money than I've ever been offered in my career. It was a tremendous opportunity and an unbelievable package. I asked for time to consider things and talk to my wife about it.

Over the next few days it became apparent that besides Stoke there were other clubs who were interested in me. I had to answer the questions I had begun to ask myself – have I taken this club as far as I can? Can I get them promoted again? Will I get the backing of chairman and fans? Do I want to leave Sunderland?

I soon had answers. Bob Murray sat me down and told me he didn't want me to go and went so far as to tell me that he would never sack me.

I also thought back to that day in May at Maine Road when our outstanding supporters had chanted my name and that if anything swayed me to stay. Obviously there was a huge pull towards Stoke but I couldn't get the images of the way the Rokerites had acclaimed myself and our relegated team. Their reaction meant so much. We'd got relegated and these incredible supporters were chanting for me. That takes some doing. Normally they would be chanting for you to get "out" on a day like that.

As I discussed my options with Kate it became clear that she had deep concerns about returning to Stoke. She felt it was the emotional tug that was drawing me not the reality of what I would be walking into. Many supporters felt it was my destiny to manage Stoke City and it had always been my burning ambition, but Kate kept telling me, "if you move back to Stoke it's going to destroy you. You care too deeply, the fans idolise you too much. It can only end badly." I realised she was right.

I decided that I wanted Stoke supporters to remember me as I was, that I could only tarnish those wonderful memories if I took charge of the club. All these factors meant there was only one decision for me. I stayed as manager of Sunderland AFC. Peter Coates, who is now Chairman of Premier League Stoke City, never lets me forget that I turned him down!

Despite the unusual euphoria and goodwill surrounding relegation and my decision to remain at the club, when the 1991/92 season began we just couldn't get going. The players were flat, I struggled to maintain their morale and levels of performance. We won just four games from the first 14. The interesting thing was that we weren't struggling to score goals, it was our defence which cost us. For example we scored three goals at Swindon Town in September, but conceded five to slump to a poor defeat. We also scored three goals at Port Vale, but still didn't win, drawing 3-3.

We kept a clean sheet at Barnsley, where our three goals gave us a good win, and at Charlton we went one better, netting four goals. Marco Gabbiadini bagged a classic striker's hat-trick in that game. He was still producing the goods and that had crystallised a plan in my mind. No funds had been forthcoming once again over the summer, the second consecutive close season where this had been the case. My hands were tied as far as bringing new players in unless I generated the cash through player sales. There was really only one option. I would have to cash in my biggest star and the most popular player at Sunderland. Magic Marco was made available for a transfer. It did not make me a popular figure with either fans or board. But I felt I had no choice. I didn't want to sell Marco, I had to for the good of the team. Management is full of tough decisions and I was not afraid to take them. If the board could not provide me with the wherewithal to piece together a new team to push for promotion then I would find a way of doing it.

To be fair to the board, there was another reason why they were reticent to invest in the team. For some months discussion had been progressing as to how to build a new stadium. Roker Park, wonderful, passionate cauldron as it was, was old, dilapidated and would cost far too much money to rebuild. The only option was to construct a new ground from scratch on a new site. That would prove to be a difficult sell to the fans, many of whom did not want to leave, and the various negotiations with the council and acquisition of land took another five years or so, before eventually the Stadium of Light, an absolutely magnificent ground which is testament to that board's vision, opened.

Because of that ambition money was tight. I decided that Marco had to go and the money generated by his sale used to bring in three or four new players. I agreed a deal with Crystal Palace manager Steve Coppell for Marco to move to Selhurst Park as the replacement for departed legend Ian Wright. Palace were at that stage regularly finishing in the top half of the First Division, and had been runners-up in the FA Cup final just 18 months earlier. It was a great move for Marco and brought in £1.8 million to our coffers which I spent immediately on bringing in three new players, Northern Irish international left-back Anton Rogan for £350,000 from Celtic and a new strikeforce of £900,000 Don Goodman from Third Division West Brom and an old face from my past John Byrne, who arrived from Brighton for £225,000 after four years at and a season at French side Le Havre. Byrnie was still part of the Republic of Ireland set up, although not a first choice as Jack Charlton's side were blessed with the likes of John Aldridge and Niall Quinn in attack. He had, however, just scored twice in Ireland's fantastic win in Turkey in Euro 92 qualification. I knew I was buying a striker in form. I also still had £325,000 to spend and, I should point out, Goodman and Byrne would later be sold at a profit.

Goodman was also in form, although I knew he had played for Albion in the early rounds of the FA Cup and so would be cup-tied when the competition came round in

January. I wasn't too bothered by that, though, as I was concentrating on boosting the team's league form.

The pair offered the pace of Gabbers in Don Goodman, and the guile and join up play of Eric Gates in John Byrne. I knew that my switch around would bring results. It's fair to say that Bob Murray did not want me to sell Marco because he had named a dog or a horse after him or something, but he understood that it was a necessity because of the board tying my hands. That was his private acknowledgment anyway.

The new players needed time to bed in, but that was something we didn't have as we were struggling in the lower reaches of the Division Two. The relegation blues needed to be blown away. A 0-1 defeat at Wolves in early December left us in 19th position. Subsequent consecutive 1-0 home victories over Leicester and Portsmouth, the former being thanks to Don Goodman's first goal for the club in a season in which he would go on to be leading goalscorer in the league with 11 goals despite only making 20 starts.

At this stage there was a huge amount of pressure on both myself and the chairman. The fans were turning and I realised that I had to try some short term measures to freshen the place up. It was at this stage that I chose to do something which still saddens me today.

I'd had a very, very close working relationship with my right-hand man Viv Busby in the ten seasons we had been together. Our partnership was extremely well balanced and had been very successful, but I now had come round to thinking that the coaching set up at Sunderland needed shaking up. I decided I wanted to promote Malcolm Crosby up the coaching set up to work more with the first team to freshen things up and maybe bring in some new ideas. Because Viv had not done his badges I wanted to see if Malcolm could bring a new approach that would galvanise what I now thought was a very good squad in this division. Viv took umbrage at this, both professionally and personally and we had a disagreement over a couple of things which will remain private. However many people believe we had a series of huge fallings out. That is not the case. I still respect Viv massively as both a person and a coach. That wasn't the issue. I felt we needed a change. Viv felt I was spending too much time in the office. I'd always been the technical man on the training ground because I'd done all the badges and courses, so perhaps I was, but that was why I wanted Crosser to do more coaching. It wasn't that I wanted to move Viv out, but we did disagree about that.

Throughout our partnership Viv was superb with the players. I always believed that I need somebody alongside me with a good sense of humour because when it comes to work I possibly have a humour bypass at times. I see blacks and whites and, as manager, believe that what I want to happen must be done. That means I need a right-hand man who can put an arm around players and say, "the gaffer's not very happy again…" That was Viv. He was a pick me up and a fantastic presence. I didn't want to lose that, I just needed to bring in the technical skills through Malcolm.

The situation came to a head and in the end Viv walked out. Perhaps if I had been able to look at the bigger picture from outside I would have seen that all I actually did was set myself up for a huge fall because now there was only my head on the chopping block.

Viv took the club to court for constructive dismissal because they didn't pay his contract up. That scenario would loom all too large in my life far sooner than I could possibly imagine. For the record I thought that after what he'd done for Sunderland AFC he should have been paid properly. When we arrived at the court I was asked by the club's lawyer if I would give evidence on their behalf but I informed him I would be backing Viv, so I was never called as a witness.

I still speak to Viv occasionally and when we meet we chat, but we are not as close as we once were. That is very disappointing and there is fault on both sides, but I will always maintain that professionally it was the right thing to do. Things were changing within the game.

By the time Viv's case came to court I would have my own claim against the club because after two away defeats between Christmas 1991 and New Year at Tranmere and Oxford, on 30 December 1991 I received a call from Chairman Bob Murray informing me that my services were no longer required. The club stood 17th in the Second Division and had won 87 of my 229 games in charge.

I was devastated. I knew that the changes which I'd instituted over the previous month or so would bear fruit and that bob was overreacting to a couple of bad results rather than looking at where the club was heading, which I felt, after a tough period following relegation, was very bright indeed. The first thing I did was invited all the local and national press lads around to our house invited them all in, gave them drinks and mince pies – it was Christmas after all – and told my side of the story. What else could I do? I think quite a few of them were sorry to see me go because I'd worked with them and made their lives and jobs easier. There would be the occasional ones who didn't like me as always happens, but the majority I got on with.

What had happened wasn't very nice. Losing your job is never nice. What I told the press was that I simply couldn't understand, and still can't understand for that matter, why Bob Murray had given me the Gabbiadini money to spend on those three new players and the give me three weeks to work with them. Why let me sell our star striker and spend the money and then not let me see what the outcome of it was? It just didn't make sense to me.

Bob has since admitted to me since that it was the worst mistake he ever made in football. I absolutely believe if he'd invested his money in the summers of 1990 and 1991 then Sunderland would have been in a far better state when he dismissed me, and arguably for the years afterwards during which they yo-yoed between the top two divisions. That was a huge missed opportunity. On top of that just six months earlier Bob had said that he would never sack me.

I think he panicked because the fans were getting very itchy feet. I'm sure if you asked him now he would say he would do things totally differently, but he he made a decision he thought was right at that time. People ask if I am still angry about it – no, Bob gave me the opportunity of managing Sunderland in the first place and plenty of water has flowed under the bridge since then. I'm not one to bear grudges at all. I will point out, though, that I did extremely well for Bob and Sunderland. We won two promotions and produced a team that reached an FA Cup final, that's not bad in four and a half years.

People make mistakes, but you get on with your life. What was hard for me was that I had huge arguments with Bob after when I left because he promised he would pay up my contract, but when it came to it I struggled to get the money. That caused a massive problem for me because I had got Becky in College, Paul at University and Tom in public school, a mortgage and now no money coming in. I wouldn't accept the low pay off the club eventually offered as it wasn't what Bob and I had initially agreed. That created a lot of financial pressure on me. That was how Bob repaid me for saving Sunderland from oblivion when I first arrived.

******

You might remember Malcolm Crosby. The little sod led my team out at Wembley.

We both joke about it now. Malcolm has always had a lovely sense of humour. He went to the Sunderland Christmas fancy party in 1992 dressed as a caretaker, and he also has in his house this massive, blown up photograph of himself leading Sunderland – my Sunderland – out at Wembley. He often invites me round just to look at it!

Once the changes I had made to the Sunderland team in the autumn bedded in after the turn of the year, the players put together a fantastic run which saw them defeat First Division West Ham and Chelsea on the way to reaching the FA Cup final. Famously John Byrne would score in every round of the competition up to and including the semi-final stage, a fantastic achievement.

Malcolm kept in touch with me during the second half of the 1991/92 season after I'd been dismissed and he had been made caretaker-manager. In fact he phoned me after just a week in charge of the club and said, "Bloody hell, Den. How do you manage to do it all. It's so hard."

That didn't surprise me, not because Malcolm was not a capable man, but because coaching is so totally different to management. Coaches are the players' best friends, but when they become managers, all at once they have to tell those same lads – "I'm going to leave you out on Saturday". They have to deal with the board, deal with the press. It's a totally different job. And yet people still keep putting coaches into manager's jobs. Recently Peter Grant was given a chance at Norwich and Chris Hutchings has twice stepped up from coach to replace Paul Jewell as manager. Apparently both men are fantastic coaches, but clearly neither are managers.

I have always been a manager, not a coach. Simply, I wanted to be in control. I wanted to be in charge. I wanted to make the big decisions and take that responsibility. I revelled in it. I f you don't it will eat you up.

Malcolm was definitely a coach, as he will readily admit. He was a bloody good one too and his influence helped my team reach the FA Cup final. What was interesting was that the fact I'd built this side stayed in the headlines because Bob Murray decided to keep Malcolm as caretaker all the way to the end of the season and this became huge national news because this team were going to Wembley without a manger. It was a strange situation.

On the day of the FA Cup final I went on holiday because I knew I had got to get away. Once Sunderland had beaten Norwich in the semi-final thanks to a goal from my signings John Byrne everyone had been phoning me up for comment. It was satisfying to see Byrnie prove my point – and I felt it wasn't fair for me to get too involved, not least because I was desperate for them to win. It would have been wonderful for the club, for Bob, Malcolm and the players if they had been able to defeat mighty Liverpool and repeat the kind of upset the 1973 side had cause in beating Don Revie's Leeds United.

But I couldn't watch the game on television. I'd spoken to Crosser to wish him and the boys luck, but it was best for me to get out the way.

Despite the 0-2 defeat by Liverpool in the final it was great for Malcolm and it was wonderful for the club. Because of that success he was made to take the job by Bob Murray, but Crosser didn't ever want to be a manager. He was forced into being there because he'd done so well. To be honest it was the cheap option for the club at the time.

I was just gutted for myself as I missed out on leading my team out at Wembley Stadium, the scene of my greatest triumph all those years before in 1972. You can argue the toss forever that if I'd have stayed as manager then the run to the FA Cup final would never have happened. That's only ifs and buts. I do regret not being able to lead my team out at Wembley for the Cup final. I'd done it for the play-offs and I would go on to lead my Wrexham team to victory at the Millennium Stadium at Cardiff while Wembley was being reconstructed, but the Cup final eluded me.

Football can be a very, very tough game.

Chapter Sixteen

SELLING COLE

TO NEWCASTLE

My career thus far had taken me from York, where I'd won promotion and had great Cup victories and only one season when things hadn't gone particularly well, to Sunderland, where we'd won two promotions in three seasons before that agonising relegation which had led so quickly to the sack. I had become used to success. To a certain extent you just believe that's the way it's always going to be. You can get fairly blasé about it and think you're good at your job. That's where the danger lies.

Leaving Sunderland meant that for the first time in my life money had become a massive issue for me. If I'd achieved the revival of a club like Sunderland in the modern era, I'd have been a multi-millionaire. And I would only have ever now been working in the Premier League because, unlike many in today's game, I've got all the coaching badges. That would have been it. I wouldn't have accepted a job anywhere else because I'd have enough money in the bank to protect myself to allow me wait for the right job to come up.

Back in 1992 I had to find work. I had my wife and family to support. I'd got to work because we had a mortgage. Can you imagine Premier League manager having a mortgage now? I wanted to work anyway, but it was a financial necessity.

This was all exacerbated by the prevarication of Sunderland chairman Bob Murray over paying me the money he had agreed the day he dismissed me from the post of manager. With what had happened with Viv's claim against Sunderland I knew I would have problems getting the money out of Bob despite his continual promises that he would pay me.

Kate never forgave him for that. I was back in work by the time both cases came to court and eventually Bob did pay up, but his prevarication altered the course of my career, causing me to take a job I shouldn't have. We have subsequently patched up our differences and Bob has acknowledged his mistakes at that time, which is a nice sentiment, but not one that was going to pay the bills. I am not one to bear grudges. I was too busy getting on with my new job anyway.

It wasn't that I'd take anything that came along, but I needed something decent to turn up fairly quickly and so when, in March 1992, I received an offer of an interview with Second Division Bristol City I jumped at the opportunity. Although I knew very little about the club, on the face of it I thought that it had a lot of potential, much like Sunderland, with a great catchment area and a solid support. Perhaps I should have got an inkling of what was to come when I was told I couldn't bring in my own backroom team as the board wanted me to work with Russell Osman, the former Ipswich and England centre-half, who they had already chosen as player-coach. Russell would not prove to be someone that I clicked with straight away.

I was fortunate enough to be offered the job, which had come free because manager Jimmy Lumsden had been sacked in late February 1992 with the team on a run of nine games without a win and languishing in 23rd position in the table, one place above bottom club Port Vale.

I took a back seat for the first match, which was the following evening at Plymouth. We lost 0-1, but I saw enough to understand what the team's short-term needs. With the experienced Nicky Morgan and raw Wayne Allison as the strikeforce the team had plenty of height but little mobility and no pace. I knew I could fix that. I'd heard of this kid who had made a massive impression in Arsenal's reserves, but who had been passed over for first team chances because manager George Graham had opted to buy Crystal Palace striker Ian Wright. Now Wright obviously went on to become an Arsenal legend, so it's hard to argue with George's decision, but the kid I'm referring to was 20 year-old Andy Cole, who went on to become one of the Premier League's most feared goalscorers over the next 15 years. Andy needed first team football and jumped at the chance to join us on loan for the rest of the season. He was raw and bursting to perform. His introduction would have a massive impact on our season.

We lost my first proper game in charge, in which Andy Cole made his debut, against Cambridge 1-2 at home, but then, three days later, in my second game, the tide began to turn in a very tight home match against Wolves. With the game locked at 0-0 going into the last ten minutes the night was lit up by Jackie Dziekanowski. The experienced Polish international was another fabulous attacking player, who had arrived from Celtic in January of that year for a £250,000 fee, which had made him the club's record signing. He'd been bought to replace striker Bob Taylor, who had been sold to West Brom for £300,000 to step into the shoes of a certain Don Goodman, the man who I'd taken from Albion to Sunderland but then never been given the opportunity to work with. Again the Bristol board had given their manager money and then sacked him a few weeks later. It must have been as frustrating for Jimmy as it had been for me at Sunderland, but we were just beginning to see the acceleration of the timescale in which boards expected to see results. That has now reached almost ridiculous proportions, and we so often see those with patience rewarded.

At Parkhead Jackie had made himself a hero by scoring four goals in a European Cup Winners' Cup tie against Partizan Belgrade, but had not established himself, become unsettled and asking for a move. At 30 he needed to be playing regular first team football and his performance that evening solidified his place in my starting line up for the remainder of the season. In the few short minutes he was on the pitch against Wolves he gave a devastating display of skill, eye for an opportunity and finishing which saw him score twice to secure a vital 2-0 victory. That was actually the team's their first win since 28 December and a crucial turning point in the players believing they could pull off the great escape and get out of a congested bottom six.

What I had to find was the way to motivate Jackie and how to use him within our team pattern. For those crucial games I played him just off a front two of the tall Leroy Rosenior and pacy Andy Cole. He loved it. Jackie only actually scored one further goal that season, the vital goal in 1-1 draw at home to Oxford, but his contribution to our attacking play was crucial.

His two late goals to defeat Wolves gave us some tremendous momentum and a lot of belief flowed into the squad once I rammed home the point that they should not be afraid of any team in this division.

We followed that up that fantastic victory by winning 3-1 at, yes, you guessed it, my old club Sunderland. It was an incredibly emotional return for me, but I was determined to win to prove a point. After racing to a three goal half-time lead the 3-1 scoreline did not flatter us. Andy Cole opened his account with the first goal in that game and would go on to finish with 8 goals in 12 games. His impact meant we moved quickly to secure his signature on a permanent transfer for club record £500,000 in the close season. Big Wayne Allison scored the other two goals that afternoon.

That win also pulled us out of the relegation zone and we extended the run to eight games unbeaten to climb to the safety of 17th place, being clear of the threat of relegation three games before the end of the season.

The team's fortunes were assisted in being turned around by two other signings I made. I brought in striker Leroy Rosenior from West Ham and Dutch midfielder Ray Atteveld from Everton for £250,000. With the new players coming in I dropped Nicky Morgan, for whom 4 goals in 19 games just wasn't enough, fellow striker Wayne Allison, who did a great job still as an impact substitute, and young midfielder Rob Edwards who would go on to have a great career with City and then Preston. Rob was only 18 and I thought too young and inexperienced for the battle. Atteveld proved to be an excellent signing as he brought solidity and experience to midfield.

Ray had a very short but eventful spell at Ashton Gate. After such a good start to life, being integral to that great run, great things were expected of him. And it's fair to say Ray had an eventful if short career at City. He scored an incredible own goal at Millwall, although thankfully it didn't cost us as we still won 3-2, he got himself sent off in spectacular fashion and also got into trouble with the law for motoring offences. I felt he had lost focus and so barely used him the following season.

A week after winning at Millwall, we defeated table-topping Ipswich Town at home 2-1 in front of nearly 17,000 fans, thanks to goals by the two strikers I'd brought in, Cole and Rosenior. Our bid for survival was complete with three games still remaining.

******

Over the summer of 1992 I worked on remodelling the defence. The fact that we'd lost the last three games of the previous campaign once we'd secured safety, including a last day capitulation at Watford, told me something about the existing players' mentality and that I would have to shake that out of them.

I brought in two new signings, Scottish right-back Brian Mitchell from Bradford to replace veteran Andy Llewellyn, and young centre-half David Thompson from Millwall. I was also helped by the return of experienced midfielder Gary Shelton from Sheffield Wednesday from a bad injury which he'd picked up prior to my arrival at Ashton Gate.

We started well enough in the new First Division (renamed following the creation of the Premiership), winning two and drawing two of the first four games, but our next home game saw us hammered 5-1 by West Ham. We won the next four home games, but lost every match on the road, including a 0-5 thrashing at Newcastle, reviving under Kevin Keegan. I was struggling to motivate the players and at the same time having problems behind the scenes. It all came to a head in the Bristol derby when we suffered a 0-4 mauling at Twerton Park. The game was played in a white hot atmosphere and the players lost their discipline a bit. After 25 minutes Justin Channing scored a goal from all of 30 yards with no player challenging him and then early in the second half Rovers put together a lovely move from which my old player Paul Hardyman to send a deep cross to the far post for Marcus Stewart to net unmarked. Two further goals followed, both exquisite shots from distance, on what was a dark afternoon for us.

Jackie Dziekanowski, who was culpable for losing the ball in midfield several times in that game, was proving to be the proverbial riddle, wrapped up in a mystery, inside an enigma. Jackie was a wonderfully talented football who many will be surprised often used to come back in the afternoons for extra training, had incredible acceleration, was great at beating his man and could pass sublimely, but conversely he all too often had the ball stripped off him, was not adept at tracking back and caused me no end of headaches with how to cover for him, whilst keeping him in the team so we could benefit from his skills. Jackie was never an out and out striker proved by the number of one on ones he missed, which was incredibly frustrating, but he provided fans with pure entertainment. He could produce tricks I'd never seen from any player before. That is maybe why Dziekanowski seems to have played his way into City fans' hearts as almost every time I meet one they cite Jackie as their favourite ever player and he was voted as the Robins' greatest cult hero in a BBC vote in 2005. Indeed John Motson once described his skills as 'like something from another planet' on Match of the Day.

Even more frustratingly Jackie also loved his social life, especially where the ladies were concerned and was forever getting himself into trouble. For example I know that the night of his goalscoring debut, just before I arrived at the club, Dziekanowski had to be taken to the Bristol Royal Infirmary after an incident in a Clifton wine bar, and there were plenty of other examples along the way. In fact Jackie was so talented and drank so much that City fans used to say he made Gazza look like a tea-totaller! Whether that was because he had found himself in this land of plenty after spending the first 27 years of his life in the stark and harsh environment of Eastern bloc Poland I don't know, but he proved a handful to manage, and this coming from someone who'd kept the lid on Billy Whitehurst! Supporter gossip had it that I had relieved Jackie of his car keys most days due to alcohol, but I can tell you that is absolutely untrue.

Another enigma who frustrated me with his lack of end product when compared to his talent and obvious enthusiasm was left winger Junior Bent. Junior had bundles of enthusiasm, loads of pace, and scored the occasional goal, but ultimately his problem was that he regularly failed to deliver a cross from the good positions his pace got him into and he didn't appreciate what was going on around him well enough. My refusal to use him in my starting line up didn't endear me to the majority of City fans. Because he was fast, direct and exciting he had become a bit of a fans' favourite, but his crossing was pretty dreadful. I thought I could develop other options, but this decision would prove to be the start of real problems for me.

I've got on well with almost all the directors at all of my clubs, especially the Chairmen. The relationship between any manager and Chairman is vital as it is what keeps the club moving forward. Central to that is the ability to make quick decisions. Sometimes opportunities present themselves in football, deals arise and you just have to take them or they disappear into the ether as someone else beats you to the punch. It is the most competitive, unremittingly cut-throat business. Ditherers will only be losers.

I was offered a very good deal for Junior Bent by Burnley manager Jimmy Mullen. All I needed was the nod from Chairman Les Kew and I could get the deal done. He ummed and aahed and then said he'd phone round the other directors. That might not sound too difficult, but this is where the unique set up at Bristol City at that time came into its own. Because of the serious difficulties the club had suffered less than a decade before, which I had ultimately benefited from by signing Alan Hay for York, a completely new structure had been agreed for the board whereby nine directors held 10% of the shares each. This, they reasoned, would stop the kind of irresponsible spending which had nearly seen Bristol City go out of existence in 1982 and would send Leeds United spiralling down the leagues in the modern era. The problem was that when the club was running perfectly reasonably it restricted me from doing the job I had been brought in to do – the job I had done so well at both York and Sunderland as it meant they had just got nobody with any power to get on to them.

So there had to be eight phone calls made to the other directors and opinions canvassed once they were contacted. I didn't hear back that afternoon, so the next morning I got straight onto the Chairman to find out what had been decided. "I haven't managed to speak to all the directors, Denis. So there's no decision as yet," he said.

I wanted to seal the deal with Burnley, but I did not get a call back for a week. That was silly. By the time I'd taken matters into my own hands and chased the Chairman up again Jimmy Mullen's interest had cooled off and he recruited Norwich winger Louie Donowa instead. We'd missed the boat. I felt undermined, although I never believed that it was deliberate, just an upshot of the way the club was organised. It did not make for effective management.

It's interesting to note that in writing this book I had to look up the names of those people who were members of the board while I was manager at Bristol City. Perhaps that tells you all you need to know. I had no idea who some of them were because there were just so many faceless chiefs without a clear process in place to assist me in my job. At most other clubs the directors become like brethren to you as you work so closely with them. Not at Ashton Gate. Frankly they were a nightmare. I just couldn't get my head round them.

All the other boards with which I'd worked had generally been extremely good. I would talk to them and explain my thoughts as to how I would progress the team and work within their plan. If anything in my career I had one possible fault which was that I didn't push any board constantly for money. On the occasions I did ask if they told me they hadn't got it, that would be it. I'd simply try and work within the budget as laid down. I'm a realist when all is said and done. Maybe that's a fault, it possibly is, not least because whenever you leave a club and a new manager comes in they always seem to come up with some cash to spend.

The problems at Bristol City deepened quite quickly as our form dipped over the Christmas period because I could just not get any decisions out of the board to strengthen the team. I have to hold my hands up and say that two of my summer signings had not worked out either. David Thompson and Brian Mitchell just did not fit well into the team. I dropped Thompson in November after a 1-2 defeat at Grimsby, but because I could not bring anyone in permanently I was reduced to plugging the gap with fringe players from the squad and the short term loan signing of Danish defender Bjørn Kristensen from Newcastle United. But at the same time the board tied my hands firmly behind my back and I felt that they were dragging the club down and I was fighting against an inexorable tide. Having had the same thing happen at Sunderland all too recently I was not going to stand by and let it happen again so I let the board know my feelings on a regular basis, ever more vociferously. The problem was they didn't want to listen. It became a living hell, such that Kate would tell me every morning not to go into the club and have another argument today. I would promise her that I would do my best, but by 10am each morning I'd be blowing my top as yet more intransigence cost me a possible signing or another type of interference undermined me.

To give you an example – and this is the kind of thing that stops managers stone dead – I more than once entered the dressing room after training to find one of the board or other with his arm round a player consoling him, only to learn that the thing they were being comforted about was the news that the manager wanted to sell them. The player had no idea what we'd discussed in the boardroom, and yet there would be a director telling him and saying there there. What kind of managerial set up is that? I was being totally undermined in what I was trying to do, but the board all had their pals amongst the squad because essentially they were just fans who had a bit of money and so had bought their 10%. They were not professional football people, they let their personal feelings dictate what went on.

The final straw was the Andy Cole situation. Andy had become the hottest striking property in the country in just a year at Bristol City. I'd made him deadly by getting him playing constantly on the shoulder of the last defender ready to hare through onto balls played in behind the defence. Andy was a very intelligent footballer who knew the talent he had, but he also wanted to contribute more. He would come to me and say, "gaffer, I'm not just a goal scorer you know".

"I do know, Andy," I said. "But we need you to just carry on sticking the ball in the net. Concentrate on getting into the gaps in between the full-backs and the centre-halves and banging in the goals." Scoring goals is the hardest job in football and every manager is searching for players with the talent and temperament to find the back of the net regularly. Having done just that I wasn't going to let Andy stop scoring just so he could fulfil his boyhood dream of becoming Glenn Hoddle or Kenny Dalglish. I've always been a big believer in having players to perform certain tasks well. Keepers are obvious, but then you've got destroyers, creators and goalscorers. Keep it simple and get the right players to do the right jobs in each part of the pitch.

I think it's fair to say my advice and decision stood Andy in good stead as it took him via hero-worship at Newcastle to the ultimate glory of the 1999 treble under Sir Alex Ferguson at Manchester United.

However I had come to realise that there was no way I would be able to hang on to Andy much longer. At the very most I might keep hold of him past the transfer deadline and then find the right club to sell him to in the summer, but he was scoring too regularly and frightening too many defenders with his pace in Division One to stay at Bristol City much longer. That was my pragmatic estimation and so I set about planning what I would do with any money we would earn from Cole's inevitable sale. I thought I needed a goalkeeper, central defender, left-sided midfielder and, of course a livewire striker to replace Andy. I felt that I could bring in five players for the money Andy's transfer would bring in, which has to be good in anyone's book.

Andy Cole had been earning rave reviews for his performances and it was a plain as baboon's backside that he would not be spending much more time at Bristol City. Everyone was watching him and I felt the best thing for all concerned was to do a deal for the most amount of money we could get with a big club and spend that on bringing in five decent quality players. I'd even identified the positions I wanted to fill and some of the targets. If tell you that one of them was goalkeeper Kevin Miller, who was then at Exeter but went on to Birmingham, Watford, Crystal Palace and Barnsley.

The other target I had my eyes beadly fixed on was much more Bristol-grown. Over at Bristol Rovers a young striker called Marcus Stewart had been catching a few eyes. Being right on the doorstep I'd watched him quite a bit and I thought he had the quality to replace Andy and score just as many goals. He'd scored 20 goals in 41 games. Marcus would eventually move on via Huddersfield Town to become the leading scorer in the top flight in 2000/01 with 19 goals for Ipswich Town. This was the way I was thinking in February 1993.

However I had reckoned without the board's reaction to the proposed sale of its prize asset. They loved Andy Cole so much and thought that it would cause a storm of protest amongst the supporters if they sold him. In fact I think they were scared of what the reaction would be both from the fans and the press if Cole left. I believe they underestimated the depth of the knowledge supporters have. No City fans would seriously have considered it possible to hold on to such a talent as Andy Cole for his entire career. He would have to be sold at some point and that he would do move on for serious money. That could only be good for the long term future of the club. Of course it would not be popular, but I was not in the job to be popular I was there to make the right decisions for Bristol City Football Club. Unfortunately the board failed to support me because of their structure and personal feelings about a player. They refused to sanction Cole's sale. It was ridiculous and snapped the thin thread of relationship that still existed between myself and the board. How did they expect me to do any kind of job for them if they wouldn't let me?

The die had been cast by that wrangling with the board over Andy Cole and the direction I wanted to take the club in. Less than 12 months after joining the club, on 21 January 1993, I was relieved of my duties, which were handed to my young assistant, player-coach Russell Osman.

At the end of it all I don't even really remember exactly how I came to leave Ashton Gate, just that it was such a relief to be out of the club when it finally happened. It certainly wasn't anything to do with results. I became probably the first and last manager to be dismissed on the back of a four game unbeaten run. It was all the more poignant that the axe fell the day after we'd travelled up to Sunderland and come back with a very creditable 0-0 draw. We may have been in 20th position, but we had a four point cushion over the relegation zone and four teams below us. It was hardly the desperate position I had dragged the club up from when I'd joined exactly a year before. To be honest it was just a relief to be out of what had become a frustrating and draining scenario.

And the upshot of it all? Within weeks of my departure Andy Cole had been sold for a new outgoing record for the Robins of £1,750,000 to Newcastle – the very thing I had been pressing for a month or so to be allowed to do. They had finally realised they could not keep hold of such a talented player given the level the club was playing at and Andy's ambition. It had taken them a while, but they had eventually realised that I was right.

Their crime was that no sell-on clause was included in the deal when Cole moved on, meaning the club missed out on a chunk of the massive £7 million that Manchester United paid the Magpies for his services in January 1995. Not only that, Jackie Dziekanowski was moved on for a free transfer when I would have got money for him. The board and my replacement Russell Osman, who had become more of a thorn in my side than an assistant over the preceding few weeks, showed their inexperience and cost the club dearly.

The thing that once again irked me was that it was Osman who got to spend that money. The money I should by rights have been given. Not that it did either him or Bristol City, for whom the phrase boardroom politics would become a familiar refrain over the next decade or so, much good. Osman lasted 18 months as manager and the club were relegated at the end of the 1994/95 season, but not before a fairly spectacular reunion.

Chapter Seventeen

ON THE BREADLINE

As grudge matches go it was one of the more spectacular ones of my career. Full of incident, controversy and a good old scrap. I loved every second of it.

Early in the 1993/94 season, six months after I had left Bristol City I was appointed manager of Oxford United by Chief Executive Keith Cox. My predecessor Brian Horton had been enticed away after six years in the job to manage Manchester City, replacing Peter Reid, who of course eventually landed the job at Sunderland thus completing a round robin of managerial changes. I was appointed on Friday 10 September 1993 and the following day brought my first game in charge of my new club, and who should it be against, but my old side Bristol City. The wounds from my departure from Ashton Gate were still raw and I relished the opportunity to set the record straight.

When those kind of coincidences come along on the fixture list the media talk it up and you do get swept up in it a bit. Passions were very high that day on all sides and a certain amount of professionalism went out of the window if I'm brutally honest. It was football at its rawest and most fanatical.

I was still getting to grips with my squad so I brought in tigerish striker David Penney instead of young defender David Collins, but otherwise kept the team the same. I knew that Bristol had lost both Coe and Dziekanowski since my departure so I was not too worried about the pace of their attacks.

The game felt like a tornado, with incidents happening all over the pitch. We lead 2-1 at half-time thanks to Chris Allen's goal and a Jim Magilton penalty. Jim scored another spot-kick after the break and Alex Dyer lashed in the clinching fourth goal to set the seal on a 4-2 win. But the controversy all surrounded David Penney being sent off for what I can only describe as a forearm jab on Junior Bent. It was a nasty foul which deserved a red card.

But the incident didn't end there. As Penney trudged off the pitch and down the tunnel, Osman accused me of winding him up to perpetrate the foul. I wasn't having that. I have never even remotely encouraged a player of mine to do physical damage to an opponent. Osman was totally out of order and I took exception to what he said and collared him in the tunnel at the end of the game. I had allowed myself to get wound up by the whole thing, it meant so much to me to put one over on my former club. A career in football gives you many scores to try and settle, but I did tend to do that on the pitch, especially as a manager. This was different. Osman had given me little option but to respond. He may well have been overwound due to all the hype surrounding the build up to the game, the tension and the fact we'd spanked them 4-2, but that was no excuse. Bearing in mind I'm at least ten years older than Russell I think he was surprised I took him on, but I pinned him to the tunnel wall and politely informed him of his mistake. Osman let it lie.

Mindful of what had happened when supported by a young coach like Osman when I was at Bristol, I opted to bring in a familiar face as coach at the Manor Ground and picked up the phone to Malcolm Crosby. Inevitably Crosser hadn't lasted at Sunderland, being sacked in February 1993 after just 13 months in charge. I was delighted as it meant he was free to come to work with me at Oxford United, where we would have some wonderful times together.

As I write Crosser is now assistant manager to Gareth Southgate at Middlesbrough, after working as reserve team manager under Steve McClaren's tenure at the Riverside. It's interesting to think that those situations could well have been reversed. When I arrived at Oxford the board told me they'd got a young coach who they wanted to give an opportunity to, but because of what had happened at Bristol with Osman, I wanted my own man and brought in Malcolm as my assistant, handing Steve responsibility for the reserve team. He did well, impressing me and many others in the game, one of whom, Jim Smith invited Steve to join him at Derby. From there, of course, he became Alex Ferguson's assistant at Manchester United and then manager of Middlesbrough before being appointed as England coach.

Oxford had survived on the final day of the previous season under Brian thanks to a 2-1 victory at Tranmere, but were already struggling when I arrived. By the beginning of October, despite that winning start, we'd hit the bottom of the division and were facing a home game against my former club Stoke City. Stoke missed a hatful of chances but we missed a penalty when Jim Magilton's kick was saved. I thought it was going to be one of those days then, but we pulled off a great victory over Lou Macari's team thanks to David Penney's header. We were off the bottom of the table.

But not for long. We slumped in the next game 1-6 at Southend and won just two of the next 17 games. It looked as if the only way was down. Realising we were seriously struggling I moved to bring in new players, although with money tight I had to be cute in the transfer market.

After the death of media tycoon Robert Maxwell in 1991 had thrown the future of the club into serious doubt, it had been bought the following year by a feller called Alan Corbett who was based in the Channel Islands. He had at least put the club back on a sound footing, while dealing with the added burden of implementing the Taylor Report at The Manor Ground, which meant further extra cost. I had been brought in because of my record of saving clubs with no money to spend and moving them up the leagues. I'd done it at York and Bristol City, and to a certain extent at Sunderland, although there was money at Roker. My reputation was a good one, but I knew now that it wasn't going to be one which propelled me towards my ultimate ambition in life – to manage England.

The task which faced us at Oxford was very difficult indeed. Essentially there was no money to spend, although we managed to prize some cash out of the board once they fully realized the peril we were in. We brought in goalkeeper Phil Whitehead on loan from Barnsley pretty much straight away. But then I pulled off what I still consider to be the best signing of my managerial career. We'd had our eyes on a big young centre-half at Scunthorpe United called Matt Elliott for some time and in November we signed him for the bargain price of £170,000. I'm often asked who my best signing was and I have no hesitation in saying Matt. For the service he gave me at Oxford and then career he went on to have with Leicester and Scotland I think that was the best £170,000 I could ever have spent.

Equally I'm often asked who my worst signing was. That's a tough one. Any manager will tell you that when they make them they try and forget them as soon as possible, but only after we've manage to unload them on someone else.

Simultaneous to Elliott's signing I paid £50,000 to sign John Byrne from Brighton. He was well worth it and I'd have him back again honestly. You don't signed a player three times if you don't think he is one hell of a player. If you want to play a passing game, as I did, then you need players like Byrne to join up the play and John was one off the best of his generation at doing that. As a manager I felt he was a pleasure to work with.

The introduction of the three new players galvanised things a little and we went four games unbeaten including back-to-back wins at home to Derby and then at Leicester to climb out of the bottom three. That was as good as it got, though. Nine games without a win followed and we were dragged down into the mire again.

It wasn't until after Christmas that we began to pull ourselves up by our bootstraps. Nick Cusack, a forward who I didn't feel was quite up to the mark when all was said and done, scored two goals to give us a much-needed 2-1 victor over Southend. That win gave us a huge confidence boost and lifted some of the gloom which had begun to descend, so much so that our next game, in the FA Cup fourth round at Leeds, became a huge focal point for the team. Leeds had won the league title just two seasons previously and were packed with stars such as Gary McAllister, Gordon Strachan and Gary Speed. We played fantastically well to lead 2-1 at the Manor Ground, but eventually conceded a late equaliser through David Wetherall's header.

But the replay at Elland Road would prove even more glorious. John Byrne and Chris Allen both scored as we took a two-goal lead over the Premier League side. But two goals in the last three minutes rescued a 2-2 result for them. We were gutted. We naturally thought our chance had gone. You don't lose a two goal lead on a top flight's home ground and still come out on top many times in your career. But we got over the mental side of that comeback and then in extra time Jim Magilton scored a superb winning goal. We'd knocked one of the biggest clubs in the country out of the FA Cup on their own patch. It was a fabulous performance and one of the best results of my career, up there with defeating Arsenal and drawing with Liverpool twice. I have always had a love affair with the Cup and those glory days were wonderful moments scattered across my career. The old cliché holds that the Cup is a great leveller, and the following season it certainly was as we lost in the first round to non-league Marlow, to a side managed by former United striker Peter Foley and which contained former Manor players Les Phillips, Ceri Evans and Peter Rhoades-Brown, who was then (and remains) an employee in the Community department at United.

The fifth round draw this time around paired us at home to Chelsea, but we would have to face the Blues without one of our major players as I had to sell midfielder Jim Magilton to Premier League Southampton for £600,000. His goal which had put paid to Leeds had brought him a lot of attention and it was inevitable that a decent bid for him would come in and I was realistic to know that if we received even a half decent offer we'd have to take it. Again I was of the opinion that we could reinvest the money wisely to improve the team in several areas. The problem was that Jim had been taking our penalties and when we were awarded one against Chelsea in the fifth round of the FA Cup we needed someone to take it. Typical of the man, my captain Mike Ford volunteered to take over the duties, but hit the bar. We played superbly well once again against Chelsea and would have got a draw if he'd scored. Joey Beauchamp netted for us but two goals before half-time had put paid to our challenge.

The big problem we had was with our league form. Three days after our wonderful victory at Elland Road, we sank to a hideous 0-4 reverse at home to Charlton in the First Division. The defeat plummeted us back down to the foot of the table again. We had our backs to the wall, 15 points off safety already, and just 16 games to somehow save ourselves. To make matters worse we lost left-back Anton Rogan with a broken leg in that game.

Going out of the FA Cup turned out to be a blessing in disguise, though. We'd used it to find some form and a cause to fight for, now we transported that feeling into all that we had left, the battle against relegation. We beat play-off hopefuls Nottingham Forest 1-0 at home thanks to Alex Dyer's goal. That game saw the debut of striker Paul Moody, who arrived from Southampton in late February for £60,000. Moody scored 12 goals in 15 games to finish as our top scorer for the campaign as we took our fresh approach into the remainder of the season.

The win over Forest sparked a run of four wins in six games, including a vital 2-0 home victory over fellow strugglers Birmingham, the last being a fabulous 4-0 victory over Wolves. That saw us move out of the drop zone, three points clear of Watford in 22nd position. Seven games remained. Could we pull off one of the most incredible escapes from relegation?

In the next three games we faced two of our relegation rivals, West Brom and Barnsley. We drew 1-1 at home to the Baggies and lost narrowly 0-1 at Oakwell. Watford managed to overhaul us over that period. Now we faced a huge uphill task again. The tos and fros were gripping. In our final four matches we faced three of the play-off sides, while the other game was at Sunderland. We drew 2-2 at home to Leicester and then came from behind to win 3-2 at Roker Park. Two games remained and two wins would keep us in the First Division.

But our penultimate match was a tough one, a visit to Derby County and we lost 1-2, with Tommy Johnson scoring the winner. Both West Brom and Birmingham won their games in hand in the midweek, so now we went into a tension-packed last day of the season needing to win and for both those sides to lose.

On a tension-packed afternoon we played really well to defeat Notts County thanks to goals from John Byrne and Joey Beauchamp. When Joey's goal hit the back of the net the explosion of noise around the Manor was truly tremendous. We held on to win 2-1, with all ears on the scores from other grounds. But it was bad news. Both teams we needed to fail recorded unlikely away victories over Portsmouth and third-placed Tranmere respectively. We were down. The post-Christmas revival had not proved enough.

Sometimes relegation devastates a club to its very core, but on this occasion we'd made such a good fist and come so close to succeeding in our unlikely quest that there was actually quite a positive feeling around the club over the summer of 1994.

For once the finances were not stretched to breaking point as, in June, I did a deal with West Ham manager Billy Bonds to pay £1,000,000 for Joey Beauchamp, our star midfielder. It was a club record outgoing fee for Oxford at the time, but I felt that was right as Joey should have been one of the real stars of football in the 1990s. When I sold him to West Ham I really thought he would go on to become a huge star. He was the perfect attacking midfielder, with a good engine, great shot, good left foot and good turn of speed off the mark. But there was a fatal flaw in his make up. Joey just loved Oxfordshire, and Oxford itself. He'd grown up there and when it came down to it he hated London. I'll never forget how it came about, soon after we'd sold him to the Hammers. I had a call from Billy Bonds asking me what on earth I'd sold him.

"How do you mean?" I replied.

"It's Joey," Billy said, "He wants to go home. He wants to go back to Oxford."

Effectively Joey point blank refused to play for West Ham because he was homesick, hated travelling from his home in Oxford to training and it soon became apparent he wanted out. Less than two months later and Joey had moved on to Swindon Town for £800,000, making it a very costly deal for Billy, especially as by the time the deal went through he had lost his job, being replaced by Harry Redknapp. To say it was one of the more bizarre transfer tales I've been involved with would be putting it mildly.

With the money from Joey's sale during the summer I spent £100,000 on midfielder David Smith from Norwich City and very early in the new season I also spent another £100,000 on bringing one of my former players David Rush down from Sunderland. Since my departure from the club David had gone from the heights of playing in the 1992 FA Cup final against Liverpool to being farmed out on loan to Hartlepool, Peterborough and Cambridge. His career was going nowhere when I made the approach to manager Mick Buxton and I think the club were happy to get any sort of fee out of us, but it would prove money well spent.

We'd started the season fantastically well with Paul Moody in rampant form in attack. He scored in eight of the first nine unbeaten games, six of them wins. Rush came off the bench to become a cult hero right from the start by scoring the winner in front of the Oxford fans in our 3-2 win over Leyton Orient. He went on to be an icon with the noisy fans in the London Road terrace who were inspired to sing: 'David Rush, David Rush, David David Rush. He has a pint, He has a fight, David David Rush.'

I can tell you a great story about David. One night he took his dog out for a walk and fancied a pint, so called in to his local pub. The problem was he was completely brassic, so he came up with an ingenious way of eliciting some beer from the bar. When he returned home his partner said, "David, where is the dog?"

"Er, I sold him in the pub to get some money to buy a few rounds."

That's David all over.

Given we were in such a seat of eminent scientific research I decided I'd develop links to the University, both in terms of using their facilities and tapping into the ideas and skills within it. I made contact with four scientists, some nutritional, some bio-mechanical, and worked with them on developing diets which we never used before. I also took computer courses because you've got to try and keep up. I'm glad I did as Prozone would become a staple for all managers within a few short years.

What I didn't do, which I probably should have done at this stage is go on enough coaching courses, although a lot of the coaching courses don't always help but I'd got people coming like Malcolm who'd done a lot of courses, so I knew what was up to date because Crossie was doing them.

Rush and Moody in attack rampaged through the first half of the season as we established ourselves amongst the early leaders. A run of five consecutive wins before Christmas sent us to the top of the table. Thanks to fantastic 4-1 victory at Peterborough on Boxing Day, in which we ripped the defence apart with some neat interpassing and deadly finishing which characterised our play over these two years, we held a lead of three points over Birmingham.

But from that high everything went wrong as we went on a long run without a win. Six out of the next seven games were lost, and we scored just four goals in the process.

The worst defeat came at Bristol Rovers when we lost a 2-0 half-time lead to go down 2-3. I knew then that we needed bolstering in defence and so I brought in quicksilver centre-half Phil Gilchrist from Hartlepool United for £60,000 in February 1995. Gilly soon became one half of the best defensive partnerships ever seen at The Manor Ground, alongside Matt Elliott.

I was lucky enough to have some fabulous dominant centre-halves during my time at Oxford, and was able to hang on to them for longer than I should have done given the parlous finances of the club. One of the most important aspects of all three men was their ability to lead the team and organise the back four. Sometimes with players when you ask them to command the line they just look at you as though you are daft. Maybe later they might come to realise it's a great gift, but ultimately that leadership has to be found from within a player. It's an innate characteristic rather than a skill to be learnt and one that seems to be found in fewer and fewer modern professionals. You might think of Roy Keane or Bryan Robson as examples of midfield generals who lead their sides with distinction, but in the last decade there has only been John Terry as a centre-half who had stood out as a true leader of men. In the 1970s I would say there were a number of players, particularly English players, who had similar qualities. The dearth of captain material is a worry of the modern game.

Predominantly left sided, Gilchrist's arrival immediately arrested our decline. We went on a run of eight unbeaten games, winning five out of the last six of them. Gilchrist himself scored the only goal of the game against Chester in late February. That run moved us back up the table into third position, just four points behind joint leaders Brentford and Huddersfield. As this season was seeing the reconstruction of the league with the Premier League being reduced to 20 clubs, only one club would go up automatically from Division Two, with a further one through the play-offs. At least at this stage we thought we'd make the first five, but it was very disappointing, given the incredible start we'd had, that we won just two of our last ten games to finish 7th. Had all else been equal I'd have been pretty annoyed by that season, but given the fact we were still balancing the club on a financial knife edge I couldn't be too annoyed.

The team was still evolving, although I was pleased with the impact the new arrivals had made. During the season we'd bade farewell to John Byrne, who was granted a free transfer to return to Brighton. Just as I had signed him three times, so this was the third occasion he had joined the Seagulls. John now lives and works down there, often commentating on the radio.

I felt that the season had at least stabilised the club financially, thanks to Joey Beauchamp's sale, which had allowed more players to be brought in at relatively low cost. Quietly I thought we'd have a very good chance indeed of winning promotion the following season.

The summer of 1995 saw a development which I felt would change the face of Oxford United, perhaps as much as the purchase of the club by Robert Maxwell in the

1980s had. Local businessman Robin Herd, who had been a Us fan all his life, bought the club, as well as a company called Biomass Recycling, which recycled waste to create energy, from owner Alan Corbett. Robin was also the founder of March engineering, a motor company which had competed in and won Formula 1 races and the Indianapolis 500. During his remarkable career Robin had also helped to design Concorde, and enjoyed considerable success in designing cars for F2 and F3000 and March Indycars, which became the dominant force in the US series in the mid-1980s. As a result of the success Herd floated the company on the Stock Exchange in 1986 – the same year in which he was awarded a CBE for his services to the motor racing industry.

I liked Robin from the start. My new chairman had the most incredible memory. I have to admit that mine is never the best when it comes to names. I'm not in the Jack Charlton league of forgetfulness, but I sometimes struggle to conjour up a first name of someone I haven't seen for a while. I always say that's what I've got assistants for! Robin is completely different. Often he will say to me, "You know we should have bought that player back then." I'm struggling to know who he's talking about because there were loads of players that I'd recommended to him, but he's got them all stored upstairs. Incredible. That's why he's a genius!

Having such an eminent motor racing man involved meant we came into contact with people such as Frank Williams, for whom he had designed a revolutionary test car which was successful in CanAm racing earning titles for McLaren in 1966, 1967 and 1968 and the 1968 F1 car, and Irish multi-millionaire Eddie Jordan, founder of the Jordan racing team.

In the summer of 1995 Robin was looking for something to do after such a long period in motor racing. One of the major reasons he was interested in the club was what he saw as its untapped potential. The ground needed redeveloping as it was nothing but a ramshackle collection of tin pot stands held together with bits of string and chewing gum. My office, for example, was known as 'the bunker', and had no natural light. We desperately needed a new ground to breath new life into the club. Plans were drawn up and my input called for and eventually the club were given full planning permission to build a new 15,000 all-seater stadium at Minchery Farm to the south of the city. It would take a long time to come to fruition, but the fact that it was underway gave the players some impetus as they felt the club was making progress off the field.

On the field the team made an indifferent start to the season. Because of the takeover going through there had been no budget available at all and I had only been able to bring in my former goalkeeper Tim Carter on loan from Millwall for a spell and Wayne Biggins, from Stoke. Neither made a huge impact, although they didn't let me down either. One player who did make me sit up and take notice was young midfielder Bobby Ford, who scored a couple of goals as we sat in 8th position in early October.

We just needed a spark to really get us going and in many ways one just fell into my lap in November 1995. Joey Beauchamp, the man who was so homesick for Oxford, wanted to return to play for us and new Swindon boss Steve McMahon wanted to change his squad around. We initially took Joey back on loan from Swindon, but soon made it permanent for just £75,000. Swindon quoted the figure as £300,000 to make it sound better to their fans, but that was what the transfer saved them including Joey's wages for the remainder of his contract. What a bargain! One of the best wingers outside the top flight, Joey would go on to play for another seven seasons for the club, make another 238 appearances, and score 43 goals. Since the club entered the Football League, no winger or striker has made more first team appearances for the club and only three men (all of whom played more centrally than Joey) have scored more first team goals. He was voted by fans as United's Player of the 1990s and the highest compliment I can pay him is that he was the closest thing I've ever seen to my wonderful former playing colleague Jimmy Greenhoff, even down to his volleying ability, which was top class. Joey really was that good, and Us fans were so lucky that circumstances contrived for him to spend most of his career at Oxford. I counted my lucky stars most matchdays.

Joey's return began well with a 2-1 victory over Stockport, but we were still inconsistent. I had been formulating a plan for some time and once all the players had bedded in around Christmas and results began to be more consistent, I moved to bring in a young striker from Northampton on a free transfer called Martin Aldridge in December 1995. I had heard good things about Martin. He was a natural finisher and so I sent one of my scouts over to have a look at him in a reserve team match. When he came back we sat down to have a chat about my transfer target over a cuppa.

"So," I said. "Tell me about Aldridge."

"Gaffer," he replied. "He's got no first touch, he ran offside too much, he doesn't contribute to team play and in all honesty he just goal hangs."

"Really. Anything else? How many did he score?"

"Well, he scored a hat-trick, but really he wasn't up to much."

That told me all I needed to know. Throughout his stay at the Manor Aldridge would be consistently criticised for his all-round contribution, but I didn't care. For me Martin Aldridge was an out-and-out goalscorer. That was his job, and he did it well. He scored his first goals at home to Brentford in a 2-1 win on his first start for the club and went on to net nine goals in 15 starts and 3 substitute appearances that season.

In January 1996 I had a sitdown meeting with Robin Herd in the Vine pub. He was asking me about how I felt the rest of the season would unfold.

"What do you think, Denis?" he said.

"I think we're good enough to get promoted," I replied. We were 17th at the time.

"Really?"

"Yes, we could look at selling a few players and start again, Robin, but I think we can go places with this squad."

"OK. In motor racing if we think a car is good we wouldn't strip it down and start again. You don't build a new car if all that needs changing is a wheel nut. Let's have a go at it."

In mid-February, after a 1-1 draw at home at home to Brighton, we stood 13th. Just 19 games remained. I don't think anyone gave us a cat in hell's chance of winning promotion at that point, but the doubters reckoned without the steely determination and outstanding ability of my squad. Slowly but surely we began to put a run of victories together, starting with an amazing 3-2 comeback victory over Walsall. That game saw the implementation of my new plan, in which Aldridge started games and Moody came on as an early impact substitute. It worked. Paul scored straight after coming on and Martin netted twice from close range, typical strikers goals you might call them, as we came from behind to nick the three points. We were now 9th, but just three points off the play-off spots. You could feel the anticipation building within the squad and supporters.

I love goalscorers. I would always defend the likes of Martin, Juan Ugarte and Marco Gabbiadini because they were fantastic at their job of scoring goals. I've had to put up throughout my managerial career with people moaning about what players can't do instead of focussing on at what they can. I suppose it's the natural human condition, which seems especially highly developed amongst many football fans, but I have always preferred to look at the positive attributes of my players rather than their failings. I suppose you might say it's the only way I could be given the clubs I was working at and the level of players I was working with, but it's more the way my mind works. I am a very positive person and I feel that rubs off on my squad.

Equally goalscoring can be a state of mind. Martin went on a run of scoring goals in games in which he possibly only touched the ball three times. I thought he was one of those little diamonds because he was blessed with the natural instinct to be in the right place at the right time and that's not something you can coach into a player. Sure goalscorers can be frustrating because they have got weaknesses in the rest of their game but what they can contribute is the vitally important part of football and that's stick the ball in the net. Everybody is looking for players capable of converting chances. It's amazing how many are neglected because of the perception, and in some cases the reality, that they can't contribute in other areas of the pitch. For me this is a problem with coaches. A coach is always looking for the perfect player. They would take one look at a goalscorer like Martin and say "oh they can't control it, they can't join in the game", just as mine had. My question to them will always be, "Ah, but did he scored any goals." If the answer is yes then you know you've got a natural talent on your hands.

So I took Martin on and he scored goals for fun for me.

Mind you, sometimes it wasn't only the fans complaining about Martin's overall contribution to the team. I remember a game up at Carlisle in late February 1996 when Mike Ford, my captain, let his frustration get to him. He came racing over to the bench after some cock up that Martin had made in joining in the play having totally lost his patience with the youngster and shouted at me, "right, boss, get him off, he's bloody useless". I ignored him and kept Martin on. I always believe that your goalscorers need time on the pitch. Just give them a chance and they will score. It's no good them sitting on the bench in the final minute when that chance finally comes along. With two minutes to go Martin toe-poked the winning goal over the line from about five yards out. To be frank he'd done bugger all else during the game. After the final whistle Fordy came in to the dressing room, held his hands up and said, "sorry gaffer, that's why you're the boss".

The first goal in that game was memorable for a different reason. We were 0-1 down at the time and Matty Elliott had the ball advancing into the Carlisle half. I could see him lining up a shot. He must have been 40 yards out if he was an inch. I shouted at him, "Matty, no! Pass, don't shoot."

The next thing that passed my lips was, "Oh, what a goal!" Elliott's shot had rocketed into the net to get us level. You can't always be right!

That victory was the first of a run of five successive wins, the other four coming over Hull, Bournemouth, Bradford and Brighton, which propelled us into 5th position. We would only lose one of our last 17 games, a 2-4 reverse at Stockport, which Matty Elliott missed. There were some fantastic performances. I remember scoring five goals in quick succession to defeat Burnley with Paul Moody coming off the bench to score a quickfire hat-trick. His introduction as an impact substitute was working like a dream. By the time he got on, early in the second half of most games, Paul was chomping at the bit and defenders were tiring. He bludgeoned his way through most defences and took advantage, scoring seven goals in our last six games.

In that run Joey Beauchamp scored one of the goals against former club Swindon Town in our 3-0 victory at the Manor. It was almost inevitable that he should score against his former club. I always thought he was something of a homing pigeon, that no matter where you sent him he would come back to Oxford. He'd loved the city of his birth ever since leaving the club and it was probably inevitable that he should come back and thrive. Joey had a chequered transfer career to say the least. Three years after returning to the Manor Ground, after I had moved on to West Brom, a fabulous run of form saw several clubs again interested in his services and Oxford agreed £800,000 deals with both Nottingham Forest and Southampton. But probably inevitably Joey failed to agree personal terms and remained at the Manor Ground. If ever a player and club were made for each other it was Joey and Oxford United.

When Joey scored spectacularly from distance to net the only goal of the game to defeat long time leaders Blackpool at the Manor in early April, knocking them off the top spot, we still had ten points to make up over the last six games on the floundering Tangerines. That was a vital victory, and was followed up by a fabulous 3-0 win at Wycombe. The team was on one of the biggest runs of form, and the biggest high in terms of confidence within the squad that I have ever been involved in. We should have had absolutely no chance of catching Blackpool, but as consistently as we were winning, so they were folding. They lost four of their next six games, picking up only two draws and by the time we had just four games remaining and Blackpool had three, we were seven points adrift. We won our game in hand by hammering Shrewsbury 6-0, with five different goalscorers fnding the net, including a brace from Paul Moody, who I was by now playing up front with Martin Aldridge and David Rush in a devastating three-pronged attack.

In our previous game we'd pulled off a fabulous 2-0 victory at Bristol City, Rush and Moody scoring once each. That victory tasted sweet. Now we had two games to go and we were only two points behind capitulating Blackpool. In our final game we won 2-1 at Crewe while Sam Allardyce's Blackpool folded once again, succumbing 1-2 at home to Walsall. Somehow we now found ourselves in second place knowing that a victory would send us up, although a slip up could let in Blackpool, who were still only a point behind, or Notts County, two points back. Thankfully our last fixture was at home against Peterborough United who had nothing to play for and we romped to a 4-0 victory with Moody, Elliott and Rush banging in the goals, the romp being started by an own goal from Posh striker Giuliano Grazioli. It's a good job we did as Blackpool won their match, although they would have to enter the play-off system while we celebrated an incredible turnaround since the turn of the year.

In the aftermath of winning promotion back into the First Division in that game against Peterborough, amidst the mayhem as supporters poured onto the pitch and I ran on to celebrate with my players, one fan stuck what I can only describe as Russ Abbott Scottish wig on my head, one of those ginger ones with a tartan cap on it. It became a bit of a symbol of that success and Oxford fans still ask me if I've got it even today! I am afraid that along with my own hair the Scottish wig has gone.

A remarkable transformation had taken place in the second half of the season. We had gone on a run of one defeat in 17 games which saw the club rise from 14th place in January to snatch the second promotion spot on the last day of the season. It was a hell of an achievement, not least because we had turned things around so well from the disappointment of relegation just two years earlier and generated a transfer surplus for the club. In truth Oxford United had punched well above their weight for years, especially those glorious ones in the mid-1980s when Maxwell's cash funded their rise to the top flight and Milk Cup victory. Even though Robin Herd's new ownership had stabilized the club's financial position we had not really been able to spend money at all. Aldridge had come in on a free transfer, Elliott £100,000, Beauchamp £75,000 and Gilchrist had cost just £60,000. It was promotion on a budget, and all the greater success for that.

Everything appeared to be quite rosy in the Oxford garden at this point. Robin Herd had huge ambitions for the new stadium, the construction of which by contractors Taylor Woodrow began during the summer of 1996. He insisted that I take a position on the board of the club. This was mostly because things were changing in the game and more chairmen were actively doing transfer deals, rather than leaving it to their managers and Robin reasoned that if I was on the board I would carry more weight in negotiations. I accepted, although I had never wanted to join the board. Subsequent events would later bring me to come to regret that decision.

******

Having won promotion, the immediate question was whether we could keep the club in the First Division with the kind of hugely restricted budget we were working within. Even in 1996 the Sky monies were beginning to have an impact and Oxford were not eating from the same table as many of the clubs against which we would be competing that season. If you think that in the First Division in 1996/97 were Bolton, Wolves, Ipswich, Sheffield United, Crystal Palace, Birmingham, West Brom and Portsmouth, you will understand how far above our weight Oxford United were punching.

In order to compete I knew we needed to replace John Byrne like for like. Great though our run in had been, I knew at the higher level we needed some guile and nous in attack. I plumped for a player who had been groomed by a man I had admired for many years, Brian Clough, in Nigel Jemson. Still only aged 27, the highlight of his career so far had been the goal he scored to win the 1990 League Cup Final for Nottingham Forest against Oldham Athletic. He'd also scored both goals at Wembley in the then Auto Windscreen Shield final whilst on loan at Rotherham United in their 2-1 win over Shrewsbury Town just a few months earlier.

Jemo was a quality forward, although not necessarily a goalscorer. That didn't bother me, it wouldn't be his job. His task would be to join up the play between our midfield and strikers Moody and Aldridge. Jemo and Moody formed a fabulous strike partnership, proving to be the perfect foil for each other. Moody was big, bustling and with a belting shot in that left foot. Jemson was cute, scheming and always had an eye for playing Moods in.

As much as their playing styles contrasted, so did their personalities. Jemson was a peculiar case, who took the most handling of almost any player I've had in my managerial career. I would say that a week did not go by with out Jemo and myself having a chat in my office about the game, his role, his future and improving himself. It was wonderful to have a player that committed to improving his game and the extra work we put in was worthwhile because of the rewards we got on the field. Jemson proved to be the missing link that I had felt he would be. He led the line linking up the play with the midfield and the wide players. I understand Jemo had had problems with many of his previous managers, but I got to like him and appreciate his care for his profession. Nigel is a very intelligent lad and just had a lot of questions to ask about his game, although at times it did border on obsession.

Moods was a totally different person all together. He was very laid back and essentially just wanted to turn up do a bit of training and leave. It was hard work to get him to do any extra or talk about his game, but he had that great gift of scoring goals, so we made sure that Jemson and the rest of the team created enough chances for him to do just that. They didn't get on particularly well off the field, but for me the fact that the relationship worked on it was all that I am interested in.

As much as the strike power of the team had propelled us through that incredible run to promotion, it was the Elliott and Gilchrist central defensive partnership that formed the basis for our success. Working to the same template of player, my favourite kind, that summer I signed Darren Purse from Leyton Orient for £100,000. Darren had impressed me because he'd been made captain of his club at the age of just 17. That is incredibly rare in professional football, and again I felt we had captured a player whose contribution would be far greater than just on the ball.

All three of them were tall, strong and athletic and imposed their presence on opponents. They were quite a sight.

In order to finance these two signings, the only ones I was able to make, I sold winger Chris Allen to Nottingham Forest for £450,000. Chris had played an important role in steadying Oxford after relegation and then in the promotion-winning side. He had impressed Forest manager Frank Clark in the FA Cup tie between us the previous season, in which we'd held them 1-1 at the Manor, and then lost 0-3 in the replay.

The first season back in the First Division proved to be an interesting one. As with many promoted sides we had patchy form early on, with a 5-0 thrashing of Southend followed by three successive defeats without scoring a goal. Our form tended to come in bursts. From mid-September we won three successive league games 2-0, but then went five games without a goal once again, losing two. But by mid-November we stood 6th after a run of four consecutive wins, scoring 11 goals. The reasons behind our fluctuations in form were pretty unfathomable, although I always felt we played better if Jemson was on form. We certainly missed him on the occasions he was injured.

In that run of wins we defeated Manchester City at Maine Road, a defeat which brought city fans onto the pitch in protest at the turmoil engulfing their club. They had just sacked manager Alan Ball and had Steve Coppell resign after a handful of days in charge. It felt to me as if their club was falling apart while my little team was on top of the world. That night we were after all in 8th position, while City languished in 19th.

We were doing extremely well in the League Cup too. After defeating Norwich in the first round, we drew Premier League Sheffield Wednesday and scored five minutes of the end of each leg, after Guy Whittingham had given Wednesday the lead, to win 2-1 over the two legs. The night we beat them at the Manor was one of those special occasions.

We saw off Port Vale in the next round, winning a replay 2-0 thanks to two Jemson goals after a 0-0 draw at Vale Park, and then in the fourth round drew top flight Southampton out of the hat. It was another of those magical manor Ground nights and we scrapped and battled all 90 minutes, but fell behind after half an hour to a Richard

Dryden goal. But my team never gave up and in injury time Paul Moody lashed home a great equaliser. It felt like the roof came off when the ball hit the back of the net, although while the place was bouncing around in celebration Southampton manager Graeme Souness was really not happy at all, blaming the referee for something or other in the lead up to the goal. It's a classic managerial gambit, concede a late goal to lose or draw and you blame the referee. Souness continued the argument on after the final whistle as we all left the pitch, and I felt that it was a sign of how much we'd rattled them over the 90 minutes.

The replay at the Dell was a game too far for us, although we pushed Southampton all the way to a 3-2 victory. Nigel Jemson scored yet another goal to equalise Eyal Berkowitz's opener, but Saints scored twice inside ten minutes early in the second half. Even though we pulled one back immediately and put their defence under a decent amount of pressure we couldn't force the equaliser on this occasion. Our fantastic cup run was over.

By the end of December we had rallied to 5th position in the league, with the atmosphere around the place, helped by our good run in the League Cup, really crackling, and incredibly we were seriously considering a play-off spot for the end of the season. But then the wheels came off spectacularly. Robin Herd was having problems with the finance for the club, and in December construction of the new stadium at Minchery Farm ceased as the contractors were not being paid. Before we knew it Robin had walked out of the club leaving us right in the mire. Robin leaving the club in that manner came as a big shock to me and really signalled the end for me at Oxford. Chief Executive Keith Cox stepped in to run the club. He tried to drum up investment to keep the club going and even though I was on the board I was so busy keeping the team running I never really found out exactly how much Robin Herd lost in doing what he did, but I know he's often been quoted as saying it was "several million".

I had always got on very well with Robin, who I found to be an intelligent and eminent man. But because of what happened when Robin left many Oxford supporters forget how he supported us to bounce back following relegation in 1994. He is painted pretty back when his name arises in conversations with Us fans, but he was not all bad. In fact there were many glorious days under his ownership and Oxford could at least compete in the second level of English football. I still speak to Robin a few times a year. He later attempted to get back into the game in the summer of 2006 by submitting a low profile bid for Liverpool when the club was put up for sale by the Moores family and eventually the American duo of Hicks and Gillett purchased the club.

Some reports held that Oxford United was now £13m in debt and close to bankruptcy and the bank got involved when the situation became gravely serious. They took control of affairs, meaning that we were working in an uncertain climate, without our own hands on tiller.

Suddenly everything changed. The news affected every aspect of the club, the mood of the players included. You can criticize them all you like, but having been through severe financial constrictions at both Oxford and then in administration at Wrexham, I can tell you that working in such conditions leaves players and staff with doubts in the back of their mind as to where the next paycheck is coming from. Imagine what that does to you on a daily basis. It was my first experience of working under such problems, with press stories flying around, rumours having to be denied and not actually knowing myself precisely what the problems were.

I was already regretting my decision to become a board member as now I had far more responsibility, in law as much as in the day to day running of the club. If Oxford United folded my name would be intrinsically involved. It was a very worrying time.

Thankfully, being the team manager meant I could also press to raise funds through the sale of players. Well aware that a firesale could wreck the club as it had done Stoke City in 1976, I opted instead to try to get the best price possible for my most marketable asset, Matty Elliott. The big defender had been scouted by a number of Premier League sides for some time, but it was Martin O'Neill at Leicester who finally made his interest plain. The club had just won promotion to the top flight and were having a good season, sitting in mid-table. I knew I had to sell him, it was just a question of how much I could get.

Right after the busy Christmas and New Year period Martin's opening bid came in at £700,000, and I took the opportunity to elicit a little bit of competition by phoning Graeme Souness at Southampton who I knew could not fail to have been impressed by Matty in our cup ties against them. Souness admitted he fancied signing Matty and opened his gambit at a round million pounds. That afternoon I was watching a reserve team game at Swansea and so began talking to both managers, negotiating one by one with them to up the price little by little. It carried on all the way back home. Each 50 miles or so it went up £100,000 as I switched between Martin and Graeme. By the time I'd got back to Oxford I'd got the price up to £1.7 million.

I still thought I'd be able to get more, but I thought I should phone both Robin and the bank official responsible for our account. The answer came back loud and clear. Sell. I tried to argue that I could up the price further, possibly even as high as two million, but my hands were tied. I phoned Martin back, who had made the highest bid and accepted his offer. Matt became a Leicester City player.

Elliott established himself as one of Leicester's all-time great defenders. He even had spells playing as a centre-forward when the squad was depleted and was intelligent enough and good enough to score goals and make life very awkward for some of the best central defenders in the country.

From my point of view to sign a player from Scunthorpe for £170,000 and then sell him a couple of years later for £1.7 million gave me a huge amount of professional satisfaction. In the short term, too, it meant that Oxford United were solvent. For Matt,

I was delighted with how his career unfolded and for him to go on and play for his country is very rewarding, although he would end up missing that season's League Cup final victory over Middlesbrough because he was cup-tied having played for us in the early rounds of the competition.

The side took a while to adjust to the loss of Elliott and I was allowed to bring in veteran defender Chris Whyte from Leyton Orient to replace him. Chris had starred in Leeds United's league title winning side of 1992, and also for Arsenal, West Brom and Birmingham. Chris did a good job for us to the end of the season, but at 36 was only a stop gap.

In such a small squad we needed everyone to contribute and it became apparent that some players had not made the step up following promotion. One example was Martin Aldridge. Much as I'd loved the way the tenacious striker had helped us out of the Second Division, this was a level too far for him. Martin did contribute 8 goals from 30 appearances, but I was now looking to move him on. Nothing materialised, but in the interim I brought in an old favourite of mine, Marco Gabbiadini, on loan from in February 1997. Marco had fallen out of favour with Jim Smith since the Rams had won promotion into the top flight. He scored once for us in five appearances, but by this time the financial constraints meant that we could not contemplate a permanent transfer.

With all the problems that we'd had and the sale of one of our best players forced by the financial situation it's perhaps no surprise that our form dipped badly. We won only six games after the turn of the year, although we were still finding the net regularly. We began an inexorable side down the table, without getting too near the danger area. Wins over Swindon and Barnsley in our final two home games boded well for the following season. Joey Beauchamp and Nigel Jemson both scored twice in that sparkling final day 5-1 thrashing of the Tykes. Given all that we'd been through during the season I felt the players had done exceptionally well to keep performances on something of an even keel.

If I had thought that the club might wrest themselves free from financial problems over the summer of 1997, I was sadly wrong. Instead it got much worse. Talk was of bank foreclosure and assets being stripped. It was a very glum time. In the autumn of 1997, it emerged that Oxford United, the company of which I was a director, had debts totalling at least £10 million. The bank were now pretty much fully in control of the finances, which resulted in the entire playing staff being put up for sale. It was made clear to me that players had to be sold to keep the club afloat. Eventually Bobby Ford, Darren Purse and Nigel Jemson would have to go, although those sales did not occur until the season was well underway, and each time money was freed up to at least bring in some kind of replacement. The situation was tight and tense, but the death knell was not yet sounding for the club.

Crazily the team did not fall apart. A spirit had grown up amongst the small group of players who had remained loyal throughout all the problems. Special mention has to go to Joey Beauchamp, Oxford through and through, who produced several sublime performances early in the new season, particularly in the 3-0 home win over Wolves, who included Steve Bull and a young Robbie Keane in their line up. Somehow we scrambled together enough results to keep our heads above the relegation zone. We picked up a great 2-1 victory at West Brom, coming from behind with goals from young Nicky Banger, who I'd brought in on a free transfer from Oldham Athletic, and Darren Purse. We then defeated a really good Ipswich side 1-0 at home thanks to David Smith's goal.

Amidst all the sales I managed to bring in central defender Phil Whelan, the former England Under 21 international from Middlesbrough, for £170,000, which was the only money I was allowed to spend on fees that season. Phil contributed well, although a broken leg at Sheffield United would end his season.

Throughout the first few months of the campaign there had been talk from Robin of a supposed new backer coming up, but ultimately nobody turned up. The board was now split over the direction the club should take. As a director myself I felt I had to dig into my own pocket to help, so I handed over £10,000 of my own money to help pay the wages. It was supposed to be a loan, but I didn't get it back.

In the end, before the situation became completely untenable for me another opportunity opened up. I received a call from West Bromwich Albion chairman Tony Hale, who had recently parted company with manager Ray Harford. They invited me for interview for the vacant post and for the second time in my career, I negotiated a unique deal in which I sold myself to the Baggies for £80,000, leaving a financial legacy at Oxford to match that on the pitch. I really should have taken my £10,000 out of the fee, but I didn't.

I left the club on a run of three wins in four, in 16th position in Division One. Considering all the upheaval and the dearth of cash over the previous seasons I consider that something of an achievement. Certainly the problems which have continued to beset the club over the last ten years have proved what a difficult proposition it is to keep football afloat at any professional level in Oxford. As I write in 2008 the club languishes in the Blue Square Conference, having suffered three relegations since my first spell in charge. I like to think that supporters appreciate what I and my team, and indeed the players who kept the club in the division that season succeeded in doing. It was against all the odds and has proved beyond anyone since. As with so many of my clubs, I left them in a far better position than when I found them, and as with all of them, the future of Oxford over the next few seasons would sadly only be down.

I left Oxford in very good hands, namely those of my assistant Malcolm Crosby, who took temporary charge before stepping down to make way for former Milk Cup final captain and Us legend Malcolm Shotton to take the reins. Malcolm inspired my players to a very decent second half of the season as they finished in a very creditable 12th position. I, meanwhile, had once again jumped out of frying pan and into the fire.

Chapter Eighteen

GRABBED BY
THE THROSTLES

So far I had made something of a speciality of turning around failing clubs, Bristol City notwithstanding, although in the four years I had worked the miracle of keeping Oxford United in the First Division the Robins had slumped back down to a 4th place finish in Division Two and play-off failure from which they would not recover for a decade in 1996/97, so I feel justified in claiming some credit for having taken them to their highest finish for 15 years, and one which was only beaten by Gary Johnson's incredible achievement in leading City to the Championship play-off final in 2008. Could I perform the same trick with West Bromwich Albion, a club who made no bones about the fact that they were totally strapped for cash?

The Throstles had slipped from their past glories, and boy didn't I know it. The board members seemed to be constantly talking about winning the FA Cup in 1968. That wonderful achievement had actually occurred before I'd made my Football League debut for Stoke City and I was no longer a spring chicken, so it was most definitely in the dim and distant past. I know in football we love to talk about the glory years, but really and truly you can't let those memories, grand as they may be, hold you back. For example I discovered when I toured the club before agreeing the deal that the training facilities were worse than useless – muddy, uneven pitches with poor dressing rooms. It immediately became a priority for me to improve them as I knew in the ever-changing world of football, if you wanted to be in the Premier League, as West Brom did, then you needed to have top class facilities. But as soon as I broached the subject I was told, "we won the FA Cup training on these pitches."

Frankly that was not a justification, thirty years later in 1998, to fail to invest in improving the facilities. Everywhere I've been a manager I have made a huge difference to the way the team have been able to prepare, not least through having far better training facilities by the time I have left compared to when I arrived. This was no different. I fought tooth and nail to get them to see sense and it became apparent that they would comply, but only if I could generate funds to spend the £2.5 million or so that the outline plans we'd had drawn up would cost to implement. This was an absolute priority for me in developing the club to the next level. Now it was down to me to generate the funds any way I could.

One thing I'd discovered soon after joining the club was that I wouldn't be raising that money by selling too many of the current squad. I'd spoken to Ray Harford, the man who had left the club after just ten months in charge publicly, at least, because he wanted to work closer to his London home, admitted to me in private that the real reason he had walked out was because he knew the West Brom squad was not good enough to compete for promotion from the First Division. On top of that he had received no cooperation from the Albion board in achieving any of his other aims for the club, which broadly mirrored mine. Ray told me he felt he'd worked wonders to keep the club in the play-off positions after a good start to the 1997/98 season which had seen them top the table in early September, but knew they were heading for a fall due to lack of investment and having an ageing team. He had therefore opted to join QPR in December 1997.

I listened to what I was being told, but I thought this was far too good an opportunity to be missed. It was a big chance and once I'd taken the job I'd just got to get on with it because I knew that I was capable of taking on the challenge.

That's not to say the entire squad I took over was a waste of space, far from it. Albion had some good, talented players. I liked the look of the Dutch midfield general with the flowing locks Richard Sneekes, his hard-working central midfield partner Ian Hamilton, left-footed striker Andy Hunt and young winger Kevin Kilbane, who has gone on to have a fabulous career with Sunderland, Everton, Wigan and the Republic of Ireland. The rest I would need to assess, and quickly if we were to take advantage of the position in which we found ourselves at the halfway point of the season.

I took up my post just before Christmas and my first game in charge couldn't have been more appropriate. My old club Stoke City were the visitors to the Hawthorns on 28 December. It was an emotion-packed day for me, although we got off to a bad start when some lax defending allowed the Potters to take the lead just after half-time. Andy Hunt scored a deserved equaliser, but we couldn't break down the resilient visitors, who actually held something of an Indian sign over the Baggies. West Brom had not beaten the Potters in a decade. It was the kind of run of results which had really begun to get under the skin of Albion fans, and a hoodoo which I looked forward to ending when the two sides met again a few days later in the FA Cup third round.

The original cup tie was postponed due to heavy snow and frost, but when we did play we ran out comfortable 3-1 winners thanks to two goals by Richard Sneekes and a late clincher by Kevin Kilbane. That made me the first Albion manager to beat Stoke in 18 games and nearly ten years, since Brian Talbot had masterminded a 6-0 victory just before Christmas 1988. Our cup run was ended unceremoniously by a 0-4 defeat at Aston Villa, but we really got up and running when we edged a very close Black Country derby against Wolves 1-0 thanks to a vital goal by Andy Hunt. Defeating both fierce local rivals surely had to stand me in great stead this early in my Albion career.

Our form in my first few months in charge of the club was nothing to write home about. In fact we won just two of our last 16 games in that 1997/98 season, although we finished a comfortable 10th. What I had been able to do in that period was assess everything about the club and come to some fairly calculated conclusions about many people and a lot of different aspects of life around the Hawthorns. In short I felt there was too much acceptance of the average around the club, there were too many people existing on reputations and there were too many people happy with the level they were at. I'd heard from within the game before I joined that the Albion had been for too long a place which accepted mediocrity, but I was someone who saw that as an opportunity and a challenge rather than a negative. I had been employed to move the club forward and in my opinion the only way to do that was by a major shake up. This ran right through the club, although I thought the squad needed major surgery and so opted to deal with things head on.

I brought in a few new faces throughout the rest of the 1997/98 campaign. First was 22 year-old centre-half and England Under 21 international Matt Carbon from Derby County for £800,000. Matt was a pacy, athletic central defender who I wanted to pair with a big muscular man in the image of Matty Elliott or Phil Gilchrist from Oxford, in fact I spent some time trying to sign Gilly, knowing that Oxford would have to accept almost any half-decent bid, but eventually, after something of a ritual dance around the subject Gilly opted to join Birmingham instead, although he would eventually sign for the Albion a few years later. Carbon replaced Paul Mardon, while I kept my hunt going for a new partner for him as I was uncertain about Daryl Burgess, the other centre-half.

I'd taken a good look at hard-working 31 year-old midfielder Peter Butler, whose previous clubs included West Ham and Notts County, but decided that he just wasn't good enough. In February we lost three consecutive games without scoring a goal, the last of which was a 0-5 hiding at Charlton. Peter did not play for me again after that. Football can be an unforgiving world, and I was the one who was being paid to make the tough decisions. Peter had to go. He joined Halifax Town and in his place I brought another young player, 23 year-old James Quinn, into the team, paying Blackpool £500,000 for this exciting talent who had been attracting the interest of a number of Permier League clubs. Quinn scored twice in a 2-1 win over Middlesbrough on 4 April, his first goals for the club. However, James found goals hard to come by and he became something of an enigma, struggling with the rigours of the step up in division.

One young man who would become an unqualified success was a young striker called Lee Hughes. Lee was a Baggie through and through. He'd grown up on the terraces at the Hawthorns and was a real Black Country lad. His hunger for the game and for goals was lovely and truly refreshing. Ray Harford had blooded Lee by giving him short bursts as a substitute throughout the first half of the season, but, much like Marco Gabbiadini and John Byrne 15 years earlier, and Andy Cole at Bristol City, I thought this kid had absolutely everything when I saw him in training. I've always been happy to put youngsters in if I thought they were good enough, and were at least as good, if not better than whoever else may be at the club and available to me. Lee may have been just 21 that Christmas, but he was certainly good enough raw material to be given his opportunity. He had made a massive impact in the second game of the season, coming on as a late substitute and turning round a 1-2 deficit at Crewe's Gresty Road with two late goals to secure a 3-2 win. Once he had established himself in the starting line up Lee ended the season with 14 goals from just 18 starts. I had a great feeling about this kid's future in the game.

After trying the two left-backs at the club David Smith and Shane Nicholson, I brought in Jason van Blerk from Manchester City for £50,000, and two defensive loanees to see us through to the end of the season, van Blerk's club colleague centre-back Paul Beesley and veteran midfielder Steve Nicol, who had made his name in the all-conquering Liverpool side of the 1980s, from Sheffield Wednesday.

Things picked up towards the end of the campaign as we lost just three of our last ten games, although ultimately for a club like West Brom to finish just two places and three points above Oxford, the club I'd left in turmoil just six months earlier, simply wasn't good enough and told me exactly how much work there was to do in order to turn the team from a group of players happy to remain within their comfort zone into one hungry enough to become promotion challengers.

The huge question mark I had in my mind was whether the board was totally behind me in assisting me to do the job they'd brought me in to do. I certainly would have been forgiven for asking when I learned that my budget for the rebuilding process was effectively zero.

When I talk to Albion fans now about my time at the Hawthorns one of the gripes that I am faced with is that I brought in too many of my own people to the club, upsetting many of the big favourites that were happy there. For example I had taken a look at the coaching set up and then moved to bring in my trusted coach Malcolm Crosby, rescuing him from the financial meltdown which Oxford United had become. Throstles fans tell me that there was a certain amount of animosity over that because I brought Malcolm and later John Gorman in over the head of huge heroes Cyrille Regis and John Trewick, who had both been appointed by Ray Harford, but who did not have any depth of experience in coaching. Again I felt that we could improve things by bringing in Malcolm to lead a team of coaches. I thought they both could learn a lot and develop their own skills, progressing on to becoming extremely good coaches in their own right, but the external perception was that I'd demoted them in some way. For a start Cyrille hadn't done his badges and in fact Cyrille and I got on really well, and I was very disappointed when Cyrille resigned to concentrate on developing the burgeoning career of his nephew Jason Roberts, who would eventually sign for West Brom, but was at this stage enjoying a fantastic first season with Bristol Rovers.

More animosity grew within the Albion support when I began to develop my squad. I had felt from the start that the man Albion fans simply refer to as SuperBob, 30 year-old striker Bob Taylor, a man who had scored nearly a century of goals in his six years at the club, was past his best. In fact it hadn't just been me who felt this. After taking a good look at Bob, Ray Harford had given him just four starts during the first half of the 1997/98 season. Bob had been struggling with an ankle injury for some time, and I, like Ray, thought his best years were behind him. For some reason I seem to take all the blame for taking that natural progression a stage further and moving Bob on to Bolton on a free transfer. Many people will tell you I got this one wrong, but I maintain that if he had not had that spell away to give him the huge kick up the backside he needed he would not have been able to return to the Albion and continue his record-breaking goalscoring as he did when he returned to the club two years later. I have nothing against Bob at all, but he never did it for me, and also he turned down the one year contract extension that we did offer to him in favour of the three proffered by Bolton. I firmly believe that it was the wake up call he needed to prolong his career when I offloaded him to the Wanderers.

Where I did perhaps create a problem for myself was with a section of the Albion support that never forgave me for the departure of their hero SuperBob. I felt the Albion fans were some of the most knowledgeable I had ever come across. Without question they loved their club, but sometimes I think certain sections of the following had this kind of idealistic devotion which led them to believe they deserved to be successful by some kind of divine right and that certain people should be left on a pedestal where past endeavours had placed them. These supporters had their huge favourites that they admirably stuck by through thick and thin. But my judgment was much more coldly professional. I thought I could do better, and needed to free up wage room on the bill to be able to bring fresh faces in as there was no money at all to spend. Bob was one of several long-standing players who had been at the club throughout years of mediocre underperforming that were moved on.

Ultimately I wonder if I tried to make too many such changes too quickly. Easing out the ageing heroes one at a time might have been more acceptable. And, to be brutally frank, if the players I'd brought in had come up to scratch.

Bob's long time strike partner had been Andy Hunt. Andy left for newly-promoted Premier League club Charlton in the summer of 1998 after scoring 67 goals in 202 games for the Baggies. This was not my decision, although the jungle drums amongst certain supporters held that it was my fault. I was desperate to keep him, but the board had simply allowed Andy's contract to run down. The Bosman ruling, which had come into effect in 1995, had not been seen in operation much before and so supporters were unused to what it meant. Previously managers and clubs had retained control over players at the end of their contracts, allowing them to demand fees. Now the European Court of Justice had declared that once a contract had reached its term a player would be a free agent and could join any team of his choice. Perhaps it was inexperience in this department that meant the board had created a situation whereby Andy could leave.

Throughout all the criticism which came my way in 1998 I maintained my belief that I was doing the right thing and telling things as they were. Sometimes the truth was uncomfortable for supporters who felt they were losing big names they adored. For example I'm often told that the players I brought in over that summer tended to be free transfers. However, with the freedom of contract which had allowed Hunt to leave without a fee, came the beginning of footballers moving without cost between clubs, changing the perception of the free transfer from that of a bargain basement giveaway to one who had merely allowed his contract to run down.

Perhaps it was more the perceived quality of our new arrivals which concerned the fans. I brought in winger Mark Angel from Oxford, lanky striker Fabian de Freitas from Spanish club Osasuna and forward Gerry Creaney, who eventually I would pass on and would sign for St Mirren. What is fair to say is that I was working within the severely restricted budget the board had given me, although this was a scenario I was well used to. It had become my stock in trade to deal in unearthing gems or dredging reserve teams for disaffected footballers and turn them into motivated forces in the game once again. I believed I was on the ame track again.

De Freitas was a very interesting case in point. The lad had so much talent, but his attitude led to him putting in such varied levels of performance, which ultimately had been the reason why he had been released by Bolton manager Colin Todd two years earlier. As a manager you want to know what you are going to get out of a player and there is nothing more frustrating than waiting on tenterhooks to see what you are going to get. With Fabian I ended up having no idea. He was strong, had pace and could score goals, but rarely seem to out the effort in. He infuriated supporters with his inconsistency. I wasn't impressed either. He was far too laid back for his own good and had an attitude that he was happy with whatever he did, good or bad. He had no performance standards. What we had to try to do is to make him become far more focused and aggressive. You'd have to be on him all the time to do anything.

But surely no-one could find fault with the other signings I made that summer. I picked up the scent of some kind of Italian superkid who had been brought over to play in a trial match at Aston Villa by his agent Gianni Paladini. As our season began earlier than Villa's and we were back in training just before them, Paladini phoned me to tell me all about this wonderkid. That left us with a small window of time within which to work. It was only then that I learned his name – Enzo Maresca. He was 18, had captained Italy at every youth age group, and was signed to Cagliari.

Maresca played in our trial game and I loved what I saw. He had ball control to die for, flair, skill, speed of thought and tactical awareness. He needed to develop physically, and improve his pace, but I knew he was going to be a hell of a player. The question was, could I get him to sign for us?

I negotiated with Paladini, persuading him that as a manager who had brought through plenty of young talent I would be best placed to bring Enzo on, and also that playing in the First Division would be less unforgiving than the Premier League, where Enzo may struggle to get even substitute appearances if he joined Villa. It worked. After consulting with Enzo and his parents, Paladini agreed the deal. We'd got our man, or should I say at that stage, boy.

I realised that a kid like Enzo would need someone to feel at home with and we heard about a smashing midfielder called Mario Bortolazzi, whose previous clubs included AC Milan and Genoa. Mario was 33 years-old and brought some style and substance, and a sweet left foot, to our midfield, as well as acting as a minder for Enzo. Unfortunately neither his English or my Italian was particularly strong, or we'd have got even more out of Mario, but he was still a hell of a good player.

I want to dispel the rumours, which I know persist, of anything fishy about how Maresca arrived at the Hawthorns. Some fans have questioned how I knew about this totally unknown talent over in Italy. The simple answer is I didn't until he came over to the UK. Paladini's involvement has also somehow become the subject of some speculation, but solely because of the subsequent shenanigans at Loftus Road where he was held at gunpoint by a fellow director of the club after they'd fallen out. No-one had heard of him back in 1998. He was then just a fully registered football agent.

The way the Maresca story is sometimes told nowadays has it that we signed Enzo then sold him almost simultaneously for a hugely inflated fee, which would, if true, have been very suspect indeed. In fact Enzo was at West Brom for 18 months, and made his first appearances in professional football during his spell with us. We were bringing him on through careful training and coaching. He was a young lad, living in a foreign country and needed some nursing through, hence my initial use of him as a substitute. I was also careful about his physical development, but all the time there was this phenomenal talent that I was so aware of.

I loved every minute of working with Enzo. He was dedicated to improving himself, worked hard, listened, even in a foreign language, and had sublime skill. He was the best free-kick taker I've ever worked with, and remember he was only 18. I had to protect him from the hardmen who would undoubtedly want to take him down if he began to exhibit his deft and magical footwork in the first team. I gave him his debut as a substitute in a 3-1 victory at Bristol City and used him sparingly at the end of games for some time to give him a chance to get used to the pace and the physicality of the matches. His first start came just before Christmas at Crewe and he would score two goals in 22 appearances in his first season in the game.

Maresca was not the only youngster I would blood. Towards the end of the campaign I gave a young defender called Daniel Gabbidon his chance. 'Des', as we called him, after England centre-half Des Walker because he was so quick, went on to play for Cardiff and West Ham, establishing himself as a top level centre-half and a regular Welsh international.

There was one man I was very disappointed to be losing. Malcolm Crosby received an offer to move to Derby County to assist Jim Smith. Malcolm knew that whatever happened at West Brom we would always be working with one hand tied behind our backs financially, so I could not say anything other than "Good luck" to him as he headed for the Premier League by the shortest possible route. He rang me to tell me about the offer and his decision to take it. I was on holiday in the close season at the time and wasn't pleased to be losing him. But then the cheeky devil asked me to make all the arrangements for him!

I looked around for an assistant and, as a short term solution, came up with a choice somewhere out of left field – my former manager at Stoke City Richie Barker. I had got nothing against Richie. My departure from the Victoria Ground had been over a difference of opinion on the way the game should be played and also his worry that I was lining myself up to take his manager's job. It was strange because Richie had been my superior, but I had always thought his true talent lay in coaching players rather than the man-management and tactical side of things.

I finally found a permanent assistant in John Gorman who I had met whilst working at Oxford when he had been involved in the England set up. John would use Oxford's youth team for coaching practice before he took the England squad, trying out different ideas and manoeuvres. We rounded off our pre-season preparations by winning 5-0 at Cardiff with Mario Bortolazzi scored a stunning free kick. We also had triallist Marco Nappi in the side that night. Nappi, a striker, had played for Genoa, Cesena and Fiorentina, ultimately didn't want to stay in England. I felt we were ready for a decent tilt at reaching the play-offs.

We kicked off the season in a blaze of goals from young Lee Hughes. He went on a record-breaking run of hitting the back of the net, scoring 25 league goals by the turn of the year. Lee was fantastic to work with. He listened to what we were teaching him and played on the shoulder of the last defender, frightening the life out of them with his pace, direct running and aggressive shooting. He hit the ground running right from the off, scoring twice in the second game of the season as we defeated Sheffield United 4-1 and then a hat-trick at Port Vale in a 3-0 win.

I felt Lee was as good as Andy Cole had been at such a young age, but he needed a partner such as John Byrne or Nigel Jemson to provide the constant stream of throughballs with which he could wreke his havoc, but I was not able to go out into the transfer market at that stage and get the right player in as we just could not compete as budgetary restrictions meant I had to look from within my existing staff and opted for big Mickey Evans, who Ray Harford had signed, but I didn't particularly see him as the future. Mickey did OK as a focal point off which Hughes could work, but did not offer any real goal threat himself, so when Fabian de Freitas announced himself with two goals after coming on as a substitute to win the home game against Norwich, I thought we may have hit on something very special.

Fantastic though we were in attack, with Hughes at his rampaging best, we were still struggling as a defensive unit. I had been forced to utilise both Australian Shaun Murphy and Paul Mardon, often out of position at right-back, players who I still thought needed to be replaced but also could not as yet afford to do so. We worked tremendously hard drilling the players, but it just didn't seem to stick. I needed to bring in new faces, but did not have the funds to do so. It was a source of endless frustration to me that we could not improve the defence beyond conceding 76 goals that season.

A case in point came in the season's fifth game. We visited Grimsby Town having won three and drawn one of our first four, and looking a real handful. Suddenly, on the August Bank Holiday Monday we capitulated to a 1-5 defeat. It was a chastening experience and one which affected the team's confidence as they went back to their old inconsistent ways over the autumn.

Around this time I renewed my acquaintance with Ian Botham, supporting the great man on one of his many charity walks from Land's End to John O'Groats. Well, not quite. I did two days on one leg of the journey with him walking from Birmingham to Gloucester. Towards the end of the day, as we entered Gloucester, I moved up beside Both behind the lead car at the front of the group, to gee him up and keep him going. After all he must be tired after doing day after day of this. As I walked alongside him he offered me an orange juice from the boot of the car in front of us. I took one swig and nearly gagged. "Both, what on earth is in this!?" I stuttered.

"Tequila," he replied. "I drink them for the last couple of miles each day to keep me going."

In a decade since those sessions in Durham Botham had barely changed and he certainly hadn't slowed down. It was some night that night, the most incredible part of it being that while I nursed my hangover on my day off the next day, Botham and his entourage were off at first light on their next 30 mile stage. The man is incorrigible. His enthusiasm and dedication are remarkable, and he thoroughly deserved the knighthood he received in 2007.

If only I had been able to bottle some of Botham's ability and desire and imbue it into many of my squad. Further limp defeats followed for my team, many of which had little to do with the talent of my players, but everything to do with their character. In September 1998 we lost 0-3 at Oxford. I had known how tough my old club would make my return and there was no reason why they should have done anything else, but what really disappointed me was my players' reaction to the whole situation. It started in the tunnel, when the sides were waiting to walk out side by side. A number of the Oxford players were telling my players how they would hurt them during the game. To be honest it was pretty standard psyching out stuff – only to be expected from a team I brought up who I would expect to do whatever they can to win – but my players wilted visibly. It was extremely disappointing and I sat them down at our next training session and explained to them exactly what I expected from them. Intimidation is a perfectly legitimate tactic, often utilised by smaller clubs. What I could not accept my players' reaction to it. Joey Beauchamp scored within five minutes and we were dead and buried. The players had lost the game in the tunnel before they'd even walked onto the pitch.

One of the key men in the team, and the most difficult to manage in many ways, was talented Dutch midfielder Richard Sneekes. I had a very interesting and up and down relationship with the man with the flowing blond hair, eye for a pass and a fabulous long range shot. Along with Nigel Jemson, I would say that Richard was the most intelligent man I worked with. But the problem for me was that he was either thinking either like a manager and wanting to control everything on the pitch rather than concentrating on doing what he could himself to the best of his ability, or he was allowing his mind to wander away from football and onto any number of fascinating and worthy topics. There is nothing wrong with being an intelligent man, and indeed Richard has gone on to become a very successful businessman in the West Midlands with a property portfolio and restaurants. But I needed him to focus on delivering the goods each and every time he took the field. Ultimately he did not provide that consistency.

What I wanted to do was blend Richard into a team pattern and build the play around him, but often he wanted to do things his way, running with the ball when it was better to pass, and ignoring the team pattern I was trying to establish, and as manager I wanted him to adhere to my way of playing, which was to play early through balls on the ground for Lee Hughes to run on to and destroy teams with his pace and finishing ability. Sneekes' maverick nature was what endeared him to the fans and also what gave him his edge that he could produce a moment of magic which could unlock a defence or conjour a goal from nothing. I was trying to find a way to harness him, but he wanted to play totally unshackled. I think there was an element of cultural difference too as, being Dutch, Richard just was not used to rigidity in either his personal life or his playing career. Where Richard was absolutely brilliant was with foreign players such as Maresca and Bortolazzi. His language skills were excellent and he helped make them feel at home.

I always found a way to include Richard, so he never developed into the same kind of problem that Bob Taylor had done. However the same could not be said of goalkeeper Alan Miller. Albion fans adored Alan. I loved him as a bloke, and he was great around the dressing Room, but I felt I needed a better all-round keeper. Alan was good shot stopper, but didn't command his area and was questionable on crosses, so I moved to replace him. That was really a mistake on my part as I failed to learn from the Bob Taylor situation and went ahead and created a problem which simply wasn't there when I already had plenty of others to solve. That was exacerbated by the fact that the keeper I brought in, Phil Whitehead from my old club Oxford in December 1998, didn't go down well. I do think in the most part that was because he wasn't Alan, who supporters had really taken to and had become, along with Taylor and Sneekes, one of the big personalities of the team. But the biggest problem I had was that was Alan was a huge boardroom favourite and consequently Whitehead attracted a lot of blame for things which simply weren't his fault. I rated Phil very highly, but now Miller had become something of a cause celebre amongst a large portion of the Albion support. No matter who came in, if they weren't Alan Miller, they were going to get short shrift. It was difficult for Phil and he didn't cover himself in glory. I would argue he didn't do that badly either, but what I would certainly agree with is that he didn't improve the team noticeably, and that was what I was looking for him to do.

At the other end of the pitch, as our form dipped and we began a slow slide down the table, problems were developing with Lee Hughes. Our extremely inconsistent form, which saw us defeat Crystal Palace at home 3-2 thanks to a Hughes hat-trick, including two late goals, one a last minute penalty winner, saw us follow that, just four days later, with an abject first half performance against Birmingham which saw us go into the break 0-3 down. Lee netted another hat-trick in the next home game to seal a 3-1 win over Huddersfield, this time slotting home two penalties, but then away defeats at Portsmouth and Bury left us in mid-table. Somehow we'd contrived to waste the fact we'd had one of the hottest strikers in Albion's history cracking home goals of every kind and not been able to build a decent team around that.

Lee's frustration began to be see in his hot-headedness and impetuosity on the field. It all boiled over in one match at home to Oxford when Lee bundled into visiting keeper Paul Gerrard, resulting in Lee badly injuring a shoulder. As hot as he'd been befre Christmas, he blew cold afterwards. An element of that was his immaturity as this was his first full season in professional football, but then he netted only six more times during the second half of the season. Lee still finished the leading scorer in the whole of the Football League with 31 goals, including 5 penalties

Although our form had begin to swing wildly, we secured a good 2-0 win at Watford in January which left us in 8th place and in what I thought was a good position to strike for the play-offs, but once again the players failed to kick on and accelerate towards the end of the season. It didn't help that with injuries such as Hughes's shoulder starting to effect the squad I was unable to move to bring in any players. I really needed a couple of new signings to shore up the defence as I ended up playing the two centre-halves I'd dropped the previous season, Paul Mardon and Daryl Burgess, meaning we hadn't progressed at all.

All through this period I had been trying to bring in a better partner for Hughes as Mickey Evans had scored just 2 goals and De Freitas 7. The heady match-winning substitute appearance of earlier in the season now seemed a long time ago as Fabian hardly made a telling contribution for the rest of that season. But without money to strengthen I could not find the right man and so Lee eventually hit his inevitable dry patch and our goals almost totally stopped flowing.

It was at this point I learned that the board had been split over my appointment right from the start. I never learned who, but I discovered that chairman Tony Hale had favoured a 'bigger name' instead of me, and I had ended up being a compromise candidate that somehow united the warring board. The problem was now that the half that had supported me – led by Vice Chairman Paul Thompson – were being slowly eased out of the club. As this scenario developed in the background, the club felt listless to myself and the supporters. There's no telling where a rudderless ship might end up and that's what West Bromwich Albion were during the second half of that season. The situation began to build to a head as I became more frustrated with not being allowed to display much leadership.

I have always believed in honesty when communicating with supporters and when times are tough I go out of my way to make myself available to talk people. At that time I was happy to go and talk to any supporters group who asked. I'd become used to having hostile receptions as a manager, and enjoyed the cut and thrust of debate and hw that could relieve a lot of tension for both sides, so the ones I was getting at West Brom at this time were nothing new. I chose to maintain my dignity and kept talking, kept communicating. You could argue that I was too honest for my own good in letting everyone know the truth about what was going on and what I thought, but I prefer to be up front about these things.

Somehow, on 6 March 1999, we still found ourselves in 6th position, the final play-off spot, on the back of consecutive home wins over Stockport and Oxford, the latter including Enzo Maresca's first goal in professional football. But we lost the next five games and then drew the next three to slump out of the play-off picture. It was a painful fall from grace. At a time of the season when I was used to my teams kicking on and charging towards its climax, I felt like the players had failed me by relaxing and failing to up their game towards the business end of the campaign. Particularly galling were the events of Easter Monday, 5 April, when we succumbed to a dreadful 1-5 home defeat to Crewe Alexandra.

I had realised it was going to be a particularly bad day when Fabian De Freitas missed the afternoon kick-off because he thought the game, being a midweek match, would begin at 7.45pm. Without De Freitas I was forced to press winger Mark Angel into rare and emergency service as a striker, a role for which he really was not suited. The afternoon just went from bad to worse. In fact it developed into a massacre. As bad as we played, Crewe were irresistible, with Jermaine Wright the star. He scored twice and Alex's symbolic fifth goal, at the death, was scored in front of a half empty stadium as fans had already left. Many of those who did stay protested about the state of the club in the Halfords Lane and towards the end, an Albion supporter invaded the pitch and headed straight for me. I saw him coming and braced myself for a confrontation, but fortunately a steward intercepted him. I remember in the after match interview I said something along the lines of, "I wasn't worried. I'm a Meir boy. I'd have taken him on." I would, and I'd have fancied my chances too. It was sad, however, that it had come to this.

Our poor run included a last day defeat at Tranmere. At that time, Albion supporters turned out en masse for the last away trip of the season, often in fancy dress, and the idea was that the team put on a show and win. At Prenton Park, the team simply curled up and died, conceding two goals in the first 20 minutes and another one towards the end to lose 1-3.

As the fans raced onto the pitch to celebrate the end of a long, hard season in the traditional fashion, I wondered if any of them would take their anger out on me. They didn't because ultimately, as I have always believed, Baggies fans are very decent people at heart. They may have vented their feelings vocally – and lord knows I shared their frustrations at how the club had pulled itself apart with internecine warfare and totally derailed a shot at the play-offs – but I understood their feelings. Rumours were already circulating that I would be sacked imminently. As it happened that never occurred, but I gave an interview early in the summer in which I said, "If I leave here now, I'll be disappointed, for the first time in my career, because I don't think I've done what I want to do yet."

In planning for the new 1999/2000 season, amidst all the turmoil, which now seemed to be dogging me everywhere I went, I really thought we could push towards the play-offs if I could revolve enough of the deadwood out of the squad. Now, looking back, I realise that the whole was very much a symptom of how English football was readjusting itself financially with so many big clubs squeezing smaller ones to sign their talent and being able to retain large squads because of the money Sky TV was putting into the game. The players simply weren't available and furthermore the money was pooling in just the largest clubs. My career had taken a turn which would characterise me as the man to sort out difficult situations and so I was attracted to bigger and bigger problems.

Somehow it seemed I had overcome the immediate one of being handed my cards by Chairman Tony Hale, but I reckoned without the craziness of board decisions. I was thinking that as we had completed our pre-season programme, with a defeat by Premier League Derby County, I would be given the opportunity to lead the team into the 1999/2000 season. In fact it never really crossed my mind that my position was in jeopardy.

I remember coming off the training pitch that morning chatting to John Gorman about how much we were looking forward to the new season because the squad were all buzzing in anticipation. So it came as a shock to both myself and the supporters, many of whom were completely befuddled by the timing of the move, when the board finally resolved its issues by ousting my supporters within it and sacking me just a week before the season started.

The manager the newly reconstituted board finally moved to bring in? Brian Little, who had just suffered a season of disappointment at Stoke and who would find the challenge of dragging the Throstles up by their bootstraps even tougher than me. Little lasted just eight months and it would not be until the club changed hands and also benefited from the good fortune of being able to employ a young manager called Gary Megson, who had been very unlucky to have been dismissed from his job, ironically also at Stoke, where he'd begun the job of rebuilding a club which had similarly failed over a long period of time, because new owners had come in and wanted their own man, that Albion's revival came about.

I'm often asked how I sum up my frustrating time at West Bromwich Albion.

I was not given enough time or budget to make the changes I wanted to. If you tie a manager's hands behind his back financially then you have to give him time to evolve things. I knew I had a fantastic player in Maresca, who would realise a significant sum of money. Once again I would not see any of the benefit of that when it came to it.'

Enzo moved on in January 2000, bringing in a club record outgoing fee of £4.3 million from Juventus. He never quite made the breakthrough there, but in 2005 he moved to Sevilla and went on to become a major player in their progression towards the top table of La Liga. He was also integral to the Spanish side winning successive UEFA Cup finals, being named as Man of the Match in the 2006 victory over Middlesbrough and scoring twice. He really was one heck of a player.

It would be Megson that was given the time to build a team from scratch, attracting new players in with the fantastic state of the art training facilities which had been constructed in the intervening period with the money the Maresca transfer had generated. Megson, who ultimately would also be forced to sell Lee Hughes for £5 million and reinvest the money, would finally bring success to the Albion, but I like to think I played a significant part in that. The Baggies' promotion to the Premier League in 2003 brought a huge smile to my face. I'm never bitter about these things. They are often out of your control, but I firmly believe that I could have worked the oracle for West Brom if I'd been given the chance. You can only work with what you are given as a manager and the only fear I have is that my time at the Albion will be judged not by what I was able to achieve against the odds, but by what supporters with great expectations thought I had failed to do. I now know I was an interim manager at a time of great upheaval behind the scenes, but that's little consolation, nor was the failure of my immediate successor.

I have never had time to dwell on such matters throughout my career as I have been fortunate enough to consistently find work within the game. It would not be long before I'd be back in a job again, a familiar one at that.

Chapter Nineteen

BACK ON THE

BREADLINE

After leaving West Brom on 27 July 1999 I was at least in a position that I could wait for a while to see what unravelled in the ever-growing merry-go-round of managerial changes. This was a very different scenario than had occurred after my dismissal from the Sunderland job. I'd got some money in the bank and my pay off from Albion came through without any problems. I had never been available for work at the start of a football season before and so I was always at the ready to seize an opportunity should one of my brethren at the League Managers' Association (founded in 1992 on the formation of the Premiership) find himself ousted from his job. I found myself keeping tabs on all sorts of different clubs who did not begin the season well, although I would never for one minute have gone so far as to want someone to lose their job. I was, however, realistic enough to know that in any given season at least 30 managers will be dismissed. My involvement would then be to apply for the position as soon as a post became free. There could not be any sentiment about it. I needed to work eventually and in this competitive world one man's downfall would become my opportunity.

Early in the season Ruud Gullit left Newcastle, while Kevin Ratcliffe (Chester City), Mick Wadsworth (Colchester United), Colin Todd (Bolton) and Sam Allardyce (Notts County) all found themselves in the same boat as me. I applied for a couple of the posts, but none of them really grabbed me. Instead, after enjoying a rare Christmas at home with the family, I began the new Millennium by receiving a phone call from Mickey Lewis, the caretaker-manager of Oxford United, my former club. Mickey was in dire straits, the club was in meltdown and he didn't know where to turn. He was doing every backroom job going himself with no support, everything from picking the team to collecting the kit after games to wash it. He'd been at the club for over a decade and thought that I might be able to offer a solution to their problems.

Since my departure to join West Brom at Christmas 1997, Malcolm Shotton and his assistant Mark Harrison had done a good job to steer the Us to a mid-table finish by the end of that season, but then a difficult 1998/99 campaign, during which the financial situation had become ever tighter at the club, saw the side struggle, picking up a couple of seven goal hammerings along the way. The club had been forced to sell more and more players to finance the debts and the construction of the new stadium, which had begun again, and all that had resulted in relegation. They'd signed off with a flourish, hammering Stockport County 5-0 on the last day of the season, in a last ditch survival attempt which was reliant on two other clubs losing. Both won, but at least that victory gave Oxford some hope for the new campaign.

However, a poor start to the 1999/00 season in Division Two saw Shotton and Harrison resign in late October, with Mickey Lewis, then a senior player and youth team coach at the club, being asked to take over the reins with the experienced Maurice Evans assisting him and offering advice. Two months later and Mickey had had enough. He didn't want to be a manager, let alone manager of struggling Oxford right now. After initially steadying the ship Mickey had realised a more experienced man was needed as the team's fortunes nose-dived.

When I took Mickey's call Oxford had won 6 games out of 26, and by the time I'd concluded discussions and appraised myself fully of the situation they'd been beaten twice more in four days, conceding six goals and failing to hit the net themselves. The team was demoralized, lacking in quality and slumping rapidly towards the foot of the table for what would be a second successive relegation. With the trap door out of the league now fully open, with automatic relegation having been in place for a decade, this slide had to be arrested or the club could simply slip out of existence. It sounded just the job for me. When I took charge of the first game of my second spell as manager we sat 21st in the Division Two table, with the worst goal difference in the league and with only 17 games in which to save ourselves.

Since my departure the squad had been divested of Phil Gilchrist, Darren Purse, Nicky Banger, Nigel Jemson, Paul Moody, Phil Whitehead and Mark Angel, the last two of which I only had myself to blame. Gilchrist had only departed earlier that season, moving on to Martin O'Neill's Leicester for £500,000. In total he had made 201 starts for the Us in his first spell, scoring eleven goals. He, along with Elliott and Purse, was one of my best ever central defensive signings.

Earlier in the book I described the circumstances of that first match back at the Manor Ground, against Blackpool, and the death of my former striker Martin Aldridge. It was an emotional day all round as both sets of fans bade farewell to Martin, but by the end of it we had lost another match and slumped to 22nd in the division.

A lot of the problems had been caused by the abrupt departure from the club of former chairmen Robin Herd towards the end of my previous time at the Manor Ground and it had been left to new owner Firoz Kassam to perform a suitably high profile rescue act for the club, taking over and clearing much of the debt through a Company Voluntary Arrangement (CVA) assisted by some complex financial deal involving how the ownership of the new ground was structured. Firoz was a very interesting character. Flamboyant, peacock-ish and most definitely rich, he had first come to Britain from his native Tanzania, where he had been born to Indian parents, as a student during the 1970s. He'd made his fortune as a hotelier in the 1980s, buying run-down London hostels and hotels to house local council homeless people and asylum seekers. In the Sunday Times Rich List 2006 he was listed with an estimated fortune of £250 million, so he could definitely afford the asking price of Oxford United F.C. in 1999 of just £1, although he also took over the club's debts, estimated to be in the region of £13 million. In 2000 he re-started construction of the 12,500 capacity three-sided stadium at Minchery Farm on the edge of Oxford, which he had perhaps inevitably renamed the Kassam Stadium, the ground which I had been involved in the planning stages of all those years before. The fourth side of the stadium was left blank ready to be filled in when the good times returned. The development included a hotel, cinema, bowling alley, gym, health centre and restaurants. It wasn't just a football club, but a community facility. That was a great idea as far as generating revenue outside the normal matchday was concerned, however the financial shenanigans that would so anger large numbers of Oxford fans soon became apparent when it became public knowledge that Kassam had sold the Manor Ground first to his own holding company for £6 million, and then on to developers for £12 million in 1999. A big fat profit of £6 million which the football club never saw. That controversy would run and run far beyond my stay under the new chairman who proved to be a very difficult man to get on with and pin down.

The immediate task was to keep the side in the Second Division and we made a great start. Two early wins, one in the last minute against Chesterfield, which gave me great hope that this group of players, unlike those I'd left at West Brom, were capable of taking on board the demands I made of them. The first thing I had done was to bring Nigel Jemson out of the wilderness of Scottish First Division side Ayr United and back to Oxford. Jemo's influence had been sorely missed since he'd been sold to Bury just after I had departed and now he brought extra attacking guile to our depleted attack.

Those back-to-back victories, the only ones of the season lifted us clear of the relegation zone, but a run of five defeats in six games soon dumped us back into it. The only bright spot of that sequence was provided by Phil Whelan's headed winner in added time at Colchester which earned a 2-1 win. We repeated the trick a couple of weeks later to secure a 2-1 victory at Bury thanks to Jamie Cook's last gasp winner. This team was responding well and fighting to the very end. I was delighted with their battling qualities and determination not to let the continuing behind-the-scenes problems affect their Second Division status during a tense run in to the end of the season.

At the death Derek Lilley scored three vital goals, the opener in the 2-1 victory over Bury, the only goal of the game to defeat Bournemouth and one in the 1-1 draw at home to Brentford. Derek was a 26 year-old Scottish striker, who had arrived after a disappointing spell at Premier League Leeds United for whom he'd signed after starting his career at Morton, where he made a great impact. He starred for me in that run in to the end of the 1999/00 season and earned himself a move to Dundee United in the Scottish Premier League on the strength of his performances

Lilley's strike gave us a half-time lead in that vital game against Brentford, but we conceded a goal to Lloyd Owusu straight from the kick-off and try as we might we couldn't find a winner. It was very disappointing as Brentford had been on a dreadful run themselves, failing to win in any of their last 13 games of the season.

Now with three games to go we had 41 points and were in a straight fight with Cardiff City, with whom we were level on points, but who had a game in hand, to avoid the last relegation spots as Scunthorpe, Blackpool and Chesterfield were already dead and buried. In our next game we pulled off a great 2-2 draw at Bristol City, coming from behind at half-time thanks to a goal by centre-half Steve Davis, and came off the pitch to hear the news that Cardiff had conceded two second half goals to lose 0-2 at Bury. We were out of the bottom four and a 2-0 win in our last home game of the season over doomed Scunthorpe put us in a great position to pull off another incredible escape. Cardiff still had three games remaining, but they were tough fixtures. They lost at play-off chasing Stoke City on the Sunday following our win over Scunthorpe and now, suddenly, we had 45 points to their 41 and they had just two games remaining. They could not afford to lose their next game at Gillingham. All Oxford eyes were on Priestfield that night, but the early news was not good. Cardiff's Jason Bowen opened the scoring in the second minute of the game. They lead 1-0 and our hopes of avoiding relegation hung by a thread, but a hat-trick from Carl Asaba and a fourth, courtesy of Nicky Southall, put paid to Cardiff's challenge. They were down and we were safe. Somehow. It was another stunning achievement of footballing survival that I am immensely proud of.

* * *

Having achieved safety against all the odds I was offered a year's extension to my contract, which I initially accepted, but it very soon became apparent that I could not work with the Chairman Kassam as we fell out over the almost total clear out of players that we were forced to undertake over the summer of 2000. We somehow muddled through, but the club descended into turmoil as we lost a full team of players and were forced to replace them with new men who would not prove their worth.

On top of that I had to go into hospital to have a major operation on my neck. I'd had problems with my balance during June 2000 and it became so bad that I went to see a specialist. He did some tests and then told me, "you have got to come in for an operation on Friday."

"I can't I've got something on this weekend," I replied.

"No, you don't understand." He said, "you will be coming in, because if you don't you might not be walking next week."

It turned out that an old and previously undetected injury I'd picked up playing had cracked a bone in my neck, which had gradually disintegrated and trapped the spinal chord at the bottom of my neck. The operation saw the specialist take a piece of bone out of my hip and place it into my neck in the hope that it would graft into my spine with no repercussions. There was, I was told, a 5% chance of being paralysed from the waist down. To wake and be able to move your toes after an operation like that is a huge relief.

By the Monday I was out of the hospital and at home, recuperating whilst making frantic phone calls to make some signings. In truth it took me nigh on two years for my legs to be working properly and I had to rest and recuperate as much as I could, whilst still keeping the club going.

The budget was unmanageable, but ultimately that is no excuse for poor signings. I had always been able to bring in a decent level of quality signing for very low cost in the past, but on this occasion we failed with the likes of Ian McGuckin, Robert Quinn and Andy Scott. We were also forced to turn to far too many kids to allow for a healthy and solid development of the team. It was all dictated by the uncooperative and difficult chairman, and, if I'm brutally honest, me being confined to my bed or the sofa for large parts of the vital summer period. In fact I remember McGuckin signed for the club at my house because I just couldn't move.

I realise now that rejoining Oxford was a mistake, irrespective of the euphoria of helping the club avoid relegation. In truth it was merely a delay of the inevitable. The 2000/01 season would prove something of a cataclysmic one. After three games of the new season we had yet to score a goal, having lost each of the games without really looking as if we were competing.

That third match was at home to Brentford and the performance and the mood of the fans, which was extremely gloomy, led me to try to buck people's spirits by standing in front of the home end and talking to the supporters. They'd been giving me stick because of the perilous situation, which was getting on top of everyone and our failure to hold on to the lead. I took some criticism for that, but I still think it was the right idea to go and try and speak to the fans who had been giving me stick all through the game. It was very much a spur of the moment thing, but I just wanted to try and make them understand that I was hurting just as much as them and that the best way to try and improve things was to work together. "That's what the players and I will be doing," I promised them. "We need your help." But it was becoming increasingly obvious that the situation was totally irretrievable.

I lasted until early October, ten games into the season. By that point I knew I simply could not continue and so resigned in the best interests of all concerned. We'd picked up just four points that season and were already plumb bottom of the division, a position from which Oxford could not recover. Relegation was a certainty and followed in due course. I had won just eight of my 30 games in charge in this spell.

After a brief period with Mike Ford as caretaker-manager, chairman Kassam appointed David Kemp as manager in November, after consultations with former Wimbledon boss Joe Kinnear, who stayed on as Director of Football. As United's season went from awful to abysmal, Kinnear left in February 2001 to become manager of Luton Town. By the end of the campaign Oxford had been relegated into the Third Division with a meager total of 27 points. It was a dreadful season for the club and a sad end to the final season of the Manor Ground, but at least Oxford would be able to begin afresh in the newly-named, on-off Kassam Stadium, which would be completed the following summer.

It was also a sad end to my time with a club that I had really enjoyed working for. It was just a shame we could not make the finances work. It hasn't got any better for Oxford since I finally departed. Firoz Kassam fell out with just about everybody during his spell in charge of the club. At least he, for all his faults, found a new buyer before he wandered off, and left Oxford United only £2 million in debt with a new ground to play in. The only problem was, by this time, they were on the way to the Blue Square Conference, two divisions below where I had left them. The new stadium had remained a pipe dream while I was there and it was not until February 2001 that work had restarted on the site again.

My resignation as manager did not lead to a total severance. I scouted for the new management team of Joe Kinnear, who was brought in as Director of Football, and David Kemp as First Team manager. Early in 2001 Kinnear left to take the vacant position of Luton Town manager, while before the end of the season Kemp left by mutual agreement with the chairman, as Oxford United plummeted towards relegation to the Third Division. I maintained my position alongside new manager Mark Wright, while keeping my ear close to the ground once again for another opportunity. I had become very realistic about where my career had taken me and the kind of experience it had given me at what particular levels. I knew that whatever my next challenge would be it would be a pretty stiff one, but I was sure it could only be better than the past trying, arduous year. Couldn't it?

Chapter Twenty

AGAINST ALL ODDS

The first thing that the board of Wrexham FC said to me at my interview for the vacant managerial post was, "We have to tell you that we have got no money. We've got to sell, the place is in a mess. "

I was by now so specialist in keeping clubs afloat and punching above their weight and status, that I had been called in to discuss taking over following their decision to relieve long-tem manager Brian Flynn of his duties.

That a lower league football club had fallen on hard times and needed a miracle worker was hardly a surprise. Since the advent of the Premier League less than ten years earlier several clubs had come close to going out of business and I was aware it was a trend which was only going to grow.

Part of the reason for the major problems at Wrexham was that to comply with the Taylor report they had constructed a wonderful new stand on the Mold Road side of the ground. The problem was they had not sold any of the executive boxes. And I always thought they'd missed a trick in the development as they merely built a brand spanking new stand, with no other facilities at all. The way the Kassam Stadium at Oxford had worked, for example, was to include other public facilities and I think if Wrexham had followed that kind of template then it would have really helped the club by bringing in other streams of income from offices, shops or cafes. Perhaps there could have been a crèche for example. Not only could players and staff have left their children there, but so could staff of the nearby North East Wales Institute of Higher Education could too. The way they'd done it, though, it wasn't working. It was earning nothing by sitting there silent during the day, only generating an income on matchdays – a white elephant really, which had become a millstone around the club's neck.

Wrexham would obviously prove to be a whole new challenge.

We'd lived in lots of lovely places around the country, York, Durham, Bristol, Oxford and Shropshire but when I told Kate we were moving to north Wales, her first question to me was, "Why on earth would you want to go to Wrexham?"

What I explained to her was the wonderful training facilities at Colliers Park which had been built on a lovely, out of town site and were good enough to be used by the England, Barcelona and Rangers squads on occasions. It had opened in June 1997 at a building cost of £750,000 and they had certainly done a super job on the buildings and pitches. It is really top class, the kind of facility that coaches dream of. Especially when compared to my bunker at Oxford.

On top of that they were running one of the new Academies, which attracted some funding from the Football Association and marked out the best clubs. It was a big status point. It was important to Wrexham to be seen as being a good club to stay with so that a youth policy could be built. Many clubs had opted to reach being a centre of excellence, but Wrexham had decided to attain the higher level and less expensive Academy status, which meant needing a hell of a lot of money to set up and run. They had been giving very good contracts out to players as well. That needed stopping or the club would go bust very quickly. There is another issue with playing in the Academy League. You are playing Man United and Liverpool and inevitably getting hammered, whilst simultaneously allowing them to watch your best players in the shop window. Having said that we made some nice money out of bigger clubs signing our kids.

Although the ambitions were laudable, this was not the best use of money. So when I took over in early October 2001 I had numerous areas of the club to work on to prune back spending. We cut back on the salaries we were offering and downgraded from an Academy to a Centre of Excellence, which saved a lot of money but did not make a great deal of difference to what could be achieved in terms of developing youngsters.

Because the training facility was so fabulous there was a bit of a split between the club and the training ground. It was them down there and those up there because people at the stadium thought the training ground was draining all the money out of the club. That was another perception I had to change as the training ground was the thing in the end which kept the club alive because it was the biggest asset in terms of selling the club to new players that we possessed. There was a lot of talk about closing it down and selling it off. Sometimes people at football clubs lose sight of the fact that everything revolves around the players and management staff. Without them you have nothing and without such a great facility Wrexham would undoubtedly have had far fewer quality players. I struck a balance between the two groups and I felt that both were happy with me.

I didn't help that the Chairman, Pryce Griffiths, was not very well at the time and was flirting with selling the club, but after he recovered I came to know him well and grew to like him a lot. Besides being the Chairman he was a great bloke and I appreciated his total honesty right from the very start. The board had been absolutely right. There really was no money.

I was obviously well versed in dealing with such situations, but in this case I was also impressed that the board had been incredibly loyal to Brian Flynn over his 11 years at the club and he had rewarded them by keeping the side in Division Two. That was perhaps no surprise given the good squad already at the Racecourse, Carlos Edwards, Dennis Lawrence, Brian Carey, Darren Ferguson, Andy Morrell, Kevin Russell, Steve Roberts, Craig Faulconbridge, and an unknown striker called Lee Trundle, who had signed from semi-professional Rhyl Town. We were also blessed with passionate support and a tradition of giantkilling in the cups. I loved the fact that there was such a big potential catchment area and it wasn't far from my natural home of north Staffordshire. The problem was that when I took over for my first match in charge we lay 23rd in the division, with only Bury below us, both clubs being way off the pace. Flynn had been dismissed after presiding over an opening sequence to the season of one win and three draws from the first eleven games, including some real hidings. It was up to me to arrest that decline and avoid relegation, whilst making the fabled profit on transfers. Water off a duck's back!

My first match was at home to promotion favourites QPR and we got off to a great start, winning 1-0, with Michael Blackwood scoring the only goal just before half-time. As we desperately clung on towards the end of the game I endeared myself to the Wrexham faithful by getting into trouble with referee Michael Ryan. In the last few moments of the game the ball was belted into the crowd by one of our players clearing a QPR attack. It took a while to come back, but when it was thrown out of the crowd it lobbed up over the dugout in my direction and so I cheekily gained a few precious seconds' relief for my defence by jumping to head it back into the fans. Mr Ryan was not amused, unlike the Racecourse faithful who fell about laughing. What wasn't quite so funny was Kate's reaction when I got home. The operation on my broken neck had been a success, but it had taken me a long time to get over it and even at this point I was having to sit on a shooting stick to watch training because my body couldn't take the strain of walking around. Now I found myself getting a severe dressing down because in the heat of battle I'd forgotten all about having a broken neck! Even when pretty much fully recovered later, the operation left me with a legacy of finding that for two days after every game I could barely move my neck because of the to-ing and fro-ing I put it through, like a tennis match, on the sidelines.

My first task was to choose a coaching team. I'd accepted the job on the basis that there was no extra budget for this, so it had to be an internal appointment. I already had a great reserve and youth coach in place in Joey Jones the former Wrexham, Liverpool, Chelsea and Wales full-back, who had played in the Reds' first European Cup-winning side in 1977. Joey is a one off, everybody loves him. He's hard work because of his enthusiasm. For example, I would tell him every morning what I wanted him to do and then he'd go out and do something totally different with the players. But his sessions are very good. What he instils in the youngsters coming through is the passion and the desire and the drive. He has that himself in spades, so he tries to rub that off on the kids.

Joey had no interest in becoming assistant manager himself. I asked him, but he turned it down, saying he wanted to work with the reserves and the youth. Joey is intelligent enough to know it's not for him. He's had a heart by-pass for a start. We always had to nag him to keep him off the weights.

"Joey, are you supposed to be doing them, mate?"

"Yeah, I'm alright."

"What's the doctor say?"

"Yeah, yeah, I'm alright."

"Your funeral!"

So I spent a few days analysing my squad to see who showed the aptitude for the task of being my number two. Three of squad had already got some of their badges under their belts, senior pros Darren Ferguson, Brian Carey and Kevin Russell. In the end I asked myself, "right, which one has got the sense of humour?" I am well aware that my intensity and serious approach – it's been called a humour bypass by some people! – to the job is well-suited to management, but to balance that I need a coach who can be the players' best friend, make them laugh and get them back up again after I deliver the inevitable bollockings that do regularly occur in this game.

When I started working with Kevin I realised he was tailor made for the job right from the start and the more I worked with him the more I realised how good he was. He made my job a hell of a lot easier, and as it went on I gave him more and more responsibility. I now believe he is one of England's finest young coaches and to see him succeeding so well at Peterborough under the management of Darren Ferguson, who would grow massively into a man capable of managing a football club and being successful into the bargain during my five-and-a-half years at the Racecourse, is fantastic. He's got his pro licence now and deservedly so. I do believe it was a mistake for Wrexham to let him go when they eventually dismissed me.

Mind you, Kev was just like all other coaches the world over. He'd take my training schedules and plans in the morning and implement them with a smile on his face and then after training come into my office and have a good old moan about the players! As long a that happens behind closed doors and my coaches are bright and bubbly on the training ground I am a happy manager as the players need to have fun and enjoyment from the day-to-day work in order to build themselves up for the serious business of playing games.

Even though I was able to walk more now, I still needed my shooting stick and consequently I was doing less coaching than I had in my previous two jobs and enjoyed organise the defence and the midfield's defensive duties, focussing on covering midfield runners and zonal marking with the central defenders. I like to simplify the game as much as possible and focus on repetition because, and I use this phrase advisedly, a lot of players are not that football savvy. The lower down the leagues you are the less you can focus on tactics and the more you have to do on basics. Get them right and you won't lose many games. That was my philosophy from the start and it brought us back-to-back wins in my first three games when first we thrashed Wigan Athletic 5-1 in the Auto Windscreens Trophy and then Craig Faulconbridge scored a late winner at the home of the same opponents to secure a 3-2 league victory.

I'd managed to draft a couple of experienced heads into my squad on loan for those first few games. Keith Hill had been a great centre-half at Rochdale, but at 32 had moved on to Cheltenham. He could not get into manager Steve Cotterill's side, so I took him for two months and he was fantastic for us, giving us stability at the back. It hasn't surprised me at all to see Keith return to Rochdale to become their manager and in 2008 take them to Wembley.

That first week I also signed Jim Whitley, the oldest of the footballing Whitley brothers of Manchester City fame, and a Zambian international. Jim, then 26, signed permanently and would be a mainstay of my Wrexham midfield until 2006 when we had to let him go aged 31. Jim did a good job for me, but he picked up so many injuries through his all-action style. Towards the end of his career Jim had begun to take up the pastime of painting and now he works as an artist for a living and sells football paintings. He also does a great Frank Sinatra cabaret act.

The win at Wigan also saw me give a first start to young Hector Sam. He scored from his role wide on the right of a front three.

The honeymoon period ended abruptly as injuries and suspensions and me getting to know the squad, which was in the most part quite young saw us slip to series of defeats. I remember losing heavily at Huddersfield, 1-5, and Bournemouth, 0-3. That result left us at the foot of the table. But I was still positive about the remainder of the season. Our problem was in defence where we missed Brian Carey for large chunks of the season. Once they were back after Christmas, from mid-January we went on a run of only one defeat in seven games. One of those was a fantastic 3-2 victory over Peterborough in which Hector Sam coolly slotted home a last minute penalty to secure the point. We were now 21st, the highest of the four relegation positions and just one point behind Bury in 20th and two behind Bournemouth in 19th. Could we pull off what supporters had begun to think of as the impossible?

That good form came after I'd introduced 29-year-old Norwegian goalkeeper Marius Rovde on a free transfer from Scottish club Ayr United to the team. Marius was a former soldier who impressed me during a short trial spell. He was a brilliant lad and being a typical goalkeeper he was a different character altogether. What was so refreshing was that he loved every second of being a professional footballer. He enjoyed training and loved the atmosphere of games. He was fantastic around the dressing room and quickly built up a rapport with the fans and players. He ended up going home to Norway to play with Lillestrøm at the end of our season, as the Norwegian season runs through the summer, but after he left I remember he once turned up out of the blue at one of our games with a load of his mates just to watch. He was an infectious character and that little incident spoke volumes to me about how someone like him could become entwined with the ethos and spirit of a small provincial football club like Wrexham.

By this point we'd already conceded 64 league goals during the season, defence being our Achilles heel. It was at this stage that we really began to struggle. We won one in ten games, drawing just three and slumped down to 23rd. Just when I thought we'd be coming strong towards the end of the season my players had wilted. I think they had given all they'd got, but eventually proved not to be good enough for that level. The patched up sides we often had to send out with kids like Shaun Pejic, Mark Evans, Kristian Rogers and Craig Morgan in them just did not have enough experience or knowhow.

The one victory during that period came thanks to two late goals by Lee Trundle when won 3-1 at Port Vale on 5 March. It proved a false dawn. A 0-3 home defeat followed and the 1-4 reverse in the next game at Northampton left us needing a minor miracle to survive. We had five games remaining, three at home, and needed to make up seven points on Northampton Town in 20th position. Two of our fixtures were against play-off chasing sides, and we drew creditably 1-1 at home to Huddersfield, and then narrowly lost 0-1 at Stoke. It wasn't enough. We went into our penultimate home game against already-relegated Cambridge knowing that if Northampton and Notts County won their matches we would be down.

Strangely that seemed to release the pressure which had been building on the players during the dark days of the poor run of form. We sparkled as we mounted wave after wave of attacks and scored five goals without reply. What made the day all the more memorable was that Lee Jones, the striker who I had signed from non-league Oswestry Town just a week beforehand, had the game of his life, netting all five.

Lee had been at Wrexham as a kid and had made quite an impression. He'd been bought by Liverpool for £300,000 at 18 in 1992, but then didn't make the breakthrough. He'd spent six years at Anfield, playing just three times for the Reds, although he'd also suffered two broken legs, returning twice on loan to the Racecourse to assist his recuperation. He'd them moved on to Tranmere, where he'd scored 16 goals in 85 games and won his two Welsh international caps, and then Barnsley. He'd dropped out of sight, however, despite the fact he was still only 28 and pitched up again learning to enjoy his football down at Oswestry. When I signed him and worked with him for a few weeks I felt that I'd unearthed another goalscoring gem, to work in tandem with Andy Morrell, who'd had a dreadful season with injury and scored only two goals. Despite our relegation being confirmed I had this great feeling that these two were capable of doing something special in Division Three, as long as I could keep hold of them.

High though Lee's five goal salvo was other results meant we were down. It's not often you win 5-0 and feel so desolate. My third relegation, as expected as it was, hurt as much as the first two at Sunderland and Oxford.

Returning to the Third Division left me back where I had started my managerial career for the very first time since I had led York to the championship of the old Fourth Division back in 1984. Turning that club around had been difficult enough, but Wrexham was a club with far deeper problems and to produce anything like that kind of success would be, I thought, one of the bigger challenges of my career. But I had great hope for my motley collection of kids and experienced pros, rejected by bigger clubs. This was exactly the kind of challenge I had loved over my career, moulding an effective team from disparate sources against the odds. Much of it stemmed down to my ability to motivate the men in the dressing room, as well as having put the right ones in there in the first place both in terms of talent and attitude.

But all of a sudden my plans had to be put on hold when chairman Pryce Griffiths, as he had been seeking to do for some time due to his continuing ill-health, sold the club to Chester-based businessman Mark Guterman. Guterman didn't get off with the fans on the best of footings because he was a former chairman of arch rivals Chester City, but on taking over in June 2002 he told supporters, "judge me on what you see, judge me on the signings and on-the-field activity".

To be fair the change of owner allowed me to cling on to all my most important players over the summer, such as Darren Ferguson, Andy Morrell, Lee Jones and Jim Whitley, although I did lose striker Craig Faulconbridge on a free transfer to Wycombe Wanderers. Despite my lack of funds to pay transfer fees I was able to add experienced goalkeeper Andy Dibble to the squad and also Paul Edwards a midfielder from Swindon, who I converted to left wing-back, both on free transfers. Paul was no relation to Carlos Edwards, a Trinidadian international, who played on the right side. Both were quick as lightning and could get up and down the pitch. The wing-back system gave us great flexibility and allowed me to have three central midfielders to other teams' two to win the ball back in the middle of the park.

Early in the season we had an opportunity for a nice payday and to show how we had progressed from the relegation fodder which had ended the previous campaign when we drew David Moyes' Everton in the second round of the League Cup. Kevin Campbell put the Toffees one up after 25 minutes, but we were holding our own ad giving Moyes' defence a rough time when David brought some kid off the bench called Wayne Rooney to make his debut for the club. Within seconds Wayne had lit up the Racecourse, scoring twice in five minutes right at the death to seal a 3-0 win. A week or so later he became the Premiership's youngest ever goalscorer when he netted that famous last minute winner against Arsenal and England keeper David Seaman. Rooney had arrived and I was privileged to have seen his first steps into the big time.

As we settled into our pattern and understood that we could compete well in this division, we had a mixed bag of results. Consecutive 4-0 wins over Swansea and Exeter at home, Andy Morrell netting a very pleasing hat-trick in the latter game, were cancelled out by a dreadful 2-5 defeat at home to Rochdale and a disappointing 0-2 Racecourse loss to Lincoln. After that result, in late October, we stood 13th, a good distance off the play-off spots.

But our season was galvanised by a magnificent comeback victory at home to Bournemouth, with Paul Edwards scoring the winner in a topsy-turvy 3-2 win late on. We won four out of five games, with Hector Sam grabbing the lat winner at Carlisle to propel us into 5th place. Perhaps the play-offs were a possibility after all.

What had galvanised the team was the goalscoring form of my three strikers, Lee Trundle, Lee Jones and the bang-in-form Andy Morrell. After trying different combinations over the first few weeks of the season I'd settled into a pattern of starting games with Andy and Lee Trundle, and then bringing Lee Jones on as a second half substitute to liven things up.

Lee Trundle was proving a revelation. He had always possessed sublime skill, as he has proved in his further career at Swansea and Bristol City, but I had always felt he needed to be right in his own mind to start a game. I found that during this campaign he loved being part of the success that we were building and he became an integral part of the team, the foil to Morrell up front, often selflessly providing crosses or through balls for Andy to score from. That's not something that's always been said about Lee. He does crave attention and wants the recognition that goes with his talent. I don't have a problem with that as long as he does the business for me, which that season he most definitely did.

Alongside him Morrell starred, banging in goal after goal. He scored goals for fun, often in pairs, or even threes. Andy's work rate was phenomenal, and he had great aerial ability. Everything he did was for the benefit of the team. Supporters often don't appreciate what that takes out of a striker to constantly be on the go like that. In fact at times it became a problem because with Lee Trundle in the side wanting to be the star, but Andy scoring the goals, there was the danger of a personality clash between my two strikers. Thankfully there is room in football supporters' hearts for more than one hero and both men earned the right to be hero-worshipped that season.

As much as the goals, and there were 84 of them that season in the league alone, were important, my other priority had been sorting out the defence which had shipped a total of 89 goals the previous season. Key to that was a giant of a man called Dennis Lawrence, who I mentioned earlier in the book would go on to play in the 2006 World Cup for Trinidad & Tobago. In 2002, when I had fully assessed my squad after failing to avoid relegation from Division Two I had come to what I had thought was a fairly easy decision that Dennis was not for me. Enormous though he was, Dennis wasn't great in the air, and for me he didn't understand his role in the game as a centre-half. But all credit to him, Dennis proved to be the player in my career who by sheer hard-work, bloody-mindedness and constant communication with me to establish what he needed to put right, changed my mind. He came to see me, listened to my opinion and made the changes I asked. I'm glad to say that as well as proving me wrong he simultaneously proved me right because by the time he made those historic appearances in Germany for the smallest nation ever to qualify for a World Cup finals, he had completely changed. He was actually almost unrecognisable as a player. He could time his tackles, impose himself on forwards such as Henrik Larsson and Wayne Rooney, and had become a key man in our dressing room. He was an absolute top man, someone I grew to love as both a man and a player.

He and I both knew his limitations, but he didn't sulk when I left him out early on, he was prepared to work round them, listen to me as I helped him overcome them and improved his game so much it felt like we'd made a new signing. No-one else in my career has ever turned my opinion round from thinking, 'no way is he ever playing in my team' to being one of the first names on the team sheet. We'd have simple conversations where he'd ask me how to improve one aspect of his game, I'd tell him and he'd go away and implement it. Not only did Dennis turn me around, he turned the supporters around too, who worshipped him in the end. Brilliant. No wonder he's gone on to great things with his national side and then helping Swansea City's resurgence by being an integral player in their 2007/08 side which won promotion into the Championship.

Dennis's renaissance, as ever in football, meant he took the place of another player in the side, about halfway through the season. That man was Shaun Pejic. Pej had caused a bit of a minor storm when he had broken into my team because accusations of nepotism were hurled at both myself and him. I have never chosen any of my teams in my entire managerial career on anything other than a totally professional basis. I just wouldn't pick a player that might put my job in jeopardy because his dad, Mel, also worked at the club as the physiotherapost, as was the case with Shaun. Occasionally the fact that I'd played so many years with his uncle Mike Pejic at Stoke was thrown at me too. But Pej was in the team on merit from the start of the season and to prove that the nepotistic claims were totally without foundation it was he that I chose to drop once Dennis Lawrence had turned himself around. In fact he also won Wales Under 21 caps, so it wasn't just me who rated him, the national set up did too. There were always those supporters who had their doubts and that's something both Shaun and I had to deal with. It was nothing major.

Pej was a good defender. In many ways, if I'm brutally honest, I had no other option but to play him if I was going to leave Dennis out as there just were no other fit defenders at the time and there was certainly no budget to bring in any new signing of any description. Shaun wasn't particularly comfortable on the ball, but he was useful because when you play with three central defenders you need people with pace to play down the sides and he was very good at that. He did the job that was asked of him well and was very strong-minded, although you have to be when you have your dad at the club and your Uncle has played for England. Pej has consequently had a lot of pressure on him throughout his career, but he has always served Wrexham well. He lost his place to

Dennis after about 20 games of the season and wouldn't get his chance again until the following season.

With the defence shored up, four wins in five games in January and February moved us up the table to 7th position. We were nicely poised for the run in, although no-one could quite work out how we were managing to do it given all the continuing financial constraints. Whatever may have been happening behind the scenes I kept it all away from the players as they began to truly believe they could achieve something truly special by winning a promotion directly after a relegation. But then came our stutter. We may have only lost one of the next nine games, but equally we only won two. A 1-1 draw at Lincoln in mid-March dropped us out of the play-off positions. I had to get through to my team that they needed to up the ante in the run in to the season. That was something I'd prided myself in achieving at every club I had been at bar West Brom, where the players' singular failure to respond left me wondering about the true level of their commitment.

But I had a willing dressing room at Wrexham, packed with players with a point to prove. They responded superbly, in fact in a manner I could only have dreamed of. The only arrival that had been possible on my shoestring budget throughout the whole season was Scott Green, an experienced midfielder who had served both Bolton and Wigan admirably. He played the last 14 games and made a telling contribution in getting the ball through for the strikers to run on to. He was also tigerish in the tackle and full of energy. He scored both goals as we defeated Hartlepool 2-0 at home on 18 March and from there we never looked back. It felt as if we could not lose, and now we were turning some of those draws into victories. Our momentum was building all the time. We were disappointed to only draw 3-3 at home to struggling Shrewsbury Town, my old player Nigel Jemson scoring for the Shrews that day. We would have the last laugh there, though, as we ended up being responsible for condemning Shrewsbury to relegation to the Conference at the end of the season. They finished bottom of the league, demotion being confirmed for them by our 2-1 win at Gay Meadow a month later, with a goal from Morrell and a 90th minute winner from substitute Lee Jones.

That victory was the second in an incredible run of eight wins which took us through to the end of a tumultuous season. As we caught up our games in hand, from eighth place in late March, and seeming out of the hunt, we somehow managed to get back into the play-off positions, and then, inexorably, move up the table as win followed win, towards the automatic spots. We beat Bristol Rovers 3-2 at home thanks to Carlos Edwards' 88th minute winner, Kidderminster 2-0 away from home through two Lee Trundle goals and then thumped Carlisle 6-1 at the Racecourse with Andy Morrell bagging a hat-trick. We were playing some super stuff, our movement and formation causing opposing defences no end of headaches. In those eight games we scored 24 goals, with just five in reply. We were flying and these were heady days. We hit third spot with four games to go and held on, finishing the campaign with a 3-0 win at Bury, comfortably ten points clear of Bournemouth in fourth position.

Not only did we secure an unfathomable promotion given the utterly parlous state of our finances, but we also won the FA of Wales Premier Cup. The competition had been organized ever since the Welsh FA had been forced to bar those Welsh clubs competing in the English Football League from entering European competition through the Welsh Cup. Many of the big Welsh clubs such as Cardiff and Swansea treated the competition as a reserve team kick-about. I am just not like that. If my team is in a competition we play to win, taking it seriously, and we did exactly that, thrashing Newport 6-1 on home turf to lift the trophy. After all the £100,000 prize money was vital to our continued existence.

******

As soon as the promotion celebrations had died down following our 5-0 thrashing of Cambridge in our final home game, I was on the lookout for players to try to improve the squad for the challenge to come in the Second Division. Essentially we'd won promotion with the same group of players who had failed at that level the season before, although confidence was obviously far higher. I needed, though, to strengthen where I could and not allow my better players to fall prey to bigger clubs, unless they were going for a hefty fee, that is.

We'd been forever scraping for players from different sources – free transfers, loans and promoting our strong youth policy by getting kids into the first team and that was also a way of generating funds by selling those players who made an impact, a vital source of income for the club. Promotion brought the inevitable Championship and Premiership clubs sniffing around. That was the stark reality of life in the basement. But I didn't mind. That meant I was being successful and if other players saw it happening then they might believe that they could be whisked into the big time and put in more effort which would only benefit Wrexham in the medium term. Plus of course the money was all important to survival.

The problem came when the club failed to keep its players under contract and allowed them to walk away under the Bosman ruling. That summer both Lee Trundle and Andy Morrell reached the end of their deals. Andy moved on to Championship club Coventry City on a free transfer, after manager Gary McAllister took the plunge. Andy had scored 40 goals in 109 games for Wrexham, 34 of them in that 2002/03 promotion season. It was gutting to lose such an important player in this way. I had become well used to selling off my best players, but I was only prepared to do so when it was on our terms and in the best interest of that player. Clearly going to Coventry was good for Morrell as they were a division higher, although the move would not work out for him in the end due to Coventry's own financial woes. But to lose him for a big fat nothing was a poor show on our part.

I've got a lot of time and a lot of respect for Andy Morrell. During the summer of 2003 he was talking to various clubs before plumping for Coventry. When they are out of contract some players become mysteriously uncontactable. Andy was quite the opposite. He would come in and tell me every week exactly what was going on, which clubs he was talking to, where he was going, so I knew the score. That's the correct way to behave for a professional footballer. If only they were all like that. As I write Andy is at Blackpool and building his popularity there. I think manager Simon Grayson plays him wide right, rather than up front, but with Andy you know what you are going to get. You know he will work his socks off for the team constantly, and often to the detriment of his own game. He remains one of my favourite players that I have managed.

Lee Trundle conducted his departure from the Racecourse totally differently. Lee just disappeared, severing all contact. Now he wasn't obliged to tell us what he was up to, but I felt he owed us the courtesy, but we didn't get it. I had no idea he was signing for Swansea until I read it on teletext. But that's Lee, he's a different kind of character and one that's full of surprises! I just prefer those he produces on the pitch.

With losing our two strikers in that manner I knew I had to keep hold of my keep players if we were to have a fighting chance of survival. That summer for example I also received a bid for Darren Ferguson from Sheffield Wednesday, but I refused to let him go. I could replace my goalscorer, but I would not be able to replace my leader in the middle of the field. Ferguson was so key to our success of the previous season on the pitch and off it and to lose him would have bee disastrous. I had to think of what was best for Wrexham, and on this occasion it was not selling our best player.

Darren, however, was not happy at all about me stopping him talking to Wednesday, but I dug my heels in and my intransigence won out. I was able to cling on onto him. Darren would see out the rest of his playing career at the Racecourse.

On a personal note I was delighted to be honoured by the LMA by being chosen by them as the Manager of the Season for the Third Division. It really was one of those occasions when I felt I was accepting an award on behalf of the entire club, let alone the team. Without the sterling work of everyone from the coaching staff to the canteen staff, the ticket office workers to the groundsmen Wrexham could well have sunk without trace at that point. That we had won promotion and given the dedicated staff, supporters and entire town something to smile about again meant everything to me.

Four games unbeaten, including three wins, was a great way to start the new 2003/04 season. I was especially pleased with a fabulous 3-2 victory at Hillsborough against Sheffield Wednesday who would finish below us that season, something I found mind-boggling given the size and stature of the two clubs.

I'd only managed to bring in two players over the summer, both on free transfers, inevitably. Experienced striker Chris Armstrong, who had begun his career at the Racecourse Ground in 1988 before going on to success with Millwall, Crystal Palace and Spurs, returned, although I used him as the third man, substituting for Lee Jones and fellow new arrival Chris Llewellyn, from Norwich City.

Armstrong's career had gone of the rails after he'd tested positive for cannabis in 1995, but I felt he deserved a chance after a failed spell at Bolton. He did well for me and stayed a couple of season.

To say I was delighted to capture the two players was an understatement. "If you had told me last May that we would be in a position to sign both Chris Llewellyn and now Chris Armstrong, well I'd have put you in a straight-jacket," I told the club's official website!

A few weeks into the season the club's finances began to be a problem once again. The first we got wind of it was when the staff were paid late. The PFA were called in and assisted us with a short term loan to ensure the players got their money, as is common with clubs struggling to pay wages in this day and age. I think the PFA is super in times of crisis such as that. Through all the dealings I've had with them as a manager they have been first class. I've never had a problem with them, which, anecdotally, is not what I believe other managers have experienced. I can only go on my own.

The PFA most certainly has a place in the modern game, just as the LMA has. I do think that they are new roles within the sport compared to their original reasons for coming into existence, but generally as a manager I found that if you speak to them they understand the issues you face as a manager and want to help because it can generally only be in the interest of their members. I had had occasion to talk to them in the past when I'd had problems with players and they knew that I would not be in touch with them unless I had exhausted every possibility. They know what I'm like, and if I'm having a problem with a player it's generally the player who has tried my patience just that bit too far. They will then deal with him quietly and he'll come back to me with his tail between his legs.

This situation at Wrexham was several notches up from an individual contract dispute, however, and it would not end there. Over the campaign players and staff were paid late on no fewer than four occasions, shifting the focus of what was going on at the club firmly off-field.

Amidst all this three consecutive wins in December over Peterborough, Stockport and Blackpool, saw us, unbelievably, climb into the play-off places. Perhaps unrealistically fan expectation had grown so much that we were expected to keep this level of form up despite everything else that was occurring. It didn't help when I lost one of my better performers of the campaign, Shaun Pejic, to a hairline fracture of his leg early in the first home game of the New Year against Sheffield Wednesday. That ended Shaun Pejic's season early and gave me defensive headaches.

That forced me to use a young lad called Craig Morgan, who had really impressed me in youth team games. I remember the first time I saw him I ran over to Joey Jones on the touchline at Colliers Row and said, "Who the hell is that?!" I really thought we had a great find on our hands and that I could make him into a top notch centre-half. He was only 16 at that point. I gave him his debut with occasional substitute outings and he scored a last minute equaliser at Cambridge in his third game in October 2002, making him the youngest goalscorer in the club's history. But Craig didn't quite cut the mustard as yet. During a 1-6 capitulation at Peterborough, I was forced to substitute him, but lack of funds to bring anyone else in meant I would still use him intermittently until the end of the campaign, even though he clearly wasn't ready yet.

I had doubts too about Craig's desire to make it as a professional footballer. I was trying to push him to do things and Craig thought he knew better a lot of the time and we did have our disagreements. The grapevine would be jingling, saying, "oh, Denis and Craig are not getting on they are arguing". Yes, I would be pulling him in. I wasn't happy always with the way he lived, ate or partied, but he was a young lad. He was still learning his trade and always had a lot of confidence in his own ability. He learned and improved and is now playing consistently now for Wales and Peterborough. He's married now with a kid, which I think has really settled him down, but he had to weather that baptism of fire and some very difficult days early in his career to emerge on the other side a stronger player and personality. That he did shows the enormous credit that should be shown to him.

That defeat at London Road put paid to any lingering thoughts of a push for the play-offs. We began to show some disturbing signs of coming off second best in too many games as we drifted towards the end of the campaign perfectly safe in mid-table, but with only two wins in our last 12 games. We also retained the FAW Premier Cup, defeating Rhyl 4-1 in the final, but that was of little consequence given the bigger fish being fried. It all boiled down to one thing – money. The club hadn't got any, and neither, it appeared did the chairman, Mr Guterman. Wages were late again and there were whispers of the Racecourse Ground being repossessed.

In the midst of a growing storm of protest, Mark Guterman resigned and we discovered that he'd had a silent backer all along – a guy named Alex Hamilton, who became chairman in his stead. Hamilton, a 78% shareholder, was a property developer and quickly made it clear that his plans for the club were to put it into liquidation, wiping away the reported £3 million debt around his neck and take control of the Racecourse Ground to use as prime development land. The club's own chairman was attempting to get the club evicted from the stadium. The ins and outs of the entire situation are intricate are fraught with potential for Mr Hamilton to recourse to the law if I am not careful, but it became apparent that he had sold the ground to a separate company, owned by himself, immediately on becoming the club's chairman and Wrexham FC were now on a years' notice to quit the historic ground.

The natives had grown extremely restless and at the end of this most disturbing of seasons began to voice their concerns ever more loudly over the situation, which had now become so public that it just would not go away. It had deeply affected the squad and saw the supporters organising meetings to debate the future of the club and, for the last home game against Brighton, a revolution.

It was 9 May 2004 and a large group of Wrexham fans organised a 'red card protest' against Guterman and Hamilton's actions. Their idea was to show their disgust at the manner of their dealings with the club by simultaneously raising the cards in a show of unity to send him a message 'Get Out'. The warm glow of promotion had faded many months before. It was now all out war between supporters and chairman.

My problem was I was supposed to be getting my players ready to play a football match, while all this was being played out in the local media, who were naturally loving it. The night before the game, which was in itself of little consequence as we could only finish 12th or 13th and visitors Brighton were safely in the play-offs and wanting to ensure they picked up no injuries, I gave a TV interview in which I gave my opinion that supporters should not mount such a protest at a game. It was distracting for the players and myself and would be better done afterwards, or at another time altogether. I was sympathetic with the supporters and I could understand people wanting to protest, but I was trying to prepare my players mentally and all this kerfuffle was not good for the team.

My outburst attracted a lot of protest from fans who read into it that I was supporting Guterman. That wasn't the case. In fact I was neither showing support for him or for the supporters against him. I just wanted the discussion removed from the time surrounding the match. People said to me, "well, that's when we all get together" and that's all well and good, but it caused no end of problems for me doing the job of giving them a team to support. The other stuff I was fighting every day, I could do without it on match days. I still get comments about that now, and I think it's unfair as what I actually said seems to have been misconstrued.

Irrespective of my wishes the protest went ahead. Ironically Brighton and Hove Albion knew exactly what we were going through after almost going to the wall themselves and having saved themselves from relegation to the Conference on a tension-riddled final day a few years earlier by drawing at Hereford. Red cards were handed out to all 4,500 supporters attending the game and the Brighton fans even joined in the showing of the cards and the derision tumbling from the dissenting element among the Wrexham faithful in the stands by chanting "Sack the board"!

I was mightily annoyed by what had gone on and refused to discuss the protest after the game, which might have been a mistake because it just fuelled the feeling amongst fans that I was siding with Guterman. I wasn't. I was just fed up with the situation.

Brighton won comfortably 2-0 to complete a perfectly wretched day and a very difficult season. Somehow we'd managed our way through it with the club intact, but there were splits everywhere and I knew it was not something that was going to go away.

******

If the 2003/04 season was challenging in almost every way, then the year that followed it knocked spots off it. I thought I had experienced just about everything there was going in professional football in my 22 years in management plus 15 as player, but I was wrong.

The 2004/05 season was the most harrowing, distressing footballing time of my life. It does not compare, of course, with the tragedies that engulfed the families of Paul Shardlow, Martin Aldridge, Keith Walwyn or Tim Carter, but for me personally it was the most trying time of my professional career.

I had centre-half Shaun Pejic back fully fit after his leg break, and he impressed in a 3–2 win in the first round of the LDV Vans trophy at Notts County in September 2004 and I said so in a post-match interview to the press. "Pejic was immense again, his defensive header in the last minute was worth a goal. He's come on again this season – that's good as we are expecting boys to do men's jobs."

We'd begun the campaign well considering all the problems which had blighted the club and continued to do so. Four wins from the first seven games left us in 7th position by the time of that visit to Meadow Lane, and we carried on through the early rounds of the LDV Vans trophy winning at home to Stockport 2-0 and at big rivals Chester 1-0, thanks to a first goal by new arrival Juan Ugarte.

But the money troubles were never far from the surface and it began to affect the team again as wages went unpaid. We won just one of the next 11 league games and dropped down to 17th after a 1-3 home reverse to Bristol City.

The battle to save the club from extinction at the hands of Hamilton was well and truly on. Directors Dave Bennett and Dave Griffiths were two men who had been on the board all the way through from Pryce Griffiths' reign and under Guterman and they truly had the club's best interests at heart. They fought Hamilton tooth and nail and I have to say that without them there would not be a football club in Wrexham. They brought lawyers in early on, out of their own pocket, to see if there were any legal loopholes with which we could challenge Hamilton.

At this point financial matters began to take a grave turn for the worse. Scottish Power-Manweb decided to turn off the power off at the Racecourse after "failing to resolve issues" with the League One club, although it was restored a few hours later. I was in the emergency board meeting which followed the discovery of this fairly key problem. The meeting was heated, unlike the boardroom. But then Hamilton made a mistake. He wanted to bring his secretary onto the board so that he would have equal voting rights and tried to bully it through, but the other directors, Dave Bennett and Dave Griffiths, who had stood up to him, were threatening to take him to High Court, something which they subsequently did do. In a moment of anger, Hamilton grabbed a scrap of paper and wrote out his resignation, flinging it down on the table as he stomped out. Alex Hamilton had resigned from Wrexham, losing many of the key rights which that status had conferred upon him. He did, however, retain his 78% share in the club, but it gave us a window of opportunity within which to work.

If Griffiths and Bennett hadn't have riled Hamilton then he would not have got angry and made that mistake. It bought their lawyers time to act. It was decided that the only way to save the club was to put it into administration. This news was met by a vociferous outcry from supporters, who hastily put together a bid via the Supporters Trust to make Hamilton an offer the club. He turned that and a subsequent offer down, but all the time, in the background, Griffiths and Bennett were working with their legal team to wrest control of the club away from Hamilton. Now with the administrator overseeing everything that went on at the club, it seemed the tide had turned in our favour. For me the two Daves are the heroes who supported me and worked so hard to save the club. They don't get enough recognition for the brilliant work they did.

Despite all this we managed a 2-1 victory at Huddersfield on 27 November 2004, although nothing could stop the inexorable process which was going on. On 3 December 2004 the club was placed in administration by the High Court in Manchester as it owed £2,600,000, including £800,000 to the Inland Revenue in unpaid taxes. Wrexham became the first Football League club to suffer a ten-point deduction under the new rule for being placed into Administration, dropping them from the middle of the League One table to the relegation zone in one fell swoop. It was a sickening blow, made all the worse for us being the first to experience this new rule being put into action. Deep down we all knew it had condemned us to relegation, but at least we had half a season to potentially avoid that disaster.

When administration came we welcomed it as it gave us protection from our creditors and allowed players to be certain that wages would be paid on time as well as vital breathing space from Hamilton. Because of the way the law dictates a business in administration is run by its appointed administrators, we knew that things would not continue the rocky course of the past two years. It was, instead, simply sink or swim. A new buyer had to be found or Wrexham would go out of business.

On the pitch, while things looked slightly perkier off it, to be honest the 10 point deduction destroyed us. It is a scenario with which we have become all too familiar in the years since. Clubs such as Leeds, Luton, Rotherham, Bournemouth and Boston have all been forced to take the legal sanctuary from their creditors which administration offers. My opinion is that the devastation of the clubs' parlous financial position is punishment enough. To deduct 10 or 15 points, as is now the rule, is far too harsh, especially when applied to the following season and compounded by other fines for not emerging form administration under new owners in a particular fashion. I understand the argument that says other clubs who do not spend outside their limitations must be allowed to compete on an even playing field, but all the points deduction actually serves to do is condemn a club to two seasons of struggle: one in the immediate aftermath of the process and then a second when the inevitable relegation follows.

As soon as it happened to us players were looking to move. It was understandable, they were worried about their livelihoods, although I tried to tell them that being in administration was better than the uncertainty which had preceded it. Before we'd suffered the deduction we'd been thinking about possible promotion as we were just four points off a play-off place following our 2-1 win at home to Stockport on 7 December, but now we not only had to play catch up on points and we had such an incredible amount of negativity around the club. The whole mind set had changed and things start going wrong and you have people realise how bad things are for them. I had a queue of people waiting to see me to voice their concerns every morning. They'd be asking, "What's going on? When are we getting paid?" It's only natural and understandable, but it wrecked the club and the team spirit. I could see so many of them thinking, 'is this the club we want to be at, or need to be at?'

I also think the deductions rule hits the wrong people. It tends to hit the fans and the players and that's unfair.

Then you've got the families and kids of the staff. The people who got you into that situation a lot of the time are not there by the time it hits and they certainly won't be around to get you out of it, but the rest of the workforce across the board are hit twice. And these people have mortgages to pay. They are not the elite of the Premier League who will have no financial worries in the future. I feel so strongly for Luton Town's new owners in the summer of 2008, led by TV presenter Nick Owen. They were punished to the tune of 30 points before they had even been in charge of a match. How can that be right?

We had a problem because our administrators, understanding and excellent at their jobs as they were, would not let us sign any new players or re-sign existing ones to anything longer than a six month contract. No player wants to do that. They want the security of at least a season. In the end I had to run to the PFA explain the problem and between us we managed to work out a solution to get it up to 12 months with the PFA guaranteeing the wages for the second half of the contract.

The irony of it all was that we would not have had to go into administration had I been able to sell my star right-winger Carlos Edwards. Carlos was a tremendous lad, who performed the wing-back role and also played on the right-hand side of midfield when we played 4-4-2, and was attracting a lot of covetous glances from Championship clubs, Stoke City and Burnley among them. Carlos was quick, athletic and could strike the ball fiercely and accurately on the run, something which is difficult to do and brings him a good return of goals. I felt to become a top Premiership player he needed to add a couple of tricks to his game to fool better defenders, but he was at least Championship material. I knew of three or four clubs interested in him and I felt I could get a decent sum for him. I ended up negotiating with new Preston manager Billy Davies and agreed a fee of £300,000, but then Carlos went and did his ligaments whilst away on international duty with Trinidad. Apparently there was a hole in some pitch wherever they were playing and he put his foot into it and badly twisted his knee. It cost us his move and that fee would have been enough to keep us going. By the time he was fit again in the summer of 2005 his contract had expired and he moved to Luton for nothing. That was gutting.

While I was losing one international star, another one, striker Juan Ugarte began to make his name by simply going on a wonderful scoring spree. In all he scored 23 goals that season, 17 in the league and 6 as we advanced in the LDV Vans trophy. Ugarte had come to us because his friend Xabi Alonso had recently joined Liverpool and he'd come over to try his luck in England. He was a stocky, out-and-out goalscorer, prone to being either on song or awful, but he had the same kind of predatory instinct as Martin Aldridge had shown. He'd been playing for Dorchester Town, but I had heard from Liverpool Chief Executive Rick Parry that he'd got talent so we had him up for a trial and I thought he had got something. He wasn't all that quick and wasn't particularly good in the air, his touch was reasonable, but then every time we had a five a side he scored. He was just an out-and-out goalscorer. No frills. When he had good days he'd be scoring threes and fours.

Or indeed more. In early March 2005 Ugarte pulled off the incredible feat of scoring five goals against Hartlepool United away from home in an amazing 6-4 victory. It was just the most incredible game, with us pegging back an early goal to lead three times before pulling two goals clear thanks to Ugarte's first four strikes and one from Mark Jones. Juan's fifth goal sealed the win and turned him into a Wrexham legend in one afternoon.

He could be so frustrating on other days. I can remember a game at Chesterfield and Kev Russell was on at me all first half to get him off because he was giving the ball away so badly. But I left him on, believing that you need your goalscorers out there for when the chances come and sure enough Juan then went and scored a goal. After another five minutes Kev came to me again, "Gaffer, OK, he's scored now. Can we get him off?" I waited again, and sure enough he scored again! It's a knack. He just found it easy to put the ball in the net. It didn't happen every week I tried that though! The lad was a goalscorer and you take gambles with your goalscorers because they win you games.

Juan's incredible run of form propelled us to the Northern Area final of the LDV Vans Trophy over two legs against Oldham Athletic. With the final being held at the Millennium Stadium, the Welsh national stadium, I was so eager to give the beleaguered Wrexham fans a great day out. The first leg was at Boundary Park and Juan had one of his fantastic night as he scored a hat-trick in a 5-3 win. We led 5-1 at one point, before two late goals brought Oldham back into it. The home leg was less of a worry than we thought as we kept Oldham on a tight rein with a good defensive display and won the game 1-0 through a Chris Llewellyn goal to reach the final 6-3 on aggregate.

Given that all this was happening while we remained steadfastly stuck in the relegation zone of Division Two, it was pretty amazing and the reaction of the fans was incredible. It was a tiny silver lining which altered the gloomy perception of the clouds surrounding the club. For some reason we could not convert that form into league points. Our form was up and down and it became obvious that we would not be able to recover from the ten point deduction. In the end, with any faint hopes of staying up ended by a 2-1 defeat to Brentford in our final home game, we finished on 43 points. Those extra 10 points would have seen us finish 19th, avoid relegation and send the MK Dons, who had 51 points, down instead.

Relegation was not so devastating this time around because there was nowhere else for my emotions to take me. The heart had been ripped out of the season by the points deduction and what had happened subsequently was entirely predictable. Try as we might we could not prevent the inevitable.

It seemed that the LDV Vans Trophy provided a release for my players and they enjoyed the cup run immensely. When it came to preparing for the final we had to take the lads away because the euphoria, I think as a complete opposite to all the doom and gloom which had surrounded the place for years, was overwhelming. We needed to keep them calm and focussed.

Come the morning of Sunday 10 April the Wrexham fans outnumbered their Southend counterparts in the 36,000 crowd by two to one. I don't think I've ever seen so many flags and banners at a game before or since. They were everywhere 'Ugarte Is King', 'Abertillery Reds' and even one from Sunderland fans proudly displaying the legend 'Denis Smiths Red and White Army'. That took me back!

The game was played in a great atmosphere, but it wasn't much to write home about. Southend, in their second consecutive LDV Vans Trophy final, both of which ended in defeat, threatened early on when Mark Bentley brought fine saves out of the on loan Ben Foster in our goal.

The game drifted along with only one real moment of excitement when Bentley's header hit his own crossbar and somehow we failed to put the ball into Darryl Flahavan's net in the ensuing scramble. The match ended goalless and we went into extra-time.

I trusted my goalscorer Juan Ugarte once again. He'd done nothing all game. In fact he'd been bloody awful. Chris Llewellyn had been doing all the donkey work up front and a couple of times Juan had been put through on goal and he hadn't even managed to get his shot away. He also should have squared the ball to a completely unmarked Llewellyn, but failed to do so. I knew it was one of those frustrating days for him then.

Everyone was on at me to get him off, but a pretty uneventful game ended up 0-0 at full time. I knew it would take one moment to decide a game like this and. I'd left him on before and he'd scored and so I felt I should do it on this biggest of all stages. Actually the main reason he remained on the pitch into extra-time was because I'm thinking he is a good penalty taker if it goes to penalties.

But then, from a corner headed on by Dennis Lawrence, the ball dropped to him a couple of yards out and, thank you very much, Juan stuck it into the back of the net. It was a classic striker's goal – a crowded goalmouth and it fell to him. For some reason it happens. There's little rhyme or reason. Goalscorers like Ugarte get the breaks. And when they come along they stick them into the net. That's also the difference between a centre-half or goalkeeper and goalscorers. A striker can be awful for 89 minutes but score and everybody loves them. A keeper or defender can be brilliant at the back but then make one small mistake and you're a plonker.

That goal won us the cup as it finished Southend, who then had to throw everything at us. We lapped up the balls they threw forward with Dennis Lawrence immense and right at the end we broke away and Llewellyn's shot was palmed aside by Flahavan, but Darren Ferguson prodded the ball home to score a deserved goal. I though he was our Man of the Match and for him to do it in front of his dad, Sir Alex, on such a big stage was fantastic for the lad, who must have found the shadow of his father difficult and frustrating at times. As captain Darren picked up the trophy and the scenes that followed were ones of true joy and emotion, given all that we'd been through over the past few years. I can't begin to describe what that achievement means to me. To win promotion the previous season had been incredible. To lift a trophy whilst in administration brought tears to my eyes. And I don't cry easily.

As Wrexham's first national trophy in their 133-year history it was a massive thing for the club to win. Not only that, brought a £250,000 windfall which helped the administrators massively.

As well as the glory of victory, the final was such a great day out for everybody associated with the club and another one followed as we toured the trophy around Wrexham. Everybody loved it. For me it took some of the pain away.

Chapter Twenty-One

DRAGONS' DEN

Wrexham Football Club, 133 years old and with a proud heritage and tradition, is a focal point for the whole of north Wales. Far more than just a provincial football club, it galvanises the supporters who are tied by their heartstrings to it, whether they follow the fortunes of the team religiously, or on an ad hoc basis, and focusses minds on what football means to this area. Back in the summer of 2005 it was on the verge of being taken away; destroyed by an arrogant man who believed he could make a fast buck out the legacy of such a community asset. Fortunately many people in the area refused to lie down and let greed win out without a fight. The battle was well and truly on to save Wrexham FC.

There were two strands to the supporters' stance. Firstly that every legal avenue be examined in order to upset Hamilton's plans, precisely as Dave Bennett and Dave Griffiths were doing, and secondly that the community rise up to decry what he was doing publicly at every possible juncture. For the first, a challenge to his right to serve notice on the club that had used the Racecourse Ground as its home for well over a century was issued in court. And for the second banners, leaflets, marches and demonstrations were held to bring to the forefront of the local news agenda the plight of the club.

In October 2005, the first chink of light emerged in favour of the survival of the club. Birmingham High Court decided that Alex Hamilton's company CrucialMove had improperly acquired the freehold of the Racecourse Ground and confirmed legal ownership of the stadium lay with the administrators. Hamilton was not the type to take this news lying down and he took this to the Appeal Court in London, but it ruled on 14 March 2006 that the stadium must remain in the hands of the club's administrators, although the stadium would be subject to a legal 'charge' in CrucialMove's favour amounting to the £300,000 it paid for the freehold of the ground and other costs.

Hamilton had to admit defeat and relinquish control. It was, as Joint Administrator Steve Williams said, "a momentous day" for Wrexham FC. On 30 April 2006 the Administrators reached an agreement with local car dealer Neville Dickens, and business partner Geoff Moss, subject to agreement by the shareholders and creditors (which was achieved on 30 May), for Mr Dickens to take over control of the club and all its assets. Had the club still been in administration by the 3 June then Wrexham would have automatically been expelled from the League because of their financial situation. Thankfully that was averted and every Wrexham fan must thank Neville for that, just as they should thank the Wrexham Supporters Trust and the Wrexham Supporters Club, and all their members for continually pressing the case in the media.

I knew both the new people who had taken over very well. Nev I've known for 30 years because I used to buy cars and sell them over at Wrexham when I was a player at Stoke and he was just starting his garages over there. We weren't close but I've known him quite a few years and I still get on okay with him. Equally I still do with Geoff. I thought they were exactly the right people to take over, but everybody seems to think I shouldn't.

There were a few corks popped and drinks downed to celebrate, but I knew that although this victory had been won, it would be a hollow one if we could not prevent the further tragedy of relegation from the Football League which now stared us in the face.

We'd dealt with whoever we had to deal with to keep the club ticking along over the last six months of torpor, but some of the people who came and knocked on the door wanting to run the club had to be seen to be believed. They would turn up at the training ground in 4 x 4's and blacked out windows. Not dodgy-looking at all!

Dickens and Moss hoped to wipe out the club's £4 million debts through the commercial redevelopment of land surrounding the Racecourse stadium, although that would prove to be more difficult than they initially thought.

As we moved towards exiting administration I felt we'd actually benefited a lot from having the two men, Dave Acland and Steve Williams, running its affairs alongside us. We'd streamlined lots of procedures and made plenty of cost savings which would only stand the club in rude health as a business. And it had not been at the cost of the vast majority of the squad. Sure there had been a high turnover of players, but that will always happen at a club such as Wrexham irrespective of the dire nature of the club's finances. I got on with both the administrators really well. Dave Acland was a Jack the lad and into football. I could relate to him. The other one, Steve Williams, was great, but he was the accountant and not interested in football particularly.

I'd convinced the administrators we could make money better if we were successful as a team, plus the players would be worth more. That was my sales pitch to try and keep the players together and give myself a chance of competing. It had won us the LDV Vans Trophy, but we'd slipped out of Division Two.

As we slumped down the table the previous season, Steve would say to me, "if you get offered another job I'd go."

"I don't want to go," I'd say. But he was only telling me how it was. "This place may not be here in six months," he'd say.

I did, in fact, get offered another job – to manage Blackpool – but I didn't go. I wanted to see the whole process through. I felt it would be wrong to leave the players I'd brought into the club in the lurch by moving on when they were in administration. Simon Grayson was later appointed to the Bloomfield Road job and managed to get the club promoted into the Championship.

At least the utter turmoil around Wrexham was nearing an end, but would it be in time to save it from extinction?

******

Amidst all this some football was being played and the battle was just as intense on the pitch as it was off it. 2005/06 started with a 2-0 victory over Boston United, and we did OK, considering all that was still going on around us. Division Two had improved in quality since our last visit and we had experienced a massive turnover of players once again. We'd lost Chris Llewellyn, Juan Ugarte, Lee Jones and Paul Edwards, plus several others who had all moved on to pastures new. In their place I'd brought in strikers Jon Walters from Hull City and Lee McEvilly from Accrington, centre-half Dave Bayliss from Luton, defender Lee Roche from Burnley and goalkeeper Mike Ingham from Sunderland. We also blooded young brothers Marc and Mike Williams. The mainstays of the team were still Dennis Lawrence, Jim Whitley, Darren Ferguson and Mark Jones.

Mark had made his debut in 2003, and made a central midfield place in our 3-5-2 formation his own alongside Darren Ferguson. Mark was best there as it gave him more freedom – he'd still got defensive work to do but he was not the best defensively and he scored goals, 13 in all that season to finish as top scorer. The following season we changed to 4-4-2 because it suited the rest of the team. I'd then got to find something for him to do and I gave him a role defensively on the right hand side, but with the ability then to float in behind the front two and pick up gaps. The problem with that is you've got no width unless your full-back bombs forward. Mark can create spaces and he gives people problems and he was probably a bit wasted out there and that got me a load of stick from the fans, but I had no choice. Mark still scored goals from playing wide right for me, but I don't think he was happy there, but it really was another flag of convenience. Was I convinced it was his best position? No. Was it the best position for him in that team? Yes. Unfortunately when you are manager you are fitting people in where there is a necessity a great deal of the time.

When we defeated Cheltenham 2-0 early in September, the second and clinching goal was scored by forward Jon Walters, his first for the club. I've got a great deal of time for Jon, I think he's a great lad. He worked his socks off for me after I brought him in from Hull City when he wanted to come back and live in the north west. Jon for me was a bit like Eric Gates or Nigel Jemson, the forward who provides opportunities for his goalscoring partner. He only scored 5 goals himself, but he provided plenty of opportunities for others with his selfless running. I'm delighted he's doing well at Ipswich.

I was disappointed with the way Jon went, though when he left at the end of the season. Jon was quite within his rights as he was out of contract, but I wasn't happy that I couldn't get to speak to him or his agent over the summer to state our case for him staying with us. Some supporters think I didn't try, but I did. I wouldn't fall out with Jon, though. He did a good job for me but he moved on to Chester, which was disappointing to say the least.

Walters' strike partner was Lee McEvilly. We got him fit after a difficult time at Accrington and he was scoring goals towards the end of the previous season, which we'd somehow managed to finish in 13th position. Lee was also now out of contract and before we knew it Bradford came in for him, making him a very good financial offer, so I had to battle to keep him. There's a story behind how I held on to Lee. Bradford were pursuing their man ever more persistently. They kept upping their offers to him, while I kept talking to him about how well he would do if he stayed at Wrexham. I spent all week on the phone persuading he'd be better off remaining with us. The only problem was I was on holiday, and so Kate wasn't too happy with me to say the least. I had a huge phone bill, but we finally kept Lee which was a fantastic thing for him to choose us over Bradford. The problem was that he then broke down in training when his metatarsal snapped again. He'd had a plate in it to fix it, and that just never happens. I can't understand why it happened again. It was devastating for Lee because after that we never got him fit. He's hard work to get fit anyway as he's a big lump. Try as we might we couldn't get him right and it led me to wonder if mentally McEvilly wanted it badly enough. He had the ability, but it's hard work to make it as a professional footballer.

Four wins in six in October got us to the heady heights of 7th position, but we couldn't sustain that level of form and spent the rest of the season fluctuating between 15th and 10th. We had a boost from the arrival on loan of striker Matt Derbyshire from Blackburn Rovers, but it was only brief respite. We knew Matt was decent and he proved he'd got that goalscoring instinct – right place at the right time. 10 goals in 16 games made him a big success for us. We were sorry to see him go back.

There was great excitement when the goalscoring hero of our LDV Vans triumph, Juan Ugarte, re-joined us on loan from Crewe in October 2005. However he broke down with a recurrence of his old knee injury and a fresh, but associated hamstring injury. That was very disappointing for everyone. I often think if he was fit enough and was playing I'd still be at Wrexham for a few years because he could score goals. But it didn't happen that way. Juan scored in his first game and got injured! Nothing you can do about that is there?

As 2005/06 came to a close, despite Matt Derbyshire's goals, we won just one of the final nine games to finish 13th. That was relegation form and we had done very well to stave it off until the back end of things. However, it did not bode well for the next campaign. I would have to come up with some more finds plucked from nowhere, and fast.

Our penultimate match of the campaign was a very poignant one for me. It pitched my current, struggling club Wrexham against the team I had managed on two separate occasions in the second tier of English football Oxford United. Oxford were in desperate straits. They had to win this match and their final game of the season and hope other results all went their way to avoid relegation from the Football League. We drew 1-1, sending Oxford out of the Football League, which was very disappointing and I am often asked by Oxford fans if I could have helped them out a bit that day. The simple answer to that it is not in my make up to ask players not to try. Can you imagine? The players would never have trusted me again and it is not in the British players' make up to throw a game. Oxford went down to join another of my former clubs York City in the Conference, to which they had been relegated in 2004. Somehow I had kept ailing Wrexham in the Football League while two of my former clubs, who I'd left in higher divisions had slumped into the non-league. The irony was not lost on me.

******

The 2006/07 season could not have begun in a more positive light. After all those years of struggle, on 4 August Wrexham emerged from the 18-month period of administration. We celebrated the news on the pitch as we went eight games unbeaten, including a 4-1 away win against Championship side Sheffield Wednesday in the League Cup first round.

In the second round we drew Birmingham City and scored first through Chris Llewellyn. We went on to take the Championship side to extra time. I remember standing in the technical area that night after geeing my players up ready for the extra half hour when Birmingham manager Steve Bruce called on one of his substitutes to warm up prior to coming on. It was Danish international striker Niklaus Bendtner. Heaven knows what he was worth or was on basic salary per week, certainly many thousands of pounds.

We, on the other hand, were sticking 19 year-old centre-half Gareth Evans on up front in a bid to win the game. His salary? £100 a week!

We'd actually had a chance to win the game right on time, a really good chance. It fell to Josh Johnson and he should have scored. Instead Birmingham, and their all-star substitutes, went on to win 4-1 after extra time. And yes Bendtner scored.

We also played quite well at Derby in the FA Cup third round, having beaten Stevenage and then Scunthorpe to get there in what was a great cup run for us. Again one of Arsene Wenger's protégées did for us as Arturo Lupoli hit a hat-trick in a 3-1 win for the Rams.

But in early September, with the usual summer influx of new faces bedding in together well, plugging the gaps left by the departures of Dennis Lawrence, Jon Walters and right-back Lee Roche, and the recurrence of the metatarsal injury to Lee McEvilly, we were sitting nicely in the play-off places. Unfortunately it all fell apart in a shock 5-0 defeat at Accrington Stanley on 13 September 2006. That was quickly followed by a 5-2 defeat at Stockport County. Both of these teams were struggling at the foot of the table and we never fully recovered from them.

It was strange. Despite the fact that the worst of the financial problems were over and the spectre of administration had been removed, it now felt as if the whole club was heaving a huge sigh of relief and relaxing so much that concentration wavered. It began a long relegation battle for us and it felt as if we were running in quicksand. I had to find ways of breaking the cycle that saw us eight out of eleven games from those defeats to slump alarmingly to 19th position.

We were really struggling with injuries. In that game at Stockport, for example, I had to use four teenagers. Not only were many players coming into the side inexperienced, but they also hadn't played much together. We'd begun the campaign with a completely remodelled strikeforce for the fourth season in a row. Having lost Jon Walters on a free transfer and with Matt Derbyshire having gone back to Blackburn I re-signed Chris Llewellyn who had spent one season at Hartlepool. Chris was in inspired form in the first half of that season and scored his first international goal for Wales against Liechtenstein in November 2006 playing alongside his ex-Norwich City strike partner Craig Bellamy. I bought and sold Chris Llewellyn twice at Wrexham, showing how highly I rated him. He went to Hartlepool for £100,000 and we got him back for £10,000 or so. He was a fearsome sight for defenders with the ball at his feet and he was capable of running teams ragged. He would give you full commitment no matter what. The funny thing for me was that he wasn't that popular with the supporters. For me he was one of our best and most consistent players. He was accused of being one of my favourites, but he was just so good and so versatile. I thought he should have been playing in the Championship. He was that good.

The one criticism I would give Chris is that he didn't score enough goals for his ability. Seeing the way he finished in training compared to what he produced in games was disappointing. That's been his let down. Chris should be scoring 20 goals a season with his ability.

In the search for goals, we had another opportunity to sign Juan Ugarte in November 2006. That was necessary because Neil Roberts, who had started the season well with Llewellyn up front, injured his ankle. That was a major blow as Neil was also our skipper. I knew it would be a gamble because Ugarte wasn't fit, but all the indicators and all the tests we did on him said he was going to be OK. I wasn't going to give him the two year contract Juan wanted, but apparently he had got offers from other clubs, so we took a gamble. I think he'd possibly done too much work on his thighs building them up so his hamstrung wasn't contracting correctly. He never really got going which was a shame. Despite coming on late on when we won at Scunthorpe and hitting the post with a free-kick, Juan lasted just three games before he was crocked again.

As we sought some sort of spark to get us going again I brought in several loanees, one of which was a lad called Maheta Molango from Brighton. I soon realised my mistake. It was a shame because he'd got pace and size and was a lovely, intelligent lad. He spoke Italian, French and German. Initially he looked the part as a footballer too, was quick and good in the air, but after a couple of games I realised I'd made a blunder.

The problem I had was that every which way I turned nothing was working for me. The loanees were injured or not good enough and most of the backbone of the promotion side of four years earlier had gone. One still remained, central midfielder Darren Ferguson. Darren is as much of a character as his father. If he was unhappy on the field he'd let the other players know in the dressing room at half or full-time. At times he caused too much bloody havoc. But you do need that kind of character.

Now Darren has taken the first steps along the road to perhaps emulating his famous father in management at Peterborough and has already won one promotion for the POSH. That all began towards the end of his career with me. I gave him some coaching responsibility and he lapped it up. He's pretty argumentative, you might not be surprised to hear, but he is also sure of his own mind. His man management skills straight away proved to be good. And from my point of view he's also proven another key point in that he's chosen one of the best coaches in the country to be his right-hand man, my former assistant, the loyal and trustworthy Kevin Russell.

It is going to be a hard job for Darren to repeat anything like his dad's success. Sir Alex had a lot harder life than Darren has ever had because of his the comfort his father's success brought, but Darren is very single minded. He also hates losing, both of which traits sound familiar when mentioned in conjunction with the name Ferguson – but if he does half as well as his dad, he'll have a great career. Everybody is going to compare him with Alex, which is not really fair, but it's absolutely inevitable.

I remember one incident in the Wrexham dressing room in January 2006. I was missing for one home game because I was having an operation on my hip, which had flared up on me. For that match I asked Brian Carey, who was by then on the coaching staff having recently retired, to manage the side. Wrexham lost and he and Darren ended up having a right falling out in front of the players over getting beaten. When I returned, Brian told me that he had hated every minute of being in charge. For my part I thought he would have handled it far better than he did, hence my reasoning behind handing him the reins.

"I never want to do this job again," he told me. "Not even for a million pounds"!

Darren was bullish about the incident when I disciplined him. He'd known I was not going to accept his behaviour. Whether it was his fault or Brian's, he knew I had put somebody in charge who had my authority and he'd challenged it. I had to take the captaincy off him. He was unhappy but he accepted it. He's a man. He may blow his top, but in the end if he knows you're right he'll hold his hands up. Much like his old man. If he thinks he's right he'll chip on and chip on and chip on. I think he learned that day that if you're enforcing something you've got to be 100% right, otherwise you're going to lose. That was something I'd learnt as a kid. Since the age of 11 I have been strong enough to do my own thing and believe in myself.

Injuries played a large part in the downturn. Shaun Pejic had missed four months of the 2005/06 season after tearing cruciate knee ligaments. On his return the partnership he formed at centre-back with Steve Evans looked as if it could be the answer to the loss of the talismanic Dennis Lawrence, who we'd missed so badly since his move to Swansea.

Evans was an interesting case. People don't realise that playing centre-half is ultimately about brains. It's what I've tried to teach all the centre-halves I've had. Sbragia and John MacPhail at York, the Oxford three: Matt Elliott, Darren Purse and Phil Gilchrist. Then at Wrexham I took Evans out of the League of Wales from TNS and he went on to play for Wales. When we picked him up Steve had won the Welsh Premier Player of the Season award for 2004/05 and made nine appearances for the Welsh semi-professional side. In February 2006, he impressed for the Saints in an FAW Premier Cup semi-final against us, scoring an equaliser in extra-time to force the game into penalties. I signed him on a two-year deal in June 2006 and he was now becoming a real towering strength at the heart of our defence. He'd scored on his home debut in a 3–0 win against Grimsby Town, but got himself sent-off for two bookings against rivals Chester City. Evans's form was so impressive he made his international debut for Wales in a friendly against Liechtenstein in November 2006 and was called up again for the game against Northern Ireland in February 2007. I really thought he could press on and make a regular place his own, but sad to say at the moment he is not in the side and doesn't seem to be progressing as I expected him to.

A couple of wins before Christmas kept the side's heads above the relegation waters, but the team was looking tired and in need of some major surgery. My problem was I didn't think I was going to be given the time necessary to fix it.

******

Geoff Moss and Neville Dickens should receive only credit for the feat they achieved in wresting control of the club away from Alex Hamilton in July 2006. But just a few weeks later I could feel they were getting cold feet. They had lost their financial partner in the proposed redevelopment of the car park, next door neighbours North East Wales Institute of Higher Education, and were beginning to get edgy when I was talking to them about the future of the club. Without the development they did not have any cash to finance the club or players.

I think, as happens normally when people come in to an existing venture, they had looked at the club and made some decisions. It was plain to me that their decision not to offer me a contract straight away was significant. They were making excuses at first, they were still trying to sort this, that and the other out. I was thinking, like anybody taking over a new business, especially when somebody has been as powerful as I was at the time, they might perhaps want a change.

I was disappointed in the end about how they went about it. The pair called a meeting in October 2006 and we talked everything through, but there was still no offer of a contract. I knew then it was probably all over and that they had decided they wanted to do things differently. The problem they had was that my team were on a cup run and doing well in the league, but from the October meeting I knew that was it.

Even so it took another three months for the axe to finally be wielded, and throughout that time the team's form suffered. In January 2007 I was relieved of my duties as manager of Wrexham after five and a half emotional, turbulent and incredible years in charge. I was disappointed and I still think they were wrong to get rid of me. I've got nothing against either Geoff or Neville. They thought, as businessmen, that was the way to do it, to get rid of the old and bring in the new and that's why I was now heading for the door. That happens in our business all too often. I think I'd got to the stage where perhaps I'd got too much to say and too much power and I can accept that. I'd been around in management for 25 years, knew the ropes and could read the signs. I had been able to tell for some time that the axe blade was being sharpened.

My final game in charge was a 1-3 defeat at home to Accrington, with Josh Johnson scoring. I was dismissed on 11 January 2007. Wrexham stood 18th in Division Three.

To give them their due Geoff and Neville had me in and sat me down and explained their thoughts, telling me that they intended to give the job to Brian Carey. Interestingly they hadn't actually asked him yet! In fact they told me they wanted Brian to work in tandem with Joey Jones. It just shows that they hadn't done their home work as I had known for years that Joey only wanted to work with the kids and reserves.

In fact as well as Joey, I was fairly sure that Brian Carey wouldn't want the job either, and so asked the board if I could have some time to talk to him about the scenario. I was right, Brian's first reaction, as with most football people in those circumstances, was to say, "Denis, if you are going then I am too." People don't realise the loyalty that exists within coaching staff at a club.

It was a very laudable reaction, but I told Brian that he had to stay and take the job. You don't often get an opportunity fall in your lap to manage a football club and you have to take advantage as I had done all those years ago at York.

I talked Brian into it. Whether I did him any favours or not I don't know. Brian had kids and a mortgage and so accepted the post on a trial basis to the end of the season because it provided for his family as much as for footballing reasons. Where I thought Moss and Dickens had made a big mistake was in not just getting rid of me but by also dismissing my coach Kevin Russell. It was strange because that left Brian with pretty much no support. He'd never done the job before and Kevin could easily have stayed on and helped him, but they moved him on too, and he soon found employment with Darren Ferguson over at Peterborough United. I tried to give Brian what help I could by speaking to him once a week or more on the phone as the season boiled to a climax.

As it was, after a very sticky start, Brian finally steered the side to safety by defeating relegation rivals Boston United 3-1 on the last day, thanks to late goals by Llewellyn and Proctor. To be honest they were always going to stay up. I knew a couple of months before the end that Boston were going to go as they had massive financial problems, on a par with those we had suffered ourselves and now come through, and so would be forced into administration and receive a consequent points deduction. That happened as they fell 1-3 behind late on during the last game of the season at the Racecourse as Wrexham survived.

Since my departure from Wrexham I've often been asked if I would have been able to avert the slump towards the relegation places had I stayed. The simple answer is yes, I think we'd have finished about 7th or 8th off bottom that season. Whether I could have kept the club afloat in the 2007/08 season, when they slid inexorably out of the Football League, I am not so sure. It would have all depended on whether money would have come into the team so we could have started building.

I took as a compliment an enquiry in the summer of 2008 I had from a person who shall remain nameless, who was interested in taking control of Wrexham from Moss and Dickens, who by now were struggling to keep the club going. This mystery investor was offering me the opportunity to go on the Board if they bought the club, but I told them I would be happy to go back as manager, but not on the board. At Board level you put a lot of money in and then lose it all just for the privilege of getting abused! I've done it once at Oxford and I am not going to go down that road again. The takeover didn't come off anyway, so I still await my return to football.

Chapter Twenty-Two

THE 1,000 CLUB

My final stats as manager of Wrexham, I think, make interesting reading. Under my stewardship we played 278 games, won 101, drew 68 and lost 109. In other words we were about 50/50 across the five and a half years of my stay. Considering that all of them were under severe financial restrictions and that three of them were in administration I'm very proud to have recorded such numbers.

I like to think I left Wrexham, like all my clubs, in a far better state than when I found it, despite all the trials and tribulations along the way. It never gives me any pleasure when my former clubs fall from grace after I have battled so hard and so long to keep them on an even keel, or even push them forwards, often against a rising tide. All I can do is point out my beliefs that barely any of them have actually progressed by opting to dispense with my services. Naturally I'll claim the credit for Sunderland's progress to the FA Cup final, because it was my team. They would not return to the top flight however until another two managers had passed through the hotseat and Peter Reid took the team by the scruff of their neck and wisely used Bob Murray's megabucks – that he'd withheld from me when we needed it after gaining promotion in 1990 – to bring in the likes of Kevin Phillips and Niall Quinn. I think if Bob hadn't panicked and sacked me I would have been able to guide the team through the building of the new stadium. I truly believe that I could have brought them success before they eventually earned it with Peter at the helm.

Equally I firmly believe that West Brom turned a corner thanks to my signing of Enzo Maresca. It would take another two managers before promotion to the top flight was finally achieved, and even then they have become a yo-yo club between the top two divisions. Could I have achieved more sustained success at the Hawthorns had I been given the chance? The truth is that I would only have been able to succeed had the West Brom board united behind me and what I was trying to do. I think it took them a fair few years and some upheavals to really understand what I was getting at and it was only when Gary Megson was given the backing of the funds from Maresca's sale that Albion won promotion into the top flight.

I'm not trying to claim all the credit for what happened in my absence, don't get me wrong. But I'd like to point out the role I played in turning around or keeping afloat the likes of York City, Oxford United, Bristol City and Wrexham. Three of which now languish in the Conference. That's a very sad state of affairs for me.

******

I have always chosen to move to any area in which I am managing a club to get the feel of people. It's an important aspect of being able to steer any football club along the right path that you understand the tradition, history, desires and needs of its supporters. It's also key that you are not always in a rush to get home because you only live five minutes away rather than two hours away. It allows you to do social things with fans, and feel part of the community and the club.

We have fallen in love with all the areas of England and Wales in which we have lived and always had a warm welcome from the people in each place. What's lovely is that people young and old still stop me when I return to York, Sunderland, Bristol, Oxford, the West Midlands and Wrexham, wishing me all the best. Both supporters and the community at large have been superb and it was for them that I wrote this book as much as it was for myself and my family. Perhaps the nicest thing I can say is that each and every time we have moved on myself and Kate have been just so sorry to leave.

But Stoke-on-Trent has always been home and that fact was reiterated to me when my brother Graham died, prompting me to return to live in Stoke in the summer of 2008. I had missed him at the gatherings since he'd died and so Kate and I decided we'd return home. It's allowed me to indulge my love for Stoke City just in time for the club to have its best season in over a quarter of a century and win promotion to the Premier League. As part of my commentaries on BBC Radio Stoke I am supposed to remain neutral, but when the Producers told me that I said, "forget it! I'm a Stokie!!" I'm afraid any pretence of neutrality went completely out of the window over the last two or three games of the 2007/08 season. City's return to the big time under manager Tony Pulis has been very emotional for so many people in north Staffordshire. Tony is a very good manager and will hopefully stabilize the club in the top flight. The revival has been wonderful to follow, but with any luck it's the beginning of something, much as my arrival at the club as an amateur back in 1963 was for me, rather than an end.

For now it's time to enjoy my extended family. My eldest son Paul lives in York with his wife Petra. Our youngest, Tom, lives in Oxford with his partner Tash, while Becky, our daughter, is married to Chris and lives in Cornwall. Each has carved their own niche in life, Paul in business as a buyer, Tom as a financial adviser and Becky as a Family Support Worker Lead in Cornwall.

Then there are the grandchildren who will kill me if I don't give them a mention! Holly, Paul's eldest daughter, is the oldest, she'll be the next woman Prime Minister I think! Then comes Emily, who is Becky's eldest daughter – she's a good athlete and they have applied for funding for sports for gifted children at school. She can swim, run, play football and do gymnastics. Next comes Will, who is Paul's eldest son. He's a good footballer, but is also very bright academically. Izzy is our character, she's crackers. She's tiny compared with Emily, her sister, and has loads of ginger hair, which is great. She plays in goal, and is brilliant. She's got her own fan club. All the boys stand there and shout "come on carrots, you can do it carrots".

Then comes Paul's third child Joe, who is so bright he does mental arithmetic like what's 6 times 1 billion 749.3 and can give you the answer off the top of his head. Joe has already been given funds for the gifted and talented for extra tuition.

Finally, for the moment, Tom's first child, Jessica, who is going to have another brother or sister in January 2009 to complete the seven – all special to me.

******

You must be wondering if I harbour any ambitions of a return to management. Frankly it's a needless question. I would love another job. 2007/08 was the first season I was not involved in professional football as either player or manager since I signed as for Stoke. It has naturally caused me to ask myself the question, 'Is it over?'

I reached 60 years of age in November 2007 and still feel I have one more big job in me. I have been offered a couple of opportunities, but so far nothing that has truly grabbed me. I also got down to the last two for a couple of Football League jobs which came vacant over the course of that season, at Carlisle United and Swindon Town. I was not successful with either of those jobs, but I firmly believe I have still got something to offer.

In the meantime I have been keeping myself busy working as an FA Premier League Match Delegate, an important, but little-known, function which enables the smooth running of the Premier League. As the official match delegate it is my job to report on every aspect of a game to which I am appointed. In January 2008, for example, I was the delegate for Manchester United versus Newcastle United at Old Trafford, the game in which the home side thrashed the visitors 6-0 with referee Rob Styles dismissing former Red Devil Alan Smith towards the end of the game. After such a tumultuous match it is my job to immediately notify the Premier League of anything which is a major newsworthy event, or else email a report the following day on the conduct of the clubs' players and officials, the crowd and the match officials. I also have to check that the drugs testing rooms and the press areas are as they should be and make sure everything is running smoothly as far as the managers are concerned.

I also appear as a co-commentator for BBC Radio Stoke and Radio Oxford, plus write a column in the Stoke Sentinel newspaper. It's enjoyable work and keeps me in touch with many of former clubs and colleagues.

I deliver management seminars at Warwick University on behalf of the League Managers' Association and talk to some young managers such as Darren Ferguson, who as I write is beginning a season in Division One having won promotion in 2007/08. I act like a kind of mentor and sounding board and point out a lot of the practicalities of situations that these managers may not have encountered before. For instance Darren used a sports scientist at Peterborough who devised a model of how his players should ideally be training, but they'd actually forgotten to factor in that as well as playing at weekends footballers also often play on midweek evenings. When Darren told me he'd had a performance when the players told him they were "knackered", it was obvious that the sports scientist was tiring the players out, hardly ideal for winning football matches. It takes some experience for a young manager to get to grips with situations like that and pre-empt them so they don't affect the results of matches.

******

Whatever the successes, failures, joy and heartbreak along the way, the sheer enormity of the fact that I have managed my teams in over 1,000 matches is a very special achievement for me personally. I am one of just 16 men to have topped that mark, the first being Sir Matt Busby, and amongst their number are Sir Alex Ferguson, Graham Taylor, Brian Clough, Jim Smith and Dario Gradi. It's an honour to be thought of in that kind of company, men for whom I have the utmost respect.

My career has a pleasing symmetry to it in the sense that I have played for and managed seven different football clubs, just as I was one of seven children and I will now have seven grandchildren. From our family home rammed with seven children through those seven clubs – Stoke City, York City, Sunderland, Bristol City, Oxford United, West Bromwich Albion and Wrexham – to now having seven expectant faces wanting me to play with them and regale with tales of Pele, broken bones, Wembley glory and promotions against the odds, it's been a hell of a lot of fun, a lot of laughs, some pain and certainly never a dull moment.

STATISTICS

Denis Smith
Born: Stoke-on-Trent, 19 November 1947
Height: 5 ft 11 ins
Playing weight: 12 st 2 lbs

As Player

Season	Club	League	FA Cup	Lge Cup	Other	Goals
67/68	Stoke City	14	0	0	0	0
68/69	Stoke City	40	3	1	0	4
70/71	Stoke City	36	8	2	2	2
71/72	Stoke City	28	9	9	8	10
72/73	Stoke City	38+1	1	2	2	4
73/74	Stoke City	41	1	3	5	5
74/75	Stoke City	30	2	4	2	4
75/76	Stoke City	19	3	0	0	4
76/77	Stoke City	30	1	0	0	2
77/78	Stoke City	41	0	1	0	1
78/79	Stoke City	38	1	5	0	2
79/80	Stoke City	34	1	4	0	3
80/81	Stoke City	0	0	0	0	0
81/82	Stoke City	17	0	2	0	0
Total	**Stoke City**	**406+1**	**30**	**33**	**19**	**41**
81/82	York City (loan)	7	0	0	0	1
82/83	York City	30	4	2	0	4
Total	**York City**	**37**	**4**	**2**	**0**	**5**
Overall Totals		**443+1**	**34**	**35**	**19**	**46**

Honours
League Cup 1971/72
Watney Cup 1972
Promotion from Second to First Division 1978/79

As Manager

York City
(15 May 1982 - 9 June 1987)

Season			W	D	L	F	A	Pts	FA Cup	Lge Cup	FL Trophy
82/83	Div 4	7th	22	13	11	88	58	79	3rd round	1st round	N/A
83/84	Div 4	1st	21	8	7	96	39	101	2nd round	1st round	1st round
84/85	Div 3	8th	20	9	17	70	57	69	5th round	2nd round	QF
85/86	Div 3	7th	20	11	15	77	58	71	2nd round	5th round	1st round
86/87	Div 3	20th	12	13	21	55	79	49	2nd round	2nd round	2nd round
Totals			**P258**		**W120**		**D59**		**L79**		

Honours
Won Fourth Division Championship 1983/84

Sunderland
(9 June 1987 - 30 December 1991)

Season			W	D	L	F	A	Pts	FA Cup	Lge Cup	FL Trophy
87/88	Div 3	1st	27	12	7	92	48	93	2nd round	1st round	QF
88/89	Div 2	11th	16	15	15	60	60	63	3rd round	2nd round	2nd round
89/90	Div 2	6th	20	14	12	70	64	74	3rd round	5th round	1st round
90/91	Div 1	19th	8	10	20	38	50	34	3rd round	3rd round	2nd round
91/92	Div 2	17th	8	5	12	33	37	29	N/A	2nd round	
(when dismissed)											
Totals			**P229**		**W87**		**D63**		**L79**		

Honours
Won Third Division Championship 1987/88
Promotion from Second to First Division 1989/90

Bristol City
(9 March 1992 - 21 January 1993)

Season			W	D	L	F	A	Pts	FA Cup	Lge Cup	FL Trophy
91/92	Div 2	1st	5	3	5	20	20	18	N/A	N/A	N/A
92/93	Div 1	18th	7	6	12	30	48	27	3rd round	2nd round	prelim rnd
(when dismissed)											
Totals			**P48**		**W15**		**D12**		**L21**		

Oxford United
(10 September 1993 - 24 December 1997)

Season				League					FA Cup	Lge Cup	FL Trophy
			W	D	L	F	A	Pts			
93/94	Div 1	23rd	12	10	20	48	66	46	5th round	2nd round	prelim rnd
94/95	Div 2	7th	21	12	13	66	52	75	1st round	2nd round	N/A
95/96	Div 2	2nd	24	11	11	76	39	83	4th round	2nd round	N/A
96/97	Div 1	17th	16	9	21	64	68	64	3rd round	4th round	N/A
97/98	Div 1	16th	7	5	11	29	33	26	3rd round	4th round	N/A
(when resigned)											
Totals	**P240**		**W96**		**D59**		**L85**				

Honours
Promotion from Third to Second Division 1995/96

West Bromwich Albion
(26 December 1998 - 27 July 1999)

Season				League					FA Cup	Lge Cup	FL Trophy
			W	D	L	F	A	Pts			
97/98	Div 1	10th	4	9	9	24	33	21	4th round	N/A	N/A
98/99	Div 1	12th	16	11	19	55	59	69	4th round	1st round	N/A
Totals	**P72**		**W22**		**D19**		**L31**				

Oxford United
(3 February 2000 - 2 October 2000)

Season				League					FA Cup	Lge Cup	FL Trophy
			W	D	L	F	A	Pts			
99/00	Div 2	20th	6	2	10	19	28	20	N/A	N/A	N/A
00/01	Div 2	24th	1	1	8	5	22	4	N/A	1st round	N/A
(when resigned)											
Totals	**P30**		**W8**		**D3**		**L19**				

Wrexham
(8 October 2001 - 11 January 2007)

Season			W	D	L	F	A	Pts	FA Cup	Lge Cup	FL Trophy
					League						
01/02	Div 2	23rd	10	7	19	42	63	37	1st round	N/A	2nd round
02/03	Div 3	3rd	23	15	8	84	50	84	1st round	2nd round	QF
03/04	Div 2	13th	17	9	20	50	60	60	1st round	1st round	2nd round
04/05	Lge 2	23rd	13	14	19	62	80	43	2nd round	2nd round	Winners
05/06	Lge 2	13th	15	14	17	61	54	59	1st round	1st round	1st round
06/07	Lge 2	18th	7	7	11	25	41	28	3rd round	2nd round	1st round
(when dismissed)											

Totals   **P278**   **W101**   **D68**   **L109**

Honours
Promotion from Third to Second Division 2002/03
LDV Vans Trophy 2004/05
FA of Wales Premier Cup 2001/02, 2003/04

TOTALS: P1155   W449   D283   L423

Milestones
1st game: York City 1 v 1 Torquay United, 28.8.1982
500th game: Watford 5 v 2 Bristol City, 2.5.1992
1,000th game: Brentford 0 v 1 Wrexham, 24.1.2004
Last game: Derby County 3 v 1 Wrexham, 6.1.2007